To Dave & Annie:

Here's the second edition of this book!

Good to see you in Sept/Oct 2006!

Best,

R. Barri 11/7/06

SEX CRIMES

Second Edition

SEX CRIMES

Perpetrators, Predators, Prostitutes, and Victims

By

R. BARRI FLOWERS

CHARLES C THOMAS • PUBLISHER, LTD.
Springfield • Illinois • U.S.A.

Published and Distributed Throughout the World by

CHARLES C THOMAS • PUBLISHER, LTD.
2600 South First Street
Springfield, Illinois 62704

© 2006 by CHARLES C THOMAS • PUBLISHER, LTD.

ISBN 0-398-07677-4   (hard)
ISBN 0-398-07678-2 (paper)

Library of Congress Catalog Card Number: 2006045237

With THOMAS BOOKS *careful attention is given to all details of manufacturing
and design. It is the Publisher's desire to present books that are satisfactory as to their
physical qualities and artistic possibilities and appropriate for their particular use.*
THOMAS BOOKS *will be true to those laws of quality that assure a good name
and good will.*

Printed in the United States of America
MM-R-3

Library of Congress Cataloging-in-Publication Data

Flowers, Ronald B.
 Sex crimes : perpetrators, predators, prostitutes, and victims. / R. Barri Flowers -- 2nd ed.
  p. cm.
 Includes bibliographical references and index.
 ISBN 0-398-07677-4 -- ISBN 0-398-07678-2 (pbk.)
 1. Sex crimes--United States. 2. Prostitution--United States. 3. Sexual abuse victims--United
States. I. Title.
 HV6592.F56 2006
 364.15'3--dc21   2006045237

PREFACE

Sex criminality represents perhaps our most disturbing and complex type of criminal behavior. Though statistics and surveys suggest that crime in general is on the decline in the United States, sex crimes appear to be on the rise and are one of the more common and frequent crimes. Each year, millions of people are victims of sexual homicides, rape, incest, child molestation, child pornography, sexual slavery, paraphilic acts, and sexual perversions such as voyeurism, exhibitionism, and sadism. Anywhere from hundreds of thousands to, some believe, well into the millions of adults and children are willing or forced participants in prostitution and pornography. These include a growing number of victims of human traffickers who are forced into sexual servitude and exploitation in this country. Most sex crimes go unreported or underreported, making it the most hidden group of crimes and thereby the most difficult to detect, assess, treat, and control. The majority of sex criminals were themselves victims of sex crimes, creating a vicious cycle.

The cost of sex crimes is enormous and includes victims' physical and psychological trauma, exposure to AIDS and other sexually transmitted diseases, medical and mental health treatment, loss of work time, and shattered innocence and idealism. Other costs can be seen in the criminal justice system. Countless law enforcement hours and considerable resources are devoted to investigating sex crimes and arresting, prosecuting, and incarcerating sex offenders. Many experts agree that rehabilitation and treatment of sex offenders often falls short of success, while recidivism remains high.

Sex crimes go to the very core of our society and speak of male and female sex roles, variance in the gender socialization process, sexual myths and misunderstandings, differential enforcement of the law, and social conditions that are conducive to the commission of sex crimes and the reluctance of victims to come forward.

The second edition of *Sex Crimes: Perpetrators, Predators, Prostitutes and Victims* offers an updated comprehensive criminological and sociological examination of sex criminality in America. It includes a new chapter that examines sex trafficking in the United States and the related international aspects. The often understated offense of statutory rape is also addressed in this edition.

The book adds to a growing body of research that, in recent years, has focused on the study of sex crimes and their dynamics apart from general crimes. However, unlike most such literature that often explores specific types of predatory sex-related crimes such as incest or rape, or sexual exploitative crimes such as prostitution and child pornography, *Sex Crimes* examines the broad range of sex crimes as both a distinct classification of crime and as individual sex offenses.

The purpose of this book is to bridge the gap of existing works on sex criminality, explore the relevant issues and dimensions of sex crimes, criminals, and victims, and shed new light on the study and implications of sex-related criminal behavior. The intended audience includes the academic and professional community in the disciplines of criminology, sociology, sexology, criminal justice, social science, psychology, psychiatry, penology, medicine, human sciences, child sexual abuse, child welfare, women's studies, international studies, and victimology. It is also recommended reading for sex crime survivors and intelligent laypersons with an interest in sexual criminality and its implications for the individual and society.

I would like to thank Charles C Thomas Publisher in recognizing the importance of this book as a contribution to the study of crime and criminal behavior. Finally, I would be remiss if I did not offer the sincerest gratitude to my brilliant assistant, Loraine, and her tireless efforts in helping to turn my research into professional published material.

R.B.F.

INTRODUCTION

In spite of the considerable attention in the literature to studying sex crimes, criminals, and victims, there is a lot we do not know about the dynamics, prevalence, and incidence of sex crimes. The primary reason for this is that, unlike certain types of offenses, most sex crimes are by their very nature committed behind closed doors or between consenting persons, hence hidden from public view and often kept private and personal by the victims. Even for such public arena sex crimes as prostitution, much of the actual sex acts are committed in secrecy and without knowledge of anyone but those directly involved. Additionally, for many sex-related homicides the emphasis is often on the homicide and *not* the sexual offense perpetrated on the victim, thereby keeping such sex crimes out of the statistics.

What we do know about sex crimes is that they are far more prevalent, heterogeneous and damaging than much of the previous research would suggest. Sex victims and offenders are adults, children, males, females, old, young, whites, minorities, lower class, middle class, upper class, foreigners and of every conceivable occupational status. Sex crimes include sexual murders, forcible rape, child molestation, incest, prostitution, child pornography, exhibitionism, voyeurism, necrophilia, and sex trafficking. Most sex criminals are influenced by alcohol and drugs, anger, hostility pornography, profit, and a history of child sexual abuse or other sexual victimization. Though there are strict laws against most sex crimes, because of its magnitude and difficulty in identifying participants, relatively few sex offenders are ever arrested, prosecuted, or serve time behind bars for their crimes.

Sex Crimes: Perpetrators, Predators, Prostitutes, and Victims will examine in depth sexual criminality, its nature, characteristics, dimensions, and ramifications in American society. Within this context, the book will address both recognized and little known sex crimes, the magnitude of such crimes, sex offenders and victims, theories on sexual criminality and sex criminals and the criminal justice system.

The book is divided into seven parts. Part I examines sex-related homicides as a reflection of sexual criminality. Part II focuses on rape crimes, including forcible rape in general, marital rape, date and acquaintance rape; female, same sex rape, and statutory rape.

Part III explores incestuous crimes, including father-daughter incest, mother-child incest, and other intrafamilial sexual abuse. Part IV studies sexual predatory crimes, including child molestation, pedophilia, pornography and sex crimes; sex trafficking and sexual slavery; and other sexual abuse and paraphilias such as exhibitionism, voyeurism, bestiality, coprolagnia, and ritual sex abuse.

Part V examines prostitution crimes, including women's prostitution, girl prostitution, and male prostitution. Part VI explores theories on sexual criminality. Part VII focuses on the criminal justice system, sex crimes and offenders, including sex crime laws, arrests and sex offenders, and incarcerated sex criminals.

Tables and figures supplement the text in illustrating relevant data on sex crimes, criminals, and victims.

CONTENTS

Chapter

PART I: SEXUAL MURDER CRIMES

PART II: RAPE CRIMES

PART III: INCESTUOUS CRIMES

PART IV: SEXUAL PREDATORY CRIMES

TABLES

FIGURES

SEX CRIMES

Part I

SEXUAL MURDER CRIMES

Chapter 1

SEX-RELATED HOMICIDES

Although this book's primary focus will be on crimes that are traditionally defined as sex crimes such as rape, incest, child molestation, child pornography, and prostitution, it seemed appropriate to open with a chapter on sex-related homicides. By their very nature, sex and murder have been well documented to be strongly related throughout history.[1] Certainly in modern times, sexual themes have played a significant role in intimate murders, stranger murders, child murders, serial murders, prostitute murders, and sexual abuse-excuse murders. Many killers are driven by sexual impulses or factors in killing and just as many sexual offenders fantasize about killing their victims. The correlation between sex and homicide make it especially important to examine in the context of sex crimes.

DEFINING SEXUAL HOMICIDE

What is a sexual homicide? The term "sexual" is defined by the dictionary as (1) of sex, sexuality, the sexes, or the sex organs and their functions, and (2) implying or symbolizing erotic desires or activity. "Homicide" is defined as (1) the killing of one person by another or (2) a person who kills another. For the purposes of this chapter, sexual homicide will be defined as homicide in which there is a sexual element, motivation, relationship, or perversion involved such as rape, molestation, prostitution, intimacy, battering, and sexual jealousy.

In the book *Sexual Homicide: Patterns and Motives,* the authors define sexual homicide as "the killing of a person in the context of power, sexuality, and brutality."[2] They further describe sexual homicide as "murders with evidence or observations that indicate that the murder was sexual in nature."[3] Murder that is sexually motivated is often referred to as *lust murder* or *erotophonophilia.*[4] In the *Diagnostic and Statistical Manual of the American Psychiatric Association*

5

(DSM III-R), sexual deviance falls under the category of paraphilia.[5] Within this is the subcategory of *sexual sadism,* including lust murder.[6]

Sex has been shown to be a major factor in many types of homicides, particularly those involving intimates, sexual workers, children, and serial killers. A relationship has also been established in the literature between sexual killers and child sexual abuse victims or violent sexual fantasies or experiences.[7]

SEX AND MURDER

One need only look at the number of homicides with a sexual basis occurring in this country to see how sex and murder often relate to one another. According to the Federal Bureau of Investigation (FBI), there were an estimated 16,137 murders and nonnegligent manslaughters in the United States in 2004.[8] Of these, supplementary data were given for 14,121 murders.

Table 1.1 shows murder circumstances by the victim's sex for victimizations attributed to sex-related causes. In 2004, there were 156 murders where the circumstances of death involved a sexual factor. These included felony murders such as rape, prostitution and commercialized vice, and other sex offenses; and romantic triangle murders in the other than felony type category. Overall, more males than females were victimized by sex-related murder circumstances. There were nearly four times as many male homicide victims due to a romantic triangle as females. However, females were much

Table 1.1
SEX-RELATED MURDER CIRCUMSTANCES, BY VICTIM'S SEX, 2004

Circumstances	Total Murder Victims	Male	Female	Unknown
Total murders	14,121	10,990	3,099	32
Felony-type total	2,089	1,718	370	1
Rape	36	0	36	–
Prostitution and commercialized vice	9	3	6	–
Other sex offenses	14	8	6	–
Other than felony type total	6,972	5,227	1,739	–
Romantic triangle	97	76	21	
Total sex-related	156	87	69	

Source: U.S. Department of Justice, Federal Bureau of Investigation, *Crime in the United States: Uniform Crime Reports 2004* (Washington: Government Printing Office, 2005), p. 23.

more likely to be murdered as rape victims or due to prostitution.

Sexual factors may have also played a role in some of the 237 murders attributed to a brawl, due to the influence of alcohol or narcotics. Studies have shown that most sex-related homicides often involve drugs or alcohol use by the victim, perpetrator, or both.[9] Many of these may be classified as due to substance abuse because of the easier categorization than the sometimes more ambiguous link between sex and homicide.

Some experts believe that there may be far more sex-related homicides than indicated by official statistics. In 2004, there were 4,943 murders where the circumstances were unknown.[10] Studies suggest that a high incidence of these may be sexual murders. For example, B. S. Cormier and S. P. Simmons' research on sexual offenders implies that sexual homicides may be more common than is reported, though they also cite studies that found violent sex crimes to be rare with a nonescalation in aggression.[11]

Long-term trends indicate that hundreds of murders each year are sex-related. According to the FBI's Supplementary Homicide Reporting Program, between 1976 and 1994, an estimated 4,807 murders in the United

Table 1.2
CHARACTERISTICS OF SEX OFFENDER MURDERERS, 1976–1994

Offender characteristic	Murders	
	All	Sexual assault
Sex		
Male	86.6%	95.0%
Female	13.4	5.0
Race		
White	47.8%	58.0%
Black	50.3	39.9
Other	1.9	2.1
Age		
12 or younger	0.2%	0.1%
13–17	8.1	9.9
18–24	30.1	39.1
25–29	18.0	22.5
30–39	23.1	21.1
40–49	11.1	5.4
50–59	5.4	1.5
60 or older	3.9	0.4
Average age	31 yrs	26 yrs

Source: Derived from U.S. Department of Justice, Bureau of Justice Statistics, *Sex Offenses and Offenders: Executive Summary* (Washington: Government Printing Office, 1997), p. 3.

States involved rape or other sexual offenses.[12] This represented about 1.5 percent of all murders. Table 1.2 shows the characteristics of sexual assault murderers from 1976 to 1994. A higher percentage of sexual assault killers are white males than with all killers. Sexual assault murderers tend to be five years younger on average than murderers in general. More than 60 percent of sexual assault killers fall between the ages of eighteen and twenty-nine, compared to less than 50 percent of all killers.

Characteristics of sexual assault murder victims over the same span can be seen in Table 1.3. Victims of sexual homicides differ considerably from other homicide victims.

Sexual assault murder victims were much more likely to be female, white, and younger than murder victims in general. More than 80 percent of victims of sexual assault murders were female and nearly 70 percent were white. More than 25 percent of sexual homicide victims were under the age of eighteen, with nearly 15 percent age twelve or younger. Nearly 73 percent of the murder victims of sexual assault were under the age of forty.

Table 1.3
CHARACTERISTICS OF SEXUAL ASSAULT MURDER VICTIMS, 1976–1994

	Murders	
Offender characteristic	*All*	*Sexual assault*
Sex		
Male	76.4%	18.0%
Female	23.6	82.0
Race		
White	51.7%	68.4%
Black	46.3	28.9
Other	2.0	2.7
Age		
12 or younger	10.1%	14.8%
13–17	4.6	9.7
18–24	21.3	21.7
25–29	15.7	12.3
30–39	22.0	14.2
40–49	11.7	8.3
50–59	6.9	5.3
60 or older	7.7	13.7
Average age	32 yrs	32 yrs

Source: Derived from U.S. Department of Justice, Bureau of Justice Statistics, *Sex Offenses and Offenders: An Analysis of Data on Rape and Sexual Assault* (Washington: Government Printing Office, 1997), p. 29.

Figure 1.1
SEX-RELATED MURDER CIRCUMSTANCES, 2000–2004

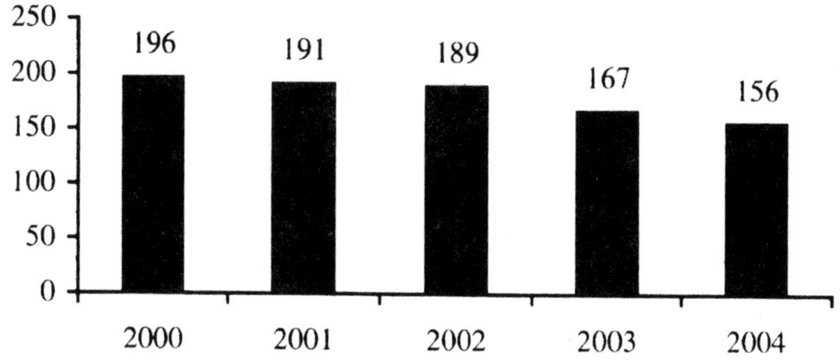

Source: Adapted from U.S. Department of Justice, Federal Bureau of Investigation, *Crime in the United States: Uniform Crime Reports 2004* (Washington: Government Printing Office, 2005), p. 23.

More recent trends support the data on sex-related murders. Figure 1.1 shows that from 2000 to 2004, there were 180 murders on average per year involving sexual issues or circumstances. Most of these murders are solved or cleared by law enforcement. However, many sexual homicides are not solved, leaving sexual murderers loose on the streets. For example, there was a 62.6 percent murder clearance rate in 2004, higher than any other serious crime.[13] That left more than 30 percent of murders not solved, possibly resulting in future homicides, sexual or otherwise.

Most sexual assault murders are intraracial. About 80 percent involve victims and offenders of the same race.[14] Sexual homicides are twice as likely as homicides in general to involve strangers, but equally likely to involve victims and offenders who are acquainted with one another.

HOMICIDE SYNDROMES

To better understand the relationship between sex and homicides requires examining what causes sexual violence to become homicidal. *Homicide Syndromes* places homicides in categories in accordance with the perpetrator's primary motive or objective at the immediate time the homicide takes place. According to Carolyn Block and Antigone Christakos, in their study of Chicago homicides over a twenty-five year period, each Homicidal Syndrome, "corresponds to a nonlethal sibling offense, and these lethal and nonlethal events are linked because they occupy the same position on an expressive versus instrumental continuum."[15]

In *Expressive violence,* the perpetrator's primary goal or motive is the act of violence; whereas in Instrumental violence, the offender's main objective is to acquire money or property. Virtually all homicides correspond to a sibling offense or similar crimes in which there was no fatal outcome. Examples of sexual-based Expressive Homicide/Violent Syndromes include:

- **Intimate violence**–between spouses, ex-spouses, girlfriends, boyfriends, or other intimates.
- **Rape/sexual assault**–where the rapist or sexual assaultist's goal is to sexually violate the victim.

Expressive and instrumental homicides are not mutually exclusive, but can occur in conjunction with one another or with other factors involved such as substance abuse, stress, and availability/use of firearms.[16] Most sex-related homicides tend to involve alcohol or drug use, and a high percentage include stressful situations such as domestic violence and use of a weapon of some type.[17]

INTIMATE MURDERS

Intimate murders often involve spouses, ex-spouses, romantic partners, ex-lovers, or other combinations of intimates. While intimate murders may involve various factors such as domestic violence, drug abuse, poverty, and stress, the underlying theme for many intimate fatal confrontations is sex. This may be in the form of actual sexual violence, anger over the end of a sexual relationship, sexual desire, or sexual jealousy. The male is typically the aggressor in domestic violence, though many women have also been the aggressor in violence between intimates. To put the problem in perspective, according to the National Crime Victimization Survey, there are more than 960,000 incidents of intimate violence in the United States every year.[18] Approximately 85 percent of the victims are female. Some estimates suggest that as many as 3.9 million women are battered by husbands or live-in boyfriends annually.19 Other findings reveal the following:

- One in four women have ever been physically abused by a partner.[20]
- Women are five to eight times more likely to be victims of battering than men.[21]
- Male intimate violence is much more damaging to the victim than female intimate violence.[22]
- Women are seven to fourteen times more likely to report being severely assaulted by an intimate than men.[23]

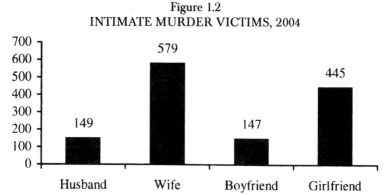

Figure 1.2
INTIMATE MURDER VICTIMS, 2004

Source: Adapted from U.S. Department of Justice, Federal Bureau of Investigation, *Crime in the United States: Uniform Crime Reports 2004* (Washington: Government Printing Office, 2005), p. 20.

- Three in four women raped or battered in adulthood are victimized by a current or former intimate.[24]
- Nearly one in five women have ever been the victims of attempted or actual rape.[25]
- More than three out of four stalking victims are female.[26]
- Twice as many females are stalked by intimate partners as males.[27]
- Eight in ten female stalking victims are physically abused by their intimate stalker, while three in ten victims are also sexually assaulted by the stalker.[28]

The relationship between intimate violence and intimate murder has been well established.[29] The number of intimate murder victims is staggering. The Bureau of Justice Statistics reported that nearly 52,000 women and men were murdered by an intimate in the United States between 1976 and 1996.[30] FBI data indicates that there were 1,320 known murders involving intimates in 2004. These are broken down in Figure 1.2. Nearly 79 percent of the murder victims were wives and girlfriends. Studies show that an estimated three in ten women murdered in this country are victims of intimate murders.[31] Around one in five female murder victims are killed by husbands or ex-husbands. One-third of all intimate murders in this country are committed by boyfriends and girlfriends.[32]

Uxoricide

Male intimate murder involving a wife or ex-wife is particularly troubling and strongly associated with sexual issues. Uxoricide is defined as (1) the killing of a wife by her husband or (2) a man who kills his wife. Studies have shown that many men who murder their wives do so out of real or perceived sexual infidelity by the wife or their own unfaithfulness, sexual jealousy, or fears that the wife and intimate partner will leave.[33] Women are more likely to be murdered by their husbands or another intimate than any other person. In a study of family homicides in Detroit, it was found that cohabitating spouses were eleven times more likely to be killed by a spouse than family members are by another relative living in the household.[34] However, living apart from a would-be spouse killer does not decrease the risk of victimization. In comparing uxoricide rates in several countries, including Australia and Canada, Margo Wilson and Martin Daly advanced that the risk of uxoricide increased after a separation.[35] This notwithstanding, some research suggests that separation and uxoricide are not entirely cause and effect but rather relative more to the overall marital discord.[36]

Some studies have found that male sexual proprietary jealousy towards younger, fertile wives increased the risk of uxoricide. Wilson and Daly noted that:

> men's proprietary jealousy is also expected to be variably aroused at least part- ly in relation to variable attributes of the woman. A man is vulnerable to cuck- oldry as a result of his wife's infidelity, for example, only when she is fertile; while he may be concerned to protect a pregnant wife from various sorts of harms, he need not protect her from insemination by rivals.[37]

M. V. Flinn's study supported this contention, finding that men appeared to be sensitive to variables related to their wives' present ability to conceive, and thus the vulnerability to cuckoldry.[38]

Other research has studied the uxoricide risk of young wives in relation to sexual proprietary jealousy and such issues as physical attractiveness, abandonment, childlessness, sexual rivals, and potential new sexual partners.[39] Wilson and Daly hypothesized that "men's sexually proprietary and coercive psychologies conflict with women's evolved psychologies of mate choice and personal autonomy."[40] For some women, this conflict will have fatal consequences.

SERIAL MURDERS

Serial murders, perhaps more than any other type of murder, are predominantly linked to sexual themes such as rape, sodomy, molestation, sadism, sexual abuse, prostitution, pornography, and other forms of sexual violence and perversions. History is replete with examples of sex-motivated serial killers.[41] In the early 1900s, German child molester serial killer Fritz Haarmann, known as the "Butcher of Hanover," murdered twenty-seven young males.[42] Another German, Bruno Ludke, combined rape, murder, and necrophilia in murdering eighty-six women in the mid 1900s.[43] More recently, the book *The Sex Slave Murders* details the "sex slave fantasies" of husband-wife serial killers Gerald and Charlene Gallego. The pair abducted, sexually assaulted, and murdered nine women in the Western U.S. in the 1970s and '80s.[44]

Other recent notable sexual murderers include "lust killer" Jerry Brudos who raped, mutilated, and murdered his female victims in Oregon during the late 1980s.[45] John Wayne Gacy had sex with and murdered thirty-three teenage boys, burying and disposing of their remains in and around his house in Chicago in the 1970s.[46]

Perhaps the prototype of a sexual serial killer was Theodore "Ted" Bundy, who raped and murdered at least forty—and possibly as many as one hundred—women in the United States during the 1970s.[47] While on death row, Bundy, not too surprisingly, was seen as an authority on the serial killer personality. The FBI Behavioral Research Unit used some of his "expertise" in their serial killer profiling.

A number of criminologists have studied sexual serial killers and drawn conclusions on their characteristics and typologies. D. T. Lunde posited that a high percentage of serial killers are sexual sadists who have associated sexuality with violence, usually starting at a young age.[48] Nearly one in five of the serial murderers examined by J. Levin and J. A. Fox from newspaper reports and FBI files were identified as sexual sadists.[49] In R. R. Hazelwood, P. E. Dietz, and J. Warren's study of sexually sadistic killers, 43 percent had been involved in homosexual acts during adulthood, and 20 percent had committed sexual offenses such as exhibitionism and voyeurism.[50] Dietz characterized one type of serial killer as a *psychopathic sexual sadist.* The researcher asserted that every known serial murderer with ten or more victims was a male diagnosed with both antisocial personality disorder and sexually sadistic tendencies.[51]

In a study of sexually motivated murderers ad serial killers, the FBI reported that twice as many were likely to be organized serial murderers as disorganized.[52]

Prostitute Murderers

The relationship between sex offender and serial homicide is particularly apropos when it comes to serial killers of prostitutes. Perhaps the most sensationalized serial murderer is "Jack the Ripper." This never-captured perpetrator murdered and mutilated at least five prostitutes in London in 1888 and has been the subject of theories and fascination ever since.[53] Other prostitute killers have followed in his footsteps. One such person was Peter Sutcliffe, dubbed "The Yorkshire Ripper." He stabbed, mutilated, and murdered thirteen women in England in the 1970s and '80s.[54] Most of his victims were prostitutes who he sought in order to "clean up the streets." Another serial killer of prostitutes was Gary Ridgway, known as "The Green River Killer," who claimed forty-eight victims in Seattle's Green River area during the 1980s.[55] All of these serial killers appear to have in common an intense hatred towards women in general and prostitutes in particular.

In a reversal of misfortunes, there have been cases where the prostitute became a serial killer. Perhaps the most widely publicized has been that of Aileen Wuornos, a prostitute who shot to death at least seven of her customers from 1989 to 1990 in Florida.[56] Though she claimed self-defense, Wuornos was sentenced to death and labeled by some as this country's first female sexual serial killer.

Signature Murderers

Another subcategory of sexual serial killers is the signature killer. What distinguishes such killers from other serial murderers is that they tend to leave behind a "calling card" or psychological signature unique to them at each crime scene. According to Robert Keppel and William Birnes' book, *Signature Killers: Interpreting the Calling Cards of the Serial Murderer,* the signature serial killer is "psychologically compelled to leave [his imprint] to satisfy himself sexually."[57] John Douglas, of the FBI's Behavioral Sciences Unit in Quantico, characterized the sexual serial killer's signature as "the person's violent fantasies which are progressive in nature and contribute to thoughts of exhibiting extremely violent behavior."[58]

Signature killers are believed to be the single greatest subcategory of serial murderers, "driven by such a primal psychological motivation to act out the same crime over and over again that their patterns become obsessive. All signature murderers seek some form of sexual gratification, and their crimes are expressions of the ways they satisfy that need."[59]

Anger appears to be a key motivating factor in sexual signature murders. Keppel and Birnes identified two types of anger-driven signature killers: (1) *anger-retaliatory killer* and (2) *anger-excitation killer.*

The anger-retaliation murderer is characterized by a sexually violent act and overkill, involving the use of more than one weapon. The killer tends to view his victim as a symbol of the frustration he feels. Prostitute murderers often fall into this category of signature killer. Although the anger-retaliation murder is an aspect of a sex offense signature, the signature killer's "fury will probably have interfered with sex before death; thus, the expression of sexuality may be through postmortem, intentional exploratory mutilation of the body."[60]

The signature for the anger-excitation sex murderer is normally sadism. The sexual assault in and of itself or leading up to the murder is typically planned in advance. The homicidal pattern of the anger-excitation murderer is characterized "by a prolonged, bizarre, ritualistic assault on the victim."[61]

The anger-driven signature killer usually starts off as a retaliatory murderer and progresses to an excitation murderer over the course of his series of crimes. The murderer's evolvement depends on the degree of his anger. The signature he leaves reflects "one or more of the core components of sadism, control, humiliation, progression of violence, posing, torture, overkill, necrophilia, and cannibalism."[62]

CHARACTERISTICS OF SEXUAL MURDERERS

Most homicidal sex offenders are male, white, with average or above average intelligence, and tend to come from dysfunctional families. According to an FBI analysis of sexual murderers, half came from families where members had criminal histories and more than half had family members with mental illness.[63] More than two-thirds of the sexual killers came from families where at least one member had an alcohol problem, one-third where a family member abused drugs, and half in which someone in the family had a sexual problem.

Two-thirds of the sex killers had childhood psychiatric problems, while the majority had cold, dominant, uncaring mothers or fathers. Nearly half reported being sexually, physically, or emotionally abused. Many of the sexual murderers had violent, sadistic, or rape fantasies while growing up, and displayed cruelty to animals or other children. Most viewed themselves as failures, had low self-esteem, and were insensitive to others' needs. Sexual murderers tended to see the world "as unjust, desired to be strong, powerful and in control, and favored autoerotic sexual activities."[64]

In their study of sexual homicide, Robert Ressler, Ann Burgess, and John Douglas further found that financial problems, relationship problems, and stress factors played significant roles in the murderer's life prior to committing the offense.[65] They reported that the offender's frame of mind was also a significant factor in committing the sexual murders. Most had highly negative mental states, including frustration, anger, hostility, agitation, and excitement.

NOTES

1. R. Barri Flowers, *The Victimization and Exploitation of Women and Children: A Study of Physical, Mental and Sexual Maltreatment in the United States* (Jefferson: McFarland, 1994).
2. Robert K. Ressler, Ann W. Burgess, and John E. Douglas, *Sexual Homicide: Patterns and Motives* (New York: Lexington Books, 1988), p. 1.
3. *Ibid.*, p. xiii.
4. J. Money, "Forensic Sexology," *American Journal of Psychotherapy 44* (1900): 26–36.
5. David Lester, *Serial Killers: The Insatiable Passion* (Philadelphia: Charles Press, 1995), p. 15.
6. *Ibid.*
7. *Ibid.*, pp. 51–52; R. Barri Flowers, *Murder, At the End of the Day and Night: A Study of Criminal Homicide Offenders, Victims, and Circumstances* (Springfield: Charles C Thomas, 2001), pp. 51–60, 159–67; U.S. Department of Justice, Federal Bureau of Investigation, "The Men Who Murdered," *FBI Law Enforcement Bulletin 62* (1985): 2–6.
8. U.S. Department of Justice, Federal Bureau of Investigation, *Crime in the United States: Uniform Crime Reports 2004* (Washington: Government Printing Office, 2005), p. 15.
9. *Ibid.*, Ressler, Burgess, and Douglas, *Sexual Homicide*, pp. 49, 52–53. See also R. Barri Flowers, *State's Evidence* (Dorchester, 2006).
10. *Uniform Crime Reports 2004*, p. 23.
11. B. S. Cormier and S. P. Simons, "The Problem of the Dangerous Sexual Offender," *Canadian Psychiatric Association 14* (1969): 329–34.
12. U.S. Department of Justice, Bureau of Justice Statistics, *Sex Offenses and Offenders: An Analysis of Data on Rape and Sexual Assault* (Washington: Government Printing Office, 1997), p. 28.
13. *Uniform Crime Reports 2004*, p. 13.
14. *Sex Offenses and Offenders*, p. 30.
15. Carolyn R. Block and Antigone Christakos, "Chicago Homicide From the Sixties to the Nineties: Major Trends in Lethal Violence," in U.S. Department of Justice, Office of Justice Programs, *Trends, Risks, and Interventions in Lethal Violence: Proceedings of the Third Annual Spring Symposium of the Homicide Research Working Group* (Washington: National Institute of Justice, 1995), p. 28.
16. *Ibid.*, pp. 39–45.
17. *Ibid.*, Lester, Serial Killers, p. 51.
18. U.S. Department of Justice, Bureau of Justice Statistics Factbook, *Violence by Intimates: Analysis of Data on Crimes by Current or Former Spouses, Boyfriends, and Girlfriends* (Washington: Government Printing Office, 1998), p. 1.
19. The Commonwealth Fund, *First Comprehensive National Health Survey of American Women*, July, 1993.
20. Lieberman Research Inc., *Domestic Violence Advertising Campaign Tracking Survey*, conducted for The Advertising Council and the Family Violence Prevention Fund, July-October, 1996.
21. *Violence by Intimates*, pp. 3–13.
22. Murray A. Straus and Richard J. Gelles, *Physical Violence in American Families: Risk Factors and Adaptations to Violence in 8,145 Families* (New Brunswick: Transaction, 1990).
23. National Institute of Justice and Centers for Disease Control and Prevention, *Prevalence, Incidence, and Consequences of Violence Against Women: Findings from the National Violence Against Women Survey*, November, 1998.
24. *Ibid.*
25. *Ibid.*

26. Center for Policy Research, *Stalking in America,* July, 1997.

27. *Ibid.*

28. *Ibid.*

29. *Violence by Intimates,* p. 6; Flowers, *Murder, At the End of the Day and Night,* pp. 51–60; U.S. Department of Justice, Bureau of Justice Statistics, Family Violence Statistics: Including Statistics on Strangers and Acquaintances (Washington: Office of Justice Programs, 2005), pp. 17–20.

30. *Violence by Intimates,* p. 6.

31. *Ibid.,* p. v.

32. *Ibid.,* p. 6; *Family Violence Statistics,* pp. 17–19.

33. J. C. Campbell, "If I Can't Have You, No One Can: Issues of Power and Control in Homicide of Female Partners," in J. Radford and D. E. Russell, eds., *Femicide: The Politics of Woman Killing* (Boston: Twayne, 1992); R. E. Dobash and R. P. Dobash, *Violence Against Wives* (New York: Free Press, 1979).

34. Martin Daly and Margo Wilson, "Homicide and Kinship," *American Anthropologist 84* (1982): 372–78.

35. Margo I. Wilson and Martin Daly, "Spousal Homicide Risk and Estrangement," *Violence and Victims 8* (1993): 3–15.

36. Margo Wilson and Martin Daly, "Uxoricide," in U.S. Department of Justice, Office of Justice Programs, *Trends, Risks, and Interventions in Lethal Violence: Proceedings of the Third Annual Spring Symposium of the Homicide Research Working Group* (Washington: National Institute of Justice, 1995), p. 172.

37. *Ibid.,* p. 173.

38. V. Flinn, "Mate Guarding in a Caribbean Village," *Ethnology and Sociobiology 9* (1988): 1–28.

39. Wilson and Daly, "Uxoricide," p. 173; D. M. Buss, *The Evolution of Desire* (New York: Basic Books, 1994); J. A. Mercy and L. E. Saltzman, "Fatal Violence Among Spouses in the United States, 1976–85," *American Journal of Public Health 79* (1989): 595–99.

40. Wilson and Daly, "Uxoricide," p. 175.

41. Flowers, *Murder, At the End of the Day and Night,* pp. 159–78; R. Barri Flowers and H. Loraine Flowers, *Murders in the United States: Crimes, Killers and Victims of the Twentieth Century* (Jefferson: McFarland, 2004).

42. Brian Lane and Wilfred Gregg, *The Encyclopedia of Serial Killers* (New York: Berkley, 1995), pp. 192–94.

43. *Ibid.,* p. 247.

44. R. Barri Flowers, *The Sex Slave Murders* (New York: St. Martin's Press, 1996). See also R. Barri Flowers, *Persuasive Evidence* (Dorchester, 2004).

45. Lane and Gregg, *The Encyclopedia of Serial Killers,* pp. 71–73.

46. *Ibid.,* pp. 164–66.

47. *Ibid.,* pp. 73–76.

48. D. T. Lunde, *Murder and Madness* (New York: Norton, 1979).

49. J. Levin and J. A. Fox, *Mass Murder* (New York: Plenum, 1985).

50. R. R. Hazelwood, P. E. Dietz, and J. Warren, "The Criminal Sexual Sadist," *FBI Law Enforcement Bulletin 61* (1992): 12–20.

51. P. E. Dietz, "Mass, Serial and Sensational Homicides," *Bulletin of the New York Academy of Medicine 62* (1986): 477–91.

52. Cited in Lester, *Serial Killers,* pp. 81–82.

53. Donald Rumbelow, *Jack the Ripper: The Complete Casebook* (Chicago: Contemporary Books, 1988).

54. Lane and Gregg, *The Encyclopedia of Serial Killers,* pp. 329–30.

55. *Ibid.,* pp. 186–87; Flowers and Flowers, *Murders in the United States,* pp. 96–97.

56. Michael D. Kelleher and C. L. Kelleher, *Murder Most Rare: The Female Serial Killer* (New York: Dell, 1998), pp. 105–20; Flowers and Flowers, *Murders in the United States,* pp. 144–45.

57. Robert D. Keppel and William J. Birnes, *Signature Killers* (New York: Pocket Books, 1997), p. 5.

58. *Ibid.*

59. *Ibid.,* p. 23.

60. *Ibid.,* p. 94.

61. *Ibid.,* p. 189.

62. *Ibid.,* p. 89.

63. FBI, "The Men Who Murdered," p. 2–6.

64. Lester, *Serial Killers,* p. 51; Flowers, *Murder, At the End of the Day and Night,* pp. 162–63.

65. Ressler, Burgess, and Douglas, *Sexual Homicide,* pp. 45–56.

Part II

RAPE CRIMES

Chapter 2

FORCIBLE RAPE

There has been a considerable body of research on rape and its dynamics and characteristics. Next to sexual murder, forcible rape is the most violent type of sex crime. It affects one in five females in this country and includes sexual violations against women and children. Most rapes are committed by offenders known by or familiar to the victim, but stranger rapes are also common. Many rapists are, in fact, serial rapists and multiple rapists. Rape is often associated with other forms of violence. Forcible rape is a common occurrence in serial murders and other sexual homicides. It is also frequently a factor in intimate murders committed by both rapists and their victims, many of whom had been long subjected to marital rape before killing their spouse rapist.[1] Studies show that rapists tend to commit sexual violence in relation to substance abuse, opportunity, learned behavior, and childhood sexual abuse.

The incidence of rape is vastly underreported, as victims often fear victimization through the criminal justice system process and stigmatization even more than the assault itself. Consequently, relatively few rapists are ever apprehended. Most rapists who do enter the criminal justice system tend to leave it with something less than satisfactory justice for their victims. This chapter will examine forcible rape and its implications.

RAPE IN HISTORY

Rape has been a part of human history for as long as men and women have coexisted. It represents the oldest means in which men seized or stole women in matrimony or forced marriage in the absence of courtship.[2] According to Susan Brownmiller, in her historical study of rape: "When men discovered that they could rape, they proceeded to do it . . . from prehistoric times to the present."[3] In *Women and Criminality,* the author notes that historically "A man simply took the woman he wanted, raped her, and brought her into his tribe. She represented little more than a trophy; she held no legal, social, or human rights."[4]

Over time, the respectability of forcible rape as a man's natural right declined and responsibility for certain types of rape shifted to the victim. This point of view was reflected in the words of Herodotus in 500 B.C., referred to by some as the "father of history," when he advanced: "Abducting young women is not, indeed, a lawful act; but it is stupid after the event to make a fuss about it. The only sensible thing is to take no notice; for it is obvious that no young woman allows herself to be abducted if she does not want to be."[5] The implication was that raped women were, in effect, asking for what they received and thus had no one to blame but themselves. Sadly, this way of thinking has transcended time and is still the foundation of many rape myths and philosophy in society.

The act of forcible rape became a crime when marriage evolved into a sanctioned tribal institution. "Women were viewed as a proprietary interest, bought and sold like cattle. The right to ownership meant that any infringement upon or damage to one person's (usually the father or husband) human property (as in rape) was a crime, often dealt with severely."[6] In particular, the rape of a virgin was considered the ultimate, irreparable damage of a man's property and often meant death for the rapist.[7]

Many scholars believe that the very institution of marriage and family are based historically on the subjugation and violation of women both inside and outside the marriage. Brownmiller argued that rapists are the "shock troops" whose existence convinced women to marry one man as a means of protection from other men.[8] She further advanced that the fundamental causes of rape and sexual inequality are the predatory nature of men and their desire for property, providing countless examples of rape throughout history.

Rape has been especially prevalent during times of war, as both the victorious and defeated have used sexual violence against women and children as a measure of revenge, power, control, domination, hatred, and humiliation.[9]

DEFINING FORCIBLE RAPE

What is forcible rape? The word *rape* derives from the Latin *rapere,* meaning to "steal, seize, or carry away."[10] The act of rape has traditionally assumed a male offender and female victim. Various definitions and interpretations of what constitutes rape have long appeared in the literature and in rape and sexual assault statutes. In spite of definitional problems with nonuniformity and gender issues, rape is generally defined as forced, nonconsensual sexual intercourse. The *American Heritage Dictionary* defines rape as "(1) the crime of forcing a person to submit to sexual intercourse, (2) seizing and carrying off by force; abduction; and (3) violation: a rape of justice."[11] Definitions of rape are typically divided into legal and nonlegal definitions.

Legal Definitions of Rape

Legal definitions of rape can be traced to traditional common law and statute law. Common law defined rape as the unlawful carnal knowledge of a female by force and against her will. Sexual penetration, regardless of how slight, was sufficient to constitute a criminal offense, assuming the other elements were present. A resistance standard was instituted "for the victim in order to distinguish forcible carnal knowledge (rape) from consensual carnal knowledge (fornication and adultery)."[12] According to common law, both forms of carnal knowledge constituted criminal acts, but if the act was forcible the victim avoided being punished for adultery or fornication.

Legal theory has long held that:

> a crime exists only when there is concurrence of an unacceptable act and a criminal intent with respect to that act. The unacceptable act is called the actus reus; the criminal intent is called the mens rea. In traditional definition of rape, the actus reus is the unconsented to sexual intercourse and the mens rea is the intention or knowledge of having the intercourse without the consent of the victim. Lack of consent of the victim is ultimately the characteristic that distinguishes rape. The concurrence of the act and the intent requires both that the victim in fact did not consent and that the perpetrator knew at the time that the victim did not consent.[13]

Thus, in accordance with legal rape theory and common law tradition, the definition of rape is dependent upon both the victim's and offender's perception that the sexual intercourse was nonconsensual. This dual legal requirement poses obvious problems with interpretation, given that in many cases no criminal intent, per se, will be present in which a sexual assault is perpetrated.

Today, in every state forcible rape is considered a crime. Most states have adopted a statutory definition of rape as the act of forced sexual intercourse with a woman other than the perpetrator's wife without her lawful consent. The marital rape exemption in state laws is discussed in Chapter 3. As in common law, only the slightest penetration is required to complete the crime of forcible rape. Excluded in this definition are oral and anal copulation and homosexual assaults, which are addressed in many statutes under broader sex crime terminology such as "criminal sexual assault" and "sexual battery."[14] Some states have redefined rape in sex-neutral terms, allowing for rape to be considered a crime beyond traditional male offender-female victim terms.[15]

Traditional legal definitions of rape have been criticized for their narrow focus, concept of force, and interpretational components. In many states, the problem of applying current legal definitions of forcible rape to a particular situation was illustrated by K. Svalastoga:

> Rape is commonly defined as enforced coitus. But this very definition suggests that there is more to the offense than the use of force alone. This must be so, since no society has equipped itself with the means of measuring the amount of force applied in the act of coitus. Hence rape, like any other crime, carries a heavy social component. The act itself is not a sufficient [criterion]. The act must be interpreted as rape by the female actee, and her interpretation must be similarly evaluated by a number of officials and agencies before the official designation of "rape" can be legitimately applied.[16]

Many rape victims fall outside the protection of the law because the sexual assault perpetrated on them falls outside the parameters of state statutes defining rape.

Nonlegal Definitions of Rape

Nonlegal definitions of rape have focused on broader concepts of sexual assault than traditional legal definitions, while addressing the issue of rape in a social context. Social scientists have redefined rape and rapists "as an extension of normative sexual attitudes and relations in a society that demands and objectifies women."[17] Influenced by the feminist movement, some rape scholars in the social sciences have emphasized the social and cultural aspects of creating sexual aggression, arguing that rape is not so much an individual pathology but "a product of the patriarchal society in which it is imbedded."[18]

Traditional views of rape have been challenged in nonlegal definitions insofar as recognizing that rape does occur in marriage, on dates, and between other acquaintances as well as strangers. Further, forcible rape by definition, has been extended by many rape experts to include various kinds of forced sex including incestuous rape and same sex rape. Other types of sexual assaults have also been studied and incorporated into definitions of forced sexual relations, including oral copulation, sodomy, molestation, and necrophilia.[19]

The victim's point of view in defining rape is perhaps most useful in exploring nonlegal definitions of rape. Traditional sex roles and normative influences tend to play a large role in how a rape victim defines her victimization. According to Susan Klenmack and David Klenmack's research on social definitions of rape, the following variables show women's perception of rape and victimization depends on various types of social conditioning and values:

- What constitutes rape is consistent with the woman's point of view on various related social issues.
- Women who are more tolerant of sex outside the marriage may conform to a definition of human sexuality that includes rape as simply forced nonconsensual sexual intercourse.
- Women with fewer stereotypically traditional perspectives on the woman's role in contemporary society tend to define rape operationally at the level of forced sexual intercourse.
- Women reared with males more often attribute responsibility for rape or sexual assault to the victim.[20]

THE INCIDENCE OF RAPE

According to the Justice Department, a forcible rape occurs every six minutes in the United States.[21] *A National Violence Against Women Survey* found that nearly one in every five women have been the victim of an attempted or completed rape, affecting 17.7 million American females.[22] D. J. Kilpatrick, C. N. Edmunds, and A. K. Seymour estimated that one out of every eight women in this country had been forcibly raped at least once during her lifetime.[23] In a national estimate of the incidence of rape of adult females, Diana Russell's survey of rape victims indicated that 1.5 million rapes and attempted rapes occurred annually.[24] Other researchers have placed the estimate at two million rape victimizations yearly.[25] By comparison, the National Crime Victimization Survey (NCVS) of persons age twelve and over estimates that there are around 260,000 attempted or completed rapes each year, with about 95,000 other types of threatened or completed sexual assaults.[26]

In spite of the prevalence of rape, it is one of the most underreported crimes in the United States, according to official sources and rape experts. Nancy Gager and Cathleen Schurr estimated that at least 90 percent of actual rapes go unreported.[27] Brownmiller estimated that only one in five rapes or possibly as few as one in twenty are reported.[28] Kilpatrick and colleagues found that only 16 percent of their nationally representative sample of rape victims reported their victimization to the police.[29] Studies show that many rape victims may also be unwilling to disclose their sexual assault to interviewers or researchers, illustrating the difficulty in assessing the true incidence of rape.[30] According to the NCVS, the most common reason for victims reporting rape is to prevent the rapist from assaulting them again; while the most common reason given for not reporting rape is that the victim considered it a personal matter.[31]

RAPE AND THE CRIMINAL JUSTICE SYSTEM

By comparison to estimates of the actual incidence of rape, only a small percentage of rapists enter the criminal justice system as arrestees, are prosecuted, convicted sex offenders, or inmates. According to the FBI, there were an estimated 94,635 forcible rapes reported to law enforcement agencies in the United States in 2004.[32] Yet there were only 26,173 arrests nationwide for forcible rape in 2004.[33] Forcible rapes account for nearly nine in ten reported rapes.[34] Arrest trends indicate that fewer persons are being arrested for forcible rape. As shown in Figure 2.1, between 1995 and 2004 arrests for forcible rape declined by just over 18 percent (see also Chapter 19).

The Justice Department reports that on a given day there are an estimated 234,000 convicted rapists and sexual assaulters under correctional authority.[35] Nearly 60 percent of these sex offenders are not incarcerated but under conditional community supervision.[36] Among convicted rapists, eight out of ten entered a guilty plea, while around two-thirds received a prison sentence.[37] It is estimated that only 2 percent of convicted rapists receive a life sentence, with the average prison term for rape defendants just under fourteen years and for convicted jail rapists eight months.

Most rape victims fail to see their attacker punished. This is partly due to underreporting and partly based on an inadequate response from the criminal justice system. A 1993 congressional report illustrates the difficulty in bringing rapists to justice:

Figure 2.1
TOTAL ARREST TRENDS FOR FORCIBLE RAPE, 1995–2004

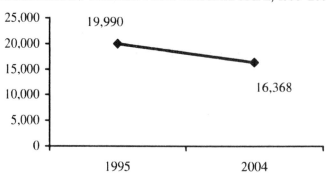

Source: Derived from U.S. Department of Justice, Federal Bureau of Investigation, *Crime in the United States: Uniform Crime Reports 2004* (Washington: Government Printing Office, 2005), p. 284.

- Ninety-eight percent of rape victims never see their rapist arrested, tried, and incarcerated.
- More than half of all rape prosecutions are either dismissed prior to trial or end up in an acquittal.
- Nearly one-fourth of convicted rapists never go to prison.
- One in four convicted rapists only receive jail sentences.
- Half of all convicted rapists serve an average of a year or less behind bars.
- A robber is 30 percent more likely to receive a conviction than a rapist.
- A convicted rapist is 50 percent more likely to be given probation than a convicted robber.[38]

THE NATURE AND CHARACTERISTICS OF FORCIBLE RAPE

Rape is a crime that affects women, children, and men from all walks of life and circumstances. Most rapists are never caught and most rapes go unreported. Victims of rape are predominantly single females under the age of thirty who know their attackers. A high percentage of forcible rapes are perpetrated against juvenile victims. According to the *Rape in America* study among females over eighteen, more than 60 percent said they were raped before the age of eighteen.[39] Similarly, more than half the rape victims in the *National Violence Against Women Survey* reported being under the age of seventeen when they were raped.[40] Russell found that 85 percent of the rape victims in her survey were single when the rape or attempted rape occurred.[41] Rape, its victims, and offenders were further characterized by criminologist Menachem Amir. In his influential work in the early 1970s, *Patterns in Forcible Rape,* he dispelled some myths.[42] He found that:

- Rape is predominantly an intraracial crime.
- Rape occurs more often between blacks than between whites.
- The majority of rapists are between fifteen and twenty-nine years of age.
- Most victims of rape fall between the ages of ten and twenty-nine.
- Sexual assaults are not occupationally bound.
- Rapists tend to more often occupy the lower end of the occupational scale.
- Rapists and rape victims generally reside in the same neighborhood.
- Alcohol is most prominent as a factor in violent rapes.
- Most group rapes involve young male offenders, are planned, and influenced by peer pressure.

Other researchers have generally supported Amir's findings. For instance, in a review of the literature on rape victimization, Sedelle Katz and Mary Mazur found, based on reported cases of rape, that "the high-risk ages are adolescents (ages 13 to 14) through young adulthood (ages 18 to 24)."[43] They also presented data to show that black women were far more vulnerable to

rape victimization than white women, correlating black female victimization
to an overrepresentation in lower income groups.[44]

In a comprehensive examination of rape in the United States, the Bureau
of Justice Statistics reported the following nature and characteristics of rape:

- Rape accounts for 3 percent of all violent crime.
- Eighty-one percent of all rape victims are white.
- Black women are disproportionately much more likely to be rape victims
  than white women.
- More than 70 percent of rape victims are unmarried.
- Two of every three rape victims are age sixteen to twenty-four.
- A woman is twice as likely to be raped by a stranger as someone she is famil-
  iar with.
- Around 15 percent of rapes involve more than one offender.
- Most victims of rape report a family income of less than $25,000 a year.
- Half the rape victims report a yearly income of below $10,000.
- Unreporting of rape by victims is motivated most often by fear of a short
  prison term for the rapist and insensitivity on the part of the criminal justice
  system.[45]

The nature of forcible rape was also studied recently by the FBI's National
Incident-Based Reporting System. Based on detailed data from three states,
it found that:

- Nine in ten rapes conformed to the male offender-female victim definition
  of rape.
- Nearly 9 percent of forcible rape victims were male.
- Around 1 percent of forcible rapists with male or female victims were
  female.
- White and black rape victims were evenly split.
- In nearly nine out of ten forcible rapes, the victim and perpetrator were of
  the same race.
- Around eight in ten rape victims were under the age of thirty; half of these
  were younger than eighteen.
- About three in ten rape victims were between the ages of twelve and sev-
  enteen.
- In nine of ten rapes involving victims under the age of twelve, the offender
  was someone they were familiar with.
- Rape victims over age thirty were about twelve times as likely as rape vic-
  tims under twelve to have been raped by a stranger.
- Two-thirds of rape victims age eighteen to twenty-nine had a previous rela-
  tionship with their rapist.
- More than 40 percent of rapists were thirty years of age and older.
- One in eight rapists were under age eighteen.
- About six in ten rapes occurred in a residence.

- Eighty percent of rapes were perpetrated through physical force only.
- Around 12 percent of rapes involved the use of a gun or knife.
- Around 40 percent of rape victims sustained a collateral injury, such as internal injuries, fractures, and unconsciousness.[46]

TYPOLOGIES OF FORCIBLE RAPISTS

Researchers have identified more than fifty types of rapists.[47] Though these represent different categories and motivational characteristics, it is important to note that many rapists fit into multiple classifications. In an analysis of sex offenders, Paul Gebhard and his colleagues found six types of rapists, whom they referred to as "heterosexual aggressors" against adult victims:

- **Assaultive rapists**–the most common type of rapist, characterized by sadistic and hostile feelings towards women.
- **Amoral delinquents**–the second most common type of rapist. This type of rapist is nonsadistic and desires to have sexual intercourse regardless of their victim's wishes.
- **Drunken variety**–rapists as common as amoral delinquents.
- **Explosive variety**–men whose past behavior gives no indication of their potential to rape. Their behavior often includes psychotic elements.
- **Double-standard variety**–these rapists divide females into good ones, to be treated with respect, and bad ones, who deserve no such respect.
- **Other types**–a mixture of the first five types of rapists, along with mental defectives and psychotics.[48]

Psychiatrist Richard Rada identified five primary types of rapists as follows:

- **Psychotic rapists**–men who are acutely psychotic and violent. Neither the victim nor perpetrator are in control of the situation.
- **Situational stress rapists**–these men are rarely very violent or dangerous. The rape is often the result of situational stress. The rapist usually does not have a history of violent behavior or sexual deviations.
- **Masculine identity conflict rapists**–a broad spectrum of rapists characterized by an actual or felt deficiency in their masculine roles. The rape is usually planned, dangerous, and violent.
- **Sadistic rapists**–represents a small percentage of rapists. They usually plan the rape, have a history of sexual persuasion, and derive pleasure in the ritualistic degrading of women.
- **Sociopathic rapists**–the most common type of rapist. These men are impulsive and motivated primarily by sex. The rape itself is merely a manifestation of general defiant behavior.[49]

Researchers Nicholas Groth, Ann Burgess, and Lynda Holmstrom, who examined rape from the standpoint of both the rapist and victim, posited that three components are present in virtually every case of forcible rape: (1) power, (2) anger, and (3) sexuality.[50] They concluded that rape "is the sexual expression of aggression rather than the aggressive expression of sexuality. Although rape is a sexual crime, it is not sexually motivated."[51] According to Groth and colleagues, sex becomes a means of expressing nonsexual needs in the psychology of the rapists, characterizing such needs as power and anger.

Power rapists make up 55 percent of all rapists.[52] Their crimes are usually premeditated, repeated, and originate from fantasies and exposure to pornography. The power rapist will employ whatever force is needed to overpower his victim, often using weapons to achieve his objective and maintain the advantage over the victim. There are two subtypes of power rapists: (1) power-assertive rapists and (2) power-reassurance rapists.[53]

- **Power-assertive rapists**–often feel powerless with the rape an expression of masculinity, command, and dominance, often accompanied by feelings of entitlement.
- **Power-reassurance rapists**–rape primarily for reassurance with respect to their masculinity and sexual adequacy. These rapists seek to make their victims feel helpless and controlled so that rejection is not possible.

Anger rapists represent the second largest group of rapists, comprising around 40 percent.[54] These sex offenders tend to be more impulsive, spontaneous, and dangerous than their power rapist counterparts. Their crimes are generally episodic and not premeditated. Anger rapists often use foul, abusive, and degrading language during their rapes, regarding themselves as superior and their victim as inferior. Two subtypes of anger rapists are (1) anger-retaliation rapists and (2) anger-excitation rapists.[55]

- **Anger-retaliation rapists**–usually commit rapes to reflect their hostility towards women. The assault is intended to degrade, hurt, and humiliate the rape victim as a retaliatory response to those women he perceives have hurt or wronged him.
- **Anger-excitation rapists**–relates anger to sexual arousal. These men gain excitement and pleasure in the victim's pain and suffering and their own aggression and violence, which becomes eroticized through their actions.

Another important type of rapist is the *rapist murderer* or *homicidal rapist.* Studies show that many sex-motivated murders involve rape or multiple rapes of the victim before or after the murder.[56] This is particularly true of intimate murders and sexual serial murders.[57] Most rapist murderers are driven by power, age, domination, control, degradation, fantasies, and sadism[58] (see also Chapter 1).

Sociologists Diana Scully and Joseph Marolla divide rapists into *admitters* and *deniers*.[59] Admitters acknowledge the sexual contact with their victims, defining the action as rape; while deniers, even when acknowledging that there was sexual contact, do not regard their behavior as rape. Both admitters and deniers tend to view their rape victims not as human beings but as objects to be used, abused, and conquered.

RAPE THEORIES

A number of theories on why rape occurs and what motivates or predisposes rapists have been formulated. Among the more prominent rape theories are: (1) interactionist theories, (2) psychoanalytic theories, (3) opportunity structure theory, and (4) biological predisposition theory.

Interactionist Theories

Symbolic interaction theories advance that "social interaction is mediated by signs and symbols, by eye contact, gestures, and words."[60] Hence, people regard and interpret one another's actions and respond accordingly. Rape is seen as the outcome of such a response. Interactionist theorists assume that rape is caused by the way males and females communicate their feelings and attitudes toward each other.

Victim-precipitation theories are interaction theories. In focusing on the rapist's reaction to the victim, supports of this school of thought refer to "those cases in which the victim—actually or so it was interpreted by the offender—agreed to sexual relations but retracted before the actual act or did not resist strongly enough."[61]

Rape experts have found fault with interactionist theories as a general explanation of rape for its inapplicability to all situations of rape. Furthermore, the theories fail to "question the oppressive sexist norms that regulate women's lives."[62] According to Julia Schwendinger and Herman Schwendinger in *Rape and Equality:*

> Rather than the victim's response, it is actually the rapist's supremacist attitude and behavior that dominate the situation and determine its violent outcome. . . . Because of the emphasis on parity, the interaction theories tacitly minimize the structural realities of the situation and the power differentials that characterize the overwhelming number of forcible rapes.[63]

Psychoanalytic Theories

Only a small percentage of rapists are considered psychotic. However, psychoanalytic theories posit that most rapists are emotionally disturbed, developed an intense hatred of women during childhood, and may have had experiences "that triggered their latent homosexual tendencies."[64] Hence rape is seen as actions undertaken by men who are "obsessively motivated by hatred of women and an overpowering need to assure themselves of their own masculinity."[65] Psychoanalytic hypotheses are also critical to some sociological theories, such as the "subculture of violence theory," which is applied to rapists by such researchers as Amir and Brownmiller."[66]

Psychoanalytic theories are limited in addressing rape due to the systematic failure to prove their theory scientifically. Psychoanalysis tends to place too much emphasis on the number of rapes attributed to personality disorders in the absence of empirical validity.

Opportunity Structure Theory

Researchers Lorenne Clark and Debra Lewis have used an opportunity structure theory in explaining rape.[67] They contend that men regard women as possessors of saleable sexual properties.

> Female sexuality is allegedly bought and sold in an open market. However, the market is dominated by male conceptions of property and therefore the best bargain a woman can achieve is still restrictive. Furthermore, when bargaining for sex, men reportedly use various forms of coercion. They may make promises they cannot or will not really fulfill. They may harass women or threaten them with physical harm.[68]

According to Clark and Lewis, while men who have money or other resources can easily make bargains with women in their own interests, those men who are poor or unattractive may use force to have sex with a woman due to an inability to bargain successfully. They further suggest that lower class rapists often choose to rape middle class women because these men are without the necessary means to attract these women and desire what they cannot have. In summary, the researchers argue that forcible rape "will always be an inevitable consequence of the fact that some men do not have the means to achieve sexual relations with women, except through physical violence."[69]

Clark and Lewis's opportunity structure theory of rape has been criticized in its concept of sex as a commodity, and for disregarding the fact that many wealthy, charming, or handsome men also rape women. Though there has been some support on the premise that habitual rapists tend to be poor, there is no evidence that they frequently prey upon middle class women. On the contrary, most studies show that the majority of rape victims also tend to come from the lower classes.[70]

Biological Theory of Rape

The biological theory of rape has mainly been forwarded by feminist researchers. Most notable in advancing a male predisposition to rape is Brownmiller in her book, *Against Our Will: Men, Women and Rape:*

> Man's structural capacity to rape and women's corresponding structural vulnerability are as basic to the physiology of both our sexes as the primal act of sex itself. Had it not been for this accident of biology, an accommodation requiring the locking together of two separate parts, penis into vagina, there would be neither copulation nor rape as we know it. . . . In terms of human anatomy, the possibility of forcible intercourse incontrovertibly exists. This single factor may have been sufficient to have caused the creation of a male ideology of rape.[71]

Brownmiller's theory of biologically created male rapists, though not without merit to some degree, has not been scientifically validated. Further, too much emphasis is placed on traditional male stereotyping while rejecting the sexist stereotyping of women. Finally, Brownmiller fails to adequately address the fact that it is man's biologically established physical strength advantage over women that is the most critical biological element in most rapes.

THE EFFECTS OF FORCIBLE RAPE

Studies show that the effects of rape on its victims can be psychological, physical, and economical, and have short and long-term duration. Physical effects associated with rape can include a variety of internal and external problems such as vaginal bleeding, broken bones, blood clots, pelvic pain, miscarriage, pregnancy, and exposure to AIDS.[72] Psychological effects for rape victims can include altered emotional states, lowered self-esteem, anxiety, depression, fear, lack of sexual desire, and posttraumatic stress disorder.[73] According to Carol Nadelson and Malkah Notman, rape victims are predictably characterized by the following:

- Feelings of helplessness.
- Heightened conflicts regarding dependence and independence.
- Self-criticism and guilt.

- Difficulty handling aggression and anger.
- Interference in developing trusting male relationships.
- Increased feelings of vulnerability.
- Increased emotional susceptibility.
- Regression to a more dependent, helpless position.[74]

The researchers also found that rape can result in a disruption of normal adaptive patterns, causing such symptoms as a lowered attention span, disturbances of appetite and sleep, and a diminished level of functioning.

Rape victimization can also increase the risk of suicide. Psychologists Dean Kilpatrick, Connie Best, and Lois Veronen found that nearly one in five rape victims reported an attempted suicide—a rate more than eight times greater than that of nonrape victims.[75] Kilpatrick and associates found a higher rate of suicidal ideation and nervous breakdowns among victims of completed rape than victims of attempted rape or other crimes.[76]

An economic impact may also be felt for victims of rape as a result of medical and legal costs associated with their victimization, lost work time and wages, loss of employment, withdrawal from school, and changes in residence or location.

NOTES

1. A. Browne, *When Battered Women Kill* (New York: Macmillan, 1987); Patricia Mahoney and Linda M. Williams, "Sexual Assault in Marriage: Prevalence, Consequences, and Treatment of Wife Rape," in Jana L. Jasinski and Linda M. Williams, eds., *Partner Violence; A Comprehensive Review of 20 Years of Research* (Thousand Oaks: Sage, 1998), pp. 122–23.
2. R. Barri Flowers, *Women and Criminality: The Woman as Victim, Offender, and Practitioner* (Westport: Greenwood Press, 1987), p. 27.
3. Susan Brownmiller, *Against Our Will: Men, Women and Rape* (New York: Simon & Schuster, 1975), pp. 13–14.
4. Flowers, *Women and Criminality,* p. 27.
5. Quoted in Carol v. Horos, *Rape* (New Canaan: Tobey Publishing, 1974), p. 3.
6. Flowers, *Women and Criminality,* p. 27.
7. Horos, *Rape,* p. 4.
8. Brownmiller, *Against Our Will.*
9. R. Barri Flowers, *Children and Criminality: The Child as Victim and Perpetrator* (Westport: Greenwood Press, 1986), p. 7.
10. R. Barri Flowers, *The Victimization and Exploitation of Women and Children: A Study of Physical, Mental and Sexual Maltreatment in the United States* (Jefferson: McFarland, 1994), p. 144.
11. The *American Heritage Dictionary,* 3rd ed. (New York: Dell, 1994), p. 683.
12. Flowers, *Women and Criminality,* p. 28.
13. Battelle Law and Justice Study Center Report, *Forcible Rape: An Analysis of Legal Issues* (Washington: U.S. Government Printing Office, 1977), p. 34.
14. Flowers, *Women and Criminality,* p. 29.

15. *Forcible Rape: An Analysis of Legal Issues,* p. 17.
16. K. Svalastoga, "Rape and Social Structure," *Pacific Sociological Review* 5 (1962): 48–53.
17. Mary E. Odem and Jody Clay-Warner, *Confronting Rape and Sexual Assault* (Wilmington: Scholarly Resources, Inc., 1998), p. xiv.
18. *Ibid.,* p. xv; Brownmiller, *Against Our Will;* Carole J. Sheffield, "Sexual Terrorism," in Jo Freeman, ed., *Women: A Feminist Perspective,* 4th ed. (Mountain View: Mayfield, 1984), pp. 3–19.
19. Flowers, *The Victimization and Exploitation of Women and Children,* pp. 54–79.
20. Susan H. Klemmack and David L. Klemmack, "The Social Definition of Rape," in Marcy J. Walker and Stanley L. Brodsky, eds., *Sexual Assault* (Lexington: Lexington Books, 1976), pp. 144–45.
21. U.S. Department of Justice, Federal Bureau of Investigation, *Crime in the United States: Uniform Crime Reports 2004* (Washington: Government Printing Office, 2005), p. 7.
22. National Institute of Justice and Centers for Disease Control and Prevention, *Prevalence, Incidence, and Consequences of Violence Against Women: Findings from the National Violence Against Women Survey,* November 1988.
23. D. G. Kilpatrick, C. N. Edmunds, and A. K. Seymour, *Rape in America; A Report to the Nation* (Charleston: Medical University of South Carolina, Crime Victims Research and Treatment Center, 1992).
24. Diana E. Russell, *Sexual Exploitation: Rape, Child Abuse, and Workplace Harassment* (Beverly Hills: Sage, 1984), p. 47.
25. Cited in Lorraine Dusky, *Still Unequal: The Shameful Truth About Women and Justice in America* (New York: Crown, 1996), p. 380.
26. U.S. Department of Justice, Bureau of Justice Statistics, *Sex Offenses and Offenders: An Analysis of Data on Rape and Sexual Assault* (Washington: Office of Justice Programs, 1997), p. 1.
27. Nancy Gager and Cathleen Schurr, *Sexual Assault: Confronting Rape in America* (New York: Grosset and Dunlap, 1976), p. 91.
28. Brownmiller, *Against Our Will,* p. 190.
29. Kilpatrick, Edmunds, and Seymour, *Rape in America.*
30. *See, for example,* L. A. Curtis, "Present and Future Measures of Victimization in Forcible Rape," in M. J. Walker and S. L. Brodsky, eds., *Sexual Assault* (Lexington: D. C. Heath, 1976), pp. 61–68.
31. *Sex Offenses and Offenders,* p. 2.
32. *Uniform Crime Reports 2004,* p. 28.
33. *Ibid.,* p. 29.
34. *Ibid.,* pp. 27–29.
35. *Sex Offenses and Offenders,* p. 15.
36. *Ibid.*
37. *Ibid.,* pp. 12–14.
38. Dusky, *Still Unequal,* p. 381.
39. Kilpatrick, Edmunds, and Seymour, *Rape in America.*
40. *National Violence Against Women Survey.*
41. Russell, *Sexual Exploitation,* p. 88.
42. Menachem Amir, *Patterns in Forcible Rape* (Chicago: University of Chicago Press, 1971).
43. Sedelle Katz and Mary A. Mazur, *Understanding the Rape Victim: A Synthesis of Research Findings* (New York: John Wiley & Sons, 1979), p. 38.
44. *Ibid.,* p. 39.
45. "U.S. Report on Rape Cases Cites Victims' Frustrations with Law," *New York Times*

(March 25, 1985), p. A 17. *See also* U.S. Department of Justice, Bureau of Justice Statistics, *Sourcebook of Criminal Justice Statistics 2003* (Washington: Government Printing Office, 2005), pp. 191–97.

46. *Sex Offenses and Offenders,* pp. 11–12.
47. Stanley L. Brodsky and Susan C. Hobart, "Blame Models and Assailant Research," *Criminal Justice and Behavior 5* (1978): 379–88.
48. Paul H. Gebhard, John H. Gagnon, Wardell B. Pomeroy, and Cornelia V. Christenson, *Sex Offenders: An Analysis of Types* (New York: Harper & Row, 1965), pp. 198–204.
49. Richard T. Rada, *Clinical Aspects of the Rapist* (New York: Grune and Stratton, 1978), pp. 122–30.
50. A. Nicholas Groth, Ann W. Burgess, and Lynda L. Holmstrom, "Rape: Power, Anger, and Sexuality," *American Journal of Psychiatry 34* (1977): 1239–43.
51. Flowers, *Women and Criminality,* p. 38.
52. Robert E. Freeman-Longo and Geral T. Blanchard, *Sexual Abuse in America; Epidemic of the 21st Century* (Brandon: Safer Society Press, 1998), p. 48; A Nicholas Groth and J. Birnbuam, *Men Who Rape: The Psychology of the Offender* (New York: Plenum, 1979).
53. Freeman-Longo and Blanchard, *Sexual Abuse in America,* pp. 48–49.
54. *Ibid.,* p. 49.
55. *Ibid.*
56. Robert K. Ressler, Ann W. Burgess, and John E. Douglas, *Sexual Homicide: Patterns and Motives* (New York: Lexington Books, 1988), pp. 6, 42–43; M. L. Cohen, R. F. Garofalo, R. Boucher, and T. Seghorn, "The Psychology of Rapists," *Seminars in Psychiatry 3* (1971): 307–27; E. Podolsky, "Sexual Violence," Medical Digest 34 (1966): 60–63.
57. D. T. Lunde, Murder and Madness (New York, Norton, 1979); J. M. MacDonald, *Rape Offenders and Their Victims* (Springfield: Charles C Thomas, 1971); J. Money, "Forensic Sexology," *American Journal of Psychotherapy 44* (1990): 26–36; David Lester, *Serial Killers: The Insatiable Passion* (Philadelphia: The Charles Press, 1995).
58. Lester, *Serial Killers,* pp. 48–82; Ressler, Burgess, and Douglas, *Sexual Homicide,* pp. 45–56; R. G. Rappaport, "The Serial and Mass Murderer," *American Journal of Serial Killers* (New York: Anchor, 1989).
59. Diana Scully and Joseph Marolla, "Incarcerated Rapists: Exploring a Sociological Mode," *Final Report for Department of Health and Human Services* (Washington: Government Printing Office, 1983), p. 63.
60. Julia R. Schwendinger and Herman Schwendinger, *Rape and Inequality* (Beverly Hills: Sage, 1983), p. 65.
61. Amir, *Patterns in Forcible Rape,* p. 346.
62. Flowers, *Women and Criminality,* p. 39.
63. Schwendinger and Schwendinger, *Rape and Inequality,* p. 68.
64. *Ibid.,* p. 71.
65. Flowers, *Women and Criminality,* p. 40.
66. *Ibid.,* pp. 72–73; Amir, *Patterns in Forcible Rape;* Brownmiller, *Against Our Will.*
67. Lorenne M. Clark and Debra J. Lewis, *Rape: The Price of Coercive Sexuality* (Toronto: Canadian Women's Educational Press, 1977), pp. 28–31.
68. *Ibid.,* Schwendinger and Schwendinger, *Rape and Inequality,* p. 78.
69. Clark and Lewis, *Rape: The Price of Coercive Sexuality,* p. 131.
70. Flowers, *Women and Criminality,* p. 41.
71. Brownmiller, *Against Our Will,* pp. 13–14.
72. J. C. Campbell and P. Alford, "The Dark Consequences of Marital Rape," *American Journal of Nursing* (1989): 946–49; R. K. Bergen, *Wife Rape: Providers* (Thousand Oaks:

Sage, 1996); K. K. Eby, J. C. Campbell, C. M. Sullivan, and W. S. Davidson, "Health Effects of Experiences of Sexual Violence for Women with Abusive Partners," *Health Care for Women International 16* (1995): 563–76.

73. L. A. Goodman, M. P. Koss, and N. F. Russo, "Violence Against Women: Physical and Mental Health Effects: Part I. Research Findings," *Applied and Preventative Psychology 2* (1993): 79–89; A Browne, "Violence Against Women by Male Partners: Prevalence, Outcomes, and Policy Implications," *American Psychologist 48,* 10 (1993): 1077–87.

74. Carol G. Nadelson and Malkah T. Notman, "Emotional Repercussions of Rape," *Medical Aspects of Human Sexuality 11* (1977): 16–31.

75. "Female Victims: The Crime Goes On," *Science News 126* (1984): 153.

76. D. G. Kilpatrick, C. L. Best, L. J. Veronen, A. E. Amick, L. A. Villeponteaux, and G. A. Ruff, "Mental Health Correlates of Criminal Victimization: A Random Community Survey," *Journal of Consulting and Clinical Psychology 53,* 4 (1985): 866–73.

Chapter 3

MARITAL RAPE

Though stranger rape receives the most attention from social scientists, criminologists, medical professionals, and the media, acquaintance rape is more prevalent and the consequences equally devastating. The form of acquaintance rape most examined by rape researchers is marital rape. Prior to the mid 1970s, there were no laws that included marital forced sexual assaults in rape definitions. Tradition and history essentially gave men the right to rape their wives.[1] The women's movement played a major role in reform legislation, making marital rape a crime across the country. However, legal definitions of marital rape are not uniform from state to state. Marital rape victims are not always certain what constitutes rape or if they believe they were raped, they are less willing to report it than stranger rape. Experts now recognize that rape in a marriage is typically an element of domestic violence that also includes such issues as sexual jealousy, sexual intimacy, and pregnancy. This chapter will examine the dynamics and characteristics of marital rape.

WHAT IS MARITAL RAPE?

The definition of marital rape, also referred to as wife rape or conjugal rape, can be defined in both nonlegal and legal terms. While the latter varies from state to state and is rooted in common law and the marital rape exemptions, rape experts define marital rape in terms similar to forcible rape (see Chapter 2). *Marital rape* is defined as "any unwanted intercourse or penetration (vaginal, anal, or oral) obtained by force, threat of force, or when the wife is unable to consent."[2] Similarly, *wife rape* is defined as "any unwanted sexual penetration (vaginal, anal, or oral) or contact with the genitals that is the result of actual or threatened physical force or when the woman is unable to give affirmative consent."[3] Many rape researchers go beyond the legally married wife in defining marital rape and include cohabitating couples, recognizing that the same dynamics apply as with couples who are in a legal marriage. In some studies, marital rape or marital sexual assault has also included forced sexual relations outside the marriage or "sexual exploitation involving sexual contact, such as when a husband coerces a wife to engage in sexual acts with someone else."[4]

Marital rape is a relatively recent phenomenon insofar as its recognition as a legitimate term and form of sexual violence. Because of its very nature, for many marital rape "is still generally regarded as a contradiction in terms; the common notion of rape is not one that includes a marital context."[5] Even victims find it hard to differentiate what is rape and what is consensual sex. Kata Issari of the National Coalition Against Sexual Assault notes the typical confusion regarding forced sexual relations among many victims: "They often don't define it as rape because of society's beliefs about what should go on in a marriage."[6] These beliefs can be seen in traditional definitions of rape such as forced male "sexual intercourse with a female not his wife without her consent"[7] or "the forcible penetration of the body of a woman, not the wife of the perpetrator."[8]

According to Patricia Mahoney and Linda Williams, these beliefs of what does and does not constitute rape are a reflection of long established notions concerning men, women, and sexuality such as

> a woman's sexuality is a commodity that can be owned by her father or husband, what happens between husband and wife in the bedroom is a private matter, a man is entitled to sexual relations with his wife, and a wife should consensually engage in sex with her husband, thus making rape "unnecessary."[9]

Many men and women still view marital sexual relations in this regard. When considered in the context of spousal exemptions from prosecution existing in many states, it in effect has given marital rapists a "license to rape."[10]

Marital Rape and the Law

Historically rape has been associated with power, proprietary interest, and enforced marriage.[11] Rape is believed to be "the oldest means by which a man could seize or steal a woman to be his wife."[12] In modern times, rape has been legally defined as the unlawful carnal knowledge of a woman forcibly and against her will. Traditionally, these laws did not pertain to men who raped their wives or included a "marital rape exemption."[13] Most scholars believe this exemption originated with a pronouncement made by Chief Justice Sir Matthew Hale in seventeenth century England, who wrote

> The husband cannot be guilty of a rape committed by himself upon his lawful
> wife, for by their marital matrimonial consent and contract, the wife hath given
> herself in kind unto the husband which she cannot retract.[14]

This way of thinking is seen as a reflection of earlier precedents that women were regarded as property by their husbands with the institution of marriage entirely for the purpose of procreation.[15] Hence, it established the belief that implicit in marriage was the man's right to sexual intercourse without the woman's right of refusal.[16] Despite the fact that Hale's opinion was not backed by legal authority, United States case law on the matter clearly accepted the Hale dictum as though "the courts were incapable of conceiving other resolutions of the issue."[17]

The marital rape exemption remained in force and largely without legal challenge until the 1970s when the women's movement successfully argued that the law failed to provide equal protection against rape for all women.[18] In 1975, Nebraska became the first state to abolish the spousal exemption.[19] In 1978, the first criminal prosecution for marital rape by a live-in husband took place in Oregon.[20] It was not until 1993 that marital rape became a crime in every state under at least one section of the sexual offense codes.[21] However, in more than half the states some exemptions exist in prosecuting men for raping their wives. For example, in many states husbands are exempt from prosecution if the wife is legally unable to consent due to reasons such as being asleep, mentally or physically impaired, or unconscious.[22] (See also Chapter 17.)

The fact that marital rape exemptions still exist in most states gives credence to the argument that rape in marriage is not regarded on the same level of criminality as other types of rape. As a result, this "perpetuates marital rape by conveying the message that such acts of aggression are somehow less reprehensible than other types of rape;" and further, suggests "an acceptance of the archaic understanding that wives are the property of their husbands and the marriage contract is an entitlement to sex."[23]

In spite of the current legal implications of marital rape, most such cases are never reported, much less result in prosecution of the rapist. However, interestingly enough, marital rapists who are prosecuted appear likely to be convicted. According to the National Clearinghouse on Marital and Date Rape, of 118 wife rape cases prosecuted from 1978 to 1985 there were 104 convictions—or an astounding 88 percent conviction rate.[24] This rate of conviction is significantly higher than that for nonmarital rape prosecutions. Rape experts have attributed the high conviction rate in marital rape cases to the more violent and abusive nature of such cases that make it to trial. The majority of wife rape cases that fall short of such severity are either never reported by the victim or not deemed as "prosecutable" by police, prosecutors, or others in the criminal justice system.[25]

Marital rape victims may also be able to receive justice through civil court action against their spouses for financial compensation for injuries, medical costs, and other expenses related to their spousal victimization.[26] In most such cases, the victims still face an uphill battle in successfully suing rapist husbands as many continue to subscribe to a marital rape exemption for sexual assaults involving spouses.

THE MAGNITUDE OF MARITAL RAPE

Most studies on marital rape and sexual assault indicate the severity of the problem that affects millions of women across the United States each year. According to the Crime Victims Research and Treatment Center (CVC), more than a million women have been victims of spousal rape during their lifetime.[27] A CVC and National Victim Center (NVC) report, *Rape in America,* estimates that more than 61,000 women are raped by spouses and ex-spouses annually in the United States.[28] In a 2003 National Crime Victimization Survey, an estimated 27,380 rape and sexual assault victimizations were perpetrated by intimates.[29]

Sex offenses of all types against married women are significantly high. The FBI estimates that twenty-five million women are victims of spousal sexual assaults each year in this country.[30] More than 12 percent of convicted jail inmates serving time for intimate violence were convicted of raping or sexually assaulting a spouse, ex-spouse, or other intimate;[31] while over 20 percent of prison inmates convicted of intimate violence committed rape or sexual assaults against spouses, ex-spouses, or others they were intimately involved with.[32]

Marital rape researchers estimate between 10 and 14 percent of married women have experienced spousal rape.[33] Studies have found that one in ten wives have been the victims of at least one sexual assault by their husband, while between 50 and 87 percent of female victims of conjugal rape report being sexually assaulted at least twenty times by their intimate mate.[34] According to Diana Russell, marital rape occurs more than twice as often as stranger rape.[35]

Marital rape prevalence studies support the high incidence of rape and sexual assault in marriage. Russell's survey of a randomly selected sample of 930 women in San Francisco yielded a prevalence rate of ever having been raped by a spouse at 14 percent.[36] David Finkelhor and Kersti Yllo's interview of 330 women in Boston revealed that 10 percent of the women who had ever been married or ever cohabitated, were survivors of marital rape or intimate rape by a partner.[37]

In relation to other forms of rape, intimate rape is proportionally high. In M. Randall and L. Haskell's study of rape, they found that 30 percent of rape cases involving adults were perpetrated by husbands, live-in partners, or boyfriends.[38] This compared to 12 percent of rapes committed by strangers to the victims. Similarly, L. K. George, I. Winfield, and D. G. Blazer found that 29 percent of sexual assaults against adult women were committed by husbands or boyfriends;[39] while S. F. Ullman and J. M. Siegel reported that 28 percent of survivors of sexual assault age sixteen and over were victimized by intimates.[40] Nearly one in five rapes involve husbands or boyfriends, according to a study by D. G. Kilpatrick, C. N. Edmunds, and A. K. Seymour.[41]

In spite of the prevalence and incidence of marital rape, it remains one of the most underreported types of rape.[42] A number of researchers have noted the reluctance of sexually violated women by intimates to disclose their victimization.[43] In a study of rape victims, L. S. Williams found that the relationship between a rape victim and her rapist appears to be the most important factor in determining if a rape is reported or not.[44]

CHARACTERISTICS OF MARITAL RAPE

Marital rape occurs across social, racial, ethnic, age, and class spectrums. Most marital rape involves other types of domestic violence—often offender substance abuse—and can have devastating long- and short-term effects on the victim. Risk factors for rape in intimate relationships include domineering men, sexual jealousy, pregnancy, separation, divorce, and alcohol and/or drug use.

Marital Rape Victim Characteristics

Most victims of marital rape tend to be younger and lower or middle class women of all racial and ethnic groups. Russell found that nearly two-thirds of the raped wives were first victimized by their spouses when under twenty-five years of age.[45] Upper middle class women were somewhat overrepresented among survivors of spousal rape. However, in Finkelhor and Yllo's study, lower class women were the most likely to report being marital rape victims.[46] Most experts believe that spousal rape among upper class groups is less likely to be reported, similar to wife battering, than other classes.[47] Russell found the rate of rape in marriage to be slightly higher among black women than white, Hispanic, and Asian women.[48]

Researchers have examined race and ethnicity of marital rape victims in relation to the decision to leave a spouse rapist. Latino women were less likely to perceive their victimization as rape and end the relationship than other victims;[49] whereas white women were more likely to leave a husband rapist than black, Hispanic, and Asian women.[50]

Many marital rape victims are victimized through social and interpersonal coercion as opposed to physical violence. Social coercion tends to be a reflection of societal beliefs with respect to appropriate male and female sex roles within the marriage. These are typically rooted in religious beliefs, family, and cultural norms.[51] Interpersonal coercion includes threats on the part of the rapist husband to leave the wife or refuse to give her money unless she complies. For many women who are economically and emotionally dependent on their spouses, this threat is more than sufficient to force them to submit to unwanted sexual relations.[52]

Research has shown that most marital rape victims are sexually violated multiple times by their spouse rapist. Half the women in Finkelhor and Yllo's sample were raped twenty times or more,[53] while M. P. Koss and associates reported that more than half the women victims of family violence were raped five or more times by the same intimate offender.[54] In D. S. Riggs and colleagues' study, though there were no victim reports of multiple rapes committed by strangers, 64 percent of raped wives reported being victims of multiple rapes perpetrated by husbands.[55] A. Browne found that women who murdered their spouses were more likely to have been raped over twenty times than a control group of battered women, suggesting a correlation between multiple rapes and homicidal women.[56]

Characteristics of Spouse Rapists

Though there has been no large scale research on husbands who rape their wives, reports from wife victims of marital rape have shed light on husband rapist characteristics. Russell's study found that marital rapists were present among all ethnic and racial groups, ages, social, economic, and educational backgrounds.[57] The husband rapist has been characterized as domineering, more accepting of wife battering, and regards his wife as personal property to sexually assault at his whim.[58]

According to Yllo and Finkelhor, there are three types of marital rapists:

- Men motivated primarily by uncontrolled anger.
- Men who use rape as a means to obtain power over their wives.
- Men who are obsessed with sex and receive gratification from perverse and sadistic acts.[59]

Nearly half the marital rapists studied fell into the uncontrolled anger category. These men tended to rape their wives during or after physically abusing them. The men who raped their spouses as a measure of having power over them typically only used the necessary force to coerce them into having sexual intercourse.

Marital Rape and Spousal Violence

Marital rape and sexual assault have been shown by many researchers to be closely associated with wife battering and other domestic violence. In one study, 33 to 46 percent of battered women reported also being sexually assaulted by their spouses.[60] Lenore Walker found that 59 percent of the battered women in her sample were forced to submit to sexual relations with their husbands, compared to only 7 percent of nonabused women.[61] It is estimated that one in three rape victims are battered women, while among rape victims over thirty, almost six in ten women are battered.[62] Russell reported that the risk of being sexually assaulted for battered women was three to five times higher than that of nonbattered women.[63]

The mere threat of violence has forced many women into having sex with their spouses, according to a number of studies. In J. C. Campbell and P. Alford's study, half of the battered women were threatened with physical violence for refusing sexual relations.[64] Other researchers have found a relationship between refusal to have sex with a spouse and wife abuse as well as forced sex to avoid beatings.[65] Some battered and sexually assaulted women are also forced into other sexual acts or sexual perversions. Campbell and Alford found that some of their sample of abused women had been forced to participate in sexual acts with other women, children, animals, as prostitutes, and in exhibitionism.[66]

A typology of wife battering and rape was developed by Finkelhor and Yllo. *Battering rape* is defined as victimization in a marriage that involves rape, physical assault, and verbal abuse.[67] In battering rape, physical abuse normally accompanies the sexual assault. The spouse batterer tends to be angry, belligerent towards the victim, and abusing alcohol or drugs. Sexual violence represents one of many ways a husband expresses violence towards his wife. "Hurting, debasing, and humiliating victims are the ways anger is expressed by these rapists, and the men may use far more actual force than would be necessary to overpower their partners."[68]

Studies show that marital rape survivors tend to be victims of a higher incidence of domestic violence than survivors of acquaintance rape.[69] Furthermore, victims of marital rape are also more likely to be forced to participate in oral and anal intercourse.[70] Some marital rape victims have reported periods of sexual assault lasting for hours and repeated rape and battering. Such rapes and violence were typically perpetrated by husbands under the influence of drugs or alcohol, or with a history of severe violence towards their wives.[71]

Not all researchers believe that marital rape and wife battering are synonymous or of cause and effect. Some studies have found that rape victims are not always battered women per se;[72] while others reported that some "force only" marital rapes are limited to the force necessary to achieve the sexual objective.[73] However, others support the correlation between spousal rape and battered women by the very nature of rape. According to Shelley Neiderback, a trauma counselor: "Marital rape is another aspect of spouse battering. It is not about sex; it's about control, violence, and humiliation."[74]

Risk Factors of Marital Rape

Women may be most at risk for marital rape if they are pregnant, ill, divorced or separated, or if their husband is domineering, jealous, or abuses alcohol or drugs. A number of researchers have found that pregnancy places women at risk for both wife rape and domestic violence.[75] Other studies have linked illness on the part of the wife to forced sexual relations by a husband.[76]

Case studies have shown an increased risk for marital sexual victimization by women just prior to, during, or following separation or divorce from their husbands. Two-thirds of the Finkelhor and Yllo sample reported being sexually assaulted towards the end of their marriage.[77] Twenty percent of separated or divorced women in the R. K. Bergen study were victims of marital sexual assaults,[78] while 15 percent of Russell's sample of wife rape survivors were sexually assaulted by a spouse just before or during a separation.[79]

Most marital rape experts believe that domineering, jealous men who regard sexual relations with their wives or "property" as an "entitlement" places the woman in their lives at higher risk of conjugal rape. Alcohol and/or drug abuse by the husband are also seen as high risk factors for wife rape and wife abuse.[80] Almost one-fourth of the wife rape victims in Russell's study reported that their rapists husband was drinking during the time of the assault, while around one-fourth of the marital rapists were identified as habitual drinkers.[81] Alcohol and drug abuse may act as uninhibitors or excuse sexually violent behavior by men towards their wives.[82] There is also some indication that substance abuse by marital rape victims may increase the risk for victimization. However, underreporting of sexual assaults in marriage makes it difficult to assess its significance in relation to other factors in marital violence.

THE EFFECTS OF MARITAL RAPE

Marital rape and sexual assault can affect victims in many ways physically and psychologically, both short- and long-term. Studies have shown that physical effects of marital rape include injuries to the vagina and anus, torn muscles, lacerations, soreness, and fatigue.[83] Battered rape victims may also suffer from injuries such as broken bones, bloody noses, black eyes, and wounds from weapons.[84] One study found that half the survivors of marital rape sampled experienced being hit, kicked, or burned during forced sexual relations.[85] Gynecological-related effects of marital rape include stretching of the vagina, miscarriages, infertility, bladder infections, and possible sexually transmitted diseases, including HIV infection.[86]

Psychological effects of rape in marriage have been compared with similar effects of other types of violence. Short-term effects of marital rape include depression, anxiety, fear, shock, suicidal tendencies, and posttraumatic stress disorder.[87] Marital rape survivors have reported higher rates of depression and anger than victims of stranger or acquaintance rape.[88]

Marital rape victims have also been found to experience severe and long-term psychological effects of their victimization. These include depression, eating disorders, sleeping disorders, self-blame, and problems with trust in a relationship.[89] Additionally, some survivors of rape in marriage have reported flashbacks, sexual dysfunction, and emotional trauma lasting for years after the sexual violence.[90]

WHY MEN COMMIT MARITAL RAPE

There have been few studies to directly address why men rape their wives, as opposed to why men rape in general. The common themes of marital rape as reported by wife victims are that they include men who are motivated by power, control, dominance, possession, obsession, humiliation, and sadism. Marital rapists have been classified into three basic types: (1) force-only rapists, (2) battering rapists, and (3) sadistic/obsessive rapists.[91]

Force-only rapists–use only the necessary force to coerce their wives into sexual relations.

Battering rapists–rape and batter their wives, either concurrently or before or after the other.

Sadistic/obsessive rapists–use torture or perverse sexual acts against their wives, often influenced by or involving pornography.

Some marital rapists have expressed feelings of weakness, powerlessness, and anger in the relationship, where forced sex was used as a weapon or viewed as an entitlement.[92] Many conjugal rapists subscribe to rape myths in justifying the sexual violence, such as that their wives really wanted the sex or enjoyed forced sexual relations.[93] Rapist husbands, in some studies, have also been found to be in denial of the rape and its harmful effects on the wife victims.[94] Further study is needed on marital rape from the perspective of husband rapists to get a more complete picture of why they choose to sexually assault their wives.

NOTES

1. R. Barri Flowers, *The Victimization and Exploitation of Women and Children: A Study of Physical, Mental and Sexual Maltreatment in the United States* (Jefferson: McFarland, 1994), pp. 143–44; Susan Brownmiller, *Against Our Will: Men, Women and Rape* (New York: Simon & Schuster, 1975).
2. VAWnet Applied Research Forum, National Electronic Network on Violence Against Women, "Marital Rape," National Resource Center on Domestic Violence, San Francisco, 1999. See also R. K. Bergen, *Wife Rape: Understanding Responses of Survivors and Service Providers* (Thousand Oaks: Sage, 1996); Diana E. Russell, *Rape in Marriage* (New York: Macmillan, 1990).
3. Patricia Mahoney and Linda M. Williams, "Sexual Assault in Marriage: Prevalence, Consequences, and Treatment of Wife Rape," in Jana L. Jasinski and Linda M. Williams, eds., *Partner Violence: A Comprehensive Review of 20 Years of Research* (Thousand Oaks: Sage, 1998), p. 116.
4. Ibid. See also Bergen, *Wife Rape;* M. D. Pagelow, *Family Violence* (New York: Praeger, 1984).
5. Mahoney and Williams, "Sexual Assault in Marriage," p. 114.
6. Quoted in Andrea Gross, "A Question of Rape," *Ladies Home Journal 110,* 11 (November, 1993), p. 170.
7. V. Barchis, "The Question of Marital Rape," *Women's Studies International Forum 6* (1983): 383.
8. Diana E. Russell, "Wife Rape and the Law," in Mary E. Odem and Jody Clay-Warner, eds., *Confronting Rape and Sexual Assault* (Wilmington: Scholarly Resources Inc., 1998), p. 71.
9. Mahoney and Williams, "Sexual Assault in Marriage," p. 114.
10. D. Drucker, "The Common Law Does Not Support a Marital Exemption for Forcible Rape," *Women's Rights Law Reporter 5* (1979): 2–3; J. Sitton, "Old Wine in New Bottles: The Marital Rape Allowance," *North Carolina Law Review 72* (1993): 261–89.
11. Russell, "Wife Rape and the Law," pp. 71–73; R. Barri Flowers, *Women and Criminality: The Woman as Victim, Offender, and Practitioner* (Westport: Greenwood Press, 1987), pp. 27–28.
12. Flowers, *The Victimization and Exploitation of Women and Children,* p. 143.
13. Bergen, *Wife Rape;* Russell, "Wife Rape and the Law," p. 71; Sitton, "Old Wine in New Bottles."
14. Quoted in Russell, "Wife Rape and the Law," pp. 71–72.
15. Hubert S. Feild and Leigh B. Bienen, *Jurors and Rape: A Study in Psychology and Law* (Lexington: D. C. Heath, 1980), p. 163.
16. Ibid.; L. Bidwell and P. White, "The Family Context of Marital Rape," *Journal of Family Violence 1* (1986): 277–87.
17. Gilbert Geis, "Rape-in-Marriage: Law and Law Reform in England, the United States, and Sweden," *Adelaide Law Review 6,* 2 (1978): 285.
18. Bidwell and White, "The Family Context of Marital Rape;" David Finkelhor and Kersti Yllo, *License to Rape: Sexual Abuse of Wives* (New York: Holt, Rinehart, & Winston, 1985).

19. National Resource Center on Domestic Violence, *Domestic Violence* (Harrisburg: Pennsylvania Coalition Against Domestic Violence, 1999).
20. Russell, "Wife Rape and the Law," pp. 73–76.
21. Mahoney and Williams, "Sexual Assault in Marriage," p. 119; Bergen, *Wife Rape.*
22. Russell, *Rape in Marriage;* Bergen, *Wife Rape;* Mahoney and Williams, "Sexual Assault in Marriage," p. 119.
23. VAWnet, "Marital Rape."
24. Cited in Russell, "Wife Rape and the Law," p. 78.
25. Mahoney and Williams, "Sexual Assault in Marriage," p. 120; Diana E. Russell, *Sexual Exploitation: Rape, Child Sexual Abuse, and Workplace Harassment* (Beverly Hills: Sage, 1984).
26. Mahoney and Williams, "Sexual Assault in Marriage," p. 120.
27. Cited in Gross, "A Question of Rape," p. 170.
28. *Ibid.*
29. U.S. Department of Justice, Bureau of Justice Statistics, *Criminal Victimization, 2003* (Washington: Office of Justice Programs, 2004), p. 9. Data includes male rape and sexual assault victims.
30. "Marital Rape: Drive for Tougher Laws is Passed," *New York Times* (May 15, 1987), p. A16.
31. U.S. Department of Justice, Bureau of Justice Statistics, *Violence by Intimates: Analysis of Data on Crimes by Current or Former Spouses, Boyfriends, and Girlfriends* (Washington: Office of Justice Programs, 1998), p. 25.
32. *Ibid.*, p. 28; U.S. Department of Justice, Bureau of Justice Statistics, *Family Violence Statistics: Including Statistics on Strangers and Acquaintances* (Washington: Office of Justice Programs, 2005), pp. 53–66.
33. Russell, *Rape in Marriage;* Finkelhor and Yllo, *License to Rape.*
34. "Marital Rape: Drive for Tougher Laws is Passed;" Finkelhor and Yllo, *License to Rape,* p. 22.
35. Russell, *Rape in Marriage.*
36. *Ibid.*
37. Finkelhor and Yllo, *License to Rape.*
38. M. Randall and L. Haskell, "Sexual Violence in Women's Lives," *Women 1,* 1 (1995): 6–31.
39. L. K. George, I. Winfield, and D. G. Blazer, "Sociocultural Factors in Sexual Assault: Comparison of Two Representative Samples of Women," *Journal of Social Issues 48,* 1 (1992): 105–25.
40. S. E. Ullman and J. M. Siegel, "Victim-Offender Relationship and Sexual Assault," *Violence and Victims 8,* 2 (1993): 121–34.
41. D. G. Kilpatrick, C. N. Edmunds, and A. K. Seymour, *Rape in America: A Report to the Nation* (Charleston: Medical University of South Carolina, Crime Victims Research and Treatment Center, 1992).
42. Ibid.; R. Bachman and L. E. Satlzman, *Violence Against Women: A National Crime Victimization Survey Report* (Washington: Bureau of Justice Statistics, 1994).
43. Russell, *Rape in Marriage;* Finkelhor and Yllo, *License to Rape;* U.S. Department of Justice, Bureau of Justice Statistics, *Sex Offenses and Offenders: An Analysis of Data on Rape and Sexual Assault* (Washington: Office of Justice Programs, 1997), p. 2; M. P. Koss, T. E. Dinero, C. A. Seibel, and S. L. Cox, "Stranger and Acquaintance Rape: Are There Differences in the Victim's Experience," *Psychology of Women Quarterly 12* (1988): 1–24.
44. L. S. Williams, "The Classic Rape: When Do Victims Report?" *Social Problems 31,* 4 (1984): 459–67.

45. Russell, *Rape in Marriage.*
46. Finkelhor and Yllo, *License to Rape.*
47. Flowers, *The Victimization and Exploitation of Women and Children,* pp. 159–61.
48. Russell, *Rape in Marriage.*
49. Bergen, *Wife Rape.*
50. Russell, *Rape in Marriage.*
51. *Ibid.*, Bergen, *Wife Rape;* Finkelhor and Yllo, *License to Rape.*
52. Russell, *Rape in Marriage,* p. 112; Mahoney and Williams, "Sexual Assault in Marriage," pp. 130–31.
53. Finkelhor and Yllo, *License to Rape.*
54. Koss, Dinero, Seibel, and Cox, "Stranger and Acquaintance Rape."
55. D. S. Riggs, D. G. Kilpatrick, and H. S. Resnick, "Long-Term Psychological Distress Associated with Marital Rape and Aggravated Assault: A Comparison to Other Crime Victims," *Journal of Family Violence 7,* 4 (1992): 283–96.
56. A Browne, *When Battered Women Kill* (New York: Macmillan, 1987).
57. Russell, *Rape in Marriage.*
58. J. C. Campbell, "Women's Response to Sexual Abuse in Intimate Relationships," *Health Care for Women International 10* (1989): 335–46; J. C. Campbell and P. Alford, "The Dark Consequences of Marital Rape," *American Journal of Nursing* (1989): 946–49.
59. Cited in Gross, "A Question of Rape."
60. Cited in "Final Report of the Supreme Court Task Force on Courts' and Communities' Response to Domestic Violence," submitted to the State Supreme Court of Iowa, August 1994, p. 10.
61. Lenore E. Walker, *The Battered Woman Syndrome* (New York: Springer, 1984), pp. 48–49. *See also* R. Barri Flowers, *Persuasive Evidence* (Dorchester, 2004).
62. "Final Report of the Supreme Court Task Force;" Evan Stark and Anne Flitcraft, *Surgeon General's Workshop on Violence and Public Health Source Book,* presented at the Surgeon General's Workshop on Violence and Public Health, Leesburg, VA, October 1985, p. 16.
63. Russell, *Rape in Marriage. See also* R. Barri Flowers *Justice Served* (Dorchester, 2005).
64. Campbell and Alford, "The Dark Consequences of Marital Rape."
65. Russell, *Rape in Marriage;* Finkelhor and Yllo, *License to Rape;* M. D. Pagelow, "Factors Affecting Women's Decisions to Leave Violent Relationships," *Journal of Family Issues 2,* 4 (1981): 391–414.
66. Campbell and Alford, "The Dark Consequences of Marital Rape." *See also* Finkelhor and Yllo, *License to Rape;* P. L. Peacock, "Marital Rape," in V. R. Wiehe and A. L. Richards, eds., *Intimate Betrayal: Understanding and Responding to the Trauma of Acquaintance Rape* (Thousand Oaks: Sage, 1995).
67. Finkelhor and Yllo, *License to Rape.*
68. Mahoney and Williams, "Sexual Assault in Marriage," p. 139.
69. Peacock, "Marital Rape." *See also* Browne, *When Battered Women Kill;* Campbell and Alford, "The Dark Consequences of Marital Rape."
70. Peacock, "Marital Rape."
71. Bergen, *Wife Rape;* Mahoney and Williams, "Sexual Assault in Marriage," p. 134; Browne, *When Battered Women Kill;* E. Pence and M. Paymar, *Education Groups for Men Who Batter: The Duluth Model* (New York: Springer, 1993).
72. Russell, *Rape in Marriage;* Finkelhor and Yllo, *License to Rape;* D. S. Riggs, D. G. Kilpatrick, and H. S. Resnick, "Long-term Psychological Distress Associated with Marital Rape and Aggravated Assault: A Comparison to Other Crime Victims," *Journal of Family Violence 7,* 4 (1992): 283–96.

73. Finkelhor and Yllo, *License to Rape;* Russell, *Rape in Marriage.*

74. Quoted in Gross, "A Question of Rape."

75. Flowers, *The Victimization and Exploitation of Women and Children,* pp. 161–62; Bergen, *Wife Rape;* Campbell, "Women's Response to Sexual Abuse in Intimate Relationships;" R. Barri Flowers, *Domestic Crimes, Family Violence and Child Abuse: A Study of Contemporary American Society* (Jefferson: McFarland, 2000); J. McFarlane, B. Parker, K. Soeken, and L. Bullock, "Assessing for Abuse During Pregnancy," *Journal of American Medical Association 267,* 23 (1992): 3176–78.

76. Campbell and Alford, "The Dark Consequences of Marital Rape;" Bergen, *Wife Rape.*

77. Finkelhor and Yllo, *License to Rape.* See also D. Kirz, *For Richer for Poorer: Mothers Confront Divorce* (New York: Routledge, 1995); R. E. Dobash and R. Dobash, Women, Violence and Social Change (London: Routledge, 1992).

78. Bergen, *Wife Rape.*

79. Russell, *Rape in Marriage.*

80. C. P. Barnard, "Alcoholism and Sex Abuse in the Family: Incest and Marital Rape," *Journal of Chemical Dependency Treatment 3* (1989): 131–44; I. H. Frieze, "Investigating the Consequences of Marital Rape," *Signs 8,* 3 (1983): 532–53; M. Whatley, "For Better or Worse: The Case of Marital Rape," *Violence and Victims 8* (1993): 29–39.

81. Russell, *Rape in Marriage.*

82. Barnard, "Alcoholism and Sex Abuse in the Family."

83. Bergen, *Wife Rape;* Campbell and Alford, "The Dark Consequences of Marital Rape;" C. Adams, "I Just Raped My Wife! What Are You Going To Do About It, Pastor?" in E. Buchwald, P. Fletcher, and M. Roth, eds., *Transforming A Rape Culture* (Minneapolis: Milkweed Editions, 1993), pp. 57–86.

84. Adams, "I Just Raped My Wife;" Bergen, *Wife Rape.*

85. Campbell and Alford, "The Dark Consequences of Marital Rape."

86. *Ibid.,* K. K. Eby, J. C. Campbell, C. M. Sullivan, and W. S. Davidson, "Health Effects of Experiences of Sexual Violence for Women with Abusive Partners," *Health Care for Women International 16* (1995): 563–76.

87. Russell, *Rape in Marriage;* Bergen, *Wife Rape;* D. G. Kilpatrick, C. C. Best, B. E. Saunders, and L. J. Vernon, "Rape in Marriage and in Dating Relationships: How Bad is it For Mental Health?" *Annals of the New York Academy of Sciences 528* (1988): 335–44.

88. Koss, Dinero, Seibel, and Cox, "Stranger and Acquaintance Rape."

89. Bergen, *Wife Rape;* Frieze, "Investigating the Causes and Consequences of Marital Rape;" Finkelhor and Yllo, *License to Rape.*

90. Whatley, "For Better or Worse;" Bergen, *Wife Rape.*

91. Finkelhor and Yllo, *License to Rape;* Bergen, *Wife Rape;* VAWnet Applied Research Forum, National Electronic Network on Violence Against Women, "In Brief: Marital Rape," National Resource Center on Domestic Violence, 1999, p. 1.

92. Mahoney and Williams, "Sexual Assault in Marriage," pp. 136–38; Finkelhor and Yllo, *License to Rape.*

93. Russell, *Rape in Marriage;* Mahoney and Williams, "Sexual Assault in Marriage," pp. 137–38; Martha R. Burt, "Cultural Myths and Support for Rape," *Journal of Personality and Social Psychology 38,* 2 (1980): 217–30.

94. *See, for example,* Russell, *Rape in Marriage,* p. 138; Pence and Paymar, *Education Groups for Men Who Batter.*

Chapter 4

DATE AND ACQUAINTANCE RAPE

In recent years, more attention has been focused on other types of rape beyond stranger and marital rape. Date rape, in particular, has been the focus of rape researchers as a serious and often hidden problem in American society. Teenage rape and rape on college campuses tends to be more a reflection of sexual assault involving intimates or acquaintances than strangers. Date rape itself seems to be a common element of the larger issue of dating violence. Another dangerous trend in nonstranger sexual violence is "date rape drugs," which render a victim helpless, often even unaware the rape occurred. Definitional problems and underreporting of date rape are further issues that affect recognition of its existence, treating victims, and prosecuting offenders.

Similarly, acquaintance rape is another rape crime that receives much less attention than stranger rape but is believed to be more prevalent. Such rapists may be friends, neighbors, colleagues, or others that the victim has some knowledge of or association with. Often victims have let down their guard or are otherwise victimized by acquaintance rapists who took advantage of trust or familiarity.

This chapter will examine the sex crimes and implications of date and acquaintance rape.

DATE RAPE

Date rape can be defined in general as rape involving boyfriends and girlfriends or others who are dating or out on a date, or previous partners. The term also tends to include rape involving acquaintances in a social setting conducive to intimate pairings and substance abuse such as campus fraternities or teenage parties. Assessing the incidence of date rape is difficult because of prevailing attitudes by males and females with respect to rape myths. Both have been socialized to believe that certain situations involving sexual relations are not rape–such as if the persons affected are dating or intimate. Other rape myths include beliefs that women secretly wish to be raped or may deserve it by their manner of behavior or style of clothing.[1] Male rapists also often subscribe to the myth that their sexual impulses are uncontrollable, hence they are not responsible for assaulting women.[2] Because so many people accept these myths as facts, victims of date rape are often blamed for their victimization or receive less sympathy than victims of stranger rape.[3]

Christine Courtois held that women who are sexually assaulted by dates are victims of an "endemic societal manifestation of the power imbalance between the sexes" whereby "men are conditioned into roles of power and domination . . . and females . . . are conditioned to be passive and dependent."[4] Martha Burt postulated that the attitudes of date rapists are greatly influenced by our culture and the status of women within it, pointing out that rape myths may act as "releasers or facilitators" of sexual aggression.[5] She argued that three attitudinal factors tend to be predictive of myths supporting rape:

- **Sex role stereotyping**–refers to accepted familial, work, and social roles as a reflection of the sex of the person.
- **Adversarial sexual beliefs**–refers to the notion that it is natural for male-female relationships to be filled with conflict and competition.
- **Acceptance of interpersonal violence**–refers to beliefs that violence is appropriate in interaction with others, particularly involving males and females.

In relating date rape to cultural biases perpetuating violence, Patricia Donat and John D'Emilio cited a social control/social conflict model of date rape:

Culturally transmitted assumptions about men, women, violence, sexuality, and myths about rape constitute a rape-supportive belief system. Furthermore, stratified systems such as the American dating situation may legitimate the use of force by those in power and weaken resistance of the less powerful. Finally, acquisition of stereotyped myths about rape may result in a failure to label as rape sexual aggression that occurs in dating situations.[6]

Other researchers have supported this date rape model.[7]

The difficulty in recognizing date rape as a criminal sexual assault–even by victims–can be seen in a recent study at the University of California in which more than half the female respondents felt that under some circumstances it was acceptable for a man to use physical aggression to receive sexual favors from his date.[8] Another study conducted by *Ms.* magazine found that nearly 75 percent of the date rape victims of rape, as legally defined, did not identify the action as such.[9]

Other studies have shown similar results on female victim interpretations of male sexual aggression or adherence to rape myths. Fifty-six percent of the adolescent females in B. Miller's survey believed that under certain conditions, it was permissible for a male to use force for sex.[10] Whereas one in six women interviewed by Miller and J. Marshall felt that once a man was sexually aroused it was impossible to prevent him from following through on that arousal.[11]

Research on date rape has characterized victims and circumstances as follows:

- Most victims are single females between the ages of fifteen and twenty-five.
- One in eight women are victims of date rape.
- Two in ten female college students are victims of date rape or attempted date rape.
- Half of female rape victims are sexually assaulted by first dates, casual dates, or romantic acquaintances.
- Rape victims are less likely to take measures to protect themselves from date or acquaintance rape than rape by a stranger.
- The majority of nonstranger rapes occur in the evening and at night.[12]

The Incidence of Date Rape

Though national date rape figures are often combined with other forms of acquaintance rape or general rape statistics, the research on date rape gives weight to its enormity as a social issue. According to the National Resource Center on Domestic Violence, more than three in four women who reported being the victims of rape or physical assault since the age of eighteen identified their perpetrator as a current spouse or ex-spouse, live-in partner, or date.[13] The Bureau of Justice Statistics reported in its factbook, *Violence by Intimates,* that more than 12 percent of convicted violent jail inmates whose victim was a spouse, former spouse, girlfriend, or boyfriend, had committed a rape or sexual assault.[14] Among violent State prison inmates, the percentage of intimate sexual violence is even higher. An estimated 21 percent of prisoners serving time for intimate violence had raped or sexually assaulted a wife, husband, girlfriend, boyfriend, or another intimate.[15]

In a 1984 study of sexual coercion by Diana Russell in San Francisco, 44 percent of the randomly selected 930 women respondents reported being the victims of an attempted or completed sexual assault.[16] Nearly one in four had been victimized through forced intercourse or sexual relations achieved by physical threats or as a result of the victim being drugged, unconscious, asleep, or otherwise incapacitated and thus unable to consent. Less than 10 percent reported the victimization to law enforcement.

It is estimated that more than half of all rapes are committed against adolescent victims, with the vast majority involving dates or acquaintances.[17] However, research shows that most adolescent date rape goes unreported and that most victims fail to even recognize their victimization as rape.[18]

DATE RAPE AND COLLEGE STUDENTS

Date rape has been particularly identified with college students and the college environment where sexual experimentation, substance abuse, and other risky behavior may increase the risk of sexual violence. Many researchers have studied rape on campus or involving college students because of the high-risk factors associated with this group, including representing the peak age range for most rape victims and perpetrators. Victim-ization data shows that rape victimization rates are highest in the sixteen to twenty-four age range,[19] while official data indicates that nearly half of the persons arrested for rape are under the age of twenty-five.[20]

Most studies of college students and rape reveal a disturbing pattern and high incidence of sexual victimization. According to the National Institute of Justice research of sexual assaults on college campuses 35 completed or attempted rapes occurred per 1,000 female students. It is estimated that one in five women were rape victims over a typical five-year college stay.[21]

In the *Ms.* magazine study, one in four of the female respondents reported being raped or attempted rape victims.[22] Eighty-four percent of the perpetrators were described as acquaintances, and 57 percent of these acquaintances were considered dates. In a study of sexual aggression, E. J. Kanin and colleagues reported that 20 to 25 percent of the women respondents were victims of attempted forced sexual intercourse by their dates, in which the victims wound up "screaming, fighting, crying, or pleading;" while just over a quarter of college men respondents admitted seeking sexual favors by force, causing distress on the part of the woman.[23]

In a survey of 2,016 female and 1,846 male students at a Midwestern university, Mary Koss and associates found that 13 percent of the females were victims of sexual intercourse by force or threat of violence; while nearly 5 percent of the males acknowledged committing an act of sexual violence that met the legal definition of rape.[24] J. Briere and N. A. Malamuth's study of the likelihood to rape and to use sexual force, found that 60 percent of male college students admitted hypothetically to the likelihood that they would rape or use force in obtaining sexual relations under certain circumstances.[25]

Most date rapes occur off campus and often involve drug or alcohol use by the perpetrators and victims. In the Koss study of hidden rape among students in higher education, the following results emerged:

- Eighty-six percent of the rapes occurred off campus.
- Fifty-seven percent of the rapists were dates.
- Ninety-five percent of the rapes were single-offender assaults.
- Seventy-three percent of the rape perpetrators were perceived as drinking or using drugs at the time of the offense.
- Fifty-five percent of the victims were using alcohol or drugs when the rape occurred.
- Forty-one percent of the victims were virgins at the time of the rape.
- Forty-two percent of the rape victims never reported the crime to anyone.
- Forty-two percent of the raped women had sexual relations again with the perpetrator.
- Forty-one percent of the women expected to experience future similar rape victimization.[26]

In addressing the problem of sexual assaults at colleges and universities in the United States, the federal Campus Sex Crimes Prevention Act was enacted into law in 2000.[27] It allows tracking convicted registered sex offenders who are enrolled, work, or volunteer at institutions of higher education.

DATE RAPE DRUGS

In recent years, date rape has been associated with so-called "date rape drugs," typically involving drugging the victim, often rendering her unconscious and helpless against her perpetrator.[28] In many instances, the victim may not even be aware a rape has occurred. Two of the more well-known date rape drugs are Rohypnol and Gamma hydroxy butyrate (GHB).

Rohypnol, also called "Roofies," is a powerful sedative that is illegal in the United States. However, it has shown up on many college campuses and in eastern and southern cities.[29] Alcohol can magnify the effects of the colorless, tasteless, odorless Rohypnol which, when ingested, can cause the person to become unconscious or physically incapacitated. Large doses of the drug can also impair the victim's ability to recall the details of an incident.[30]

GHB or "Liquid X" is used by many teens to get high. It has also come to the attention of rapists as a means to assault women with little to no resistance. Law enforcement authorities fear that GHB, known on the streets as "Easy Lay," may replace Rohypnol as a means for rendering young women unconscious for the purposes of rape and other sexual assaults.[31] More than 100 cases of date rape involving GHB have been reported in Texas,

California, and Florida.[32]

Date rape drugs are typically put in a woman's drink without her knowledge, often causing amnesia, making it difficult for the victim to recognize, much less report, that a rape had taken place. Some victims have become comatose from these drugs, while others have died from overdoses. The criminal justice system has stepped up its efforts to prosecute persons who give these drugs to others. In a recent case, three men were charged with involuntary manslaughter and poisoning in the death of a fifteen-year-old girl after her soft drink was spiked with GHB at a party.[33] In February 2000, President Clinton signed legislation that would toughen federal laws against the possession, making, or distribution of GHB.[34]

DATE RAPE AND DATING VIOLENCE

Most experts see date rape as a part of the overall problem of dating violence and often a symptom of such. Dating violence has been defined by some researchers as primarily acts of physical aggression,[35] or in relation to injuries sustained by the victim.[36] Others have defined such violence as including physical violence and verbal attacks.[37] Yet others have more broadly encompassed dating violence to include sexual violence, psychological abuse, and threats.[38]

A number of recent studies have associated physical violence with sexual violence in overall dating violence. J. E. Stets and M. A. Piroz-Good found that a significant correlation exists between physical and sexual victimization of women in dating relationships.[39] Similar findings were reported by C. K. Sigelman, C. J. Berry, and K. A. Wiles, who found a strong relationship between abusive and sexual violent male college students in dating situations.[40]

The prevalence of dating violence has been explored in various studies. More than 21 percent of the young adults in J. M. Makepeace's study reported ever having perpetrated or sustained violence in a dating relationship.[41] Other lifetime estimates of dating violence range from nine percent in one study,[42] to 60 percent in another.[43] Though a number of studies have shown a higher rate of dating violence perpetrated by males,[44] the majority of studies have reported higher rates of females inflicting violence in dating situations.[45] Most surveys show a higher prevalence rate of victimization among women than men in dating relationships.[46] Moreover, research indicates that male violence in intimate relationships tends to be more severe than female violence.[47]

A high rate of dating violence has also been found to exist among teenage couples and is related to sexual violence in teenage relationships. Surveys show that approximately one in three females will be physically abused by boyfriends prior to reaching the age of eighteen.[48] In a study of 500 young females in Des Moines over a six-month period, 60 percent reported being in a current abusive relationship.[49] Nearly all the victims had experienced dating violence in their lifetime.

ACQUAINTANCE RAPE

Many experts believe the most common form of rape is acquaintance rape. Victimization involving acquaintances such as friends, neighbors, co-workers, and others known to the victim account for nearly one-third of all reported rapes and the majority of unreported rapes.[50] According to law enforcement and rape counselors, up to 60 percent of all rapes are committed by acquaintances of the victim.[51] In the Russell survey, acquaintance rape was found to be the most prevalent type of rape assault.[52] While 55 percent of reported rapes were stranger rapes, only 17 percent of total rapes were committed by strangers to the victims. Other researchers have made similar findings on the prevalence of acquaintance rape and have further examined risk factors, causative dynamics, and long-term implications.[53]

Acquaintance rape has received greater attention in recent years by anti-rape activists as the reality of nonstranger rape is brought into focus. According to the FBI's National Incident-Based Reporting System, 90 percent of rape victims under the age of twelve were known by their rapists.[54] Rape victims in the eighteen to twenty-nine age range represent the largest group of overall and acquaintance rape victims of rape. While two-thirds of victims were in a prior relationship with the offender, they were seven times more likely to have been acquainted with the rapist than a family member.[55]

Acquaintance rape research has shown it to be characterized by the following trends:

- In 40 percent of rape attempts, the victim knows the offender other than in intimate terms.
- In more than half the acquaintance rapes, the rapist is well known to the victim.
- Casual acquaintances constitute around 40 percent of the acquaintance rapists.
- Nearly all acquaintance rapes are committed by a single offender.
- More than half of the multiple offender acquaintance rapes are committed by casual acquaintances.
- The majority of nonstranger rapes occur in the evening and at night.
- Rape victims are less likely to take self-protective measure against an

acquaintance than a stranger.[56]

NOTES

1. R. Barri Flowers, *The Victimization and Exploitation of Women and Children: A Study of Physical, Mental and Sexual Maltreatment in the United States* (Jefferson: McFarland, 1994), pp. 146–49; Mary E. Odem and Jody Clay-Warner, eds., *Confronting Rape and Sexual Assault* (Wilmington: Scholarly Resources Inc., 1998), p. xvi.
2. Kimberly A. Lonsway and Louise F. Fitzgerald, "Rape Myths: In Review," *Psychology of Women Quarterly 18* (1994): 133–64.
3. Odem and Clay-Warner, *Confronting Rape and Sexual Assault*, p. xvi; Martha R. Burt, "Cultural Myths and Support for Rape," *Journal of Personality and Social Psychology 38* (1980): 217–30.
4. Quoted in "Final Report of the Supreme Court Task Force on Courts' and Communities' Response to Domestic Abuse," submitted to the State Supreme Court of Iowa, August 1994, p. 10. *See also* Christine Courtois, *Healing the Incest Wound* (New York: W. W. Norton, 1988).
5. Burt, "Cultural Myths and Support for Rape," Patricia L. Donat and John D'Emilio, "A Feminist Redefinition of Rape and Sexual Assault: Historical Foundations and Change," in Mary E. Odem and Jody Clay-Warner,eds., *Confronting Rape and Sexual Assault* (Wilmington: Scholarly Resources Inc., 1998), pp. 43–44.
6. Donat and D'Emilio, "A Feminist Redefinition of Rape and Sexual Assault," p. 44. *See also* M. P. Koss, K. E. Leonard, D. A. Beezley, and C. J. Oros, "Non-stranger Sexual Aggression: A Discriminant Analysis of the Psychological Characteristics of Undetected Offenders," *Sex Roles 12* (1985): 981–92.
7. *See, for example,* S. Griffin, "Rape: The All-American Crime," *Ramparts 10* (1971): 26–35; Susan Brownmiller, *Against Our Will: Men, Women and Rape* (New York: Simon & Schuster, 1975); A. G. Johnson, "On the Prevalence of Rape in the United States," *Signs: Journal of Women in Culture and Society 6* (1980): 136–46.
8. "The Date Who Rapes," *Newsweek* (April 9, 1984), p. 91.
9. Cited in Ellen Sweet, "Date Rape," *Ms./Campus Times* (October, 1985), p. 58. *See also* Mary P. Koss, "Hidden Rape: Sexual Aggression and Victimization in a National Sample of Students in Higher Education," in Ann W. Burgess, ed., *Rape and Sexual Assault II* (New York: Garland Publishing, 1988), pp. 3–25.
10. B. Miller, "Date Rape: Time For a New Look at Prevention," *Journal of College Student Development 29* (1988): 553–55.
11. B. Miller and J. Marshall, "Coercive Sex on the University Campus," *Journal of College Student Personnel 28*, 1 (1987): 38–47.
12. Flowers, *The Victimization and Exploitation of Women and Children,* pp. 150–51.
13. National Institute of Justice and Centers for Disease Control and Prevention, *Prevalence, Incidence, and Consequences of Violence Against Women: Findings from the National Violence Against Women Survey,* November 1998.
14. U.S. Department of Justice, Bureau of Justice Statistics, *Violence by Intimates: Analysis of Data on Crimes by Current or Former Spouses, Boyfriends, and Girlfriends* (Washington: Office of Justice Programs, 1998), p. 25.
15. *Ibid.,* p. 28.
16. Diana E. Russell, *Sexual Exploitation: Rape, Child Sexual Abuse, and Sexual Harassment* (Beverly Hills: Sage, 1984).

17 Py Bateman, "The Context of Date Rape," in Barrie Levy, ed., *Dating Violence: Young Women in Danger* (Seattle: Seal Press, 1998), p. 94.

18. *Ibid.*, p. 95; Miller, "Date Rape."

19. Cited in Ross, "Hidden Rape." *See also*, U.S. Department of Justice, Bureau of Justice Statistics, *Criminal Victimization in the United States 1994: A National Crime Victimization Survey Report* (Washington: Government Printing Office, 1997).

20. U.S. Department of Justice, Federal Bureau of Investigation, *Crime in the United States: Uniform Crime Reports 2004* (Washington: Government Printing Office, 2005), p. 29.

21. Cited in U.S. Department of Justice, National Institute of Justice, *Sexual Assault on Campus: What Colleges and Universities Are Doing About It* (Washington: Office of Justice Programs, 2005), p. 2.

22. Mary P. Koss, "Outrageous Acts and Everyday Seductions: Sexual Aggression and Victimization Among College Students," paper presented at Romance, Rape and Relationships: A Conference on Teen Sexual Exploitation, Seattle, 1987; M. P. Koss, C. A. Gidycz, and N. Wisniewski, "The Scope of Rape: Incidence and Prevalence of Sexual Aggression and Victimization in a National Sample of Higher Education Students," *Journal of Consulting and Clinical Psychology 55*, 2 (1987): 167–70.

23. Koss, "Hidden Rape;" E. J. Kanin, "Male Aggression in Dating-Courtship Relations," *American Journal of Sociology 63* (1957): 197–204; E. J. Kanin and S. R. Parcell, "Sexual Aggression: A Second Look at the Offended Female," *Archives of Sexual Behavior 6* (1977): 67–76.

24. Koss, "Hidden Rape;" M. P. Koss and C. A. Gidycz, "Sexual Experiences Survey: Reliability and Validity," *Journal of Consulting and Clinical Psychology 53* (1985): 422–23.

25. J. Briere and N. A. Malamuth, "Predicting Self-Reported Likelihood of Sexually Abusive Behavior: Attitudinal Versus Sexual Explanations," *Journal of Research in Personality 17* (1983): 315–23.

26. Koss, "Hidden Rape," pp. 3–25. *See also* B. S. Fisher, F. T. Cullen, and M. G. Turner, *The Sexual Victimization of College Women* (Washington: National Institute of Justice, 2000); B. Bondurant, "University Women's Acknowledgement of Rape: Individual, Situational, and Social Factors," Violence Against Women 7, 3 (2001): 294–314.

27. Federal Campus Sex Crimes Prevention Act, Public Law 106–386 (2000).

28. R. Barri Flowers, *Drugs, Alcohol and Criminality in American Society* (Jefferson: McFarland, 1999), p. 150.

29. Ibid.; "What is Rohypnol?" *Oregonian* (February 25, 1997), p. E7.

30. Robert E. Freeman-Longo and Geral T. Blanchard, *Sexual Abuse in America: Epidemic of the 21st Century* (Brandon: Safer Society Press, 1998), pp. 76–77.

31. *Ibid.;* Flowers, *Drugs, Alcohol and Criminality in American Society,* p. 150; Christine Gorman, "Liquid X," Time 148 (September 30, 1996), p. 64.

32. Gorman, "Liquid X."

33. A CompuServe news report, March 14, 2000.

34. *Ibid.*

35. *See, for example,* A. Puig, "Predomestic Strife: A Growing College Counseling Concern," *Journal of College Student Personnel 25* (1984): 268–69.

36. J. M. Makepeace, "The Severity of Courtship Violence Injuries and Individual Precautionary Measures," in G. T. Hotaling, D. Finkelhor, J. T. Kilpatrick, and M. A. Straus, eds., *Family Abuse and Its Consequences: New Directions in Research* (Newbury Park: Sage, 1988), pp. 297–311.

37. W. E. Thompson, "Courtship Violence: Toward a Conceptual Understanding," *Youth and Society 18,* 2 (1986): 162–76.

38. David B. Sugarman and Gerald T. Hotaling, "Dating Violence: A Review of Contextual and Risk Factors," in Barrie Levy, ed., *Dating Violence: Young Women in Danger* (Seattle: Seal Press, 1998), pp. 100–3.

39. J. E. Stets and M. A. Piroz-Good, "Patterns in Physical and Sexual Abuse for Men and Women in Dating Relationships: A Descriptive Analysis," *Journal of Family Violence 4,* 1 (1989): 63–76.

40. C. K. Sigelman, C. J. Berry, and K. A. Wiles, "Violence in College Students' Dating Relationships," *Journal of Applied Social Psychology 14,* 6 (1984): 530–48.

41. J. M. Makepeace, "Courtship Violence Among College Students," *Family Relations 30* (1981): 97–102.

42. B. Roscoe and J. E. Callahan, "Adolescents' Self-Report of Violence in Families and Dating Situations," *Adolescence 20* (1985): 545–53.

43. K. McKinney, "Measures of Verbal, Physical, and Sexual Dating Violence," *Free Inquiry into Creative Sociology 14,* 1 (1986): 55–60.

44. Sigelman, Berry, and Wiles, "Violence in College Students' Dating Relationships;" J. M. Makepeace, "Life Events, Stress and Courtship Violence," *Family Relations 32* (1983): 101–9.

45. *See, for example,* R. E. Billingham and A. R. Sack, "Conflict Resolution Tactics and the Level of Emotional Commitment Among Unmarrieds," *Human Relations 40* (1987): 59–74; I. Arias, M. Samios, and K. D. O'Leary, "Prevalence and Correlates of Physical Aggression During Courtship," *Journal of Interpersonal Violence 2,* 1 (1987): 82–90; L. L. Marshall and P. Rose, "Gender, Stress and Violence in Adult Relationships of a Sample of College Students," *Journal of Social and Personal Relationships 4* (1987): 299–316.

46. M. L. Bernard and J. L. Bernard, "Violent Intimacy: The Family as a Model for Love Relationships," *Family Relations 32* (1983): 283–86; K. E. Lane and P. A. Gwartney-Gibbs, "Violence in the Context of Dating and Sex," *Journal of Family Issues 6,* 1 (1985): 45–59; N. O'Keefe, K. Brockopp, and E. Chew, "Teen Dating Violence," *Social Work 31* (1986): 465–68.

47. R. Barri Flowers, *Female Crime, Criminals and Cellmates: An Exploration of Female Criminality and Delinquency* (Jefferson: McFarland, 1995), pp. 93–94; Richard J. Gelles, *The Violent Home* (Beverly Hills: Sage, 1987), pp. 50–52.

48. Sheila Kuehl, "Legal Remedies for Teen Dating Violence," in Barrie Levy, ed., *Dating Violence: Young Women in Danger* (Seattle: Seal Press, 1998), p. 209.

49. Testimony at Iowa House of Representatives Public Hearing on Dating Violence by Rebecca Bettin, a counselor at the Young Women's Resource Center, Des Moines, March 31, 1992.

50. Flowers, *The Victimization and Exploitation of Women and Children,* p. 149.

51. "The Date Who Rapes," p. 91.

52. Russell, *Sexual Exploitation. See also* Andrea Parrot and Laurie Bechhofer, eds., *Acquaintance Rape: The Hidden Crime* (New York: John Wiley and Sons, 1991).

53. *See, for example,* Paula Lundberg-Love and Robert Geffner, "Date Rape: Prevalence, Risk Factors, and a Proposed Model," in Maureen Piroz-Good and Jan Stets, eds., *Violence in Dating Relationships* (New York: Praeger, 1989).

54. U.S. Department of Justice, Bureau of Justice Statistics, *Sex Offenses and Offenders: An Analysis of Data on Rape and Sexual Assault* (Washington: Office of Justice Programs, 1997), p. 11.

55. *Ibid.*

56. Flowers, *The Victimization and Exploitation of Women and Children,* p. 150.

Chapter 5

FEMALE, SAME SEX, AND STATUTORY RAPE

Historically, rape has been viewed as a sexual assault in which a male is the aggressor and a female the victim.[1] In spite of greater recognition in recent years of the heterogeneous nature of rapists and rape victims as reflected in rape laws and studies on sexual assaults, few would disagree that rape remains by and large a violent act perpetrated by males against females.[2] This notwithstanding, there has been some research and statistical data to indicate that women are capable of rape and have raped men and children. The dynamics of female rape are similar to that of male rape: an act of violent aggression, domination, control, and humiliation against a victim who is perceived to be vulnerable. In the case of statutory rape, the female rapist, like male rapists, uses the power of age differential, maturity level, and coercion to achieve sexual objectives.

Same sex rape has received relatively little attention by researchers. This is due in part to few victims of same sex rape coming forward to report the assault, usually because of societal barriers that discourage such reporting. Also, since most rape experts tend to focus on the more prevalent male-female rape patterns, same sex rape has not been considered statistically relevant.

Another form of rape that deserves greater study is statutory rape. Though sexual relations with a minor is prohibited in every state, what constitutes the age of consent is not uniform from state to state. Statutory rape occurs in this country more often than one might think and should be addressed accordingly for its implications.

This chapter will examine these somewhat hidden rape subgroups of female rape, same sex rape, and statutory rape.

THE PREVALENCE AND INCIDENCE
OF MALE RAPE IN SOCIETY

In order to put female rape of males or other females in its proper perspective, one must view the prevalence and incidence of overall rape in the United States. There were an estimated 355,000 rapes and sexual assaults reported by victims in 1995.[3] The Justice Department estimated that in 2003 there were 198,850 rape and sexual assault victimizations in this country.[4] Many rape experts believe the actual number of rapes in this country is far higher.[5] Only around one-third of rape victims report the assault to the police each year.[6] This leaves at least two-thirds or more victimizations that go unaccounted for in the statistics and other data on rape.

Females are far more likely to be the victims of male rape than males of female or same sex rape. The National Crime Victimization Survey (NCVS) defines rape as "forced sexual intercourse where the victim may be either male or female and the offender may be of the same sex or a different sex from the victim."[7] According to the NCVS, in 1994 there was one rape/sexual assault victimization of a female for every 270 females in the population at large, compared to one rape/sexual assault victimization of a male for every 5,000 males in the general population.[8] It is estimated that 91 percent of all victims of rape and sexual assault are female, with nearly 99 percent of the perpetrators of single victim rapes or sexual assaults male.[9] Nearly one in five women have reported ever being the victims of an attempted or completed rape, compared to one in thirty-three men who reported being victimized by an attempted or completed rape in their lifetimes.[10]

Arrest and incarceration data also reflect this disparity. In 2004, there were 18,406 male arrests for forcible rape. This compares to only 287 arrests of females for forcible rape.[11] The differential amounts to 98.5 percent male arrests to 1.5 percent female arrests. Similarly, 99.6 percent of the 33,800 convicted rapists in State prison in 1994 were male, while only 0.4 percent were female.[12] Various studies and statistics have consistently shown that rape is overwhelmingly a male crime perpetrated against female victims.[13]

FEMALE RAPE

Female sex offenders are relatively few in numbers. However, as noted, they do exist and therefore cannot be disregarded in the study of sex criminality. If one assumes, based on some estimates, that at least one million rapes occur each year,[14] and that females represent around 1 percent of the rapists,[15] that would suggest that approximately 10,000 rapes each year in this country are perpetrated by females. Even modest rape figures, such as the combined 355,000 yearly rape and sexual assaults, as reported by the NCVS, indicates that female offenders constitute about 3,550 rapists and sexual assaulters annually.[16] Though females constitute less than 1 percent of prisoners convicted of rape, there were still an estimated *135* inmates in State prison actually serving time for rape in 1994.[17] Another 651 female prisoners were convicted of sexual assault.

Arrest trends indicate that, on the whole, arrests for rape are declining. However, the rate of decrease has been slower for females than males arrested for rape. According to the *Uniform Crime Reports,* from 1995 to 2004 arrests of males for forcible rape declined 18.3 percent, compared to a decrease in female arrests for forcible rape of less than 3 percent.[18]

What does this data tell us about female rape? Primarily it indicates that females are not exempt from rape laws nor incapable of being rapists. Indeed, some rape experts believe that many more females may be involved in rape crimes and other sexual assaults than the statistics suggest.[19] There are a number of problems in recognizing female rape and characterizing female rapists. The first may well be the general sex-specific bias towards males as rapists. The traditional definition of forcible rape assumes a male perpetrator and a female victim. Even when the rape occurs without force or threat of force, per se, it still reflects male offender-female victim, as the following definition indicates: "Penetration of a woman not married to the offender that was nonconsensual because the victim was unconscious or in some other way physically helpless."[20]

Rape has only been recognized as a gender neutral sex offense or criminal sexual assault without narrowly defining the offender in recent years in many states. However, other states still distinguish between *male* rape and *female* sexual assaults.

Female rape or attempted rape by force or the threat thereof is not an entirely modern phenomenon. Indeed, "during a certain time in our country's history, a white woman in the South could force a black man to have sexual intercourse with her by threatening to scream "rape." Since the mere accusation could cost the black man his life, this incident would certainly qualify as rape by the very real threat of bodily harm."[21] While there have been case histories of men sexually victimized by women, only rarely have they been reported in the scientific literature.[22]

Most women charged with rape tend to be accomplices to male rapists but may not have actually physically raped the victim themselves. One recent example of such a case occurred in California in which a woman assisted her husband–a serial rapist–in finding and luring victims.[23] The wife accomplice was routinely a victim of marital rape and wife battering. By definition, females can rape children, other females, and even males, particularly if they are older, weaker, or handicapped. The female typically uses objects to rape or sodomize and physically overpower the victim into compliance.

Female Rape of Males

Female rape of males has been given little attention in the study of sex crimes. However, some study has been done on this type of rape. Sex researchers William Masters and Philip Sarrel presented clinical evidence of the actual rape of four men on separate occasions by one or more women under the threat of force, violence, or death.[24] They rejected the "sexual myth" that it would be virtually impossible for a man to achieve or maintain an erection if he was sexually assaulted by a woman, maintaining

> like most other sexual myths . . . its general acceptance has exerted an unfortunate influence on medicine, psychology and the law. Consequently, men who have been sexually assaulted by women have been extremely loath to admit this experience to anyone. They have feared that either they will be disbelieved or that they would be degraded socially and made the object of lewd jokes, not only by their peers but by representatives of the law and the health care professions.[25]

Though Masters and Sarrel acknowledge that female rape of males is rare, they suggest that many such rapes may occur but go unreported by the victims unless they seek professional help. With respect to males being raped by females, Masters noted: "Many of us have been taught that nothing of the kind could happen. Nothing is further from the truth."[26]

Male Rape Victims of Females

Few men raped by women ever report their victimization to law enforcement agencies or seek counseling. Those who do talk to therapists about what happened to them often exhibit symptoms similar to female rape victims—loss of self-esteem, depression, self-blame, and rejection of intimacy. In many cases, the law offers little, if any, protection or solace. In seven states, women are excluded from the rape statutes, thereby "even those few men with the courage to report rape may find they have no legal recourse against their attackers."[27] Even in states with female rape laws, the chances that a female rapist will ever be prosecuted for rape are very small, as reflected in the statistics. Nicholas Groth, a rape expert, summed up the difficult challenge faced by male victims of female rape and sexual aggression in terms of seeking justice: "We've seen these guys forcibly assaulted by women, but they get in front of the police or courts, and who's going to believe them?"[28]

According to Groth, 60 percent of the incarcerated rapists and child molesters were victims of child sexual abuse, with one in five of the perpetrators female.[29] Other researchers have also found a high incidence of sexual abuse perpetrated by females.[30]

Female Rape of Children

Most rapes and sexual assaults committed by females may be against child victims. This is particularly true for statutory rape or intercourse between an adult and a consenting minor, usually defined as under the age of eighteen. In the United States, it is estimated that 11.5 million teenagers have had sexual relations, including 6.5 million males and five million females.[31] Eight out of ten males have had sexual intercourse by the age of twenty. Most women involved with juveniles sexually use them as substitute lovers. These women are often in bad or abusive relationships, alone, or have a disturbed sense of reality or low self-worth.[32]

Perhaps the most blatant recent example of a female habitual statutory rapist occurred in Seattle. Mary Kay Le Tourneau, a thirty-five-year-old school teacher and married mother, was convicted in 1997 of child rape after engaging in sexual relations with a thirteen-year-old student.[33] After being released from prison on probation, Le Tourneau promptly violated parole by resuming a sexual relationship with the minor, who fathered two children with her. She was subsequently sent back to prison.

Most male victims of female statutory rape often consider the experience with an older woman to be a rite of passage, or are inhibited in reporting the experience of female sexual abuse. Therefore, relatively few male rape or sexual assault victims ever report the victimization compared to female victims.[34]

In rare instances statutory rape can cross over into forcible rape. One study found that force was used on a child victim of statutory rape in only four percent of 333 court cases.[35] In most such cases, force is usually unnecessary because the perpetrator and victim often had a prior relationship. H. Gagnon found that 1.9 percent of child statutory rape victims studied had sustained forced sexual relations and 2.7 percent were physically assaulted.[36]

Female rape can also occur in child molestation and incest cases. Many victims of child sexual abuse by females are, in fact, victims of rape or sexual assault.[37] Again, few such victims tend to come forward when the sexual assaulter is a female, allowing this to remain a largely hidden form of female sexual aggression and criminality.

WHY WOMEN RAPE

What causes females to rape or sexually assault? Experts agree that the woman rapist is driven mainly by the same elements as the male rapist—power, hostility, hatred, violence, sadism, substance abuse, mental illness, and opportunity.[38] Some female rapists and sexual assaulters are accomplices of male sex offenders or forced by males to participate in or perpetrate sex crimes.[39] Many female sex offenders were themselves rape, incest, or molestation victims, or otherwise victims of child abuse or domestic violence.[40]

Many explanations on why men commit rape also apply to women rapists. Traditional rape hypotheses posited that rape is a function of mentally ill offenders incapable of controlling sexual impulses.[41] Such a condition was attributed to such factors as early childhood experiences, biological dynamics, or fears concerning sexual inadequacy.[42]

Some believe that rape myths may also contribute to sexual assaults, such as the idea that women secretly fantasize about being raped. In reverse, female rapists may use the same justification in sexually assaulting males. Since males are socialized to respond to sex in a different way than females, the female rapist can assume that she is actually giving her victim what he really wants, whether he has expressed it verbally or not.

As women gain more equality with men in the economic and political structure, more women are also using their newfound clout, opportunities, and sexual neutrality to commit more traditional males crimes such as white collar crime, crimes of violence, and sex crimes.

Conversely, as many women continue to be homemakers and childrearers, they are generally in a position to commit sexual crimes such as incest and statutory rape without attracting as much attention as traditional male sex offenders.[43]

SAME SEX RAPE

There has been a dearth of research on same sex rape. However, most experts on rape acknowledge that same sex rape and sexual assault does occur, if rarely. In addressing rape and its heterogeneity, sociologist Stuart Miller argued that "young rape old, blacks rape whites, whites rape women and girls, juveniles rape juveniles, and women rape women and girls."[44]

The little research that has been done on same sex forcible rape and sexual assaults has focused primarily on male same sex sexual violence. Most such studies have examined male rape and sexual assault in the institutional setting where rape and other sexual violence is a common occurrence in some prisons and other correctional facilities.[45] Institutional same sex rape is seen by some authorities as "an aberration of institutional life where the sex object of choice is unavailable."[46] Prison hierarchy and an inmate subculture of violence in many correctional facilities actually promotes, if not encourages, sexual aggression and violence. According to David Briggs in his study of institutionalized sex offenders:

> Some prisons in particular have an inmate subculture of violence where aggression is not only a survival tool, but a mechanism for enhancing status, obtaining privilege, and channeling frustration at the depersonalization of prison life. Aggression here includes sexual aggression. This may manifest itself in behavior ranging from forced masturbation, through forced fellatio to buggery and gang rape. . . . Such activity provides just that negative model of the fusion of sex and violence that social learning theory would postulate as important in the genesis and maintenance of rape behavior.[47]

In 2003, the Prison Rape Elimination Act was signed into law, requiring the development of national data on the prevalence and incidence of sexual violence occurring in correctional institutions.[48] According to a Bureau of Justice Statistics survey of administrative records on sexual assaults of adult and juvenile inmates, there were an estimated 8,210 allegations of sexual violence reported nationally in 2004.[49] This represented 3.15 inmate claims of sexual violence per 1,000 prisoners. Males constituted 90 percent of the victims and perpetrators of sexual assaults in jails and prisons.

Though the vast majority of inmates serving time for rape and sexual assault victimized females, nearly three times as many males incarcerated for sexual assault had male victims as female victims, according to the Justice Department.[50]

Males sexually assaulting other males also occurs outside prison walls. In Gillian Mezey and Michael King's survey of twenty-two victims of male sexual assault seventeen reported being victims of forced anal intercourse and three of attempted sodomy.[51] Eleven of the victims were subjected to multiple types of sexual assault, including being forced to perform oral sex on their attacker. Ten of the subjects identified themselves as homosexuals, four as bisexual, and eight said they were heterosexual. In eighteen of the sexual assaults, the offender-victim makeup involved lovers or ex-lovers, acquaintances, "pickups," or intrafamilial sexual abuse. Only four of the assailants were described as complete strangers. Studies show that most sexual assaulters of males are homosexual men, while most victims of male sexual assault are homosexual.[52]

Lesbian rape or female sexual assault of females also occurs, though it is rarely documented. In one study of rape and child sexual abuse, Russell noted that five of the female respondents reported being raped by another female.[53] The study defined rape as the victim being either forced to engage in oral or anal sex, or nonconsensual sexual relations due to being unconscious, drugged, or physically incapacitated.

Women inmates are also prone to raping other female inmates in much of the same hierarchy and subculture of violence dynamics that exist in male prisons.[54] In a personal narrative, a female prison inmate described–during the course of being assaulted and burned by eight other inmates–being raped, while giving no specifics of the assault.[55] There is no evidence that institutional rape of females is as widespread as institutional rape of males. But, as in other forms of female sexual violence, there is likely more female rape among inmates and in the general public than the literature indicates.

STATUTORY RAPE

As discussed earlier, statutory rape may be a common occurrence in this country, with female and male victims and offenders. By definition, statutory rape describes "an offense that takes place when an individual (regardless of age) has consensual sexual relations with an individual not old enough to legally consent to the behavior."[56]

The age of consent tends to vary from state to state, in addition to labeling of the perpetrator, and active pursuit of statutory rapists. In general, the wider the age range between offender and victim, the more likely the statutory rape will get the attention of the authorities and action taken.

How prevalent is statutory rape in the United States? According to the FBI's National Incident-Based Reporting System (NIBRS), there was one case of statutory rape reported to law enforcement in 2000 for every three reported forcible rapes in which the victim was a minor.[57] The NIBRS estimated that there were some 15,700 statutory rapes reported nationwide in 2000. The actual number of statutory rapes occurring in this country annually is believed to be much higher.

Statutory rapists are predominantly male, whereas victims of statutory rape are largely female. The NIBRS found that 95 percent of the victims of statutory rape were female and that males comprised more than 99 percent of the perpetrators of statutory rape where the victims were female.[58]

Other noteworthy findings of the NIBRS reveal:

- Females constituted 94 percent of the perpetrators of statutory rape involving male victims.
- Seven in ten perpetrators of statutory rape against males were age 21 and over.
- Nearly half the perpetrators of statutory rape against females were age 21

and over.

- Three in ten statutory rapists were romantically involved with their victims.
- Four in ten cases of statutory rape resulted in an arrest.[59]

More research is needed to explore the dynamics of statutory rape and its relationship to date rape and other forms of sexual criminality, such as child prostitution and pornography.

NOTES

1. R. Barri Flowers, *Women and Criminality: The Woman as Victim, Offender, and Practitioner* (Westport: Greenwood Press, 1987), pp. 27–28; Susan Brownmiller, *Against Our Will: Men, Women and Rape* (New York: Simon & Schuster, 1975).

2. R. Barri Flowers, *The Victimization and Exploitation of Women and Children: A Study of Physical, Mental and Sexual Maltreatment in the United States* (Jefferson: McFarland, 1994), pp. 142–55; U.S. Department of Justice, Bureau of Justice Statistics, *Sex Offenses and Offenders: An Analysis of Data on Rape and Sexual Assault* (Washington: Office of Justice Programs, 1997), p. 2.

3. *Sex Offenses and Offenders,* p. 2.

4. U.S. Department of Justice, Bureau of Justice Statistics, *Criminal Victimization, 2003* (Washington: Office of Justice Programs, 2004), p. 2.

5. Flowers, *The Victimization and Exploitation of Women and Children,* pp. 144–45; R. Bachman and L. E. Saltzman, *Violence Against Women: Estimates from the Redesigned Survey* (Washington: Bureau of Justice Statistics, 1995); Diana E. Russell, *Sexual Exploitation: Rape, Child Abuse, and Workplace Harassment* (Beverly Hills: Sage, 1984), pp. 46–47.

6. *Sex Offenses and Offenders,* p. 2; Brownmiller, *Against Our Will,* p. 190; Nancy Gager and Cathleen Schurr, *Sexual Assault: Confronting Rape in America* (New York: Grosset and Dunlap, 1976), p. 91.

7. *Sex Offenses and Offenders,* p. 1.

8. *Ibid.,* p. 2.

9. *Ibid.*

10. National Institute of Justice and Centers for Disease Control and Prevention, *Prevalence, Incidence, and Consequences of Violence Against Women: Findings from the National Violence Against Women Survey,* November 1998.

11. U.S. Department of Justice, Federal Bureau of Investigation, *Crime in the United States: Uniform Crime Reports 2004* (Washington: Government Printing Office, 2005), p. 297.

12. *Sex Offenses and Offenders,* p. 24. See also U.S. Department of Justice, Bureau of Justice Statistics Special Report, *Profile of Jail Inmates 2002* (Washington: Office of Justice Programs, 2004), p. 4.

13. *Sex Offenses and Offenders,* p. 2; *Uniform Crime Reports 2004,* p. 24; Flowers, *Women and Criminality,* pp. 27–45; Mary E. Odem and Jody Clay-Warner, eds., *Confronting Rape and Sexual Assault* (Wilmington: Scholarly Resources Inc., 1998), pp. xi–xxi.

14. Flowers, *Women and Criminality,* pp. 31–32; Russell, *Sexual Exploitation,* p. 47.

15. *Sex Offenses and Offenders,* p. 2; R. Barri Flowers, *Female Crime, Criminals and Cellmates: An Exploration of Female Criminality and Delinquency* (Jefferson: McFarland, 1995), pp. 131–35.

16. *Sex Offenses and Offenders,* p. 2.

17. *Ibid.,* p. 21.

18. *Uniform Crime Reports 2004,* p. 285.
19. Flowers, *Female Crime, Criminals and Cellmates,* pp. 96–100, 132–35.
20. *Ibid.,* p. 132.
21. Flowers, *Women and Criminality,* p. 134.
22. Flowers, *Female Crime, Criminals and Cellmates,* p. 132.
23. Diana E. Russell, *Rape in Marriage* (New York: Macmillan, 1982), pp. 280–82.
24. Cited in Flowers, *Female Crime, Criminals and Cellmates,* pp. 132–33.
25. Quoted in "Sex Researcher's Report: The Men Raped by Women," *San Francisco Chronicle* (March 15, 1982), p. 5.
26. *Ibid.*
27. Kay M. Porterfield, "Are Women as Violent as Men?" *Cosmopolitan 197* (September, 1984), p. 276.
28. Quoted in "Sex Researcher's Report."
29. *Ibid.*
30. Flowers, *Female Crime, Criminals and Cellmates,* pp. 96–100; Flowers, *The Victimization and Exploitation of Women and Children,* pp. 54–59, 64–66; Heidi Vanderbilt, "Incest: A Chilling Report," *Lears* (February, 1992), pp. 62–63.
31. Pamela Hersch, "Coming of Age on City Streets," *Psychology Today* (January, 1988), p. 35.
32. Flowers, *Female Crime, Criminals and Cellmates,* pp. 97–101.
33. Cited from a news report on America Online (March 3, 2000).
34. David Finkelhor, *Child Sexual Abuse: New Theory and Research* (New York: Free Press, 1984); A. Nicholas Groth, *Men Who Rape* (New York: Plenum, 1979).
35. H. Gagnon, "Female Child Victims of Sex Offenses," *Social Problems 13* (1965): 191.
36. *Ibid.,* p. 183.
37. Flowers, *Female Crime, Criminals and Cellmates,* p. 132; Vanderbilt, "Incest: A Chilling Report," p. 63.
38. Flowers, *Female Crime, Criminals and Cellmates,* p. 134; Flowers, *Women and Criminality,* pp. 37–42.
39. Flowers, *Female Crime, Criminals and Cellmates,* pp. 98–99, 134.
40. *Ibid.,* pp. 98, 134; Russell, *Sexual Exploitation.*
41. Flowers, *Women and Criminality,* pp. 37–42; Menachim Amir, *Patterns in Forcible Rape* (Chicago: University of Chicago Press, 1971).
42. Flowers, *Women and Criminality,* pp. 39–42; Emanuel Hammer and Bernard Glueck, "Psychodynamic Patterns in Sex Offenders: A Four-Factor Theory," *Psychiatric Quarterly 31* (1957): 167–73; John MacDonald, *Rape Offenders and Their Victims* (Springfield: Charles C Thomas, 1971).
43. Flowers, *Female Crime, Criminals and Cellmates,* p. 97; Vanderbilt, "Incest: A Chilling Report," pp. 62–63.
44. Stuart J. Miller, "Foreword," in Anthony M. Scacco, Jr., ed., *Male Rape: A Casebook of Sexual Aggression* (New York: AMS Press, 1982), p. ix.
45. David Briggs, "The Management of Sex Offenders in Institutions," in Tony Morrison, Marcus Erooga, and Richard C. Beckett, eds., *Sexual Offending Against Children: Assessment and Treatment of Male Abusers* (London: Routledge, 1994), pp. 131–35.
46. Gillian Mezey and Michael King, "The Effects of Sexual Assault on Men: A Survey of Twenty-two Victims," in Mary E. Odem and Jody Clay-Warner, eds., *Confronting Rape and Sexual Assault* (Wilmington: Scholarly Resources Inc., 1998), p. 83; E. Sagarin, "Prison Homosexuality and Its Effect on Post-Prison Sexual Behavior," *Psychiatry 39* (1976): 245–57.
47. Briggs, "The Management of Sex Offenders in Institutions," p. 132.

48. U.S. Department of Justice, Bureau of Justice Statistics Special Report, *Sexual Violence Reported by Correctional Authorities, 2004* (Washington: Office of Justice Programs, 2005), p. 1.

49. *Ibid.*

50. *Sex Offenses and Offenders,* p. 24.

51. Mezey and King, "The Effects of Sexual Assault on Men," pp. 85–86.

52. *Ibid.,* p. 88; A. N. Groth and A. W. Burgess, "Male Rape: Offenders and Victims," *American Journal of Psychiatry 137* (1980): 806–10.

53. Russell, *Sexual Exploitation,* p. 67.

54. *Sexual Violence Reported by Correctional Authorities, 2004,* p. 8.

55. Dorothy West, "I Was Afraid to Shut My Eyes," in Anthony M. Scacco, Jr., ed., *Male Rape: A Casebook of Sexual Aggression* (New York: AMS Press, 1982), p. 171.

56. Karyl Troup-Leasure and Howard N. Snyder, *Statutory Rape Known to Law Enforcement* (Washington: Office of Juvenile Justice and Delinquency Prevention, 2005), p. 2.

57. Cited in *Ibid.,* p. 1.

58. *Ibid.*

59. *Ibid.*

Part III

INCESTUOUS CRIMES

Chapter 6

FATHER-DAUGHTER INCEST

S exual abuse of children has reached epidemic proportions in recent years as child molestation, prostitution, and pornography have found ways to expand their reach in the sexual misuse and exploitation of children. It is most frightening when this maltreatment hits close to home. Intrafamilial child sexual abuse—incest—exists in more families than most people could imagine. Note the authors of *Incest as Child Abuse:* "Adult-child incest strikes at the very core of civilization," which they then refer to as "one of the most heinous forms of rape."[1] Experts agree that the results of incest can be devastating to all parties involved, especially the victim. Aside from the physical and psychological ramifications, incest has been linked to other forms of sexual abuse, crimes of violence, substance abuse, suicide, and other cause and effect symptoms. This chapter will focus on the predominant incestuous relationship between a father and daughter.

INCEST IN A HISTORICAL CONTEXT

Incestuous relationships are not a modern day phenomenon; it traces back to ancient civilization. The word *incest* comes from the Latin term *incestum,* which means unchaste and low. Incest is commonly defined as "sexual intercourse between relatives within the prohibited degrees of relationship defined by the law."[2] No other sexual act or form of abuse has been more condemned throughout history than incest. Anthropologists have found that there is an almost universal incest taboo.[3] The severity of prohibitions against incestuous activity can be clearly seen in Leviticus, the Book of Laws (18:6; 20:11–21). The description of "consanguinity defined the nature of punishment to be inflicted upon those guilty of incest, including burning, flogging, exile, and death. Incest, along with murder and idolatry, was forbidden even if for medical reasons or to save one's life."[4]

In spite of the strong taboos against incest, particularly in Western societies, its long history as a form of maintaining bloodlines from generation to generation has been well documented. Moses was the progeny of an aunt-nephew marriage (Numbers 26:59; Exodus 6:20), while Abraham wed his paternal sister Sarah (Genesis 29:12), and Jacob married his two sisters (Genesis 29:15–30). In ancient Peru, the Incas wed their sisters; while African Kings in Golzales and Gaboon married their daughters and the Queens their eldest sons.[5] In some nonliterate societies, incest was allowed by only the privileged classes. Among sectarian groups, the Mormons sanctioned nearly every type of incestuous relationship before prohibiting such practices in 1892.[6]

Today, incest is considered a criminal offense in most societies, though definitions of incest are not uniform from country to country or even within the United States. Consequently, incest continues to affect millions of children and families around the world, with no end in sight.

DEFINITIONS OF INCEST

The definition of incest has expanded over the years. It often encompasses legal and nonlegal definitions, direct family members and extended family, step or foster family members, and various types of sexual acts, misuse, and exploitation. Legally, incest falls under the Child Abuse Prevention and Treatment Act, which defines *child sexual abuse* as

(a) the employment, use, persuasion, inducement, enticement, or coercion of any child to engage in, or assist any other person to engage in, any sexually explicit conduct or simulation of such conduct for the purpose of producing any visual depiction of such conduct, or (b) the rape, molestation, prostitution, or other such form of sexual exploitation of children, or incest with children.[7]

Intrafamilial child sexual abuse can generally be broken down into three categories: (1) familial sexual abuse, (2) extended familial sexual abuse, and (3) other familial sexual abuse.

Familial Sexual Abuse typically involves incestuous relations in which the aggressor is a member of the nuclear family such as a father or father substitute, mother or mother substitute, or a sibling.

Extended Familial Sexual Abuse typically concerns incest in which the aggressor is a nonnuclear family member such as a grandparent, uncle, aunt, or cousin.

Other Familial Sexual Abuse relates to incestuous acts in which the aggressor is a stepparent or stepsibling, foster parent or foster sibling, or any other perpetrator that is considered part of the family that may fall outside the other categories.

The dictionary defines incest as "Sexual relations between persons so closely related that their marriage is illegal or forbidden by custom." Many professionals have stretched the latitude of incestuous "sexual relations" to not only include intercourse but oral sex, sodomy, fondling, masturbation, exhibitionism, voyeurism, and other inappropriate sexual contact or acts. While incest was once considered limited to sexual relations within the immediate family, it is now common to include grandparents, aunts, uncles, cousins; as well as stepfamily or foster family members. Some of these incestuous combinations may fall into gray areas as it relates to incest laws, but they are generally recognized as illegal or wrong in the court of public opinion.

THE NATURE OF INCEST

According to most of the research, the vast majority of incestuous relations occur between fathers and daughters. Indeed, since the late 1970s, intrafamilial child sexual abuse has become almost synonymous with father-daughter incest. In a publication of the National Center for Missing and Exploited Children, it is noted that the "vast majority of training materials, articles, and books on this topic refer to child sexual abuse only in terms of intrafamilial father-daughter incest."[8] There is good reason for this. It is estimated that in 90 to 97 percent of all cases of incest, the active aggressor is an adult male, while more than 85 percent of incest victims are passive child females.[9] H. Stoenner found the ratio of female-to-male victims of incest ten to one.[10] Approximately 78 percent of reported incest today concerns father-daughter incest, 18 percent sibling-sibling incest, 1 percent mother-son incest, and 3 percent grandfather-granddaughter incest and multiple incestuous relationships.[11]

Adele Mayer identifies other types of incestuous pairings as follows:

Type of Incest	Motivations (Individual Psychopathology)
Father-Son	Homosexual conflict.
Sibling-Sibling	Expression of unconscious conflict.
Mother-Daughter	Psychosis or infantilism.
Mother-Son	Substitute satisfaction for missing father.
Grandfather-Granddaughter	Assertion of manhood.[12]

Incest occurs in all levels of society. According to social worker Susan Forward: "We know that incest cuts across every social, economic, and educational barrier."[13] As a result, incest victims "come from all walks of life and share a common bond of betrayal and exploitation by those often closest to them."[14] Though victims of intrafamilial sexual abuse can be any age, studies show that most incestuous relationships begin when the victim is between six and eleven years of age, and generally lasts for at least two years.[15]

HOW BIG IS THE PROBLEM OF INCEST?

Assessing the extent of incest in America is virtually impossible given the secrecy surrounding this type of sexual abuse in so many incestuous families. David Finkelhor estimated that anywhere from 75 to 90 percent of all incest cases go unreported.[16] Some experts believe that the incidence of incest is staggering. Early estimates of incest in the United States ranged from one to two cases per million population in the early 1900s,[17] to 5,000 cases per million per year in the mid 1900s,[18] to over 5,000 cases per million per year by the 1970s.[19] One study estimated that there were 5,000 cases of father-daughter incest alone each year.[20]

Recent studies indicate that the problem is far more widespread. G. Pirooz Sholevar estimated the number of incest victims in the United States to be between eleven and thirty-three million.[21] Social worker Mary Donaldson estimated that between 5 and 28 percent of all females in this country are incest or other sexual abuse victims.[22] In a report from the Family Violence Research Program at the University of New Hampshire, it was estimated that 5 to 15 percent of all females under seventeen have been victimized by intrafamilial sexual abuse.[23] As many as one in ten females in the United States are thought to be affected by incest.[24]

CHARACTERIZING FATHER-DAUGHTER INCEST

By some estimates father-daughter incest accounts for three-quarters of all incest cases.[25] In *The Broken Taboo: Sex in the Family,* Rita Justice and Blair Justice describe the typical incestuous father as "white and middle class, has a high school education and often some college, and holds a white-collar job or skilled trade. He's most often in his late thirties, married more than ten years. His wife is slightly younger than he is."[26] In *Children and Criminality,* the incestuous father and daughter are characterized as follows:

Incestuous Father
- The median age is thirty-five.
- His is in a state of reassessment of his life.
- He suffers from depression.
- Has experienced rejection of a spouse.
- Suffers from diminished potency.

Incest Victim-Daughter
- The median age is eight.
- She is typically entering adolescence.
- She is usually the oldest daughter.[27]

Intrafamilial daughter sexual abuse can start in infancy and last well into the victim's adulthood. The incestuous father tends to be middle-aged (thirty to fifty years old), with an introverted personality, intrafamily background, and is socially isolated. Many sexually abusive men gradually move towards incestuous relations with their daughters. In some instances, the wife may unknowingly encourage the intrafamilial sexual abuse by arranging situations that leave the father and daughter alone.

One of the most comprehensive examinations of incestuous men was conducted by Finkelhor and Linda Williams.[28] In studying 118 men who molested their daughters, the researchers divided the abusers into five categories as follows:

- **Sexually Preoccupied** men have a subconscious or obsessive sexual interest in their daughters.
- **Adolescent Regressive** men become sexually attracted to their daughters as they reach puberty.
- **Instrumental Self-Gratifier** fathers regard their daughters in nonerotic terms, feeling guilty about the incestuous contact.
- **Emotionally Dependent** fathers are emotionally needy, depressed, and/or lonely.
- **Angry Retaliator** men sexually abuse their daughters out of anger towards them or their mother who may have neglected or abandoned them.

Angry retaliators represented around 10 percent of the incestuous fathers and were the most likely to have violent criminal records involving rape or assault. The largest group of sexual abusers was adolescent regressives, accounting for about one-third of the sample, followed by sexually preoccupied molesters, representing around one-fourth of the intrafamilial sex offenders.

Finkelhor and Williams also found that substance abuse played a role in the incestuous relationship for 43 percent of the fathers, while marital discord was cited as a factor in 43 percent of the incest cases. A correlation was found between the father molesters and their own history of sexual victimization. Seventy percent of the men reported being victims of childhood sexual abuse.

A high rate of father-daughter incest has been found to exist between stepfathers and stepdaughters.[29] A typical scenario involves a man married to a woman who has a daughter by a previous marriage. His sexual attraction to the daughter as a sex object can often continue for years, even though he may still regard her as a dependent.

FATHER-SON INCEST

Fathers sexually molesting their sons is very rare, but can happen. When father-son incest does occur, it is generally though to reflect "interactional family disturbances and intrapsychic conflicts of the incestuous father."[30] Studies have found that incestuous relations between father and son often involve individual and family pathologies.[31] In a recent case of parricide in which two teenage boys were charged with killing their wealthy parents, the boys alleged that their actions stemmed from years of being sexually molested by their father.[32] The following is an example of a male child victim of a ritually sadistic incestuous father:

> Harry . . . was the victim of ritualistic and sadistic sexual abuse committed by his father as early as he could remember until about age twelve. His first memory of sex involved his father taping a crayon on his penis and making him insert it in the vagina of his younger sister. . . . He stated that his father sodomized him on several occasions, starting when Harry was five. . . . He recalled bleeding heavily . . . vomiting afterwards, and thinking he was going to die. . . . For Harry, sexual contact with his father was a way of life, something that happened virtually every day.[33]

MULTIPLE SEX OFFENSES, RECIDIVISM,
AND INCESTUOUS MEN

A high percentage of incestuous men are also involved in other sexual offenses. In many instances, the men began offending before the age of eighteen;[34] often with multiple victims.[35] In G. Abel and colleagues' study of sex offenders with multiple paraphalias, the following findings were made on incestuous sexual offenders:

- Nearly 26 percent of incestuous offenders with female victims engaged in at least two types of paraphilic acts.

- Seventeen percent of incestuous offenders with female victims committed at least three types of paraphilias.
- More than 8 percent of offenders with female victims committed at least five kinds of paraphilic acts.
- Nearly 4 percent of incestuous men with female victims perpetrated ten types of paraphilias.
- Almost 16 percent of incestuous offenders with male victims committed at least two paraphilic acts.
- Nearly 14 percent of offenders with male victims committed at least five paraphilias.
- More than 9 percent of incestuous offenders targeting male victims perpetrated ten different sex offenses.[36]

Some studies on recidivism rates among incestuous offenders have been undertaken. W. L. Marshall and H. E. Barbaree found that reoffense rates for untreated incest sex offenders varied from 4 to 10 percent.[37] Rates of recidivism are greater for untreated incestuous men than those who receive treatment. One study of recidivism among incest offenders found that 21.7 percent of the untreated men reoffended, compared to only 8 percent of the treated intrafamilial sex offenders.[38] Because of the limitations in the methodology of such research, many believe that the actual rate of recidivism among incestuous sex offenders is much higher.

There is also evidence that a high percentage of intrafamilial sex abusers also commit a fair share of nonsexual offenses. In examining the criminal histories of ninety-nine imprisoned sex offenders, M. R. Weinrott and M. Saylor found that many more incest offenders admitted committing nonsexual criminal offenses than previous research had disclosed.[39] This finding was consistent with results of the Abel and associates study.[40]

THE VICTIM ROLE IN PARENT-CHILD INCEST

Victim culpability, provocation, and precipitation have been studied as factors in incestuous relationships. Some researchers such as L. Bender and A. Blau[41] have accused children as young as four years old of "unusual attractiveness, seduction, and outright instigation of incest in the home."[42] According to Marshall Schecter and Leo Roberge, physiological and social changes undergone by the female incest victim during adolescence results in an increased sex drive, which in turn "produces an acceptance of the incestuous relationship if not at times seductive partner whose tenuous oedipal resolution make her especially vulnerable."[43]

Most behavioral scientists studying victim-provocation in incestuous relationships believe that only a small percentage of incest victims actively seek or encourage incestuous contact with adults.[44] Others reject the notion of any culpability on the part of the child victim, placing the burden of responsibility entirely upon the incestuous adult's shoulders. However, it would be naïve to assume that even young children are incapable of instigating sexual contact with an adult. Thus said, they can never be blamed for inappropriate sexual contact with an adult. Based on a recent case in which a convicted child molester was given a minimum sentence by a judge who believed that the five-year-old victim was guilty of sexual promiscuity, one expert on incest commented:

> The sad reality is that most people were outraged for the wrong reason—because they thought it was impossible for a five-year-old child to be sexually promiscuous. Although not typical, it is possible for such a child to be sexually promiscuous. Of course, this is the *result* of abuse, not the cause. . . . It in no way lessens the offender's crime or responsibility.[45]

A social worker further reflected on the power imbalance and adult role in a parent-child incestuous relationship: "It's always the responsibility of the adult to control any destructive interaction, no matter what the child's behavior is."[46]

THE EFFECTS OF INCEST

Incest can have a traumatic effect on its victims. For some, the effects may be more short-term, for others they can last a painful lifetime. Young incest victims, in particular, can face a number of physical and psychological problems as a result of their victimization such as: internal bleeding; injuries to the vagina, anus, and stomach; sexually transmitted diseases; bed wetting; nightmares; and suicide.[47] Incest can also lead to aberrant behavior on the part of the victim including running away, child prostitution, child pornography, and precociousness.[48]

Adult survivors of incestuous relations typically suffer from flashbacks, eating disorders, sexual problems, and emotional and social issues. Studies have also shown a strong relationship between incest victimization and incest offending, other forms of child abuse, and domestic violence.[49]

Victims of incest share feelings of guilt, self-blame, denial, anger, and distrust. A typical example of a female sexually molested by her father from the age of twelve on is described as follows:

> Lisa doesn't want to think she's been damaged by what happened to her, but . . . she's had a real problem with trust. She was vulnerable at twelve, and look

what happened to her. For the next two years . . . she had sexual problems. She had a problem being touched. She had an overreaction to anything sexual or exploitative of women. She couldn't stand to see nudity in movies. She was really fearful about having children of her own, especially girls. . . . But Lisa minimized what happened to her and put all her efforts and energies into appearing normal. That was her coping mechanism.[50]

At the age of nineteen, Lisa filed a civil suit against her father, charging him with incestuous assault and battery. The case was settled out of court.

NOTES

1. Brenda J. Vander Mey and Ronald L. Neff, *Incest as Child Abuse: Research and Applications* (New York: Praeger, 1986), pp. I, 3, 38.
2. Patricia Beezley Mrazek, "Definition and Recognition of Child Sexual Abuse: Historical and Cultural Perspectives," in Patricia Mrazek and C. Henry Kempe, eds., *Sexually Abused Children and Their Families* (New York: Pergamon Press, 1981), p. 7.
3. M. Sidler, *On the Universality of the Incest Taboo* (Stuttgart: Enke, 1971).
4. R. Barri Flowers, *The Victimization and Exploitation of Women and Children: A Study of Physical, Mental and Sexual Maltreatment in the United States* (Jefferson: McFarland, 1994), p. 60.
5. Ibid., p. 61; H. D. Jubainville, *La Familie Celtique: Et de Droit Compare* (Paris: Librarie Emile Bouillon, 1905); Edward Westermarch, *The History of Human Marriage,* 5th Ed. (New York: Macmillan, 1921).
6. Theodore Schroder, "Incest in Mormanism," *American Journal of Urology and Sexology 11* (1915): 409–16.
7. Public Law 100–294.
8. U.S. Department of Justice, *Child Sex Rings: A Behavioral Analysis, For Criminal Justice Professionals Handling Cases of Child Sexual Exploitation* (Arlington: National Center for Missing & Exploited Children, 1992), p. 2.
9. R. Barri Flowers, *Women and Criminality: The Woman as Victim, Offender, and Practitioner* (Westport: Greenwood Press, 1987), p. 61.
10. H. Stoenner, *Child Sexual Abuse Seen Growing in the United States* (Denver: American Humane Association, 1972).
11. S. Kirson Weinberg, *Incest Behavior* (New York: Citadel Press, 1966), pp. 34–40.
12. Adele Mayer, *Incest: A Treatment Manual for Therapy with Victims, Spouses, and Offenders* (Holmes Beach: Learning Publications, 1983), p. 22.
13. Quoted in Julie Howard, "Incest: Victims Speak Out," *Teen* (July, 1985), p. 31.
14. Flowers, *The Victimization and Exploitation of Women and Children,* p. 62.
15. *Ibid.*
16. Cited in Jean Renvoize, *Incest: A Family Pattern* (London: Routledge & Kegan Paul, 1982), p. 51.
17. Weinberg, *Incest Behavior.*
18. A. C. Kinsey, W. B. Pomeroy, and C. E. Martin, *Sexual Behavior in the Human Male* (Philadelphia: W. B. Saunders, 1948); P. H. Gebhard, J. H. Gagnon, W. B. Pomeroy, and C. V. Christenson, *Sex Offenders: An Analysis of Types* (New York: Harper & Row, 1965).

19. Stoenner, *Child Sexual Abuse Seen Growing in the United States.*

20. American Humane Association, *Child Victims of Incest* (Denver: American Humane Association, 1968).

21. Cited in Carol L. Mithers, "Incest; The Crime That's All in the Family, *Mademoiselle 96* (June, 1984), p. 127.

22. Cited in Flowers, *The Victimization and Exploitation of Women and Children,* p. 62.

23. Cited in Kathy McCoy, "Incest: The Most Painful Family Problem," *Seventeen 43* (June, 1984), p. 18.

24. Julie Howard, "Incest: Victims Speak Out," *Teen* (July, 1985), p. 30.

25. Flowers, *The Victimization and Exploitation of Women and Children,* p. 63.

26. Quoted in Howard, "Incest: Victims Speak Out," p. 31. *See also* Susan Forward and C. Buck, *Betrayal of Innocence: Incest and Its Devastation* (Los Angeles: J. P. Tarcher, 1978).

27. R. Barri Flowers, *Children and Criminality: The Child as Victim and Perpetrator* (Westport: Greenwood Press, 1986), p. 79.

28. Cited in Flowers, *The Victimization and Exploitation of Women and Children,* pp. 63–64.

29. Herbert L. Packer, *The Limits of the Criminal Sanction* (Stanford: Stanford University Press, 1968), pp. 296–316.

30. Flowers, *The Victimization and Exploitation of Women and Children,* p. 66.

31. *See, for example,* P. Machotka, F. S. Pittman, and K. Flomenhaft, "Incest as a Family Affair," *Family Process 6* (1967): 98.

32. Charles P. Ewing, *Fatal Families: The Dynamics of Intrafamilial Homicide* (Thousand Oaks: Sage, 1997), pp. 5–6.

33. Douglas W. Pryor, *Unspeakable Acts: Why Men Sexually Abuse* Children (New York: New York University Press, 1996), p. 38.

34. G. Abel, M. Mittleman, J. Becker, J. Rathner, and J. Rouleau, "Predicting Child Molesters' Response to Treatment," *Annals of the New York Academy of Sciences 528* (1988): 223–34.

35. W. L. Marshall and A. Eccles, "Issues in Clinical Practice with Sex Offenders," *Journal of Interpersonal Violence 6* (1991): 68–93.

36. Abel, Mittleman, Becker, Rathner, and Rouleau, "Predicting Child Molesters' Response to Treatment."

37. W. L. Marshall and H. E. Barbaree, "Outcome of Cognitive-Behavioral Treatment," in W. L. Marshall, D. R. Laws, and H. E. Barbaree, eds., *Handbook of Sexual Assault* (New York: Plenum, 1990).

38. *Ibid.*

39. M. R. Weinrott and M. Saylor, "Self-Report of Crimes Committed by Sex Offenders," *Journal of Interpersonal Violence 6,* 3 (1991): 286–300.

40. Abel, Mittleman, Becker, Rathner, and Rouleau, "Predicting Child Molesters' Response to Treatment."

41. L. Bender and A. Blau, "The Reactions of Children to Sexual Problems with Adults," *American Journal of Orthopsychiatry 8,* 4 (1937): 500–18.

42. Mayer, *Incest: A Treatment Manual,* p. 13.

43. Marshall D. Schecter and Leo Roberge, "Sexual Exploitation," in Ray E. Helfer and C. Henry Kempe, eds., *Child Abuse and Neglect: The Family and the Criminality* (Cambridge: Ballinger, 1976), p. 131.

44. L. Burton, *Vulnerable Children* (New York: Schocken Books, 1968); David Finkelhor, *Sexually Victimized Children* (New York: Free Press, 1979).

45. *Child Sex Rings: A Behavioral Analysis,* p. 8.

46. Quoted in Flowers, *The Victimization and Exploitation of Women and Children,* p. 68.

47. *Ibid.*

48. *Ibid.*; Joel Greenberg, "Incest Out of Hiding," *Science News 117*, 4 (1980): 218–20; R. Barri Flowers, *Runaway Kids and Teenage Prostitution: America's Lost, Abandoned, and Sexually Exploited Children* (Westport: Greenwood Press, 2001), pp. 111–120.

49. Flowers, *Children and Criminality*, pp. 3–12; E. Sue Blume, *Secret Survivors: Uncovering Incest and Its Aftereffects in Women* (New York: Random House, 1998).

50. Quoted in Mithers, "Incest: The Crime," p. 216.

Chapter 7

MOTHER-CHILD INCEST

A lmost all of the literature on intrafamilial sexual relations has focused on father-daughter incest and, more recently, sibling-sibling incest. Mother-child incest has gone virtually unnoticed for the most part in our society. The main reason for this is that it is perhaps the most secretive of all types of incest by both victims and perpetrators. A second reason is that women as homemakers often care for their own children and are in a position to sexually abuse them in the normal course of rearing, drawing little suspicion. As a result, mother-child incest rarely comes to the attention of authorities or researchers on incest. This chapter will examine incestuous women as part of intrafamilial sexual abuse of children.

DEFINING ADULT FEMALE INCEST

General legal and social definitions of incest can be found in Chapter 6. Incest itself is broadly defined today as sexual relations between persons closely related or living in the same household, such as parent-child, siblings, cousins, grandparent-child, aunt or uncle-child, and step or foster family members. The nature of such sexual relations includes sexual intercourse, masturbation, anal sex, fondling, kissing, exhibitionism, voyeurism, and other sexual contact. With respect to incestuous women, possible molesters include birth mothers, foster mothers, adoptive mothers, stepmothers, aunts, or other females of adult age living in the household with children. Mother-child incest can be broken down into two types: (1) mother-son and (2) mother-daughter. Each will be explored.

TYPES OF FEMALE CHILD SEXUAL ABUSERS

Adult female child sexual abusers exist in every social class, race, ethnicity, age group, and educational level. Most women who commit incest molest their sons, though mother-daughter incest does occur. Adele Mayer identifies the motivations of incestuous mothers:

Type of Incest	*Motivations*
Mother-Son	Substitute gratification for absence of father.
Mother-Daughter	Psychosis/infantilism.[1]

In a study of more than one hundred female child sexual abusers, psychologist Ruth Matthews broke them down into four types:

Teacher-lover: typically older women who have sexual relations with a young adolescent.
Experimenter-exploiter: females from strict families where sex education is forbidden.
Predisposed abusers: women who are predisposed to sexually abuse children due to their own history of severe sexual and/or physical abuse.
Male-coerced abusers: women who sexually abuse children because they are forced to by men.[2]

According to Matthews, teacher-lover sexual abusers are the most likely to go undetected because the behavior is usually socially sanctioned. She gave two examples from Hollywood such as *Summer of 42* and *The Last Picture Show.*

Experimenter-exploiter abusers often use such situations as babysitting jobs to "explore" young children. "Many of these girls don't even know what they are doing, have never heard of or experienced masturbation, and are terrified of sex."[3]

Predisposed sex offenders sexually abuse not only their own children but young siblings as well. One incestuous woman tried to rationalize her behavior: "I was always treated as an animal when I was growing up. I didn't realize my kids were human beings."[4]

Matthews also found that male-coerced abusers experienced childhood sexual abuse, though not as severe as predisposed abusers. Many are married to child molesters who were the first to sexually abuse their children, often long before the wife became aware of it and made to be an active incest participant.

More than one in three of the incest victims Matthews interviewed admitted being molested by their mothers. However, she found *true female pedophiles* to be rare, representing only around 5 percent of her sample.[5] Matthews also found that intrafamilial female sex abusers tended to take more responsibility for their behavior than male molesters. Seventy percent of the female sex abusers acting alone took full blame for the incestuous relationship; while 50 percent of the female molesters acting in cooperation with an incestuous male took 100 percent of the blame for their joint child molestation.

THE EXTENT OF WOMEN INTRAFAMILIAL SEX OFFENDERS

Studies show that anywhere from 11 to 33 million people may be active participants in incestuous relationships in the United States.[6] As many as one in three people may be incest victims prior to reaching adulthood.[7] Most available data indicates that intrafamilial sexual abuse is largely committed by male offenders. It is commonly believed that incestuous relations involving a mother-son or mother-daughter represent less than 2 percent of all intrafamilial sexual abuse cases.[8] However, many professionals dealing with incest believe that the actual number of adult female molesters may be much higher.

Nicholas Groth advanced that the incidence of "sexual offenses against children perpetrated by adult women is much greater than would be suspected from the rare instances reported in crime statistics."[9] He attributed this to the relative ease in which women sexual abusers can escape detection "under the guise of normal child rearing."[10] Kathy Evert conducted a 450-question survey of ninety-three woman and nine men who had been molested by their mothers. From this, she stated: "I believe no one, including me, knows the extent of sexual abuse by females, especially mothers. About 80 percent of the women and men reported that the abuse was the most hidden aspect of their lives."[11]

There have been some studies that have supported a high rate of incest committed by women. Matthews reported that mothers were the perpetrators in over 33 percent of the sexual abuse experienced by her sample.[12] David Finkelhor and Diana Russell examined data on female sexual abuse from two incidence studies. They found that the rate of incest offenses by women was higher when considering females who "allowed" as well as "committed" intrafamilial sexual abuse.[13]

The American Humane Association study of sexual abuse found that 14 percent of male incest victims and 6 percent of female incest victims were molested by females acting on their own.[14] Some researchers believe that male incest victims of females are less likely to regard the molestation as victimization than female victims of males and may actually consider it a pleasurable experience.[15] As a result, such victims would be unlikely to ever report the abuse, thus giving a false impression of the extent of female incest.

There are studies that suggest that many women who do sexually abuse their children act in conjunction with men. S. Barnett, F. Corder, and D. Jehu found that all the female sexual abusers in their treatment group had partnered with men in committing the offense.[16] Similarly, L. McCarthy reported that each of the seven women abusers in his sample had male accomplices;[17] while half of the sixteen women R. Matthews, J. K. Matthews, and K. Speltz sampled committed their intrafamilial sex offenses with male partners.[18]

MOTHER-SON INCEST

The vast majority of mother-child incestuous relations is mother-son incest. Many experts feel that women who are incestuous with their sons are often seriously disturbed. However, Matthews and Evert found only a fraction of the women in their samples to be severely psychotic.[19] In mother-son incest, the father is usually absent and the mother uses her adolescent son for sexual gratification. A mother who has sexual relations with her son—oftentimes referring to him as her "lover"—may be more socially acceptable than a father sexually molesting his daughter. Usually, only the most blatant examples of mother-son incest result in societal condemnation and official intervention.

Even if the husband/father is present and coerces the wife/mother into molesting her children, she may begin to sexually abuse a son on her own. One incestuous mother with a five-year-old son victim recalled: "Having sex with my son was more enjoyable than with my husband."[20]

In Matthews' study of female sex abusers, she found that the majority had adult sexual partners living with them during the time the incestuous relations were occurring.[21] Evert reported that women who molested their sons often "abused their daughters violently, beat and terrorized them, and raped them with objects. But they treated their sons like substitute lovers."[22]

MOTHER-DAUGHTER INCEST

Incest between a mother and daughter is thought to be even more rare than incest involving a mother and son. However, there are still documented cases of mother-daughter incest.[23] Little is known about the cause of mother-daughter incest. Experts contend that when it does occur, the female sexual abuser is often "extremely disturbed and exhibits infantile and/or psychotic tendencies."[24] By sexually exploiting her daughter for emotional nurturance, the molesting mother may effect a complete role reversal in the mother-daughter dynamics.

R. Medlicott cited a case of mother-daughter incest where the mother slept with her daughter to avoid her husband, resulting in incestuous relations with the daughter.[25] R. Lidz and T. Lidz studied the adverse effects of a mother's homosexual attraction to her daughter. In three such cases, they found that the incest involved molestation while the daughter was asleep, touching and anal contact, and aloofness. All three daughters suffered from schizophrenia in adulthood.[26]

In her article "Incest: A Chilling Report," Heidi Vanderbilt depicts the often sadistic nature of mothers sexually abusing their daughters. She notes that they "wash, fondle, lick, and kiss the child's breasts and genitals, penetrate the vagina and anus with tongue, fingers, and other objects: dildos, buttonhooks, screwdrivers—one even forced goldfish into her daugher."[27] According to a victim of mother-daughter incest: "My mom would play with my breasts and nipples and insert things into my vagina to see if I was normal. 'I'm your mother,' she'd say. 'I need to know if you're growing properly.' She'd give me enemas and make me dance for her naked. It lasted until I was twenty. . . . I was petrified of her. Absolutely."[28]

WOMEN AS PASSIVE COLLABORATORS IN FATHER-DAUGHTER INCEST

Some women who are not active participants in child sexual molestation are guilty of being passive or silent collaborators to fathers who sexually abuse their daughters. The wife/mother may unwittingly "aid and abet in an incestuous relationship between a father and daughter by allowing or arranging situations that isolate the father and daughter; or otherwise promote unnatural closeness, intimacy, or opportunities for father-daughter incestuous contact."[29]

There are mothers who blame the daughter victim for initiating sexual contact with the father or who actually create circumstances that allow the incestuous relationship to continue. Vanderbilt notes one such example:

When Mariann's mother caught her husband fondling their daughter, she called Mariann a whore and accused her of trying to seduce her father. Yet when Mariann's father got a job in another state that required him to move early one spring, her mother stayed behind until summer but insisted that Mariann go with him.[30]

Some mothers play a silent or inactive collaborative role in father-child incest by ignoring the warning signs that the molestation is taking place. Others falsely accuse the child victim of outright lying about it.

INCEST AS THE FAMILY SECRET

Maintaining a cloak of secrecy in intrafamilial sexual abuse often bands family members together. This is true whether the incestuous aggressor is a father, mother, or child. Such unity in the face of sexual abuse and exploitation is not surprising, given the stakes in revealing the incest to the outside world. Perhaps it is even more difficult for the nuclear family to come to terms with the incest behind closed doors. Researcher Sandy Rovner recently wrote:

> Incest has always been something nobody wants to talk about. The taboo is so deep-seated, and the act so steeped in humiliation, rage, shame, and guilt that perpetrator and victim may be caught in a this-is-happening-but-it's-not-happening twilight zone. For the rest of the family, all of the human mind's boundless capacity to not "see," to deny, rationalize or reject reality comes into play.[31]

The silence and secrecy of incest for the victim is often a reflection of fear above all else. It is the fear of the sexual abuser, being believed, not being believed, self-doubts, shame, confusion, ridicule, and just about every other thought that goes through the incest victim's mind. As a result, many victims never speak out or even admit to themselves their violation-continuing the silent torture, self-blame, and denial.

The process of recovery can often be as difficult as the victimization of incest itself. As Vanderbilt writes:

> Recovery . . . requires [a] heartbreaking commitment to truths nobody wants to hear...things nobody wants to say . . . memories nobody wants to have. . . . Confronted by memories . . . the victim can swing wildly between denial that the abuse ever happened and acceptance of the fact that it did. With acceptance comes grief . . . rage, and finally, self-forgiveness followed by resolution.[32]

NOTES

1. Adele Mayer, *Incest: A Treatment Manual for Therapy with Victims, Spouses and Offenders* (Holmes Beach: Learning Publications, 1983), p. 22.
2. Cited in R. Barri Flowers, *Female Crime, Criminals and Cellmates: An Exploration of Female Criminality and Delinquency* (Jefferson: McFarland, 1995), p. 98.
3. Quoted in *Ibid.*

4. *Ibid.*
5. *Ibid.*, p. 99.
6. Cited in Carol L. Mithers, "Incest: The Crime That's All in the Family," *Mademoiselle 96* (June, 1984), p. 127.
7. Flowers, *Female Crime, Criminals and Cellmates,* p. 97.
8. *Ibid.*
9. Quoted in *Ibid.*
10. *Ibid.*
11. *Ibid.*
12. *Ibid.*
13. David Finkelhor and Diana Russell, "Women as Perpetrators," in David Finkelhor, ed., *Child Sexual Abuse: New Theory and Research* (New York: Free Press, 1984).
14. American Humane Association, *National Reporting Study of Child Abuse and Neglect* (Denver: American Humane Association, 1978).
15. *See, for example,* M. Fromuth and B. Burkhart, "Childhood Sexual Victimization Among College Men: Definitional and Methodological Issues," *Violence and Victims 2,* 4 (1987): 241-53.
16. S. Barnett, F. Corder, and D. Jehu, "Group Treatment for Women Sex Offenders," *Practice 3* (1989): 148-59.
17. L. McCarthy, "Investigation of Incest: Opportunity to Motivate Families to Seek Help," *Child Welfare 60* (1981): 679-89.
18. R. Matthews, J. K. Matthews, and K. Speltz, *Female Sexual Offenders: An Exploratory Study* (Orwell: Safer Society Press, 1989).
19. Flowers, *Female Crime, Criminals and Cellmates,* p. 99.
20. Quoted in *Ibid.*
21. *Ibid.*
22. *Ibid.*
23. R. Barri Flowers, *The Victimization and Exploitation of Women and Children: A Study of Physical, Mental and Sexual Maltreatment in the United States* (Jefferson: McFarland, 1994), pp. 65-66. See also Beverly A. Ogilvie, *Mother-Daughter Incest: A Guide for Helping Professionals* (Binghamton: Haworth Press, 2004).
24. Flowers, *Female Crime, Criminals and Cellmates,* p. 99.
25. R. Medlicott, "Parent-Child Incest," *Australian Journal of Psychiatry 1* (1967): 180.
26. R. Lidz and T. Lidz, "Homosexual Tendencies in Mothers of Schizophrenic Women," *Journal of Nervous Mental Disorders 149* (1969): 229.
27. Heidi Vanderbilt, "Incest: A Chilling Report," *Lears* (February, 1992), p. 63.
28. Quoted in *Ibid.*
29. Flowers, *Female Crime, Criminals and Cellmates,* p. 100.
30. Quoted in Vanderbilt, "Incest: A Chilling Report," p. 54.
31. Sandy Rovner, "Healthtalk: Facing the Aftermath of Incest," *Washington Post* (January 6, 1984), p. D5.
32. Vanderbilt, "Incest: A Chilling Report," p. 74.

Chapter 8

OTHER INTRAFAMILIAL SEXUAL ABUSE

Contrary to the public perception of incest as mainly an adult parent molester-child victim problem, the truth is intrafamilial sexual abuse often involves child siblings and cousins or other incestuous combinations. Because of our societal focus on parents who molest their children, little attention is placed on other sexual abuse within the family that may occur in greater numbers. For many incest perpetrators and victims–consensual or not–the sexual abuse forever remains a family secret, making its incidence that much harder to determine. Experts on sex offenders know that many began their sexual assaultive training through childhood sexual abuse and intrafamilial nonparent/guardian incestuous relations. This chapter will examine the nature and implications of sibling sexual abuse and other relatives who commit incest.

SEXUAL ABUSE WITHIN THE FAMILY

As discussed in earlier chapters, intrafamilial sexual abuse is a major problem in our society, affecting millions of families. Estimates of incest cases range from hundreds of thousands to over a million in the United States annually.[1] Some believe such estimates may be conservative when assessing the true incidence of incest. Recent studies estimate that between 8 and 62 percent of females were sexually abused prior to reaching adulthood;[2] while 3 to 16 percent were victims of child sexual abuse.[3] In studies of homosexual men and women, the incidence of childhood incest was 37 percent and 38 percent, respectively.[4] For bisexual men, 46 percent had been the victims of intrafamilial incest.

Broadly defined, incest is sexual relations involving inappropriate touching, masturbation, intercourse, or other sexual acts between persons "too closely related to marry each other." As such, incestuous relationships are not limited to fathers or mothers abusing children but include all family members: siblings, cousins, stepchildren, grandparents, aunts, uncles, and multiple combinations. Even nonparticipating family members can be affected by incest through related issues such as substance abuse, domestic violence, delinquency, and suicide. Noted one expert: "The family as a whole supports actively or passively their own incestuous equilibrium."[5]

The ramification of intrafamilial sexual abuse often reaches well beyond the nuclear family, manifesting itself in a cycle of intrafamilial incest, sexual abuse and exploitation beyond the family, sexual violence, and other forms of dysfunction and deviant behavior. Official data suggest that sex-related offenses are on the rise in many jurisdictions,[6] as well as the number of people imprisoned for sex crimes.[7] Similarly, with the explosion of material available on sexual abuse–including the rapidly expanding and informative Internet–the dangers of incest and sexual misuse of children are becoming more and more evident. "Sexual abuse in childhood has been shown to be very traumatic, upsetting, and life altering in its impact. . . . Evidence suggests that the closer the relationship between victim and offender, and the longer and more involved the sexual encounter, the greater the devastation overall."[8]

SIBLING INCEST

Incestuous sibling relationships appear to be far more prevalent than once believed. Some studies have suggested that brother-sister incest may actually be five times as common as father-daughter incest.[9] In L. H. Pierce and R. L. Pierce's review of forty-three juvenile intrafamilial offenders, sibling-sibling incest was found to be the predominant incestuous pairing.[10] Twenty percent of the victims were natural, adoptive, or stepsisters; 19 percent foster sisters; 16 percent foster brothers; and 5 percent of victims were natural brothers. In another study of 150 adult survivors of child sibling abuse, 67 percent identified the abuse as sexual.[11] T. J. Kahn and M. A. Lafond found that 95 percent of the adolescent sexual offenders studied knew their victims, with the most common association being a sibling or child the molester was babysitting.[12]

In spite of such evidence, the extent of sibling incest remains by and large a hidden form of child sexual abuse. Sandra Arbetter posited:

> Sibling sexual abuse is an underreported phenomenon, partly because parents resist recognizing it and partly because there's confusion about where normal sex play ends and incest begins. Sex play usually occurs between children who are close in age, and before puberty. If there is an age difference of even a few years, there is an imbalance of power and the younger child is being coerced.[13]

In most sibling incest, the older male child is typically the aggressor, while the younger child, usually a female, is the victim.[14] The aggressor incestuous partner has often been a victim of sexual abuse.[15]

With respect to brother-sister incest, the female (in many instances) has had prior sexual contact, often with an incestuous father or other male relative. Young female siblings are most at risk to be the object of an incestuous sibling. "The brother may have coerced the sister into sexual relations after having assumed a father role in the family (usually after the biological father has abandoned the family). The idolizing sister may succumb to her brother's request while experiencing little guilt at the time."[16]

A typical example of coercive incest was described in the book, *Unspeakable Acts:*

> Phil . . . admitted to having sex with his sister, six different times, when she was ten or eleven and he was thirteen. The contact escalated to vaginal intercourse, and as he saw it, she initially was a willing partner. At first his sister returned his kisses and apparently told him, "You can do what you want," but later she had to be persuaded to participate. He continued to initiate even though he knew she had become uncomfortable with the interaction. He indicated that he felt remorse a few years later, but had buried the feelings and never really gave them much thought again.[17]

Some men who were incestuous with siblings or cousins as children have reported that the sexual relationship was more mutual than coercive.[18] In most cases—even when there is mutual consent, per se, to engage in sibling or adult-child incestuous acts—there remains an element of coercion or force simply by the power imbalance between male and female or older and younger incestuous partners.

Incest: A Training Ground for Adolescent Sex Offenders?

Evidence suggests that children who are sexually abused may be at a higher risk to sexually offend outside the family. To put the incidence of juvenile sex offenders into perspective, a number of studies have found that they represent a high percentage of all sex offenders. In R. Dube and M. Herbert's examination of 511 cases of sexually abused children, 26 percent of the abusers were under the age of fifteen and 22 percent between the ages of fifteen and twenty.[19] One-third of the child sexual abuse victims in B. Gomes-Schwartz and colleagues' sample identified a juvenile as the sexual abuser.[20] In one of the most comprehensive studies of child sexual abuse in the United Kingdom, adolescents were the perpetrators in more than 36 percent of 408 cases of sexual abuse.[21]

The relationship between adolescent sexual offenders and intrafamilial sexual victimization has been well documented in the literature. In M. Kaplan, J. Becker, and J. Cunningham-Rathner's study of adolescent intrafamilial sexual offenders, 30 percent reported being victims of sexual abuse.[22] Sixty percent of the adolescent sexual abusers in Kahn and Lafond's study were themselves sexually molested,[23] while 48 percent of Pierce and Pierce's sample disclosed previous sexual victimization.[24]

Other studies have linked juvenile sexual abusers with intrafamilial incest involving others. D. Lankester and B. Meyer's study of 153 adolescent sex offenders revealed that 64 percent of family members had been sexually or physically abused in childhood.[25] Similarly, in Kahn and Lafond's study, in half the cases of incest the abuser was someone in the family other than the juvenile sex offender identified.[26]

In a comparative evaluation of intrafamilial and extrafamilial adolescent sexual abusers, Michael O'Brien identified incestuous abusers as:

- More likely to participate in sexual relations involving penetration.
- More likely to abuse more than one child victim.
- Having a history of sexual abuse offending that went undetected for a longer period of time.[27]

C. Bagley found that adolescent sexual abusers tended to come from families exhibiting high levels of instability, marital tension, and mental illness.[28] Further, such sex offenders were more likely to be characterized by hyperactivity, depression, anxiety, low self-esteem, and suicidal tendencies than nonsexual adolescent offenders.[29]

GRANDFATHER INCEST

There have been several reports of grandfather-grandchild incest. One study found that grandfather-granddaughter incest represented between 9 and 11 percent of all cases of intrafamilial sexual abuse.[30] The characteristics of this form of incest mirror those of father-daughter incest (see Chapter 6). This is especially true when the incestuous relations involve younger grandfathers. When grandfather molesters are older, the incest is more likely to be initiated in order to "bolster the molester's ego and help him reassert his manhood and self-esteem which have decreased due to his natural physical deterioration."[31]

According to A. W. Burgess and associates, incestuous grandfathers can be identified as one of two types of incest offenders: *passive-dependent* or *aggressive-dominant.*[32]

- **Passive-dependent molesters** are characterized as timid, docile, and emotionally weak. These men tend to lack self-confidence, assertion, and ego strength; and feel insecure, inadequate, and depressed. Many are unemployed or substance abusers. Incestuous fathers and grandfathers often abandon friends in favor of family to meet their social, sexual, and economic needs. In most instances, these abusers use sympathy and guilt to manipulate family members, without the need for violence. In role reversals, children of grandfather or father incest offenders often, in effect, become the parents.

- **Aggressive-dominant molesters** are seen as strong-willed and confident, compared to passive-dependent abusers. Yet this type of molester is, as one put it, a "cast-iron marshmallow," or one who manages to mask his "vulnerable inner emotional condition."[33] Aggressive-dominants use intimidation, threats, and/or violence (such as child abuse and wife battering or rape) to get what they want. The family as a whole typically maintains the family secret of incestuous relations and domestic violence, fearing the implications of the discovery more than the molester himself.

The aggressive-dominant father or grandfather is often charming, easygoing, and well-liked by his peers; unlike the controlling "reign of terror" he presents behind closed doors. Similar to passive-dependents, the aggressive-dominant is characterized as feeling depressed, inadequate, worthless, helpless, and powerless. He is also likely to abuse alcohol or drugs in coping with his deficiencies and unhappiness.

There is some evidence that suggests incest is trigenerational—that is, the grandfather may have sexually molested his own daughter, followed by his granddaughter in a cycle of incestuous relations.[34]

MULTIPLE INCESTUOUS RELATIONS

Although rarely reported, there have been confirmed cases of multiple incestuous relations involving more than two family members either at once or during different incestuous encounters. In K. C. Meiselman's study of incest, 30 percent of the sample reported being incestuous with more than one member of the immediate family or was aware of incest taking place within the family.[35] The implication of this finding is that "once the incest taboo is broken in a family, it may become more acceptable amongst family members, thereby increasing the chances of it spreading beyond the initial incestuous relationship."[36] Clearly there is not enough known about the incidence of multiple incest abuse and it may occur much more often than current research would suggest.

NOTES

1. R. Barri Flowers, *Women and Criminality: The Woman as Victim, Offender, and Practitioner* (Westport: Greenwood Press, 1987), pp. 61–62.
2. David Finkelhor, Gerald Hotaling, I. A. Lewis, and Christine Smith, "Sexual Abuse in a National Survey of Adult Men and Women: Prevalence, Characteristics, and Risk Factors," *Child Abuse and Neglect 14* (1990): 19–28; Diana E. Russell, *The Secret Trauma: Incest in the lives of Girls and Women* (New York: Basic Books, 1986), pp. 60–74; Mary Wellman, "Child Sexual Abuse and Gender Differences: Attitudes and Prevalence," *Child Abuse and Neglect 17* (1993): 539–47.
3. Douglas W. Pryor, *Unspeakable Acts: Why Men Sexually Abuse Children* (New York: New York University Press, 1996), p. 2.
4. Ibid.; C. Georgia Simari and David Baskin, "Incestuous Experiences Within Homosexual Populations: A Preliminary Study," *Archives of Sexual Behavior 11* (1982): 329–44.
5. Quoted in Marshall D. Schechter and Leo Roberge, "Sexual Exploitation," in Ray E. Helfer and C. Henry Kempe, eds., *Child Abuse and Neglect: The Family and the Community* (Cambridge: Ballinger, 1976), p. 129.
6. U.S. Department of Justice, Federal Bureau of Investigation, *Crime in the United States: Uniform Crime Reports 2004* (Washington: Government Printing Office, 2005); U.S. Department of Justice, Bureau of Justice Statistics, *Sex Offenses and Offenders: An Analysis of Data on Rape and Sexual Assault* (Washington: Government Printing Office, 1997).
7. Sex Offenses and Offenders.
8. Pryor, *Unspeakable Acts,* p. 2. See also, Anthony J. Urquiza and Maria Capra, "The Impact of Sexual Abuse: Initial and Long-Term Effects," in Mic Hunter, ed., *The Sexually Abused Male* (New York: Lexington Books, 1990), pp. 105–36; Jen Goodwin, "Suicide Attempts in Sexual Abuse Victims and Their Mothers," *Child Abuse and Neglect 5* (1981): 217–21.
9. See, for example, A. C. Kinsey, W. B. Pomeroy, and C. E. Martin, *Sexual Behavior in the Human Male* (Philadelphia: W. B. Saunders, 1948).
10. L. H. Pierce and R. L. Pierce, "Adolescent/Sibling Incest Perpetrators," in L. Horton, B. Johnson, L. Roundy, and D. Williams, eds., *The Incest Perpetrator: A Family Member No One Wants to Treat* (Beverly Hills: Sage, 1990).
11. Vernon R. Wiehe, *Sibling Abuse: Hidden Physical, Emotional and Sexual Trauma* (Lexington: Lexington Books, 1990).
12. T. J. Kahn and M. A. Lafond, "Treatment of the Adolescent Sex Offender," Child and Adolescent Social Work Journal 5 (1988).
13. Sandra Arbetter, "Family Violence: When We Hurt the Ones We Love," *Current Health 22,* 3 (1995): 6.
14. R. Barri Flowers, *The Victimization and Exploitation of Women and Children: A Study of Physical, Mental and Sexual Maltreatment in the United States* (Jefferson: McFarland, 1994), p. 62.
15. *Ibid.,* p. 57.
16. *Ibid.,* p. 66.
17. Pryor, *Unspeakable Acts,* p. 46.
18. *Ibid.,* p. 47.
19. R. Dube and M. Herbert, "Sexual Abuse of Children Under 12 Years of Age: A Review of 511 Cases," *Child Abuse and Neglect 12* (1988): 321–30.
20. B. Gomes-Schwartz, J. M. Horowitz, and A. P. Caldarelli, *Child Sexual Abuse: The Initial Effects* (Beverly Hills: Sage, 1990).
21. Northern Ireland Research Team, *Child Sexual Abuse in Northern Ireland* (Belfast:

Greystone, 1991).

22. M. Kaplan, J. Becker, and J. Cunningham-Rathner, "Characteristics of Parents of Adolescent Incest Perpetrators: Preliminary Findings," *Journal of Family Violence 3,* 3 (1988): 183–91.

23. Kahn and Lafond, "Treatment of the Adolescent Sex Offender."

24. Pierce and Pierce, "Adolescent/Sibling Incest Perpetrators."

25. D. Lankester and B. Meyer, "Relationship of Family Structure to Sex Offense Behavior," paper presented at First National Conference on Juvenile Sexual Offending, Minneapolis, 1986.

26. Kahn and Lafond, "Treatment of the Adolescent Sex Offender."

27. Michael O'Brien, "Taking Sibling Incest Seriously," in M. Quinn-Patton, ed., *Family Sexual Abuse: Frontline Research and Evaluation* (Beverly Hills: Sage, 1991).

28. C. Bagley, "Characteristics of 60 Children and Adolescents with a History of Sexual Assault Against Others: Evidence from a Comparative Study," *Journal of Forensic Psychiatry 3,* 2 (1992).

29. *Ibid.*

30. Jean Goodwin, Lawrence Cormier, and John Owen, "Grandfather-Granddaughter Incest: A Trigenerational View," *Child Abuse and Neglect* 7 (1983): 163–70.

31. Flowers, *The Victimization and Exploitation of Women and Children,* p. 67.

32. A. W. Burgess, A. N. Groth, L. L. Holmstrom, and S. M. Sgroi, *Sexual Assault of Children and Adolescents* (Lexington: Lexington Books, 1978).

33. Robert E. Freeman-Longo and Geral T. Blanchard, *Sexual Abuse in America: Epidemic of the 21st Century* (Brandon: Safer Society Press, 1998), p. 43.

34. Flowers, *The Victimization and Exploitation of Women and Children,* p. 67.

35. K. C. Meiselman, *Incest: A Psychological Study of Causes and Effects with Treatment Recommendations* (San Francisco: Jossey-Bass, 1978).

36. Flowers, *The Victimization and Exploitation of Women and Children,* p. 67.

Part IV

SEXUAL PREDATORY CRIMES

Chapter 9

CHILD MOLESTATION

In the last section, intrafamilial child sexual abuse was examined. Equally common are sex offenses against children that occur outside the nuclear family. These include child rape, child molestation, sexual perversions against children, and the sexual exploitation of children such as through child pornography and child sex rings. In some instances, the perpetrator might be a family member or otherwise connected to the child or family as an acquaintance, neighbor, teacher, coach, or other trusted person. Child sex offenders can also be total strangers with a sexual fixation on girls or boys.

Child victims of sexual abuse and exploitation range from completely accidental victimization with little victimogenesis to a seductive sexual partner with extensive victimogenesis. In many cases of child molestation, the victim may consent to the sexual contact unintentionally or unwittingly, or offer only passive resistance. In other instances, the victim and sex abuser are in a symbiotic relationship or form a cooperative dyad.[1] In the worst case scenario, the molested or sexually exploited child is totally powerless, vulnerable and subject to the abuse, control, and exploitation of the more powerful, nonvulnerable sex perpetrator. The type of therapy for child sexual abuse victims is often dependent upon "where they are situated along the victim continuum in conjunction with such factors as the degree of physical force or violence used by the offender and the intensity of the victim-offender relationship prior to the sex offense."[2]

In this chapter, the focus will be on the dynamics involving the sexual abuse and exploitation of children by child molesters and pedophiles.

THE INCIDENCE OF CHILD SEXUAL ABUSE

Many studies have been conducted on the incidence of child sexual abuse, providing some perspective, if not a consensus, on its magnitude. In the

103

1960s estimates of child sexual abuse in large urban areas were placed at 4,000 cases annually;[3] in one large city with advanced victim services, 24 percent of all sexual offenses were reported as involving children under the age of fourteen.[4] Another study estimated that there were 200,000 to 500,000 cases of sexual molestation of girls age four to fourteen.[5]

More recently, estimates of child sexual abuse cases have ranged from 50,000 to over one million annually.[6] In a review of nineteen studies on the prevalence of child sexual abuse, rates for female victims ranged from 6 percent to 62 percent and male victims from 3 percent to 31 percent.[7] Most experts in the study of child sexual abuse agree that the vast majority of child sexual abuse cases have gone unreported and, as a result, unrecorded.[8]

Studies of child molesters have revealed that most have committed not only multiple child molestation offenses but other types of sex offenses as well. In one of the most comprehensive self-report surveys of 561 nonincarcerated sex offenders to date, Gene Abel and associates found 377 of the subjects had committed a total of 48,297 completed acts of nonincestuous child molestation, involving 27,416 victims.[9] The vast majority of pedophilia acts were directed towards male victims. Another study of two hundred nonincarcerated child molesters yielded similar results.[10] In Abel and colleagues' study of sex offenders with multiple sex offenses, 26.8 percent of pedophiles with male victims and 23.7 percent with female victims had committed at least two types of sexual offenses.[11] Nearly 20 percent of molesters with male and female victims had committed at least three types of sex crimes, while more than 2 percent had committed ten different sex offenses.

Most studies of child sexual abuse have found higher rates of abuse among girls.[12] However, rates of abuse involving boys has been significant as well. In data obtained from eight random surveys of child sexual abuse, girls were the victims in 70 percent of the cases and boys in 30 percent.[13] A study of 148 child molesters showed that 51 percent of the molesters chose only girls as victims, 28 percent only boys, and 21 percent molested girls and boys.[14]

Other studies that have focused on male victims of sexual abuse give further evidence of its severity. In a study of nearly 3,000 male college studies, 216 disclosed having sexual contact that fit the researchers' criteria for sexual abuse.[15] In another study of eighty-nine male runaways, 38 percent reported being sexually abused.[16] Experts believe that many more boys may be victims of child molestation than studies indicate, but they are less likely to report the victimization than girls.[17]

Studies of adolescent sexual abusers have found a high rate of prior sexual victimization. Nearly 60 percent of T. J. Kahn and M. A. LaFond's sample reported being molested;[18] while L. H. Pierce and R. L. Pierce[19] and M. O'Brien[20] reported victimization rates of 48 percent and 40 percent, respectively. Prisoner studies have supported these findings. In one study of imprisoned child molesters, more than half reported being victims of child sexual abuse.[21]

DEFINING CHILD MOLESTATION

When referring to *child molestation,* the term is often used interchangeably with the term *pedophilia.* Many professionals today prefer to separate the two by definition. In general, child molestation refers to the actual sexual abuse of a child (usually outside of incest). Pedophilia, on the other hand, refers to a sexual preference for children over adults that often includes fantasies but may not result in child molestation, per se. In both instances, the sex offender is usually an adult male, but can also be an adult female or adolescent. Pedophilia will be discussed in more detail later on.

The *American Heritage Dictionary* defines molestation as "to subject to unwanted or improper sexual activity." When considering child molestation, this definition applies every time, with "improper sexual activity" relating to any form of child sexual abuse or exploitation. Child molestation is defined under the Child Abuse Prevention and Treatment Act as falling within the broader definition of child sexual abuse or "the rape, molestation, prostitution, or other such form of sexual exploitation of children."[22] (See also Chapter 6.)

In the National Center for Missing and Exploited Children's publication, *Child Molesters: A Behavioral Analysis,* a child molester is defined as "a significantly older individual who engages in any type of sexual activity with individuals legally defined as children."[23] Law enforcement authorities generally regard a child molester as a person "who engages in illegal sexual activity with children," but in applying the term, child molester "is more likely to conform to a legal definition of sexual molestation set forth in the penal code."[24]

Nicholas Groth, a leading authority on child sexual abuse, defines a child molester as "having a sexual attraction toward prepubertal children (pedophilia) or sexual attraction toward pubertal children (hebephilia)."[25] He developed a classification typology for child molesters, dividing them into two groups, dependent upon if the child sexual abuse represents a persistent pattern (fixation) or a new experience or change (regression).[26]

- **Fixated Child Molester** is a molester who favors children as sexual partners, identifying closely with them.
- **Regressed Child Molester** is a molester who prefers people his own age as sexual partners but, due to stress, departs from his normal sexual involvement with adults.

Another classification typology of child molesters was established by Raymond Knight and Robert Prentky, based upon five elements:

- Social competence.
- Sexual preoccupation with children.
- Nonoffense contact with children.
- Physical injury to a child.
- Sadism.[27]

The typology was empirically established based on statistical analysis of the research. Both classification typologies are used by psychologists in evaluating and treating individuals who molest children, and by criminal justice officials in classifying sexual offenders.

TYPES OF CHILD MOLESTERS

Researchers have divided child molesters into two general categories: *situational* molesters and *preferential* molesters.[28] Each contains subtypes and often combination child molesters.

Situational Child Molesters

Situational child molesters generally do not have a sexual preference for children but become sexually involved with children for various reasons. Such child molesters often require tension and conflicts in their adult relationships before turning their focus to children. Under extreme stress and sometimes self-doubt, the situational child molester may come to regard children as adult substitutes, thus thinking of the child as a peer. When the child victim is responsive to the molester's emotional needs, a sexual relationship often develops.

Situational child molesters tend to molest fewer children than preferential child molesters and may also sexually victimize other types of vulnerable people including the elderly, ill, or disabled. Some researchers have found that situational child molesters are overrepresented among lower socioeconomic classes.[29]

Four subgroups of situational child molesters have been identified: (1) regressed, (2) morally indiscriminate, (3) sexually indiscriminate, and (4) inadequate.[30] The characteristics of each are as follows:

- **Regressed Child Molester** typically has a low self-esteem and poor coping skills. He uses a child substitute for his preferred adult sexual partner, often coerces the victim into having sex, and may collect child pornography. His primary victim criterion is availability, which is often the molester's own children. This is one of the more common types of child molesters.

- **Morally Indiscriminate Child Molester** will often use and abuse others, including their wife and friends. He molests children primarily because of an urge to, opportunity, and vulnerability of the victim. Force or manipulation are often used to acquire victims who may be strangers or family members. The morally indiscriminate molester lacks a conscience, is impulsive, and collects detective magazines or adult pornography, and sometimes child pornography.
- **Sexually Indiscriminate Child Molester** is typically motivated to molest children mostly by sexual experimentation and boredom. This molester often includes children in prior sexual involvements, such as with other adults, group sex, and sometimes ritual sexual abuse. His own children may be the victims of the molestation. Sexually indiscriminate molesters are the most likely of situational child molesters to have multiple child victims, a higher social and economic background, and collect erotica and pornographic materials.
- **Inadequate Child Molester** is a social misfit and includes molesters suffering from psychoses, mental retardation, eccentric personality disorders, and senility. Inadequate child molesters are motivated by insecurity and curiosity, finding children to be non-threatening for exploring sexual fantasies. This type of molester may molest due to built up impulses, which could result in violence and sexual torture. The elderly and children are at risk. The offender is likely to collect primarily adult pornography.

Preferential Child Molesters

Preferential child molesters have a decided sexual preference for children, including sexual fantasies and erotic images of children. They molest minors not due to situational stress, but rather because of a sexual attraction to children who they find "to be safer partners who can provide adoration, have lower expectations, and are less inclined to reject the adult. These abusers fear rejection intensely."[31] Though they possess a number of character traits, their sexual behavior tends to be "highly" predictable and referred to as "sexual ritual and are frequently engaged in even when they are counterproductive to getting away with the criminal activity."[32]

Preferential child molesters represent a smaller group of offenders than situational child molesters, however they have the potential to sexually abuse greater numbers of children. The preferential child molester is characterized not only by "the nature of the sex drive (attraction to children) but also the quantity (need for frequent and repeated sex with children)."[33]

There is an overrepresentation of preferential child molesters among the upper socioeconomic classes, according to studies.[34] These molesters tend to prefer boys over girls as victims. The *true* pedophile is classified as a preferential child molester.[35]

At least three subtypes of preferential child molesters are known to exist: (1) seduction, (2) introverted, and (3) sadistic.[36]

- **Seduction Child Molesters**–involve children in sexual contact through seducing them with attention, affection, and anything else to win them and lower the victim's sexual inhibitions. These molesters are often involved simultaneously with multiple victims in child sex rings. The seduction child molester's success is based on his ability to identify with the victim, such as a trusted choir leader or scoutmaster, as well as being an adult and an authority figure. Victims of seduction molesters are often also victimized by emotional or physical neglect. Victim disclosure of the molestation most often occurs when the molester seeks to end the relationship. The seduction child molester is likely to use intimidation or violence to prevent disclosure or premature ending of the sexual abuse.
- **Introverted Child Molesters**–have a sexual preference for children and do not have the interpersonal skills to seduce them. Consequently, the introverted molester uses nonverbal communication in sexually abusing strangers or young child victims. This abuser fits the stereotypical image of the child molester who hangs around playgrounds, parks, or schools, or wherever children gather–often watching them or having brief sexual contact. Some introverted child molesters are exhibitionists or may exploit a child prostitute for gratification. Such molesters may even marry, have children, and sexually abuse them starting at infancy.
- **Sadistic Child Molesters**–have a sexual preference for children. However, arousal or gratification can only be achieved through inflicting physical or psychological pain on the victimized child. It is the victim's suffering or pain that arouses the sadistic child molester. These sexual abusers often use force or lures to reach their victims and are more likely than other preferential child molesters to abduct or even murder the molested child. Sometimes seduction child molesters become sadistic child molesters. The sadistic molester is believed by experts to be few in number.

PEDOPHILIA

Defining Pedophilia

Pedophilia generally refers to child molestation where a child is the favored sexual object of an adult, through sexual fantasies and arousal or actual sexual situations. The layperson's definition of pedophilia is "a sexual perversion in which children are the preferred sexual object."[37] The National Center for Missing and Exploited Children uses the term *preferential child molester* in referring to pedophiles.[38] Pedophilia normally consists of nonviolent adult (or older child) sexual contact with a child and includes "genital viewing or fondling, orogenital contact, penetration, and any other immoral or indecent behavior involving sexual activity."[39]

According to the American Psychiatric Association's *Diagnostic and Statistical Manual of Mental Disorders (DSM-III-R)*, in defining pedophilia:

> The essential feature of this disorder is recurrent, intense, sexual urges, and sexually arousing fantasies, of at least six months' duration, involving sexual activity with a prepubescent child. The person has acted on these urges, or is markedly distressed by them. The age of the child is generally 13 or younger. The age of the person is arbitrarily set at age 16 years or older and at least 5 years older than the child.[40]

The *DSM-III-R* classifies pedophiles as a *paraphilia,* or a psychosexual disorder. Pedophiles often have other psychosexual disorders or personality disorders accompanying a sexual interest in children such as exhibitionism, sadism, coprophilia, voyeurism, bondage, and necrophilia (see Chapter 12).

Although pedophilia is a psychiatric term it, is commonly used by other professionals and laypeople in depicting the pedophile or child molester as a sexual abuser of children who are usually young.

Characterizing Pedophilia and Pedophiles

Pedophilia is the most common form of child sexual abuse. It is estimated that anywhere from one to more than two million children are sexually molested in the United States each year.[41] In an eighteen-month study of reported child molestation cases in Brooklyn and the Bronx, New York, the following characterizations of pedophilia and child molesters emerged:

- Child molestation is statistically more prevalent than child physical abuse.
- The median age of a child molestation victim is eleven.
- Younger children, including infants, are also at risk for molestation.
- Female victims of child molestation outnumber male victims ten to one.

- Child molesters are male in 97 percent of the cases.
- The median age of a molester is thirty-one.
- In three out of four cases, the molester was known to the child victim or the victim's family.
- In more than 40 percent of the molestation cases, the sexual abuse had taken place over a period varying from a few weeks to seven years.
- Sixty percent of the molested children were victimized through force or threat of force.
- Two-thirds of the victims of child molestation suffered some type of identifiable emotional trauma while 14 percent become severely disturbed.[42]

Preferential child molesters/pedophiles are capable of molesting hundreds or even thousands of children over a life span. In Abel and associates' study of 561 sex offenders, it was found that pedophiles who molested young boys outside the home perpetrated the greatest number of offenses—averaging 281.7 acts with 150.2 victims on average.[43] Incestuous child molesters perpetrated an average of 81.3 acts, averaging 1.8 child victims. Nearly one in four of the sexual offenders committed offenses against both family and nonfamily victims.

According to Kenneth Lanning, there are four major characteristics of the preferential child molester/pedophile: (1) a long and persistent behavioral pattern, (2) children as preferred sexual objects, (3) well-established techniques used in getting child victims, and (4) sexual fantasies that focus on children.[44] Researchers have found the pedophile (or pedophiliac) to frequently be passive, immature, and insecure with respect to an inability to participate in normal heterosexual adult relations.[45] J. M. Reinhardt advanced that some young or middle-aged pedophiles turned to children only after failing to achieve sexual satisfaction with adults.[46] Older pedophiles, usually over fifty, have been shown to "molest children due to diminishing physical and mental abilities brought about by the aging process."[47]

Types of Pedophiles, Pedophilia, and Victims

Albert Cohen identified three groups of child molesters: (1) immature child molester who seeks only to fondle, touch, or caress the child victim, (2) the regressed child molester, characterized by feelings of self-doubt and sexual inadequacy, and (3) the aggressive child molester who is often sadistic and violent in his quest for sexual excitement and arousal.[48] Johan Mohr, R. E. Turner, and M. B. Jerry described five types of pedophilia committed by child molesters as follows:

- **Heterosexual Hebephilia**–sexual relations of any kind where the female victim is pubescent.
- **Heterosexual Pedophilia**–sexual relations of any nature when the female victim has not shown any pubertal changes.
- **Homosexual Hebephilia**–sexual relations of any type where the male victim is pubescent.
- **Homosexual Pedophilia**–sexual relations of any nature when the male victim of the same sex has shown no pubertal changes.
- **Undifferentiated Pedophili**–sexual relations of any kind where the victim's gender is not differentiated.[49]

Some studies have examined the victim's role in pedophilia. In one study of seventy-three female child molestation victims, the females were divided into two categories: (1) participant victims and (2) accidental victims:

- **Participant victims**–those who played an active role in initiating and maintaining the relationship.
- **Accidental victims**–those who did not have an active role in their molestation.[50]

A significant factor in participant child sexual victimization appears to be the victim's seductive behavior towards adults. Evidence indicates that when participant victims of child molestation are "deprived of the care, affection, and approval they need at home, they are more likely than accidental victims to seek such nurturance elsewhere."[51]

CHILD SEX RINGS

Child sex rings are an important component in the sexual abuse and exploitation of children through child molestation, prostitution, and pornography. A *child sex ring* or *sex ring crime* is defined as child sexual victimization in which "there are one or more adult offenders and several children who are aware of each other's participation."[52] It is difficult to assess the true extent of these child sex rings because of the secrecy involved as well as inadequate law enforcement and study into the problem. However, many experts believe that child sex rings are a common form of child sexual misuse around the world. One study reported on eleven such child sex rings throughout the United States. These consisted of at least fourteen adult male sex offenders and eighty-four identified sexually abused children ages eight to fifteen.[53] Another study in the United Kingdom presented details on eleven child sex rings involving fourteen adult male sexual abusers and 175 child sexual abuse victims ages eight to fifteen.[54]

According to Ann Burgess and Christine Grant, there are three primary types of child sex rings: (1) solo sex rings, (2) transition sex rings, and (3) syndicated sex rings.[55] These are described as follows:

- **Solo Sex Rings** are characterized by the participation of multiple children in sexual acts with an adult, generally a male. The child sex offender usually has ready access to the victim for sexual entrapment and relies on isolation and secrecy to control the child and continue the victimization.
- **Transition Sex Rings** involve multiple adults in sexual activities with children, usually adolescents. The child victims are often runaways, abducted children, and child sexual or physical abuse victims. Transition sex rings often precede advancement to syndicated sex rings or sex-for-hire operations.
- **Syndicated Sex Rings** are well-structured organizations that involve recruitment of children for child prostitution and pornography, delivery of sexual services, and establishing an extensive network of clients. Victims of syndicated sex rings are often between the ages of eleven and sixteen, and may involve transportation across state lines.

The solo sex ring and transition sex ring can "constitute different stages in the evolution of a syndicated child sex ring, or they may represent only a loosely organized association of adults exploiting small groups of children."[56] In most child sex rings there is usually an element of adult or child pornography used or collected by the sexual offender (see Chapter 10).

ADVOCATING CHILD SEXUAL ABUSE

There are a number of organizations worldwide that openly support sexual activity between children and adults and seek to end statutory rape and age of consent laws.[57] The North American Man-Boy Love Association (N.A.M.B.L.A.) promotes men having sexual relations with boys. Their efforts have included protesting child sexual abuse-related events, producing a journal, and using the Internet to promote their cause. Another organization supporting the molesting of young children is The Rene Guyon Society. Once based in Beverly Hills, California, the group whose slogan is "Sex by year eight, or else it's too late," had as many as 5,000 members at one time.

In the United Kingdom, the Paedophiliac Information Exchange (PIE), based in Wales, is organized for the sole purpose of advocating consensual sexual activities between adults and children. Other organizations promoting adult-child sexual relations include the Childhood Sensuality Circle, which boasts more than 10,000 members.

Additionally, some organizations—such as Victims of Child Abuse Laws (V.O.C.A.L.)—indirectly support child sexual abuse through their fight against laws that protect children from sexual abuse and allow state agencies to investigate allegations of sexual abuse. V.O.C.A.L. was created in the 1980s by persons alleging they were falsely accused of sexually abusing children. Most experts believe that children who falsely accuse others of molesting them are in the minority, compared to those who truly were sexually abused. Moreover, studies show that accused child molesters are far more likely to never be prosecuted than to be prosecuted as a result of false accusations.[58]

NOTES

1. Leroy C. Schultz, "The Child as a Sex Victim: Socio-Legal Perspectives," in Israel Drapkin and Emilo Viano, eds., *Victimology: A New Focus,* Vol. 5 (Toronto: D. C. Heath, 1975), p. 178.

2. R. Barri Flowers, *Children and Criminality: The Child as Victim and Perpetrator* (Westport: Greenwood Press, 1986), p. 75. *See also* Kathryn Brohl and Joyce Potter, *When Your Child Has Been Molested: A Parent's Guide to Healing and Recovery* (New York: Wiley, 2004).

3. *Protecting the Child Victim of Sex Crimes* (Denver: American Humane Association, 1966), p. 2.

4. Schultz, "The Child as a Sex Victim," p. 177.

5. *Sexual Abuse of Children: Implications for Casework* (Denver: American Humane Association, 1967), p. 10.

6. R. A. Eve, "Empirical and Theoretical Findings Concerning Child and Adolescent Sexual Abuse: Implications for the Next Generation of Studies," *Victimology: An International Journal 10* (1985): 97–109.

7. Cited in U.S. Department of Justice, *Children Traumatized in Sex Rings* (Arlington: National Center for Missing & Exploited Children, 1988), p. 2; David Finkelhor, *A Sourcebook on Child Sexual Abuse* (Beverly Hills: Sage, 1986).

8. D. Russell, *Intra-family Child Sexual Abuse: Final Report to the National Center on Child Abuse and Neglect* (Washington: U.S. Department of Health and Human Services, 1983); L. Berliner and J. R. Wheeler, "Treating the Effects of Sexual Abuse on Children," *Journal of Interpersonal Violence 2* (1987): 415–24.

9. G. Abel, J. Becker, J. Cunningham-Rathner, and J. Rouleau, "Self-Reported Sex Crimes of 561 Nonincarcerated Paraphiliacs," *Journal of Interpersonal Violence 2,* 6 (1987): 3–25.

10. Cited in *Children Traumatized in Sex Rings,* p. 2.

11. G. Abel, M. Mittleman, J. Becker, J. Rathner, and J. Rouleau, "Predicting Child Molesters' Response to Treatment," *Annals of the New York Academy of Sciences 528* (1988): 223–34.

12. *Children Traumatized in Sex Rings,* p. 4; R. Barri Flowers, *The Victimization and Exploitation of Women and Children: A Study of Physical, Mental and Sexual Maltreatment in the United States* (Jefferson: McFarland, 1994), pp. 53–59.

13. Finkelhor, *A Sourcebook on Child Sexual Abuse.*

14. A. N. Groth, *Men Who Rape* (New York: Plenum, 1979).

15. Ibid.; L. I. Risin and M. P. Koss, "Sexual Abuse of Boys: Prevalence and Descriptive

Characteristics of the Childhood Victimizations," *Journal of Interpersonal Violence 2* (1987): 309–19.

16. M. D. Janus, A. McCormack, A. W. Burgess, and C. R. Hartman, *Adolescent Runaways* (Lexington: Lexington Books, 1987).

17. *Children Traumatized in Child Sex Rings,* p. 4; Groth, Men Who Rape; D. Finkelhor, *Child Sexual Abuse: New Theory and Research* (New York: Free Press, 1984).

18. T. J. Kahn and M. A. LaFond, "Treatment of the Adolescent Sex Offender," *Child and Adolescent Social Work Journal 5* (1988).

19. L. H. Pierce and R. L. Pierce, "Adolescent/Sibling Incest Perpetrators," in L. Horton, B. Johnson, L. Roundy, and D. Williams, eds., *The Incest Perpetrator: A Family Member No One Wants to Treat* (Beverly Hills: Sage, 1990).

20. M. O'Brien, "Taking Sibling Incest Seriously," in M. Quinn-Patton, ed., *Family Sexual Abuse: Frontline Research and Evaluation* (Beverly Hills: Sage, 1991).

21. T. K. Seghorn, R. A. Prentky, and R. J. Boucher, "Childhood Sexual Abuse in the Lives of Sexually Aggressive Offenders," *Journal of the American Academy of Child and Adolescent Psychiatry 26* (1987): 262–67.

22. Child Abuse Prevention and Treatment Act, P.L. 100–294.

23. U.S. Department of Justice, Office of Juvenile Justice and Delinquency Prevention, *Child Molesters: A Behavioral Analysis, For Law Enforcement Officers Investigating Causes of Child Sexual Exploitation* (Arlington: National Center for Missing & Exploited Children, 1992), p. 1.

24. *Ibid.,* p. 1–5.

25. *Ibid.,* p. 1.

26. *Ibid.,* p. 4.

27. *Ibid.*

28. *Ibid.,* pp. 5–10; Robert E. Freeman-Longo and Geral T. Blanchard, *Sexual Abuse in America: Epidemic of the 21st Century* (Brandon: Safer Society Press, 1998), pp. 40–41.

29. *Child Molesters: A Behavioral Analysis,* p. 6.

30. *Ibid.,* pp. 6–7; Freeman-Longo and Blanchard, *Sexual Abuse in America,* p. 44.

31. Freeman-Longo and Blanchard, *Sexual Abuse in America,* p. 40.

32. *Child Molesters: A Behavioral Analysis,* p. 8.

33. *Ibid. See also* Carla van Dam, *Identifying Child Molesters: Preventing Child Sexual Abuse by Recognizing the Patterns of the Offenders* (Binghamton: Haworth Press, 2001).

34. *Child Molesters: A Behavioral Analysis,* p. 8.

35. *Ibid.,* pp. 15–21.

36. *Ibid.,* pp. 8–9.

37. *Children Traumatized in Sex Rings,* p. 6.

38. *Ibid.*

39. Flowers, *The Victimization and Exploitation of Women and Children,* p. 73.

40. *Diagnostic and Statistical Manual of Mental Disorders,* 3rd Ed. (Washington: American Psychiatric Association, 1987).

41. E. P. Sarafino, "An Estimate of the Nationwide Incidence of Sexual Offenses Against Children," *Child Welfare 58,* 2 (1979): 127–34.

42. Flowers, *The Victimization and Exploitation of Women and Children,* p. 73; Susan Brownmiller, Against Our Will: Men, Women, and Rape (New York: Simon & Schuster, 1975), pp. 278–79.

43. Cited in *Child Molesters: A Behavioral Analysis,* p. 15.

44. *Ibid.*

45. Flowers, *The Victimization and Exploitation of Women and Children,* p. 74.

46. J. M. Reinhardt, *Sex Perversions and Sex Crimes* (Springfield: Charles C Thomas, 1957).
47. Flowers, *The Victimization and Exploitation of Women and Children,* p. 74.
48. Albert K. Cohen, "The Sociology of the Deviant Act: Anomie Theory and Beyond," *American Sociological Review 2* (1965): 5–14.
49. van Dam, *Identifying Child Molesters;* Johan W. Mohr, R. Edward Turner, and M. B. Jerry, *Pedophilia and Exhibitionism* (Toronto: University of Toronto Press, 1964).
50. J. M. MacDonald, *Rape Offenders and Their Victims* (Springfield: Charles C Thomas, 1971); J. L. Mathis, *Clear Thinking About Sexual Deviations* (Chicago: Nelson-Hall, 1972).
51. Flowers, *The Victimization and Exploitation of Women and Children,* p. 74.
52. *Children Traumatized in Sex Rings,* p. 7.
53. Cited in *Ibid.*
54. *Ibid.*
55. *Ibid.,* pp. 7–14; U.S. Department of Justice, *Child Sex Rings: A Behavioral Analysis, For Criminal Justice Professionals Handling Cases of Child Sexual Exploitation* (Arlington: National Center for Missing & Exploited Children, 1992), p. 11.
56. *Children Traumatized in Sex Rings,* p. 10.
57. Flowers, *The Victimization and Exploitation of Women and Children,* pp. 74–75; Freeman-Longo and Blanchard, *Sexual Abuse in America,* pp. 72–73; Tom O'Carroll, Paedophilia: The Radical Case (Boston: Alyson Publications, 1980).
58. Freeman-Longo and Blanchard, *Sexual Abuse in America,* pp. 73–74.

Chapter 10

PORNOGRAPHY AND SEX CRIME

The impact of pornography with respect to sex criminality has manifested itself in several ways. Many believe that pornography, through its graphic and sometimes violent depiction of women, promotes male sexual and physical aggression towards females. There have been a number of studies that have shown a relationship between use of pornography and rape, child sexual abuse, sexual intimidation, murder, and sexual serial murder.[1] A correlation has also been established between pornography and prostitution.[2]

The most persuasive aspect linking pornography and sex crime is child pornography. Although illegal in all fifty states, pornographic material involving children is widespread and a flourishing enterprise in this country and around the world. The use of the Internet for distributing child pornography has increased in recent years, setting up legal battles between free speech advocates and those wishing to protect children from online smut. Child prostitution and child sex rings are integral parts of child pornography and must be dealt with in any effort to combat this sex-related crime. This chapter will address the issue of pornography and its association to sexual crimes and predators.

DEFINITIONS OF PORNOGRAPHY

The word *pornography* historically reflects female prostitutes and prostitution. Pornography derives from the Greek term *pornographos,* a combination of *porne,* which means prostitute or female captive, and *graphein,* meaning to write–thus, writings on prostitution and prostitutes.[3] In current times, the definition of pornography has widened to include the many ways in which sexually explicit material can be provided and disseminated such as pornographic literature, movies, videos, live shows, photographs, and computer-related pornography.

Definitions of pornography can be found from a number of sources. The dictionary defines it as "writings, pictures, films, or other materials that are meant to stimulate erotic feelings by describing or portraying sexual activity." In the *Academic American Encyclopedia,* pornography or obscenity is defined as "any material, pictures, films, printed matter, or devices dealing with sexual poses or acts considered indecent by the public."[4] Philosopher Helen Longino's definition of pornography is material that "explicitly represents or describes degrading and abusive sexual behavior so as to endorse and/or recommend the behavior as described."[5]

> In *Women and Criminality,* pornography is defined as
> any sexually explicit and/or titillating, arousing, written, photographic, pictorial (including moving pictures), or live depiction of women or children as objects for commercial exploitation, sexual abuse, degradation, regression, or humiliation that is offensive in its sexual content or acts to the population-at-large and that has a negative effect on certain elements of society.[6]

Some experts believe that pornography promotes in sex abusers and sexually aggressive men what is know as objectification or "an attitude that others are nothing more than objects—not human beings. Women and children may be seen as eager, yet passive, sexual toys whose function in life is to satisfy a man."[7]

The debate about pornography in society concerning its constitutionality and broad or narrow scope adds to the confusion over its definition. For example, pornography is commonly associated by definition with *obscenity,* which is defined as "something condemnatory, offensive, indecent, disgusting, or lewd to prevailing concepts of decency." However, not everything that is considered obscene is pornographic and not all pornography is obscene or reflects obscenity, per se. Yet there does seem to be some consensus that pornographic material depicting children or viewed by children is harmful or potentially harmful.

THE PORNOGRAPHY BUSINESS

Pornography is a big business both in the United States and abroad. It is estimated to be a seven to ten billion dollar a year enterprise in this country alone.[8] This includes hard-core pornography, sold mostly through mail order, adult bookstores, computer websites, and the black market; and soft-core porn that can be found in trade bookstores, supermarkets, and magazine and newsstands everywhere.[9] Cable TV has long since offered soft- and hard-core entertainment, competing with traditional adult theaters. Recent years have seen more and more examples of soft porn on network television from daytime soap operas to prime time dramas.

Many see this explosion in pornography-related entertainment as harmful to the public, particularly to women and children. The pornography industry itself is regarded by some experts as being supported through "systematically eroticizing violence against women by producing and marketing images of men humiliating, battering, and murdering women for sexual pleasure. . . . Pornography is about power imbalances using sex as a weapon to subjugate women. In pornography, the theme is assailant vs. victim."[10]

According to the organizer for Women Against Pornography, Francis Patai: "Pornography objectifies women by caricaturing and reducing them to a sum of their sexual parts and functions–devoid of sensibilities and intelligence. . . . Objectifying the sexual anatomy of women renders them inferior and nonhuman, thus providing the psychological formulation for committing violence against them."[11] Feminist Catherine MacKinnon argues that pornography "is one of the ways in which the system of dominance and submission is maintained, a system whose underlying dynamic depends on the sexual objectification of women."[12]

Unfortunately, given the many women who choose to participate in pornography, including the production of it, there appears to be little end in sight to this growing and lucrative sex industry.

PORNOGRAPHY AND ITS EFFECTS ON ANTISOCIAL BEHAVIOR

In an attempt to study the effects of pornography on antisocial behavior towards women and children, two government commissions were formed in the 1970s and 1980s. In 1970, the Presidential Commission on Obscenity and Pornography came to the conclusion that

> empirical research designed to clarify the question has found no evidence to date that exposure to explicit sexual materials plays a significant role in the causation of delinquency or criminal behavior among youths or adults. The Commission cannot conclude that exposure to erotic materials is a factor in the causation of sex crime or sex delinquency.[13]

However, fifteen years later, the Attorney General's Commission on Pornography reached a markedly different conclusion in its effort to determine the "nature, extent, and impact on society of pornography in the United States, and to make specific recommendations . . . concerning more effective ways in which the spread of pornography could be contained, consistent with constitutional guarantees."[14] The Commission found that there was a relationship between certain types of pornography and sexual violence and abuse towards women, noting that even nonviolent sexually explicit material "bears some causal relationship to the level of sexual violence."[15]

The Commission's report read, in part:
When clinical and experimental research has focused particularly on sexually violent material, the conclusions have been nearly unanimous. In both clinical and experimental settings, exposure to sexually violent materials has indicated an increase in the likelihood of aggression. . . . The research . . . shows a causal relationship between exposure to material of this type and aggressive behavior towards women. . . . The assumption that increased aggressive behavior toward women is causally related . . . to increased sexual violence is significantly supported by the clinical evidence, as well as by much of the less scientific evidence.[16]

The Commission called for a nationwide crackdown on hard-core pornography purveyors; further recommending amending federal obscenity laws "for distributing obscene materials through interstate commerce and enacting legislation to prohibit transmitting obscene material by phone or similar common carrier."[17]

Although the report was not without its critics, given the vast amount of data used, most experts on pornography agreed that the findings and recommendations, "clearly justify the conclusion that there is at least some relationship between the pornography industry and the victimization of women."[18]

PORNOGRAPHY AND SEXUAL VIOLENCE

The correlation between pornography and sexual violence against women has been supported through a number of studies. In a study of one hundred battered wives, 15 percent reported that their batterers "seemed to experience sexual arousal" after viewing hard-core pornography, "since the demand for sexual intercourse immediately followed the assault."[19] Pauline Bart, who studied rape victims, observed: "I didn't start out being against pornography; but if you're a rape researcher, it becomes clear that there is a direct link. Violent pornography is like an advertisement for rape. . . . Men are not born thinking women enjoy rape and torture. They learn from pornography."[20]

According to Larry Baron and Murray Straus in their study of mass-circulation sex magazines and the incidence of rape: "Rape increases in direct proportion to the readership of sex magazines."[21] Co-editor of *Pornography and Sexual Aggression,* Neil Malamuth asserted: "In a culture that celebrates rape, the lives of millions of women will be affected."[22]

In correlating pornography with sex crimes during a public lecture titled "Does Pornographic Literature Incite Sexual Assault?" a Michigan State police detective cited:

> numerous cases where the assailants had immersed themselves in pornographic films or pictures and then gone out and committed sex crimes. These crimes included rape, sodomy, and even the bizarre erotic crime of piquerism (piercing with a knife till blood flows, a kind of sexual torture). In some cases the attacker admitted that the urge to rape or torture erotically came over him while reading an obscene picture magazine or attending a movie showing rape and erotic torture.[23]

Sex crimes such as female prostitution have also been linked to pornography-inspired sexual violence against prostitutes who are "already in a high-risk lifestyle involving illicit sex, physical assaults, and often substance abuse" and especially "susceptible to customer, pimp, or stranger rape as part of the sex industry cycle of victimization."[24] The Los Angeles Police Department recently found a direct correlation between the "clustering of adult entertainment establishments in Hollywood and an increase in the incidence of rape and other violent crimes."[25] The department further found that prostitution in the Hollywood adult entertainment district had risen at a rate fifteen times the city average over a six-year period, putting prostitutes right in the path of sex offenders.[26]

Other experts have also noted the correlation between pornography and sexual violence. Laura Lederer maintained in her book, *Take Back the Night: Women on Pornography:* "Pornography is the ideology of a culture which promotes and condones rape, woman battering, and other crimes against women."[27] When asked the question: "What do men want?" MacKinnon responded: "What men want is: women bound, women battered, women tortured, women humiliated, women degraded and defiled, women killed . . . women sexually accessible, have-able, there for them, wanting to be taken and used."[28]

Pornography and Sexual Homicide

Pornography has been associated with sex killers and sexual serial murders in the literature. Such killers as Ted Bundy, Jeffrey Dahmer, and Gerald Gallego confessed to using or being influenced by pornography in some fashion.[29] Common triggering factors among most sexual murderers are fantasies of rape, sexual torture, or other forms of violent behavior.[30] These fantasies are often rooted in childhood sexual and physical abuse, sexualized rituals, and pornographic or violence-oriented materials.[31]

In studying the childhood sexual experiences of sex killers, Robert Ressler, Ann Burgess, and John Douglas found a "strong reliance on visual sexual stimuli" among the killers.[32] Highest on the list was pornography, with more than eight in ten offenders reporting this experience. More than seven in ten killers were into fetishism, voyeurism, and compulsive masturbation. An analysis of the correlation between child sexual abuse and sexual experiences found that 92 percent of the serial killers who were sexually abused used pornography versus 79 percent of those not sexually abused.[33] In both instances, pornography still proved to be a strong element.

Studies have shown that pornography can increase sexual desires in some sex offenders;[34] while those who are predisposed to sexual aggression may use hard-core and soft-core pornography "to increase their arousal or justify their behavior."[35] While pornography cannot be blamed in and of itself for sexual homicide or other murders, its impact on the psyche of the unstable personalities of sex-related killers cannot be ignored.

CHILD PORNOGRAPHY

Child pornography is a very serious form of pornography than can affect potentially millions of children and their families with various implications, including child prostitution, child molestation, other sexual victimization, and graduation into adult pornography and sex criminality. An expert on the sexual exploitation of children described child pornography as "the most inhuman of crimes. For pleasure and profit, pornographers have murdered the childhood of a million boys and girls, victims who must live with the dreadful memories of their experience."[36]

It is generally believed that the modern era of child pornography began during the 1400s in China with the sex manual, *The Admirable Discourses of the Plain Child,* in which sexual intercourse and other sex acts involving children were graphically described.[37] Today, there are countless forms of child pornography easily available around the world to any pedophile or child molester or, for that matter, any prechild molester or pedophile.

Defining Child Pornography

Child pornography, often called "kiddie porn," "child porn," or "chicken porn," is typically defined as "photographs, videos, books, magazines, and motion pictures that depict children in sexually explicit acts with other children, adults, animals, and/or foreign objects."[38] In the book, *The Sexual Abuse of Children and Adolescents,* the authors define child pornography as "any visual or written depiction, on film or in print, of the sexual abuse of children."[39] To both of these definitions one could add what is a growing concern to professionals in the field of child sexual exploitation—any sexually explicit material appearing on or transmitted through the rapidly expanding Internet involving children or available to children.

Definitional problems exist in understanding what constitutes or should constitute child pornography. This can been seen in Federal law, which defines child pornography as "sexually explicit visual depictions of minors. A minor is defined as someone who has not yet reached his or her eighteenth birthday."[40] Hence, at least technically, a sexually explicit image in picture form or any other means of a mature, sexually experienced seventeen-year-old female would legally be considered child pornography. Even with such a gray area of pornography, there is little dispute among experts that child pornography is a serious problem involving the sexploitation of minors that shows little sign of abating.

In a U.S. Department of Justice publication, *Child Molesters: A Behavioral Analysis,* the definition of child pornography seems to address inconsistencies in its meaning. It defines child pornography as

> the sexually explicit reproduction of a child's image—including sexually explicit photographs, negatives, slides, magazines, movies, videotapes, and computer disks. In essence, it is the permanent record of the sexual abuse or exploitation of an actual child. In order to be legally child pornography, it must be a visual depiction (not the written word), or a minor (as defined by statute), which is sexually explicit (not necessarily obscene, unless required by state law).[41]

Child pornography can be broken down into four subtypes: (1) commercial, (2) homemade, (3) technical, and (4) simulated. Each reflect different aspects in recognizing this type of child sexual victimization and exploitation.[42]

- **Commercial child pornography** is produced mainly by child molesters and pedophiles and meant for commercial sale.
- **Homemade child pornography** is not originally produced for purposes of commercial sale by pedophiles, but usually swapped and traded with other pedophiles.
- **Technical child pornography** is pornography involving persons under eighteen as legally defined. It is typically produced, distributed, and purchased by nonchild molesters or pedophiles.
- **Simulated child pornography** involves individuals over the age of sev-

enteen in pornographic situations designed to stimulate child pornography.

Commercial and homemade child pornography can sometimes merge. For example, in some instances homemade child porn is sold or ends up in commercial child pornography files, videos or magazines.

Child pornography is often confused with *child erotica,* which is defined as "any material, relating to children, that serves a sexual purpose for a given individual."[43] Child erotica, also known as *pedophile paraphernalia,* includes drawings, toys, games, sexual aids, books, diaries, manuals, and souvenirs related to children. Possessing and distributing child erotica is not illegal–as long as it does not cross over into what is legally defined as child pornography.

Victims of child pornography are subjected to virtually every form of abuse, perversion, humiliation, and sexual exploitation. These include paraphilias such as rape, incest, sadism, pedophilia, bestiality, triolism, torture, and sexual murder. One magazine graphically depicts adults in various sexual acts with toddlers.[44] In at least one audiotape, the screams of a young girl being raped can be heard, accompanied by graphic narrative description.[45]

Although child pornography is illegal in the United States, most experts agree that current laws and law enforcement are seriously inadequate in confronting the problem and going after child pornographers and molesters.

The Scope of Child Pornography

Child pornography, like adult pornography, is a multimillion dollar worldwide enterprise. For example, in Germany the annual sales of child pornography are estimated to exceed $250 million, with the number of customers said to be somewhere between 30,000 and 40,000.[46] The United States has the largest market for child pornography, with an estimated six billion dollars taken in each year.[47] Eighty-five percent of worldwide sales of child porn-related items take place in this country.[48] In Los Angeles alone, it is estimated that 30,000 children are victimized by child pornographers annually.[49] Child pornography makes up approximately 7 percent of the pornography market in the United States.[50]

Data from the National Incident-Based Reporting System on child pornography revealed that between 1997 and 2000, approximately 2,900 incidents of pornography involving minors or child sexual exploitation were known to law enforcement nationwide.[51] The proportion of total pornography involving children or juveniles rose over the span from 15 percent to 26 percent. The perpetrator of the majority of child pornography crimes tended to be a single adult offender; with six in ten juvenile victims female and teenagers, and one in four victims members of the perpetrator's family.[52]

Much of the kiddie porn magazines and films come from abroad from countries such as Germany, Sweden, Switzerland, and Denmark. A recent study found that at least 264 different magazines depicting sexual acts involving children are produced and distributed each month in the United States.[53] A magazine of sexually explicit pictures of children can be produced for as little as fifty cents and sold for many times that amount.[54] The profit margin is even greater for child porn sold over the Internet.[55]

In spite of tough antipornography laws on the books in this country, "several hundred magazines, international mailing lists, videotapes, and other forms of child pornography are still being sold. Producers find a steady supply of actresses and actors for their 'kiddie porn' on the streets where runaways and throwaways search for money to provide themselves with food and shelter."[56]

Recently the ABC television program 20/20 did a story on a U.S. Postal Service sting operation called "Operation Special Delivery," which identified and arrested child pornography distributors and consumers. Many of the perpetrators were described as "respected members of their community;" while the confiscated photographs and videotapes contained children who were crying, sexually or physically abused, and tortured.[57] Other recent examples of child pornography or pornographers include:

- A woman was alleged to have made a half million dollars annually by supplying 80 percent of the child porn market.
- Houston police raided a warehouse loaded with child pornographic materials including 15,000 color slides of children performing sexual acts, more than 1,000 magazines and paperback books, and over 1,000 reels of film.
- A child pornography consumer was arrested in a police raid. Confiscated was a scrapbook, which contained articles about child rapes and murders. Also included were photographs of young girls.[58]

Child pornographers and child sexual predators have little trouble recruiting children for sexual exploitation. The pool of susceptible victims includes runaways, throwaways, homeless youth, teenage prostitutes, drug addicted youth, thrill-seeking minors, children from unstable families, neighbor children, and even family members who seek "easy" money, drugs, or other compensation for their trouble. Not all children enter pornography voluntarily or with minimal coercion. Some are forced into child pornography or abducted as child sex slaves, indentured sexual servants, or by child sex rings.[59] Many of these sexually exploited children are kept in line through intimidation, drugs, torture, blackmail, and/or guilt.

Characterizing Child Pornographers and Child Sexual Exploiters

The producers and consumers of child pornography are almost always men (though children can be lured into watching other children in pornographic pictures, movies or performances as part of the child porn or child sex rings). These child sexual exploiters come from all walks of life and backgrounds. While they are mostly strangers to the victims, some producers and purveyors of child pornography are family members or relatives of the victims. "The men who support this industry do so to rationalize and seek justification for their perverted and deviant mentality, whereas the pornographers who bring children into this seedy world are primarily interested in capitalizing monetarily from the sickness of disturbed, immature pedophiles who receive their only sexual satisfaction with children."[60]

The FBI's pedophile profile describes typical child pornographers and sexual exploiters of children as men who are "intelligent enough to recognize they have a problem" yet somehow manage to rationalize that "what they're doing is right."[61] According to one FBI agent in explaining the mindset of pedophiles: "Pedophilia is a way of life. They believe there's nothing wrong with it, so naturally they're looking for other individuals who support their thinking."[62]

Pedophiles and child pornographers have powerful allies in such groups as the North American Man-Boy Love Association and the Rene Guyon Society. These organizations openly advocate child pornography and consensual sex between children and adults. In spite of the existence of such groups and local affiliates across the United States, law enforcement is often powerless to intervene in their activities "without an allegation or a reason to conduct" an investigation.[63] (See also Chapter 9.)

Child Sex Rings and Child Pornography

As described in Chapter 9, child sex rings are an important component of child sexual abuse. These rings often involve one or more child molesters having sexual contact with several children and also usually include child pornography activities. According to Ann Burgess, who wrote *Child Pornography and Sex Rings,* there are three types of sex rings: (1) solo, (2) transition, and (3) syndicated.[64]

Solo child sex rings–offenders keep their activities and photographs a secret from others. There is one offender and multiple victims.
Transition child sex rings–offenders share their experiences, pornography, and child victims amongst each other.

Syndicated child sex rings–well-structured organizations that recruit child victims, produce pornography, supply sexual services directly, and have an extensive network of consumers.

Each of these child sex rings can progress to the next level or operate within their parameters.

FBI supervisory special agent Kenneth Lanning identified two distinct types of child sex rings: (1) historical child sex rings and (2) multidimensional child sex rings.[65] The former refers to more traditional child sex rings, typically involving solo, transitional, and syndicated dynamics. The vast majority of historical child sex ring offenders are male molesters with more than half their victims boys. Child pornography and child erotica are commonly collected by these offenders.

Multidimensional child sex rings tend to be more difficult to define, but typically involve the following components: (1) multiple child victims, (2) multiple offenders, (3) fear as an instrument of control, and (4) bizarre, ritualistic, or satanic activity. Victims often report that pictures and videotapes were taken of the multidimensional episodes; while law enforcement authorities have confiscated huge amounts of child pornography and paraphernalia in recent years.[66] Overall, multidimensional child sex rings can be the most difficult for law enforcement to investigate given their complexity, unpredictability, and skepticism about the existence of these sex rings.

Child Pornography and Child Prostitution

Child pornography is strongly associated with the prostitution of children.[67] Many of the victims share the same dynamics: runaways or throwaways, a history of sexual or physical abuse, drug or alcohol addiction, coerced into being sexually exploited by pimps, pornographers, and hustlers–as a means to support themselves, their perpetrators, or drug habits. Often child prostitution leads to child pornography, or vice versa, as sexual predators and pedophiles use every means available to sexually exploit and profit from their young victims. One study found that nearly one in three teenage prostitutes interviewed reported involvement in child pornography.[68] In some cases, a pimp may take sexually explicit photographs of a girl and threaten to expose her to family or school officials as a means of maintaining control and breaking her resistance to his authority.[69] Child sex rings typically use boys and girls for sex and pornography, often swapping each among themselves.[70] Customers of child prostitutes may also use child pornography "to describe the sexual act they want and to rationalize their behavior and their demands of the child."[71]

Child Pornography and the Internet

Recent years have seen an explosion of child pornography on the Internet. Pedophiles and sex offenders have found easy access to child victims through chat rooms on services such as America Online and Compu-Serve. Also there are countless websites that cater to pedophiles, purveyors of smut, and supporters of child pornography. "Cyber sex" has become a common phrase on the web and can often involve adults (sometimes pretending to be children) with child victims—and has at times led to actual meetings and child molestation or child rape.

The government's attempts to control children from the "patently offensive" pornographic material available on the Internet has had mixed results. The Communications Decency Act of 1996 made it a crime for anyone who "by means of a telecommunications device knowingly makes, creates or solicits, and initiates the transmission of any comment, request, suggestion, proposal, image or other communication which is obscene or indecent, knowing that the recipient of the communication is under eighteen years of age."[72] Penalties for such would have included up to two years in prison and a $250,000 fine.

The law was quickly challenged by free speech advocates, civil libertarians, and computer users. In 1997, the Supreme Court struck down the law as a violation of the First Amendment right to free speech.[73] This affirmed a Pennsylvania federal court ruling blocking enforcement of the Communications Decency Act. The president of the Christian Coalition warned that the ruling leaves "millions of children vulnerable to exploitation by pornographers."[74]

A further blow to the protection of children from Internet pornography came in 1998 when a federal judge found the Child Pornography Prevention Act of 1996 to be unconstitutionally vague.[75] The law's aim was to combat computer technology used to alter child images to make them appear sexually explicit. See Chapter 17 for more on laws against the sexual exploitation of children.

In 2000, the Child Online Protection Act was enacted with the intention of protecting minors from sexual material deemed harmful on the Internet.[76] The law was struck down as unconstitutional by the courts, including the Supreme Court, in June 2004 in *Ashcroft v. American Civil Liberties Union.*[77]

Congress enacted the Children's Internet Protection Act (CIPA) in 2000, addressing access on library and school computers to offensive material on the Internet and requirements for receiving federal funding.[78]

NOTES

1. *See, for example,* R. Barri Flowers, *The Prostitution of Women and Girls* (Jefferson: McFarland, 2005), pp. 115–25; U.S. Department of Justice, *Children Traumatized in Sex Rings* (Arlington: National Center for Missing & Exploited Children, 1988); Robert K. Ressler, Ann W. Burgess, and John E. Douglas, *Sexual Homicide: Patterns and Motives* (New York: Lexington Books, 1988), pp. 24–25.

2. Flowers, *The Prostitution of Women and Girls,* pp. 119, 121–25; U.S. Department of Justice, Office of Juvenile Justice and Delinquency Prevention, *Prostitution of Children and Child-Sex Tourism: An Analysis of Domestic and International Responses* (Arlington: National Center for Missing & Exploited Children, 1999), p. 6.

3. R. Barri Flowers, *Women and Criminality: The Woman as Victim, Offender, and Practitioner* (Westport: Greenwood Press, 1987), pp. 47–48.

4. Quoted in R. Barri Flowers, *The Victimization and Exploitation of Women and Children: A Study of Physical, Mental and Sexual Maltreatment in the United States* (Jefferson: McFarland, 1994), p. 180.

5. Helen E. Longino, "Pornography, Oppression, and Freedom: A Closer Look," in Laura Lederer, ed., *Take Back the Night: Women on Pornography* (New York: William Morrow, 1980), p. 44.

6. Flowers, *Women and Criminality,* p. 48.

7. Robert E. Freeman-Longo and Geral T. Blanchard, *Sexual Abuse in America: Epidemic of the 21st Century* (Brandon: Safer Society Press, 1998), p. 66.

8. Ibid., p. 96; Flowers, *The Victimization and Exploitation of Women and Children,* p. 180.

9. Freeman-Longo and Blanchard, *Sexual Abuse in America,* p. 96.

10. Frances Patai, "Pornography and Woman Battering: Dynamic Similarities," in Maria Roy, ed., *The Abusive Partner: An Analysis of Domestic Battering* (New York: Van Nostrand Reinhold, 1982), p. 91–92.

11. *Ibid.,* pp. 93–94.

12. Quoted in Alice Leuchtag, "The Culture of Pornography," *The Humanist 55* (1995): 5.

13. Commission on Obscenity and Pornography, *Technical Report of the Commission on Obscenity and Pornography: Legal Analysis,* Vol. 2 (Washington: Government Printing Office, 1971), p. 223.

14. U.S. Department of Justice, *Attorney General's Commission on Pornography: Final Report,* Vol. 1 (Washington: Government Printing Office, 1986), p. 215.

15. *Ibid.,* p. 216.

16. *Ibid.,* pp. 324–25.

17. *Ibid.,* pp. 465–81, 483–90; Flowers, *The Prostitution of Women and Girls,* p. 118.

18. Flowers, *Women and Criminality,* p. 53.

19. Kathleen Barry, *Female Sexual Slavery* (Englewood Cliffs: Prentice-Hall, 1979), p. 145.

20. Quoted in Hillary Johnson, "Violence Against Women: Is Porn to Blame?" *Vogue 175* (September, 1985): p. 678.

21. Larry Baron and Murray A. Straus, "Sexual Stratification, Pornography, and Rape in the United States," in Neil M. Malamuth and Edward Donnerstein, eds., *Pornography and Sexual Aggression* (Orlando: Academic Press, 1984), p. 206.

22. Quoted in Johnson, "Violence Against Women," p. 678.

23. Quoted in William A. Stanmeyer, *The Seduction of Society* (Ann Arbor: Servant Books, 1984), pp. 29–30.

24. Flowers, *The Prostitution of Women and Girls,* p. 118.

25. Stanmeyer, *The Seduction of Society,* p. 49; Flowers, *Women and Criminality,* p. 54.

26. Stanmeyer, *The Seduction of Society,* p. 49.
27. Laura Lederer, ed., *Take Back the Night,* pp. 19–20.
28. Quoted in Leuchtag, "The Culture of Pornography," p. 6.
29. R. Barri Flowers, *The Sex Slave Murders* (New York: St. Martin's Press, 1996); Brian Lane and Wilfred Gregg, *The Encyclopedia of Serial Killers* (New York: Berkley, 1995).
30. Ressler, Burgess, and Douglas, *Sexual Homicide,* pp. 50–52.
31. *Ibid.,* pp. 42–43; Flowers, *The Victimization and Exploitation of Women and Children,* pp. 182–85.
32. Ressler, Burgess, and Douglas, *Sexual Homicide,* p. 25.
33. *Ibid.,* p. 26.
34. Freeman-Longo and Blanchard, *Sexual Abuse in America.*
35. *Ibid.;* J. Rosenberg, *Fuel on the Fire: An Inquiry into "Pornography" and Sexual Aggression* (Orwell: Safer Society Press, 1989).
36. Rita Rooney, "Children for Sale: Pornography's Dark New World," *Reader's Digest* (July, 1983), p. 53.
37. Reay Tannahill, *Sex in History* (New York: Stein and Day, 1980), p. 320.
38. *Ibid.,* p. 90.
39. Margaret O. Hyde and Elizabeth H. Forsyth, *The Sexual Abuse of Children and Adolescents* (Brookfield: Millbrook Press, 1997), p. 18.
40. U.S. Department of Justice, *Child Sex Rings: A Behavioral Analysis, For Criminal Justice Professionals Handling Cases of Child Sexual Exploitation* (Arlington: National Center for Missing & Exploited Children, 1992), p. 7.
41. U.S. Department of Justice, Office of Juvenile Justice and Delinquency Prevention, *Child Molesters: A Behavioral Analysis, For Law Enforcement Officers Investigating Cases of Child Sexual Exploitation (Arlington: National Center for Missing & Exploited Children,* 1992), p. 24.
42. *Ibid.,* pp. 24–26.
43. *Child Sex Rings: A Behavioral Analysis,* p. 12.
44. Flowers, *The Prostitution of Women and Girls,* p. 121.
45. *Ibid.;* Tannahill, *Sex in History,* p. 90.
46. Cited in Michael S. Serrill, "Defiling the Children," *Time 141* (June 21, 1993), p. 52.
47. Cited in Flowers, *Women and Criminality,* p. 48.
48. Cited in Joan J. Johnson, *Teen Prostitution* (Danbury: Franklin Watts, 1992), p. 90.
49. R. Barri Flowers, *The Adolescent Criminal: An Examination of Today's Juvenile Offender* (Jefferson: McFarland, 1990), p. 64.
50. Shirley O'Brien, *Child Pornography* (Dubuque: Kendall/Hunt, 1983), p. 19; M. Guio, A. Burgess, and R. Kelly, "Child Victimization: Pornography and Prostitution," *Journal of Crime and Justice 3* (1980): 65–81.
51. David Finkelhor and Richard Ormrod, *Child Pornography: Patterns From NIBRS* (Washington: Office of Juvenile Justice and Delinquency Prevention, 2004), pp. 1–3.
52. *Ibid.,* p. 2.
53. Cited in R. Barri Flowers, *Children and Criminality: The Child as Victim and Perpetrator* (Westport: Greenwood Press, 1986), p. 82.
54. Flowers, *The Adolescent Criminal,* p. 64.
55. Flowers, *The Prostitution of Women and Girls,* p. 122.
56. Hyde and Forsyth, *The Sexual Abuse of Children and Adolescents,* p. 18.
57. Cited in Freeman-Longo and Blanchard, *Sexual Abuse in America,* p. 99.
58. Flowers, The Prostitution of Women and Girls, p. 122.
59. *Ibid.,* pp. 122–23; *Child Sex Rings: A Behavioral Analysis; Children Traumatized in Sex Rings.*
60. Flowers, *Children and Criminality,* pp. 82–83.

61. "Child Pornography on the Rise Despite Tougher Laws," *Sacramento Union* (April 7, 1984), p. E6.
62. *Ibid.*
63. Flowers, *The Prostitution of Women and Girls,* p. 123.
64. Ann W. Burgess, *Child Pornography and Sex Rings* (Lexington: Lexington Books, 1984).
65. *Child Sex Rings: A Behavioral Analysis,* pp. 10–30.
66. *Ibid.*
67. Flowers, *The Prostitution of Women and Girls,* pp. 123–24; *Prostitution of Children and Child-Sex Tourism,* p. 6.
68. Johnson, *Teen Prostitution,* p. 91.
69. *Prostitution of Children and Child-Sex Tourism,* p. 6; Evelina Giobbe, "Juvenile Prostitution: Profile of Recruitment," in Ann W. Burgess, ed., *Child Trauma I: Issues and Research* (New York: Garland Publishing, 1992), p. 124.
70. *Children Traumatized in Sex Rings.*
71. *Prostitution of Children and Child-Sex Tourism,* p. 6; Cathy S. Widom and Joseph B. Kuhns, "Childhood Victimization and Subsequent Risk for Promiscuity, Prostitution and Teenage Pregnancy: A Prospective Study," *American Journal of Public Health 86* (1996): 1611.
72. The Communications Decency Act of 1996.
73. Flowers, *The Prostitution of Women and Girls,* p. 125.
74. Quoted in an Associated Press news report (June 26, 1997).
75. Cited by the Associated Press news report (April 2, 1998).
76. The Child Online Protection Act (Public Law 106–554).
77. *Ashcroft v. American Civil Liberties Union* (June 30, 2004).
78. The Children's Internet Protection Act (Public Law 106–554).

Chapter 11

SEX TRAFFICKING

A growing and serious problem in the United States is human trafficking. Referred to as a "modern day form of slavery," the trafficking of persons for forced labor and sexual misuse and exploitation is a global concern.[1] It is estimated that as many as one million women and children are trafficked across international borders every year.[2] Many of these are forced into prostitution and other types of sexual degradation and exploitation. Victims are typically poor, undereducated, and susceptible to sex traffickers who offer false promises of a better life but end up delivering a much worse fate in conjunction with pimps, johns, pornographers, pedophiles, and others involved in the commercial sex trade industry. (See also the other chapters in this part and Part V.)

With sex trafficking and involuntary servitude becoming as much of a domestic issue in the war against child sexual abuse and exploitation, illegal prostitution, and slave labor as internationally, efforts have been stepped up to go after human traffickers and sexual predators and protect and assist victims.

This chapter will look at the dynamics of sex trafficking in this country and abroad.

HUMAN TRAFFICKING

What is human trafficking? In the simplest terms, it relates to the recruiting and transporting of persons through deception, coercion, or other means of manipulation for purposes of forced labor, involuntary servitude, sexual abuse and exploitation, and/or enslavement. The trafficking of persons is more broadly defined by the United Nations Protocol to Prevent, Suppress, and Punish Trafficking in Persons as:

131

The recruitment, transportation, transfer, harboring or receipt of persons, by means of threat or use of force or other forms of coercion, of abduction, or fraud, of deception, of the abuse of power or of a position of vulnerability or of the giving or receiving of payments or benefits to achieve the consent of a person having control over another person, for the purpose of exploitation. Exploitation shall include, at a minimum, the exploitation of the prostitution of others or other forms of sexual exploitation, forced labor or services, slavery or practices similar to slavery, servitude or the removal of organs.[3]

In the United States, "severe forms of trafficking in persons" has been defined by the government through the Victims of Trafficking and Violence Protection Act of 2000 and again in the Act's reauthorization in 2003, as

(a) sex trafficking in which a commercial sex act is induced by force, fraud or coercion, or in which the person induced to perform such act has not attained 18 years of age; or
(b) the recruitment, harboring, transportation, provision, or obtaining of a person for labor or services, through the use of force, fraud, or coercion for the purpose of subjection to involuntary servitude, peonage, debt bondage, or slavery.[4]

Traffickers or slave traders tend to target the most vulnerable—especially young women and children—and exploit their often dire circumstances in life, including impoverishment, discrimination, political instability, corruption, and even terrorism.

In seeking a better life and higher standard of living, many victims may leave home voluntarily before realizing too late that they were duped and find themselves forced into domestic servitude, labor in sweatshops or agriculture, sex-for-sale industry, pornography, and other forms of slavery. Whether a victim consents to the initial trafficking is seen as irrelevant in defining them as a victim of human trafficking because of the deception, coercion, sexual exploitation, violence, and solution that typically occurs as a result of trafficking.[5]

THE SCOPE OF HUMAN TRAFFICKING

Just how widespread is the trafficking in persons? Because of the hidden aspects of global human trafficking and inconsistent methods of tracking and assessing its scope, no one knows for certain just how many people are being trafficked worldwide. However, there are indications that the numbers are staggering.

UNICEF estimated that 1.75 million women and children were trafficked globally each year,[6] while the FBI put the figure in 2001 at around 700,000 annually.[7] The International Organization on Migration estimated that 400,000 children and women were trafficking victims each year.[8] In contrast, the United Nations estimate of persons trafficked across international borders every year was one million in 2000, which was down from their previous estimate of four million but significant nonetheless.[9] An estimated 50,000 people are trafficked into the United States from Mexico alone each year.[10] One in three of these are Latin Americans.[11]

According to the Justice Department's *Trafficking in Persons Report,* an estimated 600,000 to 800,000 children, women, and men are trafficked involuntarily or through deceptive practices across international borders each year.[12] Seventy percent of those trafficked are female and at least half are children—with the majority of victims forced into prostitution or otherwise sexually abused and exploited.

It is estimated that between 14,500 and 17,500 foreign nationals are brought into the United States annually by way of human trafficking.[13] The number of Americans trafficked each year is much higher. As many as 300,000 American children are seen as at risk to become victims of sex trafficking each year.[14]

In 2004, the *Assessment of U.S. Government Activities to Combat Trafficking in Persons,* reported that most of the persons trafficked into the United States annually originate from East Asia and the Pacific, with between 5,000 and 7,000 trafficking victims, followed by Latin America, Europe and Eurasia, with victims numbering between 3,500 and 5,500.[15]

In one of the few major studies of human trafficking in the United States, it was found that the trafficking of women for forced labor, sexual exploitation, and enslavement often lasted for years without detection. Forced labor or services tended to last anywhere from 4.5 to 6.5 years, while prostitution went on for an estimated 2.5 years, and other types of sexual exploitation persisted between ten months and three years before being detected. Upon discovery, it took approximately a year and a half for completion of an official investigation and prosecution of the traffickers.[16]

The Business of Human Trafficking

The supply and demand of human trafficking makes it an attractive enterprise for traffickers, recruiters, pimps, and others who profit from the trafficking in persons. This includes those who pay to sexually exploit children and women such as johns, molesters, pedophiles, and pornographers through child sex tourism, streetwalkers, arranged forced sex acts, and child pornography.[17]

It is estimated that 9.5 billion dollars are generated in annual revenue from human trafficking.[18] Recent criminal trafficking investigations in the United States found traffickers' profits were between one and eight million dollars over a span of one to six years of trafficking.[19]

The trafficking of persons is closely associated with organized crime and other criminal activity, often funneling through profits from trafficking, including drug trafficking, money laundering, pornography, human smuggling, document forgery, and homicide.[20] Human traffickers typically "operate through a spectrum of criminal organizations—from major crime syndicates, to gangs, to smuggling rings, to loosely associated networks. Major trafficking organizations are Asian criminal syndicates, Russian crime groups and syndicates, and loosely associated Latin American groups."[21]

Given the enormous profits derived from the trafficking in persons, traffickers and related offenders are willing to engage in any type of psychological manipulation or physical violence to control victims and continue the vicious cycle of deception, slavery, and exploitation.

Entry For Trafficking Victims Into The United States

Victims of trafficking typically gain entry into the United States in one of three ways: (1) proper travel documents that are illegally used, (2) fake passports, and (3) through avoiding inspection.[22]

According to law enforcement authorities, most trafficked women enter the United States by plane.[23] However, it is noted that victims of trafficking can also gain entry into the country by automobile, boat, train, swimming, and on foot.

Traffickers use various entry points to smuggle children and women into the United States. These include primary immigration ports of entry that run along the U.S. and Canadian border and such entry points as New York, Detroit, Los Angeles, Miami, and Chicago. Trafficked women have also been reported to gain entry into this country through military bases.[24]

In Donna Hughes and colleagues' study of sex trafficking of women in the United States, the process is described as often involving:

> the use of many transit nations before [victims] arrive at the country of destination. An Asian crime investigator noted that many Asians might have been in South America before coming over the Mexican border into the United States. . . . These entry points for trafficking, however, are fluid and when the Immigration and Naturalization Service conducts crackdowns in particular areas of the country, the entry points shift to another location.[25]

Upon successful entry into the United States for trafficking victims, the trafficking routes within the country vary from regional to national to one coast to the other, depending on the traffickers' intentions for victims. For example, in the Midwest, it was reported recently that Russian women were "trafficked from Chicago to the escort services and clubs of Minneapolis; especially after the crackdown of a Latvian-American trafficking ring in Chicago."[26]

For women and children victimized by sex traffickers, typical destinations for sexual exploitation include Detroit, New York, Tampa, Houston, Miami, Seattle, Denver, and Las Vegas.

SEX TRAFFICKING

Sex trafficking as a part of the trafficking of persons is defined as, "the recruitment, harboring, transportation, provision, or obtaining of a person for the purpose of a commercial sex act in which a commercial sex act is induced by force, fraud, or coercion, or in which the person forced to perform such an act is under eighteen years of age."[27]

The trafficking of women and children for sexual exploitation is a worldwide crisis. Millions are victimized by sex traffickers through prostitution, molestation, child sex tourism, pornography, and related sex offenses. The following findings illustrate the gravity of the problem:

- The trafficking of persons is third only to drug and arms trafficking in revenue generated worldwide.
- As many as four million women may be actively involved in the sex-for-sale business in the United States.
- Thirty million women are estimated to have been sold into prostitution since the mid-1970s.
- An estimated four billion dollars is generated annually by brothels globally.
- Half a million women have been trafficked from developing countries and forced into prostitution.
- At least two million youth in Asia alone are actively being sexually exploited in the sex trade.
- Between 50 and 60 percent of child victims of sex traffickers are under sixteen years of age.
- Child pornography brings in an estimated one billion dollars a year.
- One in four child sex tourists globally are American citizens.[28]

Sex trafficking has interconnected nations worldwide in its expansion and victimization of women and children by recruiters, traffickers, pimps, and customers who have criss-crossed international borders, often with impunity or indifference.[29]

Who Are The Sex Traffickers of Persons?

Sex traffickers are not easily identifiable because they can be anyone. These include victims' family members, intimates, friends, and acquaintances, who may operate as traffickers, recruiters, pimps, or even customers. Traffickers are also often part of an organized crime syndicate, gang members, drug dealers, child sexual abusers, white-collar criminals, pornographers, and other criminal elements. The exploiters of trafficking victims may have a legitimate front as businessmen or women, diplomats, or coworkers, while operating as traffickers behind the scenes.

In the study on sex trafficking by Hughes and associates, the researchers found that 60 percent of international women and 40 percent of American women in the sex trade industry were recruited and controlled by persons representing organized criminal enterprises, such as escort services, brothels, gangs, and the mafia.[30] Twenty percent of the international prostitutes and 28 percent of American prostitutes reported having a husband or boyfriend as pimp, while a small percentage pointed to drugs as the primary reason for entering the sex-for-sale business.

The relationship between members of the U.S. military, and trafficking/pimping of females was found to be strong. Many servicemen married or promised to marry international or American women who were previously involved in the sex trade industry, only to force them into prostitution in massage parlors or elsewhere in the United States. Such women were often made vulnerable to their pimp intimate's demands due to such issues as displacement, language issues, substance abuse, domestic violence, or threats of abuse.[31]

Sex Trafficking and Prostitution

The correlation between global and domestic sex trafficking and the prostituting of women and children has been explored in a number of studies.[32] As posited by one group of researchers: "Trafficking for sexual exploitation is, for the most part, trafficking for prostitution. Domestic trafficking is, for the most part, trafficking for prostitution. . . . Traffickers rely on local and existing sex industries, whether women are trafficked domestically or internationally."[33]

Marisa Ugarte and colleagues held that females are trafficked by pimps to any place with a demand for prostitution services.[34] In a study of prostitution and trafficking in women, Dorchen Leidholdt concluded that trafficking was "global prostitution," whereas the more common type of prostitution was seen as "domestic trafficking."[35]

Few trafficked persons wish to prostitute themselves. In a 2003 study in the *Journal of Trauma Practice,* 89 percent of female prostitutes wished to escape the business. The study found that 65 to 75 percent of the prostitutes were the victims of rape; 70 to 95 percent had been physically assaulted; and 68 percent suffered from posttraumatic stress disorder.[36] (See also Chapters 13 to 15.)

Child Sex Tourism

A key component of international sex trafficking is child sex tourism, defined by the United Nations as "tourism organized with the primary purpose of facilitating the effecting of a commercial-sexual relationship with a child."[37] Child sex tourism (CST) also refers to "the opportunistic use of prostituted children in regions while traveling on business or for other purposes."[38]

Child sex tourists typically seek to evade laws against child sexual abuse and exploitation in their own countries by journeying to developing countries in search of child prostitutes to victimize. CST is a multibillion dollar enterprise in such countries as Thailand and the Philippines, where "sex-tour promoters feed the stereotype that Asian [females] are submissive and have a strong desire to please men."[39]

Other countries frequented by sex tourists include South Africa, Brazil, Cambodia, Russia, Vietnam, Germany, and the United States. In this country, sex tourism involving juvenile and young women and men prostitutes generates millions of dollars for traffickers, pimps, and organized criminals in such cities as Las Vegas, New York, and Los Angeles.[40]

The global success of the CST industry tends to reflect permissive governments, corrupt law enforcement, impoverishment, inexpensive international travel, the Internet, and the availability of untold numbers of potential victims to sexually exploit.

Recent years have seen an increase in pursuing and prosecuting sex tourists worldwide. Extraterritorial laws exist in at least 32 countries to date, allowing for the prosecution of child sex tourists who sexually exploit children abroad.[41] In 2003 in the United States, the Prosecutorial Remedies and Other Tools to end the Exploitation of Children Today Act of 2003 (PROTECT Act) was enacted into law, leading to the arrest of more than a dozen sex tourists.[42]

COMBATTING SEX TRAFFICKING

In an effort to combat sex trafficking in the United States and worldwide, in 2006 the Trafficking Victims Protection Reauthorization Act of 2005 became law.[43] It reauthorized and strengthened the antitrafficking programs of the Trafficking Victims Protection Act of 2000, aimed at reducing sex trafficking and prostitution in this country, new funding for investigating and prosecuting domestic trafficking and related criminal activity, and fighting international human trafficking.[44]

Other tools used to fight sex trafficking in this country include the PROTECT Act, new and strengthened antitrafficking statutes on the state and local levels, initiatives for battling trafficking in persons internationally; as well as aggressive prosecution of traffickers and other sexual exploiters of trafficking victims.[45] As of January 2006, according to the U.S. Immigration and Customs Enforcement (ICE), since 2003 more than 5,400 arrests were made involving the trafficking of persons and smuggling. These resulted in 2,300 convictions.[46] (See also Chapter 17.)

NOTES

1. Office of the Press Secretary, "Fact Sheet: Human Trafficking: A Modern Form of Slavery," (July 16, 2004), http://www.whitehouse.gov/news/releases/2004/07/20040716-3.html; Marjan Wijers and Lin Lap-Chew, *Trafficking in Women: Forced Labor and Slavery-like Practices in Marriage, Domestic Labor, and Prostitution* (Utrecht: STV, 1997); Patricia H. Hynes and Janice G. Raymond, "Put in Harm's Way: The Neglected Health Consequences of Sex Trafficking in the United States," in J. Stillman and A. Bhattacharjee, eds., *Policing the National Body: Sex, Race, and Criminalization* (Cambridge: Southend Press, 2002), pp. 197–229.
2. Cited from the United Nations in Frontline, "Sex Slaves," (February 7, 2006), http://www.pbs.org/wgbh/pages/frontline/salves/etc/stats.html.
3. UN Protocol to Prevent, Suppress and Punish Trafficking in Persons, Article 3 (February 14, 2006), http://www.unodc.org/unodc/en/trafficking_human_beings.html.
4. P.L. 100–386, Sec. 103 (8) (2000); U.S. Department of State, *Trafficking in Persons Report, Office to Monitor and Combat Trafficking in Persons* (June 3, 2005), http://www.state.gov/g/tip/ris/tiprpt/2005/46606.htm.
5. U.S. Department of Justice, *Assessment of U.S. Activities to Combat Trafficking in Persons* (August, 2003).
6. Cited in "Sex Slaves."
7. Ibid.; "Trafficking in the United States," http://www.floridafreedom.org/Pages/Trafficking.htm.
8. Cited in "Sex Slaves."
9. *Ibid.*
10. Marisa B. Ugarte, Laura Zarate, and Melissa Farley, "Prostitution and Trafficking of Women and Children From Mexico to the United States," *Journal of Trauma Practice 2,* 3/4 (2003): 147–65.
11. *Ibid.*
12. *Trafficking in Persons Report.*
13. U.S. Department of Justice, *Report to Congress from Attorney General John Ashcroft on U.S. Government Efforts to Combat Trafficking in Persons in Fiscal Year 2003* (Washington:

Department of Justice, 2004).

14. *Ibid.*; Richard J. Estes and Neil A. Weiner, "The Commercial Sexual Exploitation of Children in the U.S., Canada and Mexico, Executive Summary," Philadelphia: Center for the Study of Youth Policy, September 19, 2001.

15. *Assessment of U.S. Government Activities to Combat Trafficking in Persons.*

16. Amy O'Neill-Richard, *International Trafficking in Women in the United States: A Contemporary Manifestation of Slavery and Organized Crime* (Washington: Center for the Study of Intelligence, 1999), p. 13.

17. R. Barri Flowers, *The Prostitution of Women and Girls* (Jefferson: McFarland, 2005), pp. 39–47, 165–84; Donna M. Hughes, Janice G. Raymond, and Carol J. Gomez, *Sex Trafficking of Women in the United States: International and Domestic Trends* (North Amherst: Coalition Against Trafficking in Women, 2001); Penny Venetis, "International Sexual Slavery," *Women's Rights Law Reporter 18,* 3 (1997): 263–70.

18. *Trafficking in Persons Report.*

19. *International Trafficking of Women in the United States. See also* Kevin Bales and Steven Lize, *Trafficking in Persons in the United States,* unpublished report to the National Institute of Justice, Washington, U.S. Department of Justice, November 2005, pp. 14–15.

20. *Trafficking in Persons Report.*

21. Bales and Lize, *Trafficking of Persons in the United States,* p. 15.

22. *Ibid.*

23. Hughes, Raymond, and Gomez, *Sex Trafficking of Women in the United States,* p. 55.

24. *Ibid.*

25. *Ibid.*

26. *Ibid.,* p. 56.

27. *Trafficking in Persons Report. See also* "Child Sex Trafficking: The Facts," from Oprah talk show: Ricky Martin on Children Being Sold into Sexual Slavery, Oprah.com.

28. Flowers, The Prostitution of Women and Girls, pp. 122, 165; National Institute of Justice, http://www.ojp.usdoj.gov/ovc/ncvrw/2005/pg51.html.

29. Flowers, *The Prostitution of Women and Girls,* pp. 8–9, 165–95; Venetis, "International Sexual Slavery;" Siriporn, Skrobanek, S. Boonpakdee, and C. Jantateroo, *The Traffic in Women: Human Realities of the International Sex Trade* (New York: Zed Books Ltd., 1997).

30. Hughes, Raymond, and Gomez, *Sex Trafficking of Women in the United States,* p. 48.

31. *Ibid.*

32. *Ibid.,* p. 25; Dorchen A. Leidholdt, "Prostitution and Trafficking in Women: An Intimate Relationship," *Journal of Trauma Practice 2,* 3/4 (2003): 167–83; Wijers and Lap-Chew, *Trafficking in Labor and Slavery-like Practices in Marriage, Domestic Labor and Prostitution.*

33. Hughes, Raymond, and Gomez, *Sex Trafficking of Women in the United States,* p. 25.

34. Ugarte, Zarate, and Farley, "Prostitution and Trafficking of Women and Children From Mexico to the United States."

35. Leidholdt, "Prostitution and Trafficking in Women."

36. Cited in *Trafficking in Persons Report.*

37. Quoted in R. Barri Flowers, *Runaway Kids and Teenage Prostitution: America's Lost, Abandoned, and Sexually Exploited Children* (Westport: Greenwood Press, 2002), p. 179.

38. *Ibid.*

39. Carol Smolenski, "Sex Tourism and the Sexual Exploitation of Children," *Christian Century 112* (1995): 1080.

40. Flowers, *Runaway Kids and Teenage Prostitution,* p. 179.

41. *Trafficking in Persons Report.*

42. *Ibid.*; "U.S., Moldovan, Romanian Cooperation Leads to Sex Tourist Arrests," (January

13, 2006), http://www.USInfo.state.gov; "Americans Who Sexually Abuse Children Abroad Face Criminal Prosecution," (January 13, 2006), http://www.usembassy.at/en/policy/human_traff.htm.

43. "President signs H.R. 972, Trafficking Victims Protection Reauthorization Act, (January 10, 2006), http://www.whitehouse.gov/news/releases/2006/01/20060110-3.html.

44. *Ibid.*; P.L. 100–386 (2000). *See also* Joan Fitzpatrick, "Trafficking as a Human Rights Violation: the Complex Intersection of Legal Frameworks for Conceptualizing and Combating Trafficking," *Michigan Journal of International Law 24* (2003): 1143; Stephanie Farrior, "The International Law on Trafficking in Women and Children for Prostitution: Making it Live Up to its Potential," *Harvard Human Rights Journal 10* (1997): 10–12.

45. "Fact Sheet: Human Trafficking: A Modern Form of Slavery;" "U.S., Moldovan, Romanian Cooperation Leads to Sex Tourist Arrests."

46. U.S. Immigration and Customs Enforcement, "2,300 Smuggling, Trafficking Convictions Since 2003, ICE Reports," (January 11, 2006), http://www.usembssy.at/en/policy/human_traff.htm.

Chapter 12

OTHER SEXUAL ABUSE AND PARAPHILIAS

There are a number of sexual crimes, abuses, and perversions that often go unnoticed or undetected by law enforcement and the general public. These include exhibitionism, voyeurism, satanism, cannibalism, and necrophilia, among others. Many of these are aimed directly at children and young adults by men who also participate in more common sexual offenses such as child molestation, child pornography, and child rape. Because of the nature of sexual perversion crimes, assessing their incidence is difficult. However, some experts believe that these types of offenses may be at least equally as prevalent as other sex crimes. This chapter will examine some of these offenses and their characteristics.

PARAPHILIA

Most sexual deviance falls under the psychiatric term *paraphilia,* which originates from the Greek *para,* meaning "beyond, amiss, or altered," and *philia* that means love.[1] According to the American Psychiatric Association, paraphilia is characterized by

> arousal in response to sexual objects or situations that are not part of normative arousal activity patterns and whose essential features are intense sexual urges and sexually arousing fantasies generally involving nonhuman objects, the suffering or humiliation of one's self or one's partner, or children or other nonconsenting persons.[2]

A high percentage of sex offenders and sexually motivated murderers are paraphiliacs. In G. Abel and associates' study of self-reported sex crimes of fifty-six nonincarcerated sex offenders, the incidence and range of completed paraphilic episodes was substantial.[3] In all, there were 291,737 completed paraphilic episodes involving 195,407 victims. Completed paraphilic episodes were highest for exhibitionism, frottage, nonincestuous pedophilia, and voyeurism. The range of paraphilia included such sexual deviant behavior as sadism, bestiality, coprolagnia, urolagnia, fetishism, and public masturbation.

G. Abel and colleagues found a high rate of multiple paraphilias among paraphiliacs.[4] Nearly one-fourth of the paraphiliacs committed offenses against family members and nonfamily victims. More than one-fourth used touching and nontouching in their paraphilia, while 20 percent committed offenses against both sexes. More than half the paraphiliacs had at least one sexually deviant interest before the age of eighteen. In W. L. Marshall and A. Eccles' study of sex offenders, they found that 80 percent of the paraphiliacs who had committed at least four victimizations, had perpetrated their first act before the age of twenty.[5]

EXHIBITIONISM

Exhibitionism by definition refers to (1) the intentional, inappropriate exposure of genitalia, usually to a child or woman, and (2) the practice of behaving as such so as to attract attention as a means of sexual gratification. Although the vast majority of exhibitionists are adult male, there have also been cases of female and child exhibitionists.[6]

Typically the act of male exhibitionism ranges from "exposure of the flaccid penis in which sexual stimulation is not present, to exposure of the erect penis in which masturbation often occurs along with intense sexual gratification."[7] J. L. Mathis reported that the "exhibitionist does not expose himself as a prelude to sex or as an invitation to intercourse; rather, the exhibitionist seems more intent on evoking fear or shock."[8] Exhibitionists tend to favor strangers for exposure over nonstrangers. However, when his target is a child, he often prefers a group of children.

How prevalent is exhibitionism? It is believed to be one of the more common sex crimes against children, along with pedophilia.[9] Estimates put the number of child victims of exhibitionists between 20 and 50 percent.[10] In G. Abel and associates' study, exhibitionism ranked highest among paraphilic episodes. There were 71,696 recorded completed acts of exhibitionism, with 72,974 victims.[11] Nearly four in ten completed paraphilic episodes involved exhibitionism.

The recidivism rate of exhibitionists is among the highest of sex offenders. Using official and child protective agencies' data, along with self-report studies, W. L. Marshall and H. E. Barbaree compared the reoffending rates of treated and untreated sex offenders. Among treated exhibitionists, 47.8 percent reoffended, while 66.7 percent of those untreated were recidivists.[12]

In spite of being among the most frequent sexual offenses known to law enforcement, exhibitionism also ranks as one of the least reported.[13] The majority of reports of exhibitionism come from parents of child victims.

The most frequent place for exposure tends to be public such as parks, theaters, or streets. However, when a child is the exhibitionist's intended victim, the exposure occurs most often in or near schools, playgrounds, and in cars.[14]

Characterizing the Exhibitionist

Exhibitionism is viewed as a compulsive behavior by a person who feels driven to exhibit their body in order to relieve "unbearable anxiety." Mathis posited that the exhibitionist is compelled by uncontrollable forces within.[15] Exhibitionists are typically classified as (1) invitational exhibitionists and (2) shocking exhibitionists.

- **Invitational exhibitionists** tend to offend from a distance. They view the impersonal nature of exhibiting themselves as a form of intimacy, in seeking a positive response from the victim. Invitational exhibitionists are generally considered the least dangerous.
- **Shocking exhibitionists** are primarily motivated by power and anger. "By exposing themselves they can control their victims in a sexual way. Additionally, they can frighten and emotionally scar people. Sexual satisfaction comes from instilling fear in others and in that way, they feel potent and powerful."[16] Shocking exhibitionists will sometimes degrade victims, accompanied by threats and possible stalking—all of which increase the possibility of sexual assault or child sexual molestation.

Exhibitionism tends to begin in the late teens, peak in the twenties, and lessen or end by the time the exhibitionist reaches the age of forty.[17] Exhibitionists typically possess inadequate personalities. They lack social skills and maturity and are fearful of intimacy and rejection.

P. H. Gebhard and colleagues characterized the exhibitionist as follows:

- He is fairly normal aside from his exhibitionism.
- He has little rationale for being an exhibitionist.
- He attaches special significance to his victim's reaction.
- He has an irresistible compulsion to be an exhibitionist and a kind of stupefaction during the sex offense.
- His childhood was usually very difficult in some respect.[18]

J. C. Coleman related exhibitionism to personal immaturity (such as shyness, self-doubts regarding masculinity, and an inferiority complex in approaching the opposite sex), and interpersonal stress and acting out (such as being unable to cope with an intense conflict). With respect to the latter relationship, Coleman stated:

> Often the married exhibitionist appears to be reacting to some conflict or stress situation in his marriage, and his behavior is in the nature of a regression to adolescent masturbatory activity. In some instances, an exhibitionist may state that exhibiting himself during masturbation is more exciting and tension reducing than utilizing pictures of nude women.[19]

Exhibitionism has been associated with such mental disorders as schizophrenia and brain deterioration.[20]

Generally speaking, exhibitionism is regarded as more of a nuisance than anything. However, many social scientists and criminologists have now begun to recognize the correlation between exhibitionist behavior and other sexual offenses, including rape and child sexual abuse.

COPROLAGNIA/UROLAGNIA

Coprolagnia/urolagnia is a sexually deviant behavior closely associated with child molestation. It typically involves sexual gratification through smelling, eating, throwing, and/or handling urine, excrement, or other filth. In the book *Psychopathia Sexualis,* Richard von Krafft-Ebing characterized the coprolagnia/urolagnia sex offender as "driven by an irresistible urge to touch or swallow feces, sputum, nasal mucus, earwax, or menstrual blood."[21]

This sexual perversion has proven to be one of the most commonly encountered offenses for law enforcement agencies.[22] The strong correlation between coprolagnia/urolagnia addiction and child sexual abuse has been documented in a number of cases.[23] In one telling example, a police officer

> who was aware that in many instances child molesters handle filth (in one form or another), arrested a local person for a minor offense. During the booking, the officer found the offender in possession of pictures and written material that referred to urine and excrement. The man later admitted to molesting local children. He was ultimately confined to a mental institution.[24]

Robert Morneau and Robert Rockwell made an interesting observation regarding the link between coprolagnia/urolagnia and child molestation:

> An officer who is booking a suspect for any crime and discovers excrement on his person (many times carried in dried form) should realize, at the very mini-

mum, he may have a child molester on his hands. . . . Just as a child molester might be recognized from his interest in filth, anyone who is arrested as the result of a complaint that he is a child molester should be interviewed about unrelated cases where coprolagnia or urolagnia were part
of the offense.[25]

BESTIALITY/ZOOERASTIA

The terms *bestiality* and *zooerastia* are legal and medical ones, respectively,
but refer to the same form of paraphilia–sexual relations between a human
and an animal. The dictionary definition of *bestial,* "marked by brutality or
depravity," is an apt one. In spite of laws that prohibit this sexual deviance
and its rarity in society, bestiality/zooerastia does occur–often involving children with adult pedophiles. It is most frequent in rural areas where animals
are often present and detection less likely.

One case of bestiality/zooerastia cited involved a boy coerced into entering a man's shanty, shortly after which the boy was made to "play" with the
man's dog. This led to the dog orally copulating the boy victim.[26] In Gebhard
and associates' study, 17 percent of farm boys reported experiencing an
orgasm from contact with animals.[27] Most of the contacts occurred during
preadolescence and lasted over a two or three-year period.

Many sexual serial killers practice bestiality in the course of their killings,
often as a reflection of a childhood history of cruelty towards animals.[28] In
one such example, serial murderer Henry Lee Lucas tortured animals to
death, often having sex with them afterwards. Claiming to have raped and
murdered hundreds of women and children, Lucas began practicing bestiality and sadism as a young teenager.[29]

The incidence of bestiality/zooerastia is unknown. However, some experts
believe it may be much more prevalent than some conservative estimates of
the problem.

NECROPHILIA

Necrophilia refers to the desire to have or engaging in sexual relations with
the dead. This sexually deviant behavior typically involves deceased children and adult male necrophiliacs. Researchers have identified four primary
types of necrophiliac sex offenders: (1) true necrophiliacs, (2) sadonecrophil-
iacs, (3) sadomasochistic necrophiliacs, and (4) necrofetishists.[30] Because
these types can frequently overlap, it is often difficult for law enforcement
authorities to identify or differentiate necrophiliac sex offenders or their par-

ticular motivation.

Necrophiliacs tend to be morticians or others who work or have worked in a mortuary, hospital, or otherwise with the dead. A frightening example of necrophilia can be seen in a police report in which a recidivist sexual offender is being questioned regarding the sexual assault and murder of a young female:

> He admitted he had worked years before as a mortician's assistant . . . fascinated by the bodies, especially those of young girls. . . . The mortician's vehicle was pressed into service as an ambulance. This man described how he became sexually aroused when driving back into town because of the screams and crying of the injured and dying children he was transporting.
> That night, working late and alone in the mortuary, he was seized with a compulsion to have intercourse with the corpses. He spoke . . . of having intercourse with one young girl who was mutilated and, since additional wounds would not likely be noticed, he cut her stomach open at some point so he could see his penis down inside her.[31]

A key aspect of necrophilia is the complete passivity of the female victim, allowing the necrophiliac to sexually violate her as he pleases without resistance or fear of detection or reprisal.[32] Another element of this sexually deviant behavior often relates to religious fanaticism and the necrophiliac's belief that he is following God's commands. Many male child sex offenders and sexual murderers use this delusional, irrational reasoning as justification for their necrophilia and murder.[33]

The act of necrophilia is often accompanied by disfigurement of the corpse. Necrophiliacs receive gratification from the sexual offense in two ways: (1) from mutilating the dead and (2) in realizing that others (family members, in particular) will be repulsed by the actions. Defenselessness, helplessness, and decomposition of the victim are key elements in carrying out necrophilia acts.

Some sexual serial murderers are known to be (or have been) necrophiliacs. German born serial murderer Bruno Ludke had a long history of sexual assault, murder, and necrophilia in the first half of the twentieth century.[34] In the seventies, John Gacy practiced necrophilia and molestation when he murdered thirty-three boys in Illinois.[35] More recently, signature serial murderer George Russell raped and murdered several women in Bellevue, Washington before sexually assaulting them in death and leaving them in humiliating sexual positions.[36] D. Sears theorized that serial killer necrophiliacs may be driven by a need for power, excitement, and feeling the social pressure to be virile and masculine.[37] He also suggested that the media—through violent movies and sensationalized news stories on violence—may help influence sexual serial killers and copycat murderers.

CANNIBALISM

Cannibalism refers to a cannibal who eats the flesh of human beings. It is also defined as an animal that feeds on others of its own kind. Like other kinds of paraphilia, cannibalism is difficult to conceive. However, this practice has a long history dating back to the Neanderthal man, ancient Incas, and the Aztecs.[38] Sexual offenders and sexual serial killers are especially prone to cannibalistic tendencies. In the early 1900s, American serial murderer Albert Fish, dubbed the "Cannibal killer," practiced necrophilia and cannibalism, among other sexual perversions. In all, Fish murdered twelve young girls and violently assaulted over a hundred victims.[39] Similarly, George Karl Grossman, the "Berlin Butcher," murdered and cannibalized at least fifty girls in the early 1900s to satisfy his sexual appetite.[40]

In 1981, a Japanese student named Josei Sagawa, turned his morbid sexual fantasies into reality when he raped and murdered a young woman in Paris. Sagawa reportedly "cut slices off her buttocks and ate it raw, experiencing intense sexual satisfaction."[41]

Perhaps the most shocking case of sexual cannibalism occurred in the early 1990s with serial killer Jeffrey Dahmer. He lured young men—who were usually racial and ethnic minorities—to his Milwaukee, Wisconsin apartment and confessed to having sex with, drugging, murdering, and eating body parts of seventeen victims. In a search of Dahmer's apartment, police investigations found grisly evidence of cannibalism:

> Nine severed heads were found—two in the refrigerator, seven in various stages of having flesh boiled off the skull. Four male torsos had been wedged into a barrel, and several pieces of male genitalia had been stored in a pot. The apartment was littered with scraps of human bodies and limbs, and the smell of putrefaction was unbearable.[42]

In confessing to cannibalism—along with necrophilia, pedophilia, and substance abuse—Dahmer claimed to have cooked parts of his victims, seasoning them with salt, pepper, and steak sauce. In his own words: "My consuming lust was to experience their bodies. I viewed them as objects, as strangers."[43]

SATANISM AND RITUALISTIC SEXUAL ABUSE

One of the more recently recognized and disturbing forms of sexual abuse, particularly against children, involves *satanism* and/or *ritual abuse*. Though authorities often use these terms interchangeably, they are not necessarily synonymous. Generally speaking, satanic or ritualistic sexual abuse refers to abusive behavior or accompanying religious practices, the supernatural, witchcraft, or black magic. Lawrence Pazder, an expert on ritualistic abuse, defined *ritualized child abuse* as "repeated physical, emotional, mental, and spiritual assaults combined with a systematic use of symbols and secret ceremonies designed to turn a child against itself, family, society, and God."[44] He further posits that the sexual assault "has ritualistic meaning and is not for sexual gratification."[45] Victims of ritualistic sexual abuse report activity involving "ceremonies, chanting, robes and costumes, drugs, use of urine and feces, animal sacrifice, torture, abduction, mutilation, murder, and even cannibalism and vampirism."[46]

How widespread is satanic and ritualistic child abuse? It is estimated that 1 to 5 percent of all child sexual cases may involve some form of ritualistic or satanic practice.[47] Some child abuse professionals contend that as many as 50,000 children are abducted each year by satanic devil worshipers and sexually molested and exploited in child pornography.[48]

Three basic types of ritualistic child sexual abuse patterns have been identified: (1) cult-based–where the sexual abuse is secondary to the primary goal, (2) pseudo-ritualistic–where sexual abuse is the primary goal, and (3) psychopathological–where there is a sole perpetrator.[49] Ritualistic abuse offenders consist of:

- Organized groups, including families and communes.
- National and international organizations with local and regional affiliates.
- Persons who participate in ritualism or satanism for fun, curiosity, or sexual experimentation, often while using drugs and/or alcohol.
- Mentally unbalanced individuals.

Many groups that engage in ritualistic or satanic abusive practices are highly structured and may even involve the child victim's parents, siblings, or other relatives as well as their "cult parents" in their indoctrination. "Children may be taken from natural parents and placed in the care of other group members as a means of ensuring continued group involvement by natural parents."[50]

There is evidence that some sexual serial murderers practice satanism or ritualistic patterns of abuse in their crimes. Serial killer David Berkowitz, known as the "Son of Sam," reportedly belonged to a satanic network.[51] Larry Eyler murdered twenty-three young males in the Midwest, mutilating them with "ritualistic signs and buried four in a barn marked with an inverted pentagram."[52] Richard Ramirez, California's "Night Stalker," alleged he was a satanist and had a tattoo of a pentagram on his left palm, as if for proof.[53] Other cases of satanic serial killers have also been documented.[54] M. Newton estimated that 8 percent of serial killers in America were motivated by reasons related to the occult or satanism.[55]

VOYEURISM

A *voyeur* is defined as a person who derives sexual pleasure from observing the sexual acts of others. *Voyeurism* is often related to other sexual deviant behavior such as exhibitionism, child molestation, and viewing child pornography.[56] Voyeurs or "peeping Toms" are usually males who tend to favor strangers or "forbidden fruit" over real relationships with women.

Voyeuristic tendencies often arise in early adulthood. Approximately one in four men arrested for voyeurism are married, while half of all arrested voyeurs are repeat offenders. Voyeur offenders are seen as sexually immature, similar to exhibitionists. They tend to have a low self-esteem and few sexual experiences. Real intimate relationships frighten voyeurs, evoking a fear of rejection and/or loss of control. Most voyeurs live in a "fantasy world where they successfully conquer and satisfy all partners or vicariously identify with someone they've observed."[57]

TRIOLISM

Triolism is a variation of exhibitionism and voyeurism through which the adult triolist achieves sexual pleasure by viewing others, as well as himself, in group sexual activity.[58] It is when triolism involves children that most concerns law enforcement authorities. Triolism has also been linked to child pornography.[59]

Children are easily lured into participation in triolism. Triolists may offer them money or other incentives for a minimum amount of work. The sexual molester is often addicted to child triolism and its relatively low cost and risk of detection compared to other illicit sexual activities such as prostitution. The typical pattern of a triolist who targets children can be seen as follows: To earn his extra money, the child gets others from among his friends to go to the offender's house or the back of his store and engage in acts which are in themselves fun, while the pervert watches.[60]

NOTES

1. David Lester, *Serial Killers: The Insatiable Passion* (Philadelphia: The Charles Press, 1995), p. 17.

2. American Psychiatric Association, *Diagnostic and Statistical Manual of the American Psychiatric Association (DSM III-R)*, 1987.

3. G. Abel, J. Becker, J. Rathner-Cunningham, and J. Rouleau, "Self-Reported Sex Crimes of 561 Nonincarcerated Paraphiliacs," *Journal of Interpersonal Violence 2*, 6 (1987): 3–25. See also R. Barri Flowers, *State's Evidence* (Dorchester, 2006).

4. G. Abel, M. Mittleman, J. Becker, J. Rathner, and J. Rouleau, "Predicting Child Molesters' Response to Treatment," *Annals of the New York Academy of Sciences 528* (1988): 223–34.

5. W. I. Marshall and A. Eccles, "Issues in Clinical Practice with Sex Offenders," *Journal of Interpersonal Violence 6* (1991): 68–93.

6. L. Kelly, L. Regan, and S. Burton, *An Exploratory Study of the Prevalence of Sexual Abuse in a Sample of 16–21 Year Olds* (London: CSAU, North London Polytechnic, 1991); D. Finkelhor and D. Russell, "Women as Perpetrators," in David Finkelhor, ed., *Child Sexual Abuse: New Theory and Research* (New York: Free Press, 1984); Dave O'Callaghan and Bobbie Print, "Adolescent Sexual Abusers: Research Assessment and Treatment," in Tony Morrison, Marcus Erooga, and Richard C. Beckett, eds., *Sexual Offending Against Children: Assessment and Treatment of Male Abusers* (London: Routledge, 1994), pp. 146–77.

7. R. Barri Flowers, *The Victimization and Exploitation of Women and Children: A Study of Physical, Mental and Sexual Maltreatment in the United States* (Jefferson: McFarland, 1994), p. 76.

8. Quoted in Harold J. Vetter and Ira J. Silverman, *The Nature of Crime* (Philadelphia: W. B Saunders, 1978), p. 115.

9. Flowers, *The Victimization and Exploitation of Women and Children*, p. 75.

10. *Ibid.*, p. 76.

11. Abel, Mittleman, Becker, Rathner, and Rouleau, "Self-Reported Sex Crimes of 561 Nonincarcerated Paraphiliacs."

12. W. L. Marshall and H. E. Barbaree, "Outcome of Cognitive-Behavioral Treatment," in W. L. Marshall, D. R. Laws, and H. E. Barbaree, eds., *Handbook of Sexual Assault* (New York: Plenum, 1990).

13. R. Barri Flowers, *Children and Criminality: The Child as Victim and Perpetrator* (Westport: Greenwood Press, 1986), p. 80.

14 Flowers, *The Victimization and Exploitation of Women and Children*, p. 76.

15. J. L. Mathis, *Clear Thinking About Sexual Deviations* (Chicago: Nelson-Hall, 1972), p. 37.

16. Robert E. Freeman-Longo and Geral T. Blanchard, *Sexual Abuse in America: Epidemic of the 21st Century* (Brandon: Safer Society Press, 1998), p. 45.

17. M. Dyer, "Exhibitionism/Voyeurism," in D. M. Dailey, ed., *The Sexually Unusual* (New York: Harrington Press, 1988).

18. P. H. Gebhard, J. H. Gagnon, W. B. Pomeroy, and C. V. Christenson, *Sexual Offenders: An Analysis of Types* (New York: Harper & Row, 1965).

19. J. C. Coleman, *Abnormal Psychology and Modern Life* (Glenview: Scott, Foresman and Co., 1972).

20. Flowers, *The Victimization and Exploitation of Women and Children*, p. 76.

21. Richard von Krafft-Ebing, *Psychopathia Sexualis* (New York: Stein and Day, 1965).

22. Flowers, *The Victimization and Exploitation of Women and Children*, p. 77.

23. *Ibid.*

24. *Ibid.*
25. Robert H. Morneau and Robert R. Rockwell, *Sex, Motivation and the Criminal Offenders* (Springfield: Charles C Thomas, 1980), pp. 87–89.
26. Flowers, *The Victimization and Exploitation of Women and Children,* p. 77.
27. Gebhard, Gagnon, Pomeroy, and Christenson, *Sex Offenders.*
28. Lester, *Serial Killers,* pp. 98–99; M. A. Heller, S. M. Ehrlich, and D. Lester, "Childhood Cruelty to Animals, Firesetting and Enuresis as Correlates of Competence to Stand Trial," *Journal of General Psychology 110* (1984) 151–53.
29. Lester, *Serial Killers,* p. 99.
30. J. M. Reinhardt, *Sex Perversions and Sex Crimes* (Springfield: Charles C Thomas, 1957); Clifford Allen, *The Sexual Perversions and Abnormalities* (London: Oxford University Press, 1949).
31. Morneau and Rockwell, *Sex, Motivation and the Criminal Offender,* p. 142.
32. Magnus Hirschfield, *Sexual Anomalies: The Origins, Nature and Treatment of Sexual Disorders* (New York: Emerson, 1956).
33. Morneau and Rockwell, *Sex, Motivation and the Criminal Offender,* p. 145; Lester, Serial Killers, pp. 73–74.
34. Brian Lane and Wilfred Gregg, *The Encyclopedia of Serial Killers* (New York: Berkley, 1995), p. 247.
35. *Ibid.,* p. 165.
36. Robert D. Keppel and William I. Birnes, *Signature Killers: Interpreting the Calling Cards of the Serial Murderer* (New York: Pocket Books, 1997), pp. 217–62.
37. D. Sears, *To Kill Again* (Wilmington: Scholarly Resources, 1991).
38. Lane and Gregg, *The Encyclopedia of Serial Killers,* pp. 160–62; Colin Wilson, *The Mammoth Book of True Crime* (New York: Carroll & Graf, 1998), p. 73.
39. *Ibid.,* p. 77.
40. Lane and Gregg, *The Encyclopedia of Serial Killers,* pp. 188–89.
41. Wilson, *The Mammoth Book of True Crime,* p. 78.
42. Lane and Gregg, *The Encyclopedia of Serial Killers,* p. 126.
43. *Ibid.,* p. 129.
44. Quoted in U. S. Department of Justice, *Child Sex Rings: A Behavioral Analysis, For Criminal Justice Professionals Handling Cases of Child Sexual Exploitation* (Arlington: National Center for Missing & Exploited Children, 1992), p. 21.
45. *Ibid.*
46. *Ibid.* p. 18.
47. Flowers, *The Victimization and Exploitation of Women and Children,* p. 79.
48. *Child Sex Rings: A Behavioral Analysis,* p. 3.
49. Flowers, *The Victimization and Exploitation of Women and Children,* p. 79.
50. U.S. Department of Health and Human Services, *Research Symposium on Child Sexual Abuse: May 17–19, 1988* (Washington: National Center on Child Abuse and Neglect, 1988), p. 3.
51. Lester, *Serial Killers,* p. 166.
52. *Ibid.,* p 167.
53. *Ibid.;* L. Kahaner, *Cults That Kill* (New York: Warner, 1988).
54. E. W. Hickey, *Serial Murderers and Their Victims* (Pacific Grove: Brooks/Cole, 1991); G. Ivey, "Psychodynamic Aspects of Demonic Possession and Satanic Worship," *South African Journal of Psychology 23* (1993): 186–94.
55. M. Newton, *Raising Hell* (New York: Avon Books, 1993).
56. Flowers, *The Victimization and Exploitation of Women and Children,* p. 76; Freeman-Longo

   and Blanchard, *Sexual Abuse in America,* p. 46.
57. *Ibid.*
58. Flowers, *The Victimization and Exploitation of Women and Children,* p. 76.
59. *Ibid.*
60. Morneau and Rockwell, *Sex, Motivation and the Criminal Offender,* p. 73.

Part V

PROSTITUTION CRIMES

Chapter 13

WOMEN AND PROSTITUTION

S ome have called prostitution "the world's oldest profession." Others see it as less of a profession, per se, and more of a means to exploit, victimize, and humiliate those forced to sell sexual favors. Few would argue that prostitution is mostly identified with adult and teenage females, though male prostitution is roughly equal in numbers. Recent years have seen several high profile upper class women prostitute stories such as that of Heidi Fleiss, the "Hollywood Madam," and Sydney Barrows, the "Mayflower Madam," that sought to glamorize the industry. Women as prostitutes have also long been associated with streetwalkers, substance abuse, pornography, sexual serial offenders and killers, and other forms of violence and victimization.[1] The rate of AIDS among women prostitutes is high, increasing the risks associated with the sex trade industry. This chapter will examine the relationship between women and prostitution.

DEFINITIONS OF PROSTITUTION

Historically, prostitution has been defined as a sex-specific act or offense, or related to women selling sexual favors as prostitutes. Today, prostitution is recognized as including child prostitutes, male prostitutes, and various types of pimps, madams, and customers. Some define prostitution as a form of sexual victimization, others as a sex crime. There are others still who see it as a victimless offense, or "at most only a marginal type of vice."[2] Typically, most definitions of prostitution are broken down into two categories: (1) legal definitions and (2) social definitions.

Legal Definitions of Prostitution

Early legal definitions of prostitution focused on the prostitution of women combined with immorality and promiscuity. Near the turn of the twentieth century, the U.S. Supreme Court defined prostitution as involving "women who for hire or without hire offer their bodies to indiscriminate intercourse with men."[3] In *Prostitution in the United States,* Howard Woolston advanced that before 1918, the only statutory definition of prostitution was Section 2372 of the Indiana Law, which read: "Any female who frequents or lives in a house of ill-fame or associates with women of bad character for chastity, either in public or at a house which men of bad character frequent or visit, or who commits adultery or fornication for hire shall be deemed a prostitute."[4]

A study of court decisions prior to 1918 illustrates the legal dilemma in attempting to define prostitution. "In some cases, the element of a gain was considered an essential ingredient of prostitution, and in others it was not the case. Dictionary definitions, whether those of Webster or of the Law Dictionaries, are equally confusing. In Webster, the definition varies according to the edition."[5] Indeed, as recently as 1968, the Oregon Supreme Court tried to differentiate the prostitute from the nonprostitute when it ruled: "The feature which distinguishes a prostitute from other women who engage in illicit intercourse is the indiscrimination with which she offers herself to men for hire."[6]

Today, prostitution is legally recognized in all fifty states as a sexual offense involving female and male prostitutes, and mostly male clients. The penalties vary from state to state as well as the specific prostitution-related charges. However, studies show a clear bias against females in the prostitution business when it comes to arrest and detention. This gender bias in prostitution laws and arrest data caused one researcher to suggest: "Prostitution is really the only crime in the penal law where two people are doing a thing mutually agreed upon and yet only one, the female partner, is subject to arrest."[7]

Social Definitions of Prostitution

Social definitions of prostitution have typically defined prostitution as "sexual relations that include some form of monetary payment or barter and are characterized by promiscuity and/or emotional apathy."[8] One sociologist defined prostitution as "sexual intercourse on a promiscuous and mercenary basis, with emotional indifference."[9] Edwin Lemert added barter as an element of the interaction preceding sexual relations. As early as 1914, Abraham Flexner subscribed to these principals in writing that prostitution is characterized by three elements variously combined: barter, promiscuity and emotional indifference. The barter need not involve the passage of money. . . . Nor need promiscuity be utterly choiceless: a woman is not the less a prostitute because she is more or less selective in her associations. Emotional indifference may be fairly inferred from batter and promiscuity. In this sense any person is a prostitute who habitually or intermittently has sexual relations more or less promiscuously for money or other mercenary consideration. Neither notoriety, arrest nor lack of other occupation is an essential criterion.[10]

Flexner further related prostitution to four societal problems: (1) economic waste, (2) spread of sexually transmitted diseases, (3) personal demoralization, and (4) social disorder and criminality.

Charles Winick and Paul Kinsie defined prostitution as the "granting of nonmaterial sexual access, established by mutual agreement of the woman, her client, and/or her employer for remuneration which provides part or all of her livelihood."[11] Paul Goldstein's definition of prostitution is "nonmarital sexual service for material gain;"[12] while Richard Goodall defines prostitution as the selling of sexual favors by one who "earns a living wholly or in part by the more or less indiscriminate, willing and emotionally indifferent provision of sexual services of any description to another, against payment, usually in advance but not necessarily in cash."[13]

Such social definitions of prostitution continue to be slanted towards female offenders, influencing legal definitions and enforcement of prostitution laws.

THE EXTENT OF WOMEN'S PROSTITUTION

The actual number of females working in the sex-for-sale industry in the United States is difficult to estimate. This is due, in part, to the different types of prostitutes, many of whom operate inconspicuously such as call girls. Also, official data tell us only about arrested prostitutes and not the many who evade the law or others who are never targeted by police. Most estimates of prostitutes range anywhere from one to two million women who are actively selling sexual favors in this country at any given time.[14] More than a million female teenagers are also estimated to be in the prostitution business and perhaps just as many males.[15] In Portland, Oregon alone, there are more than two hundred known escort services, most, if not all, fronts for prostitution—illustrating the extent of the problem on a national scale.[16] Hundreds of thousands ply their trade on the street, others in massage parlors, hotels, bars, and other places where customers are available and willing. All are at risk for HIV infection and other perils of the sex trade industry.

RACE AND ETHNICITY OF FEMALE PROSTITUTES

The vast majority of female prostitutes are white, according to most experts.[17] However, in inner city red-light districts, the number of minority prostitutes may increase by as much as 50 percent.[18] Arrest statistics reveal that poor, black streetwalkers are most often targeted by law enforcement as a reflection of being the most likely prostitutes to be "forced onto the streets and into blatant solicitation where the risk of arrest is highest."[19] Most such arrests tend to occur in inner cities where "living standards are low, the level of depression high, and police prejudice endemic."[20]

Studies on streetwalking prostitutes show that black females are overrepresented. In Joyce Wallace's study of more than 3,000 New York City prostitutes, half were black, one-fourth Hispanic, and one-fourth white.[21] Other studies have yielded mixed results, finding that eight in ten female prostitutes are white;[22] 10 to 50 percent black;[23] with Hispanic, Asian, and Native American prostitutes accounting from anywhere from 2 to 11 percent of all females in the prostitution business.[24]

TYPES OF WOMEN PROSTITUTES

Prostitute typologies have focused mostly on motivational, situational, and occupational variables of prostitution. In *Prostitution and Morality,* Harry Benjamin and R. E. L. Masters described prostitutes as two types: voluntary and compulsive.[25] Voluntary prostitutes tend to act rationally and freely chose to enter the business. Compulsive prostitutes act under compulsion because of "psychoneurotic" needs or drug addiction. The researchers found that some prostitutes fit into both typologies.

Goldstein broke down prostitutes in terms of *occupational commitment* and *occupational milieu.*[26] Occupational commitment relates to the frequency of a woman's prostitution and is subcategorized into three types:

Temporary prostitute–a discreet prostitution episode, lasting not more than six months in a specific occupational milieu.
Occasional prostitute–two or more discreet instances of prostitution in a specific occupational milieu, each lasting no longer than six months.
Continual prostitute–prostitution lasting more than six months in a particular occupational milieu on a regular basis.

Occupational milieu refers to the specific types of prostitution in which a woman is involved. Goldstein breaks these down into seven types:

- **Streetwalker**–a woman who overtly solicits men on the street and offers sexual services for pay.
- **Call girl**–a woman who works in a hotel or residence soliciting clients or who solicits by phone.
- **Massage parlor prostitute**–a woman who offers sexual favors in a massage parlor, and not always limited to massages or fondling.
- **House prostitute**–a woman who works in an establishment created specifically for prostitution services and where male clients are provided sexual favors for payment.
- **Madam**–a woman who supplies other prostitutes with male clients for a percentage of the fee.
- **Mistress**–a woman who is primarily supported by one man at a time or who sees only one man at a time for money.
- **Barterer**–a woman who exchanges sexual favors for professional or other services, or for material items (such as drugs or clothes).[27]

In *Female Crime, Criminals and Cellmates,* two other types of prostitutes are identified:

- **Bar girl prostitute**–a woman who works in a bar, lounge, or other club where men are solicited or the woman is willingly solicited by men for sexual services.
- **Online prostitute**–a woman who sells sexual favors through the Internet, either for online sex or in person meetings.[28]

As discussed in Chapter 11, another type of female prostitute in the United States is the *sex slave.*[29] These women and girls are the victims of sex trafficking, in which they are often brought into this country through force, coercion and/or deception for purposes of sexual exploitation through prostitution and related forms of sexual enslavement.

According to anthropologist Jennifer James, there are two primary types of prostitutes: *true prostitutes* and *part-timers.* From these she identified roles played by prostitutes.[30] True prostitutes' roles are as follows:

- **Outlaws** are prostitutes independent of pimps.
- **Rip-off artists** are thieves disguised as prostitutes. Prostitution is not their primary source of income.
- Hype refers to prostitutes who work to support drug habits.
- **The Lady** prostitute is identified by her carriage, finesse, class, and professionalism.
- **Old-timers** are seasoned pros, lacking the class of The Lady.
- **Thoroughbreds** are young, professional prostitutes.

Part-timers include prostitutes who have no style and amateurs or "hos."

Neither true prostitutes, part-timers, nor the roles within are mutually exclusive of the others, as they describe different elements of prostitution as opposed to complete behavioral characteristics.

Streetwalkers

Streetwalker prostitutes, often referred to as *hookers,* occupy the lowest level of the prostitution hierarchy. It is estimated that 10 to 15 percent of all prostitutes,[30] to as many as 75 percent, are streetwalkers.[31] In New York City, there are an estimated 5,000 to 8,000 women who sell sexual favors on the street.[32]

Most streetwalkers are in their mid to late twenties, graduated from teenage prostitution, and "come from a range of backgrounds: rich or poor; well-educated or illiterate; urban, suburban, or rural."[33] Many are "born and raised in an environment of poverty, drugs, and violent crimes."[34] Virtually all streetwalkers have been victims of physical and/or sexual abuse and have problems with substance abuse.[35]

Streetwalkers are often associated with pimps. Studies show that women street prostitutes are less likely to have pimps than girl prostitutes.[36] However, nearly all streetwalkers, independent or not, have some contact with pimps during the course of their prostitution. Once in a pimp's stable, a prostitute is typically controlled through misplaced "love, drug dependency, pregnancy, fear, degradation, and anything else the pimp can use to hold on to his 'property'."[37]

There is some debate among experts as to just how big a role intimidation and violence play in a pimp forcing a woman into prostitution. Some researchers have found that as many as nine in ten females entering prostitution did so based on the coercive charms of a pimp.[38] However, James disputed this finding that, for the most part "it is not true that pimps force women to work against their will . . . turn women into drug addicts for the purpose of control [and] keep them from ever leaving their stable. . . ."[39] Instead many streetwalkers' ties to a pimp are seen as a reflection of the "severe isolation that pre-prostitutes feel [that] predisposes them to join up with someone who 'plugs' them into the world, gives them a set of social relations, a place to call their own, and an ideology to make the world intelligible."[40]

Call Girls

Call girls represent the elite of female prostitutes. Often in their late teens to mid-twenties, they usually work out of expensive apartments or hotels and have a steady clientele of high-paying customers. It is estimated that 20 to 25 percent of the prostitutes in the United States are call girls.[41] Some experts believe that there are at least as many call girls as streetwalkers, if not more.[42]

Along with the "traditional" high class call girl, we have seen the emergence of middle class call girls. These women can work for pimps, madams, brothels, escort services, or are independent. They include college students, college graduates, struggling actresses, single mothers, "nursing students, housewives in the process of getting a divorce, a teacher with a sick husband who is trying to raise money to bring a relative to the United States."[43] Notes an author about middle class prostitution: "For women who are short on money and unconventional, hooking has become like waitressing–a means of getting by."[44]

Call girl prostitutes have been found to have few pathologies compared to their streetwalking counterparts.

> At the upper level, among the full-time call girls and part-time housewives who appear to lead economically secure, stable, arrest-free lives, there is no evidence of special pathology. At the lower levels, inhabited by streetwalkers, drug addicts, juvenile runaways, and deviants of many different stripes, the population is so prone to psychological pathology that it is difficult to know what part, if any, prostitution contributes to their many difficulties.[45]

However, there have been studies that contradicted this belief. In *The Elegant Prostitute,* Harold Greenwald found severe personality disorders among his call girl patients, noting that he had "never known a call girl who had strong bonds of love and affection with her family."[46] In her study of call girls and streetwalkers, James found that more than four in ten had been sexually abused and a high percentage came from broken homes.[47]

AIDS AND WOMEN'S PROSTITUTION

Acquired Immunodeficiency Syndrome (AIDS) has been strongly associated with women's prostitution through sexual contact and drug use.[48] Streetwalkers typically have the highest risk of exposure to the AIDS virus, call girls the lowest. In a University of Miami study of streetwalkers and escort service call girls, 41 percent of the streetwalkers tested positive for the Human Immunodeficiency Virus (HIV), compared to none of the call girls.[49] Studies of HIV infection among streetwalkers in selected cities showed rates of positive testing to be 57 percent in Newark, nearly 50 percent in Washington, D.C., and 35 percent of the sample of prostitutes in New York City.[50] Intravenous (IV) drug using prostitutes are also at high risk for becoming infected with AIDS. Studies have found the proportion of HIV infection among IV drug using prostitutes to be a staggering 61 percent.[51] Wallace found that 46 percent of her sample of New York City streetwalkers who were also IV drug addicts tested positive for HIV.[52] Based on their study of prostitutes and AIDS, M. Rosenberg and J. Weiner posited: "Prostitutes are considered a reservoir for transmission of certain sexually transmitted diseases . . . sexual activity alone does not place them at high risk . . . prostitutes who use intravenous drugs are far more likely to be infected with HIV."[53]

Minority prostitutes appear to have a higher rate of HIV infection than white prostitutes.[54] This is particularly true among IV drug addicted prostitutes. A Baltimore study of streetwalkers who were HIV-seropositive with a history of IV drug use, found the rate of exposure to be highest among black prostitutes in lower class areas.[55]

FEMALE PROSTITUTION AND VIOLENCE

Along with the risks of AIDS and sexually transmitted disease, women prostitutes put themselves at greater risk for violence and victimization such as rape, sexual assault, physical attacks, and even death. Studies have found that an estimated 70 percent of all female prostitutes are raped, often repeatedly, by customers–thirty-one times a year on average.[56] Gang rapes of prostitutes have also been reported.[57] According to an article in a law journal, 65 percent of women prostitutes are regularly subjected to frequent, severe abuse by customers, johns, and pimps.[58] It is estimated that 5 percent of prostitutes die in the line of duty each year.[59] The Justice Department reported that the mortality rate among female prostitutes is forty times the national average.[60]

Prostitutes have often been the targets of serial killers and sex murders.[61] They are also at risk for sexual violence through pornography and sexual abuse. Many prostitutes are also victimized through drug-related violence and robbery.

Female prostitutes have also been shown to perpetrate violence–assaults on or robberies of customers, often related to drug addiction, manipulation by pimps, or even retaliation for being victims of violence.

WHY DO WOMEN BECOME PROSTITUTES?

Over the years various theories have been used to explain why women enter and remain in the sex-for-sale industry. Early theorists tended to blame female prostitution on biological inferiority and sexual motivations. In *The*

Female Offender, Cesare Lombroso and William Ferrero hypothesized that female prostitutes were "biologically predisposed" to criminal behavior,[62] while Sigmund Freud believed prostitutes were biologically deficient.[63] Sociologist William Thomas attributed women's prostitution to a need for excitement and response,[64] while Otto Pollak, who wrote *The Criminality of Women,* argued that female criminals such as prostitutes are sexually motivated.[65] These theories have since been discredited based on their weak methodologies, biases, and sexism.

Recently other theorists have focused more on the social structure and cultural transmission in explaining prostitution. Winick and Kinsie contend that the social structure is threatened by prostitution because "people tend to equate sexual activity with stable relationships, typified by the family."[66] Kingsley Davis held that "the function served by prostitution is the protection of the family unit, maintenance of the chastity and purity of the 'respectable' citizenry."[67] According to cultural transmission theory, prostitution is the result of a "weakening of family and neighborhood control and the persistence and transmission from person to person of traditional delinquent activities."[68]

Much of the current prostitution research has found that economic motivations appear to be the most influential as it relates to a woman's decision to enter and remain in prostitution. Winick and Kinsie advanced that the decision to become a prostitute is based highly on few employment opportunities and the recognition of the potential income of prostitution.[69] Lemert proposed that women's inferior power and control over societal material gains make prostitution a viable means to balance the resulting status differential.[70]

In her study of prostitutes, James described five aspects of the social-economic structure that draws women into prostitution:

- No other occupations that are available to unskilled or low-skilled women provide income comparable to that found in prostitution.
- Almost no other occupations for unskilled or low-skilled women offer the independent, adventurous lifestyle of prostitution.
- The traditional "woman's role" is virtually synonymous with the culturally defined female sex role, which focuses on physical appearance, service, and sexuality.
- The cultural importance of wealth and material items leads some women to seek advantages normally out of reach due to their socioeconomic position in society.
- The discrepancy between culturally accepted male and female sex roles creates the "Madonna-whore" view of female sexuality, so that women sexually active outside the boundaries of their normal sex role expectations are labeled as deviants, thereby losing social status.[71]

NOTES

1. R. Barri Flowers, *The Prostitution of Women and Girls* (Jefferson: McFarland, 2005); Neil McKeganey and Marina Barnard, *Sex Work on the Streets: Prostitutes and Their Clients* (Bristol: Taylor and Francis, 1996); David Lester, *Serial Killers: The Insatiable Passion* (Philadelphia: The Charles Press, 1995).

2. Robert E. Faris, *Social Disorganization* (New York: Ronald Press, 1955).

3. *U.S. v. Bitty,* 208 U.S. 393, 401 (1908); Charles Rosenbleet and Barbara J. Pariente, "The Prostitution of the Criminal Law," *American Criminal Law Review 11* (1973): 373.

4. Howard B. Woolston, *Prostitution in the United States* (New York: Century, 1921).

5. Ibid.; Isabel Drummond, *The Sex Paradox* (New York: Putnam, 1953); p. 208.

6. *State v. Perry,* 249 Oregon 76, 81 436, P. 2d, 252, 255 (1968); Rosenbleet and Pariente, "The Prostitution of the Criminal Law," p. 381.

7. Kate Millett, "Prostitution: A Quartet for Female Voices," in Vivian Gornick and Barbara K. Moran, eds., *Women in a Sexist Society* (New York: New American Library, 1971), p. 79.

8. Flowers, *The Prostitution of Women and Girls,* p. 6.

9. Marshall B. Clinard, *Sociology of Deviant Behavior* (New York: Holt, Rinehart & Winston, 1957), p. 249.

10. Abraham Flexner, *Prostitution in Europe* (New York: Century, 1914), p. 11.

11. Charles Winick and Paul M. Kinsie, *The Lively Commerce: Prostitution in the United States* (Chicago: Quandrangle Books, 1971), p. 3.

12. Paul J. Goldstein, *Prostitution and Drugs* (Lexington: Lexington Books, 1979), p. 33.

13. Richard Goodall, *The Comfort of Sin: Prostitutes and Prostitution in the 1990s* (Kent: Renaissance Books, 1995), p. 1.

14. Flowers, *The Prostitution of Women and Girls,* p. 15.

15. R. Barri Flowers, *Female Crime, Criminals and Cellmates: An Exploration of Female Criminality and Delinquency* (Jefferson: McFarland, 1995), p. 141.

16. Flowers, *The Prostitution of Women and Girls,* p. 15.

17. *Ibid.,* pp. 20–21.

18. *Ibid.,* p. 21; Jennifer James, *Entrance into Juvenile Prostitution* (Washington: National Institute of Mental Health, 1980), p. 19.

19. Marilyn G. Haft, "Hustling for Rights," in Laura Crites, ed., *The Female Offender* (Lexington: Lexington Books, 1976), p. 212.

20. *Ibid.,* p. 129.

21. Cited in Barbara Goldsmith, "Women on the Edge: A Reporter at Large," *New Yorker 69* (April 26, 1993), p. 65.

22. Flowers, *The Prostitution of Women and Girls,* p. 21; The Enablers, *Juvenile Prostitution in Minnesota: The Report of a Research Project* (St. Paul: The Enablers, 1978), p. 18.

23. James, *Entrance into Juvenile Prostitution,* p. 19.

24. Flowers, *Female Crime, Criminals and Cellmates,* p. 151; Mimi H. Silbert, *Sexual Assault of Prostitutes: Phase One* (Washington: National Institute of Mental Health, 1980), p. 10.

25. Henry Benjamin and R. E. L. Masters, *Prostitution and Morality* (New York: Julian Press, 1964).

26. Goldstein, *Prostitution and Drugs,* pp. 34–37.

27. *Ibid.*

28. Flowers, *Female Crime, Criminals and Cellmates,* p. 106.

29. Kevin Bales and Steven Lize, *Trafficking in Persons in the United States,* unpublished report to the National Institute of Justice (Washington: U.S. Department of Justice, March, 2005), pp. 11–15; Gad Bensinger, "Trafficking of Women and Girls," *Crime & Justice*

International 17, 56 (2001): 11–13; Donna M. Hughes, Janice G. Raymond, and Carol J. Gomez, *Sex Trafficking of Women in the United States: International and Domestic Trends* (North Amherst: Coalition Against Trafficking in Women, 2001), pp. 25, 48, 55–56.

30. Jennifer James, "Two Domains of Streetwalker Argot," *Anthropological Linguistics 14* (1972): 174–75; Jennifer James, "Prostitutes and Prostitution," in Edward Sagarin and Fred Montanino, eds., *Deviants: Voluntary Actors in a Hostile World* (Morrison: General Learning Press, 1977): pp. 390–91.

31. Cited in Linda Lee, "The World (and Underworld) of the Professional Call Girl," *New Woman* (January, 1988), p. 61; Adrian N. LeBlanc, "I'm a Shadow," *Seventeen 52* (March, 1993), p. 216.

32. Cited in Goldsmith, "Women on the Edge," p. 65.

33. LeBlanc, "I'm a Shadow," p. 214.

34. *Ibid.*

35. Flowers, *The Prostitution of Women and Girls,* pp. 48–53.

36. *Ibid.,* p. 50.

37. *Ibid.,* p. 51.

38. Joan J. Johnson, *Teen Prostitution* (Danbury: Franklin Watts, 1992), p. 75.

39. Jennifer James, "Prostitute-Pimp Relationships," *Medical Aspects of Human Sexuality 7* (1973): 147–63; Lee H. Bowker, *Women, Crime, and the Criminal Justice System* (Lexington: Lexington Books, 1978), p. 155.

40. Bowker, *Women, Crime, and the Criminal Justice System,* p. 155.

41. Flowers, *The Prostitution of Women and Girls,* p. 55.

42. Flowers, *Female Crime, Criminals and Cellmates,* p. 110.

43. Robert Karen, "The World of the Middle Class Prostitute," *Cosmopolitan 217* (March, 1987), p. 205.

44. *Ibid.*

45. Freda Adler, *Sisters in Crime: The Rise of the New Female Criminal* (New York: McGraw-Hill, 1975), p. 73.

46. Quoted in Flowers, *The Prostitution of Women and Girls,* p. 59; Harold Greenwald, *The Elegant Prostitute: A Social and Psychoanalytic Study* (New York: Walker and Co., 1970), p. 242.

47. Cited in Lee, "The World (and Underworld) of the Professional Call Girl," p. 62.

48. Flowers, *The Prostitution of Women and Girls,* pp. 30–36, 61–63; Martin A. Plant, ed., *AIDS, Drugs, and Prostitution* (London: Routledge, 1990).

49. Cited in Flowers, *The Prostitution of Women and Girls,* p. 52.

50. Cited in James Bovard, "Safeguard Public Health: Legalize Contractual Sex," *Insight on the News 11* (1995): 20.

51. Goldsmith, "Women on the Edge," p. 65.

52. Cited in *Ibid.,* p. 74.

53. M. J. Rosenberg and J. M Weiner, "Prostitution and AIDS: A Health Department Priority," *American Journal of Public Health 78* (1988): 418.

54. Flowers, *The Prostitution of Women and Girls,* pp. 32–33.

55. W. R. Lange, et al., "HIV Infection in Baltimore: Antibody Seroprevalence Rates Amongst Parenteral Drug Abusers and Prostitutes," *Maryland Medical Journal 36* (1987): 757–61.

56. Cited in Anastasia Volkonsky, "Legalizing the 'Profession' Would Sanction the Abuse," *Insight on the News 11* (1995): 20.

57. Susan Moran, "New World Havens of Oldest Profession," *Insight on the News 9* (1993): 14.

58. Volkonsky, "Legalizing the 'Profession' Would Sanction the Abuse."

59. Cited in Flowers, *The Prostitution of Women and Girls,* p. 64.

60. *Ibid.*

61. Lester, *Serial Killers;* Brian Lane and Wilfred Gregg, *The Encyclopedia of Serial Killers* (New York: Berkley, 1992).

62. Cesare Lombroso and William Ferrero, *The Female Offender* (New York: Appleton, 1900).

63. Sigmund Freud, *New Introductory Lectures in Psychoanalysis* (New York: W. W. Norton, 1933).

64. William I. Thomas, *Sex and Society: Studies in the Social Psychology of Sex* (Boston: Little, Brown, 1907).

65. Otto Pollak, *The Criminality of Women* (Philadelphia: University of Philadelphia Press, 1950).

66. Winick and Kinsie, *The Lively Commerce.*

67. Flowers, *The Prostitution of Women and Girls,* p. 25; Kingsley Davis, "The Sociology of Prostitution," *American Sociological Review* 2 (1937): 744–55.

68. Faris, *Social Disorganization,* p. 271.

69. Winick and Kinsie, *The Lively Commerce,* p. 271.

70. Lemert, *Social Pathology.*

71. Jennifer James, "Motivations for Entrance into Prostitution," in Laura Crites, ed., *The Female Offender* (Lexington: Lexington Books, 1976), p. 194.

Chapter 14

GIRL PROSTITUTION

C hild prostitution can be found at all levels of society and every corner of the world as sexual exploiters, predators, and molesters seek youthful victims for sexual gratification and exploitation. The prostitution of girls in particular is big business worldwide, often involving runaways, throwaways, and homeless youth and a variety of flesh peddlers including traditional pimps, sex trade operators, child pornographers, and even family members.[1] Most young female prostitutes are forced into the sex trade industry as a means of survival, though it comes with a heavy price. The sexual exploitation of girls in the United States typically leads to selling sex on the streets, substance abuse, exposure to AIDS and other diseases, and other hazards such as child pornography, rape, victimization, and even serial murder. Few are able to escape without permanent scars inside and out. This chapter will focus on the characteristics of girl prostitution and its implications.

A HISTORY OF GIRL PROSTITUTION

Young women and girls being forced into prostituting themselves is not a new phenomenon but is deeply rooted in historical tradition, customs, and sexual exploitation. "Many societies considered it proper and actually encouraged treating children as marketable commodities and selling them into slavery or prostitution."[2] In ancient Egypt, the "most beautiful and highest born Egyptian maidens were forced into prostitution . . . and they continued as prostitutes until their first menstruation."[3] Children were routinely sold into prostitution in India and China, while child brothels "flourished in Europe during the nineteenth century, and freelance child prostitution was rampant in both Europe and America during the early 1800s, as men demanded more esoteric forms of sexual titillation."[4]

167

Throughout the twentieth century, girl prostitution continued to exploit young females domestically and internationally, as demand has shown little sign of slowing down in spite of tougher child sexploitation laws worldwide. The victims have been as young as three, sometimes actually abducted and/or forced into sexual slavery; in other instance they were recruited in government-sponsored "packaged sex tours."[5] Most female prostitutes in this country have entered the business voluntarily, though as a direct result of the need for adequate food, clothing, or shelter; or through the charms or coercion of pimps or customers.

However, as seen in Chapter 11, a rising number of girls and young women are being brought into the United States by sex traffickers for purposes of sexual exploitation, including prostitution.[6]

DEFINING CHILD PROSTITUTION

Definitions of prostitution in general were explored in Chapter 13. It is important to differentiate what constitutes child prostitution as opposed to adult prostitution. State definitions of prostitution tend to vary from state to state but are generally defined as

> performing, offering, or agreeing to perform any act of sexual penetration as defined by state statute or any touching or fondling of the sex organs of one person by another person, for any money, property, token, object, or article or anything of value, for the purpose of sexual arousal or gratification.[7]

The prostitution of a child by definition refers to a minor, or a person under the age of mandatory, usually eighteen. Though most juvenile prostitutes are older teenagers, some are preteens, some even under the age of ten. Experts on child prostitution typically define it as the use of or participation for payment of minors (usually persons age seventeen and under) in sexual relations or acts with adults or other minors where no force is present. This can include sexual intercourse, oral sex, anal sex, multiple partner sex, gay sex, sadomasochism, urination, defecation, triolism, and pornographic sexual performance. Child prostitution differs from child incest or statutory rape in that it involves some form of payment for sexual favors such as money, drugs, or clothing, and often does not involve intrafamilial sexual abuse.

Most child prostitutes are female, according to professionals in child sexual exploitation. It is estimated that as many as two-thirds of the children selling sex in the United States are girls.[8] The vast majority of these girls are streetwalking prostitutes. Estimates are that at least one in five streetwalkers are teenage girls.[9] Most can be easily identified by their "working the streets" attire and overdone makeup consisting of "thickly painted red lips and extravagant wigs . . . ankle-length coyote and raccoon coats over Victoria's Secret®-type chemises of shimmering satin" or "G-strings with sparkling pasties on their nipples, or in lace bras and panties . . . fishnet stockings, and totter on the inevitable five-inch heels."[10]

THE EXTENT OF GIRL PROSTITUTION

How many girls are there in the prostitution business in the United States? Accurate figures have been hard to ascertain due in part to the often hidden homeless, missing, and runaway youths in society. Many of these youth turn to prostitution to make ends meet. In addition, definitions of prostitution-related activities are not uniform. Some young prostitutes move from place to place, unreported as missing by parents who abandoned them. Others openly ply their trade, but sometimes the small samples used in studies make it impossible to extrapolate to the country at large.[11]

This notwithstanding, research does exist to give some gravity to the number of girls selling prostitution services. According to the Department of Health and Human Services, there are as many as 300,000 prostitutes under the age of eighteen in the United States.[12] Police sources place the figures at between 100,000 and 300,000 juvenile prostitutes.[13] Some experts believe that up to half a million children under the age of sixteen are prostituting themselves; with double or triple that amount of sixteen and seventeen-year-old prostitutes.[14]

Juvenile prostitutes come from the lower class, middle class, and upper class as well as big and small cities and towns. Some evidence suggests that there may be "an increase in the recruitment of middle class youths from schools and shopping malls in the suburbs."[15] Many young prostitutes are runaways and throwaways, while some are kidnapped and forced into the sex trade industry, and others sell sex part-time while continuing to live at home.[16] Most have been sexually and physically abused, neglected, and otherwise come from unstable, dysfunctional families.[17] Though most girl prostitutes work on the streets, many teenage prostitutes operate out of escort services, massage parlors, brothels, hotels, and even private homes.

Services offered by underaged female prostitutes include every conceivable sexual act. However, according to one study, an estimated 75 percent of teenage streetwalkers' sexual contacts consist only of fellatio, or oral sex.[18] One expert observed that the girl prostitute's primary motivation for this sexual service is that it's "what her customers want and the most practical for working in the cars. It's also quick, which is a concern, because street prostitution is illegal, and when the cops show up, it's sometimes necessary to run."[19]

ENTRY INTO PROSTITUTION FOR GIRLS

Most girls who enter prostitution do so in their early teens, though many girl prostitutes are preteens.[20] Mimi Silbert and Ayala Pines found in their study of child prostitution that the average age of a girl's first prostitution experience is fourteen.[21] In the book *Entrance into Juvenile Prostitution,* Jennifer James reported that the median age of girl prostitutes is 16.9 years.[22] Another study found the median age of prostitution to be even younger at 15.5 years.[23]

The majority of prostituted children enter the business as part-time prostitutes—usually hoping to earn money for food, cigarettes, shelter, drugs, and pocket money. For many this part-time gig becomes a full-time way of life. Research indicates that the typical girl prostitute will be turning tricks on a regular basis within eight months to a year following her initial experience as a prostitute.[24] Joan Johnson described the conditions in which a girl becomes a full-time prostitute, noting that they first undergo a change in self-image. In adapting to the reality of being prostitutes and the negative self-image it brings, adolescent females become, in effect, what they are labeled by society—sluts, hookers, whores.[25] "The more they become a part of the prostitution subculture . . . the more they come to regard themselves as prostitutes and the more committed they become to working the streets, selling their bodies full-time."[26]

The vast majority of girl prostitutes have been turned out—or brought into the business—by pimps or other dominant figures. It is estimated that as many as 90 percent of all female juvenile prostitutes entered the sex trade through the coercions and charms of a pimp or eventually established a working relationship with a pimp.[27] One study indicated that virtually every girl prostitute had some type of relationship with a pimp, either directly or indirectly.[28]

The stereotypical pimp figure is not the only means by which girls are brought into the world of prostitution. "Some, abducted by con men, are raped and psychologically pummeled into submission. . . . Their pimps lurk in the shadows, calculating the night's take. But not all pimps are gangsters. Often it is the father who sits in the backup car or mother who negotiates the deal for her daughter."[29] Studies show that in four out of every one hundred cases of girls entering prostitution, the "pimp" was a relative.[30] In some instances, the influential person was the girl prostitute's mother or sister, who may also be in the business.

Around 20 percent of homeless girl prostitutes enter the profession though their acquaintance with other juvenile streetwalkers;[31] while 10 percent become prostitutes through direct propositions by johns.[32] What almost all girl prostitutes have in common, irrespective of how they entered the business, is that they usually come from unstable backgrounds and are placed in situations that are at least as bad and often worse.

RUNNING AWAY AND GIRL PROSTITUTION

Running away from home is perhaps the strongest indicator of a prostitution-involved lifestyle. It is estimated that up to two million children run away or are thrown out of the home each year in the United States.[33] More than half the children who run away from home are recidivists, having left home on at least three occasions.[34] Approximately 300,000 runaways have been identified as "hard core" street kids, who are habitual runaways.[35]

The relationship between running away and child prostitution has been well documented. In a study of child prostitution in all fifty states, it was concluded that the majority of prostitutes were runaways with drug or alcohol problems.[36] The rate of teen prostitution had increased in 37 percent of the "affected" cities, which was attributed to greater numbers of teenagers running away from troubled homes. A study of runaway and homeless youth revealed that up to one-third reported participating in street prostitution or "survival sex," in order to acquire basic necessities.[37] More than three-quarters of children involved in prostitution activities report running away from home at least one time.[38]

Girl runaways are especially vulnerable to becoming prostitutes. Studies indicate that two-thirds of all runaway girls wind up as prostitutes.[39] Arrest data reveals that girls are much more likely to be arrested as runaways than

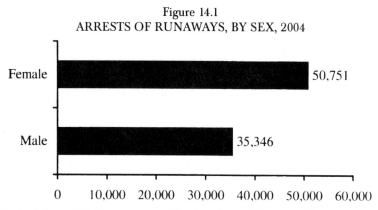

Figure 14.1
ARRESTS OF RUNAWAYS, BY SEX, 2004

Source: Derived from U.S. Department of Justice, Federal Bureau of Investigation, *Crime in the United States: Uniform Crime Reports 2004* (Washington: Government Printing Office, 2005), p. 297.

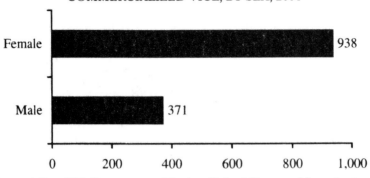

Figure 14.2
JUVENILE ARRESTS FOR PROSTITUTION AND
COMMERCIALIZED VICE, BY SEX, 2004

Source: Derived from U.S. Department of Justice, Federal Bureau of Investigation, *Crime in the United States: Uniform Crime Reports 2004* (Washington: Government Printing Office, 2005), pp. 292, 294.

boys. In 2004, there were 50,751 arrests of females for running away compared to 35,346 arrests of males (see Figure 14.1). Nearly 59 percent of runaway arrestees were female. Girls were more than twice as likely as boys to be arrested for prostitution and commercialized vice. As shown in Figure 14.2, there were 938 arrests of females under the age of eighteen for prostitution and commercialized vice, compared to 371 arrests of males under eighteen for prostitution-related charges in 2004.

Most girl runaways "leave home with little money or direction and quickly find themselves homeless and literally living on the streets, in alleys, or on park benches. . . . Within weeks (sometimes days or hours), many of these runaway girls have become prostitutes–selling their bodies for money, food, drugs, shelter, companionship, or false promises."[40] According to one sociologist: "The rule for runaway girls everywhere is often 'ball for bed'–meaning that implicit in an offer of lodging is the expectation of sexual intercourse."[41]

Girls who run away from home often gravitate to sexual exploiters, predators, and pornographers almost by design. In an article called "Coming of Age on City Streets," the author notes: "Runaway girls, scared and alone, are welcomed by pimps who watch them as they arrive at bus and train stations. They offer them a roof over their heads, a 'caring adult,' clothes, makeup and promises of love and belonging."[42] According to an expert on runaways, most of these prostituted girls end up suffering from "malnutrition, venereal disease, a high incidence of suicide, and are frequently sexually exploited."[43]

GIRL PROSTITUTES' INVOLVEMENT WITH PIMPS

Pimps or hustlers play a key role in the sexual exploitation of girls. The vast majority of pimps are adult males, but they can be women (often former or current prostitutes) or older teenagers.[44] Almost all runaway prostitute streetwalkers have a relationship of one kind or another with a pimp (or more than one). Few of these girls are actually abducted or forced into prostitution, per se. A number of studies have found that only around 5 percent of young females enter prostitution as a result of a pimp's threats or intimidation.[45] However, a pimp's use of more subtle persuasion—romancing the naïve and vulnerable girl, charming her with gifts and attention, pretending to be her friend and confidante—is a powerful enticement. In studying the pimp-prostitute relationship, Johnson found that pimps largely rely on two ways to manipulate their target: love and fear.[46] Few girls, who are already at a disadvantage in the unfamiliar street life, can resist these powerful emotions.

Girl prostitutes are also prone to emotional and psychological dependence on pimps, who often act as substitutes for the family that maltreated or discarded her. A primary way in which pimps maintain their hold on girl prostitutes is through supplying them with drugs and turning them into addicts, assuring their need for and loyalty to the pimp.[47]

In spite of these physical and psychological ties, most girl prostitutes do not remain with one pimp forever. Studies show that more than two-thirds of teenage prostitutes move from one pimp to another within a few months of entering the business.[48] Ninety percent of girl prostitutes leave a pimp within a year's time; some having as many as four pimps in their early years in the business before settling for one.[49]

CHARACTERIZING GIRL PROSTITUTES

Most girls who turn to prostitution are white, middle class, and come from broken or dysfunctional homes. Studies conducted in San Francisco[50] and Minneapolis[51] found that 80 percent of the girl prostitutes were white. In James's sample, 62 percent of the teen prostitutes were white girls.[52]

Black girls make up the second largest number of teenage female prostitutes, with the estimated number varying from 10 to 50 percent of the sample group.[53] The black female percentage appears lower the larger the sample. Hispanic and Native American prostitutes represent anywhere from 2 to 11 percent of adolescent female prostitutes.[54]

Some smaller studies have reported a higher rate of girl prostitutes from lower and working class backgrounds.[55] However, research involving larger prostitute samples has found that most teenage prostitutes come from the middle and upper middle classes. Nearly one in four girl prostitutes sampled in Minnesota had parents with some college education, with many of the fathers in professional or skilled occupations.[56] Seventy percent of the girl prostitutes in Silbert's study came from families where there was average or above average income.[57]

Girl prostitutes are more likely to come from broken, unstable homes than homes with both parents present in a living environment. Maura Crowley reported that 85 percent of the girl prostitutes sampled reported the absence of at least one parent when living at home.[58] Seventy percent of the teen prostitutes in the Huckleberry House Project[59] and James's study[60] indicated leaving homes with one or both parents missing.

According to many studies, most teenage prostitutes' relationship with their parents has been characterized by conflict and stress. The Huckleberry House study found that few girl prostitutes had caring, positive relationships with their parents.[61] In a study of teen prostitution, Diana Gray found that 75 percent of her sample depicted their relationship with parents as "poor" or "very bad."[62] In Crawley's study, mothers were nearly twice as likely as fathers to be the source of daughter-parent dysfunction.[63]

CHILD SEXUAL AND PHYSICAL ABUSE AND GIRL PROSTITUTION

Most girls selling sexual favors have been victims of sexual and physical abuse. Ninety percent of those in the Huckleberry House Project had been sexually molested;[64] while two-thirds of Silbert's sample experienced intrafamilial sexual abuse.[65] Early childhood sexual abuse appears to be a key factor in increasing the probability of entrance into prostitution as a result of running away from the abuse.[66] As one sociologist contends: "It is not so much that sexual abuse leads to prostitution as it is that running away leads to prostitution."[67]

Similarly, physical abuse can often lead to running away and prostitution as a consequence. In the Huckleberry House findings[68] and the Crowley study,[69] two out of every three girl prostitutes reported being victims of childhood physical abuse. According to Anastasia Volkonsky, an expert on child sexual exploitation, most runaway girls turned prostitutes have experienced a major trauma such as incest, domestic violence, or rape prior to entering prostitution.[70]

GIRL PROSTITUTES AND SUBSTANCE ABUSE

Substance abuse is common among girl prostitutes, often as a coping mechanism, through introduction by a pimp or john, or due to addiction. Many began using alcohol or drugs before becoming prostitutes. In one study, nearly eight in ten teenage prostitutes were already alcohol or drug involved prior to entry into the sex trade industry.[71] Virtually all teen prostitutes have tried at least one illegal drug, with between 20 and 50 percent regular drug users.[72] At least 70 percent of all adolescent female prostitutes consume some type of alcohol.[73]

Marijuana is the drug of choice for most teenage prostitutes, along with alcohol.[74] However, many young prostitutes use other mind altering drugs such as heroin and cocaine. Some girl prostitutes trade sex for crack cocaine to feed their addiction. The addictive qualities of crack can be such that some call it the "new pimp" as crack addicted prostitutes "are seen as willing to do anything to feed their habits."[75]

Alcohol and drugs are easily obtained by teenagers in the prostitution subculture. Many share dirty needles and tainted blood in IV drug use, leading to HIV exposure and other diseases. Some girl prostitutes use alcohol and/or drugs to "deaden memories" of child sexual or physical abuse, while others turn to substance abuse to "desensitize present experiences" in the often cruel and violent world of child prostitution.[76]

GIRL PROSTITUTES, AIDS, AND VICTIMIZATION

Girl prostitutes face a high risk for exposure to the AIDS virus as well as other hazards endemic to street life and child sexual exploitation. Frequent unprotected sexual encounters, multiple drug use, and IV drug use place teenage prostitutes in the greatest danger for HIV exposure. Notes one expert of runaway prostitutes: "They have sex with strangers. They use intravenous drugs or love somebody who does. . . . Girls may have lovers who earn a living that way. Some try to practice safe sex 'if the john doesn't object'."[77] Researchers have found that client resistance is the girl prostitute's biggest obstacle to practicing safe sex, or safer sex.[78] James Farrow referred to the dire situation of teenage prostitutes and AIDS as "a time bomb. . . . Because of their activity, their potential for spreading [AIDS] far and wide is pretty great."[79]

According to an AIDS specialist at New York City's Covenant House, a runaway shelter, an estimated 40 percent of runaway and homeless prostituted children may be exposed to the AIDS virus.[80] Other studies have shown a high rate of HIV exposure among IV drug-using streetwalkers.[81]

Girls in the sex trade are also at high risk for other sexually transmitted and infectious diseases such as syphilis, gonorrhea, and chlamydia.[82]

Prostitution-involved girls further place themselves as high risk for violence by customers, sexual predators, pimps, gang members, and/or drug addicts. Studies show that upwards of two-thirds of girl prostitutes are frequent victims of rape, sexual perversions, physical assaults, and other forms of mistreatment.[83] Most of these attacks go unreported by victims who fear police will not take the charges seriously or that they themselves will be arrested.[84] Girl prostitutes are at increased risk for sexual exploitation by child pornographers[85] and victimization from sexual murderers and serial killers who prey on prostitutes.[86]

As a direct result of the involvement in the sex-for-sale industry, many girl prostitutes actually victimize others (including customers and other prostitutes) through assaults, thefts, and exposure to AIDS or other sexual diseases.[87]

WHAT ARE THE REASONS FOR GIRL PROSTITUTION?

Most experts agree that girls enter and remain in the prostitution business primarily for money and to support drug habits–but also for love, sex, companionship, adventure, and even peer pressure.[88] James broke girl streetwalkers' motivations for prostitution into three areas (1) conscious, (2) situational, and (3) psychoanalytic as follows:

- **Conscious**–economics, working conditions, adventure, and a coercive pimp.
- **Situational**–early experiences in life, child abuse and neglect, occupation.
- **Psychoanalytic**–general factors, oedipal fixation, latent homosexuality, and retardation.[89]

Situational motivation research has associated girl prostitution to such situational determinants as incest, molestation, rape, and early sexual experiences.[90] Psychoanalytical studies have focused on the role of mental disorders such as depression, emotional deprivation, and schizophrenia in teenage prostitution.[91]

Economic factors have been given the most attention in prostitution studies. James asserted: "The apparent reason for prostitution among adolescents is for economic survival and to meet other needs."[92] In surveys, most girl prostitutes have listed money and material items as the most common reasons for being in the business.[93]

NOTES

1. R. Barri Flowers, *Runaway Kids and Teenage Prostitution: America's Lost, Abandoned, and Sexually Exploited Children* (Westport: Greenwood Press, 2001), pp. 51–57, 89–90; R. Barri Flowers, *The Prostitution of Women and Girls* (Jefferson: McFarland, 2005), pp. 69–103.
2. R. Barri Flowers, *Children and Criminality: The Child as Victim and Perpetrator* (Westport: Greenwood Press, 1986), p. 7.
3. Henry Benjamin and R. E. L. Masters, *Prostitution and Morality* (New York: Julian Press, 1964), p. 161.
4. *Ibid.*, p. 162; Flowers, *Children and Criminality*, p. 7; Reay Tannahill, *Sex in History* (New York: Stein and Day, 1980), p. 374.
5. Flowers, *The Prostitution of Women and Girls*, pp. 70–71, 76, 84; U.S. Department of Justice, Office of Juvenile Justice and Delinquency Prevention, *Prostitution of Children and Child-Sex Tourism: An Analysis of Domestic and International Responses* (Arlington: National Center for Missing & Exploited Children, 1999).
6. *See, for example,* Marisa B. Ugarte, Laura Zarate, and Melissa Farley, "Prostitution and Trafficking of Women and Children from Mexico to the United States," *Journal of Trauma Practice 2,* 3/4 (2003): 147–65; Gad J. Bensinger, "Trafficking of Women and Girls," *Crime & Justice International 17,* 56 (2001): 11–13; Richard J. Estes and Neil A. Weiner, "The Commercial Sexual Exploitation of Children in the U.S., Canada, and Mexico, Executive Summary," Philadelphia: Center for the Study of Youth Policy, September 19, 2001.
7. *Prostitution of Children and Child-Sex Tourism,* p. 9.
8. Flowers, *Runaway Kids and Teenage Prostitution,* p. 107; R. Barri Flowers, *The Adolescent Criminal: An Examination of Today's Juvenile Offender* (Jefferson: McFarland, 1990), p. 55.
9. Flowers, *The Prostitution of Women and Girls,* p. 79.
10. Barbara J. Goldsmith, "Women on the Edge: A Reporter at Large," *New Yorker 69* (April 26, 1993), pp. 66–67.
11. Flowers, *The Prostitution of Women and Girls,* pp. 71–79; *Prostitution of Children and Child-Sex Tourism,* p. 2; Beth E. Molnar et al., "Suicidal Behavior and Sexual/Physical Abuse Among Street Youth," *Child Abuse and Neglect 22* (1998): 213–14.
12. *Ibid.; Report of the Special Rapporteur on the Sale of Children, Child Prostitution and Child Pornography,* United National Economic and Social Council, Commission on Human Rights, 52nd Sess. (1996).
13. R. Barri Flowers, *Female Crime, Criminals and Cellmates: An Exploration of Female Criminality and Delinquency* (Jefferson: McFarland, 1995), p. 149; Michael Satchel, "Kids for Sale: A Shocking Report on Child Prostitution Across America," *Parade Magazine* (July 20, 1986), p. 4.
14. Flowers, *The Adolescent Criminal,* pp. 54–55.
15. *Prostitution of Children and Child-Sex Tourism,* p. 2.
16. Flowers, *The Prostitution of Women and Girls,* pp. 176–84; Debra Whitcomb, Edward DeVos, and Barbara E. Smith, *Program to Increase Understanding of Child Sexual Exploitation,* Final Report, Education Development Center, Inc. and ABA Center on Children and the Law, 1998, p. 74.
17. R. Barri Flowers, *The Victimization and Exploitation of Women and Children: A Study of Physical, Mental and Sexual Maltreatment in the United States* (Jefferson: McFarland, 1994), pp. 81–86.
18. Cited in Goldsmith, "Women on the Edge," p. 65.
19. Adrian N. LeBlanc, "I'm a Shadow," *Seventeen 52* (March, 1993), p. 216.
20. Flowers, *The Prostitution of Women and Girls,* p. 81; *Prostitution of Children and Child-Sex*

Tourism, p. 2.

21. Mimi H. Silbert and Ayala M. Pines, "Occupational Hazards of Street Prostitutes," *Criminal Justice Behavior 8* (1981): 397; Mimi H. Silbert and Ayala M. Pines, "Entrance into Prostitution," *Youth & Society 13* (1982): 471–73.

22. Jennifer James, *Entrance into Juvenile Prostitution* (Washington: National Institute of Mental Health, 1980), p. 17.

23. *Prostitution of Children and Child-Sex Tourism,* p. 2.

24. Joan J. Johnson, *Teen Prostitution* (Danbury: Franklin Watts, 1992), p. 108.

25. *Ibid.*

26. Flowers, *The Prostitution of Women and Girls,* p. 80.

27. Johnson, *Teen Prostitution,* p. 75.

28. Cited in *Ibid.,* p. 78; Flowers, *Runaway Kids and Teenage Prostitution,* pp. 119–26.

29. Margot Hornblower, "The Skin Trade," *Time 141* (June 21, 1993), p. 44.

30. Johnson, *Teen Prostitution,* p. 87.

31. *Ibid.*

32. Flowers, *The Prostitution of Women and Girls,* p. 80.

33. *Ibid.,* p. 89; Flowers, *Runaway Kids and Teenage Prostitution,* p. 107.

34. Flowers, *Female Crime, Criminals and Cellmates,* p. 141.

35. Cited in Patricia Hersch, "Coming of Age on City Streets," *Psychology Today* (January, 1988), pp. 31, 34.

36. Sam Meddis, "Teen Prostitution Rising, Study Says," *USA Today* (April 23, 1984), p. 3A.

37. *Prostitution of Children and Child-Sex Tourism,* p. 3; Jane Rotheram-Borus et al., "Sexual Abuse History and Associated Multiple Risk Behavior in Adolescent Runaways," *American Journal of Orthopsychiatry 66* (1996): 390–91.

38. Magnus J. Seng, "Child Sexual Abuse and Adolescent Prostitution: A Comparative Analysis," *Adolescence 24* (1989): 671.

39. Flowers, *Female Crime, Criminals and Cellmates,* pp. 141–56.

40. Flowers, *The Prostitution of Women and Girls,* pp. 71, 97.

41. *Ibid.*

42. Hersch, "Coming of Age on City Streets," p. 32. *See also* David Finkelhor and Richard Ormrod, *Prostitution of Juveniles: Patterns From NIBRS* (Washington: Office of Juvenile Justice and Delinquency Prevention, 2004), p. 2.

43. Quoted in Dotson Rader, "I Want to Die So I Won't Hurt No More," *Parade Magazine* (August 18, 1985), p. 4.

44. *Prostitution of Children and Child-Sex Tourism,* p. 5; Silbert and Pines, "Occupational Hazards of Street Prostitutes," p. 498.

45. *See, for example,* Jennifer James, "Prostitute-Pimp Relationships," *Medical Aspects of Human Sexuality 7* (1973): 147–63; *The Enablers, Juvenile Prostitution in Minnesota: The Report of a Research Project* (St. Paul: The Enablers, 1978), p. 57; Dorothy H. Bracey, *"Baby-Pros": Preliminary Profiles of Juvenile Prostitution* (New York: John Jay Press, 1979), p. 23.

46. Johnson, *Teen Prostitution,* p. 79.

47. Flowers, *The Prostitution of Women and Girls,* pp. 100–4.

48. *Ibid.,* p. 103; Flowers, *Runaway Kids and Teenage Prostitution,* p. 125.

49. Johnson, *Teen Prostitution,* p. 83.

50. Sparky Harlan, Luanne L. Rodgers, and Brian Slattery, *Male and Female Adolescent Prostitution: Huckleberry House Sexual Minority Youth Services Project* (Washington: U.S. Department of Health and Human Services, 1981), p. 7.

51. *The Enablers, Juvenile Prostitution in Minnesota,* p. 18.

52. James, *Entrance into Juvenile Prostitution,* p. 19.

53. *Ibid., The Enablers, Juvenile Prostitution in Minnesota*, p. 18; Flowers, *The Adolescent Criminal*, p. 56.
54. James, *Entrance into Juvenile Prostitution*, p. 10; Mimi Silbert, *Sexual Assault of Prostitutes: Phase One* (Washington: National Institute of Mental Health, 1980), p. 10.
55. Flowers, *The Adolescent Criminal*, p. 56; Bracey, *"Baby-Pros": Preliminary Profiles of Juvenile Prostitution*, p. 19.
56. Ellen Hale, "Center Studies Causes of Juvenile Prostitution," *Gannet News Service* (May 21, 1981).
57. Silbert, *Sexual Assault of Prostitutes*, p. 15.
58. Maura G. Crowley, "Female Runaway Behavior and Its Relationship to Prostitution," Master's thesis, Sam Houston State University, Institute of Contemporary Corrections and Behavioral Sciences, 1977.
59. Harlan, Rodgers, and Slattery, *Male and Female Adolescent Prostitution*, p. 14.
60. James, *Entrance into Juvenile Prostitution*, p. 88.
61. Harlan, Rodgers, and Slattery, *Male and Female Adolescent Prostitution*, p. 15.
62. Diana Gray, "Turning Out: A Study of Teenage Prostitution," Master's thesis, University of Washington, 1971, p. 25.
63. Crowley, "Female Runaway Behavior," pp. 74–77.
64. Harlan, Rodgers, and Slattery, *Male and Female Adolescent Prostitution*, p. 21.
65. Mimi H. Silbert, "Delancey Street Study: Prostitution and Sexual Assault," summary of results, Delancey Street Foundation, San Francisco, 1982, p. 3.
66. *Prostitution of Children and Child-Sex Tourism*, p. 3; Ronald Simons and Les B. Whitbeck, "Sexual Abuse as a Precursor to Prostitution and Victimization Among Adolescent and Homeless Women," *Journal of Family Issues 12* (1991): 375.
67. Seng, "Child Sexual Abuse and Adolescent Prostitution," p. 673.
68. Harlan, Rodgers, and Slattery, *Male and Female Adolescent Prostitution*, p. 15.
69. Crowley, "Female Runaway Behavior," p. 63.
70. Anastasia Volkonsky, "Legalizing the 'Profession' Would Sanction the Abuse," *Insight on the News 11* (1995): 21.
71. Cited in Johnson, *Teen Prostitution*, p. 97.
72. Flowers, *The Adolescent Criminal*, pp. 59–60; D. Kelly Weisberg, *Children of the Night: A Study of Adolescent Prostitution*, pp. 117–19.
73. Flowers, *Runaway Kids and Teenage Prostitution*, p. 112; Paul W. Haberman and Michael M. Baden, *Alcohol, Other Drugs, and Violent Death* (New York: Oxford University Press, 1978), pp. 18–19.
74. Flowers, *Female Crime, Criminals and Cellmates*, p. 153; Crowley, "Female Runaway Behavior," p. 80.
75. *Prostitution of Children and Child-Sex Tourism*, p. 6; Finkelhor and Ormrod, *Prostitution of Juveniles*, p. 2; Jean Faugier and Mary Sargeant, "'Boyfriends,' 'Pimps' and 'Clients',￼" in G. Scambler and A. Scambler, eds., *Rethinking Prostitution: Purchasing Sex in the 1990s* (London: Routledge, 1997), pp. 125–26.
76. Flowers, *The Prostitution of Women and Girls*, p. 85.
77. John Zaccaro, Jr., "Children of the Night," *Women's Day* (March 29, 1988), p. 137.
78. *Prostitution of Children and Child-Sex Tourism*, p. 8.
79. Quoted in Johnson, *Teen Prostitution*, p. 125.
80. Cited in Flowers, *The Prostitution of Women and Girls*, p. 98.
81. *Ibid.*, pp. 52–53, 62–63.
82. *Ibid.*, p. 98; Flowers, *The Victimization and Exploitation of Women and Children*, p. 88; *Prostitution of Children and Child-Sex Tourism*, p. 8; Gary L. Yates et al., "A Risk Profile

Comparison of Homeless Youth Involved in Prostitution and Homeless Youth Not Involved," *Journal of Adolescent Health 12* (1991): 547.

83. Flowers, *The Prostitution of Women and Girls,* p. 83; *Prostitution of Children and Child-Sex Tourism,* pp. 6–7; Silbert and Pines, "Occupational Hazards of Street Prostitutes;" Faugier and Sargeant, "'Boyfriends,' 'Pimps,' and 'Clients'," p. 124.

84. Silbert and Pines, "Occupational Hazards of Street Prostitutes;" Minouche Kandel, "Whores in Court: Judicial Processing of Prostitutes in the Boston Municipal Court in 1990," *Yale Journal of Law and Feminism 4* (1992): 346; Byron Fasset and Bill Walsh, "Juvenile Prostitution: An Overlooked Form of Child Sexual Abuse," *The APSAC Advisor 7,* 1 (1994): 30.

85. Flowers, *The Prostitution of Women and Girls,* pp. 121–25; *Prostitution of Children and Child-Sex Tourism,* p. 6.

86. R. Barri Flowers, *Murder, At The End of The Day and Night: A Study of Criminal Homicide Offenders, Victims, and Circumstances* (Springfield: Charles C Thomas, 2002), pp. 159–67; Brian Lane and Wilfred Gregg, *The Encyclopedia of Serial Killers* (New York: Berkley, 1995).

87. Flowers, *The Prostitution of Women and Girls,* pp. 85–86; Simons and Whitbeck, "Sexual Abuse as a Precursor to Prostitution and Victimization," pp. 370–71; Arlene McCormack et al., "Runaway Youths and Sexual Victimization: Gender Differences in an Adolescent Runaway Population," *Child Abuse and Neglect 10* (1986): 392–93; Cathy S. Widom and M. Ashley Ames, "Criminal Consequences of Childhood Sexual Victimization," *Child Abuse and Neglect 18* (1994): 303, 310, 312.

88. Flowers, *Female Crime, Criminals and Cellmates,* pp. 154–56; Flowers, *Runaway Kids and Teenage Prostitution,* pp. 112–13.

89. Jennifer James, "Prostitutes and Prostitution," in Edward Sagarin and Fred Montanino, eds., *Deviants: Voluntary Actors in a Hostile World* (Morrison: General Learning Press, 1977), pp. 390–91.

90. Flowers, *Children and Criminality,* pp. 81–83.

91. *Ibid.*; Flowers, *The Prostitution of Women and Girls,* p. 87.

92. James, *Entrance into Juvenile Prostitution,* p. 68.

93. Flowers, *The Adolescent Criminal,* p. 58.

Chapter 15

MALE PROSTITUTION

M uch of the literature on prostitution has focused on female prostitutes and the dynamics involving women and girls who sell sexual favors. Consequently, less is known about the characteristics and extent of male prostitution. Most male prostitutes are teenagers and come from the same types of backgrounds as female teen prostitutes. Many are homeless runaways or throwaways, have been physically or sexually abused, and face a number of difficulties in street life including substance abuse, sexual violence, and exposure to the AIDS virus. This chapter will examine the issue of male prostitution in American society.

THE MAGNITUDE OF MALE PROSTITUTION

How many males are involved in the sex trade industry as prostitutes? The answer is unclear, as male prostitution has not received the same attention as female prostitution from researchers or criminologists. However, some experts believe that there may be as many male prostitutes as female prostitutes.[1] It is estimated that there are at least two million women and girls selling their bodies in the United States,[2] and perhaps twice that number.[3] In Robin Lloyd's book, *For Love or Money: Boy Prostitution in America,* the author estimated that there were 300,000 male prostitutes under the age of sixteen in this country.[4] There is evidence that the vast majority of male prostitutes are over the age of eighteen, giving rise to the magnitude of male prostitution.[5]

Females are more likely to be arrested for prostitution and commercialized vice, as indicated through recent arrest trends, while total male prostitution arrests are decreasing at a greater rate than total female arrests for prostitution (see Figure 15.1). According to FBI statistics, between 1995 and 2004, overall male arrests for prostitution and commercialized vice dropped

Figure 15.1
ARREST TRENDS FOR PROSTITUTION AND
COMMERCIALIZED VICE, BY SEX, 1995–2004

■ 1995
□ 2004

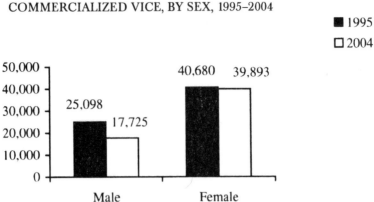

Source: Derived from U.S. Department of Justice, Federal Bureau of Investigation, *Crime in the United States: Uniform Crime Reports 2004* (Washington: Government Printing Office, 2005), p. 285.

Figure 15.2
JUVENILE ARREST TRENDS FOR PROSTITUTION
AND COMMERCIALIZED VICE, BY SEX, 1995–2004

■ 1995
□ 2004

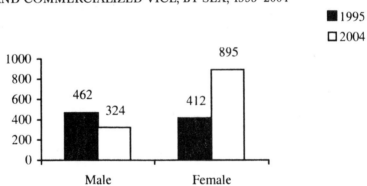

Source: Derived from U.S. Department of Justice, Federal Bureau of Investigation, *Crime in the United States: Uniform Crime Reports 2004* (Washington: Government Printing Office, 2005), p. 285.

29.4 percent. Comparatively, overall female prostitution arrests decreased just 1.9 percent over the period. The differential was even greater for arrestees under the age of eighteen. Male juvenile arrests for prostitution declined nearly 30 percent over the span, while female juvenile arrests for prostitution rose by more than 117 percent (see Figure 15.2). These figures may be more of a reflection of differential law enforcement, visibility, and other factors that tend to favor male prostitutes, hence underplaying their true involvement in the sex-for-sale industry.

MALE PROSTITUTION TYPOLOGIES

Different types of male prostitutes have been identified by a number of researchers. According to S. Caukins and N. Coombs, male prostitutes can be broken down into four categories: (1) street hustlers, (2) bar hustlers, (3) call boys, and (4) kept boys.[6] They postulated that a "gay sex market thrives in every big city . . . a profit-oriented street corner college for the recruiting, training, and selling of boys and men to older, affluent homosexuals."[7] In a psychological study, Donald Allen described the male prostitute types as follows:

- **Street hustlers**–usually drifters who may support a family through selling sexual favors.
- **Bar hustlers**–drifters who may also support a wife or children.
- **Call boys**–often serve as companions for upscale clients for social occasions such as dinner or the theater.
- **Kept boys**–houseboys who perform nonsexual domestic chores.[8]

Dan Waldorf and Sheigla Murphy, who studied the relationship between male prostitution and IV drug use, divided male prostitutes into two general categories: (1) hustlers and (2) call men. Hustlers tended to find johns in typical cruising places for male prostitution such as arcades, adult bookstores, gay bars, and theaters.[9] The researchers subcategorized hustlers into three types: (1) trade hustlers, (2) drag queen hustlers, and (3) youth hustlers.

- **Trade hustlers**–usually heterosexual or bisexual males who sell sex for money; rarely do they admit to being homosexual or enjoying sexual relations with male customers.
- **Drag queen hustlers**–transvestites and transsexuals specializing in oral sex. They typically frequent known gay red-light districts.
- **Youth hustlers**–young, admittedly gay males who appear naïve and innocent but, in fact, are often experienced in a range of sexual activities.[10]

Call men tend not to reflect erotic styles, per se, but are more defined by the ways they find customers as well as the sexual services offered by them. These male prostitutes are subdivided into four types: (1) call book men, (2) models and escorts, (3) erotic masseurs, and (4) porn industry stars.

- **Call book men**–often self-identified as homosexual or bisexual. They often get clients from a call book or have regular johns. *Drag queen call girls* are transvestites working from a call book.
- **Models and escorts**–men who find customers through local advertising in general or special interest publications. They often establish a network of regular johns and may also use a call book.

- **Erotic masseurs**–men who seek new clients through advertisements even while maintaining established customers. Most are certified by licensed massage schools and combine massages with sexual favors, often for lower fees than other call men.
- **Porn industry stars**–the upper class or elite among male prostitutes. These include erotic dancers and pornography actors. Clients (including female) are often solicited at work and serviced elsewhere. These male prostitutes are the highest paid in the male sex trade.[11]

MALE PROSTITUTION DYNAMICS

Male prostitutes, similar to their female counterparts, tend to come from all walks of life and backgrounds, including "delinquent school dropouts to well-educated, refined college students; they come from inner city projects and middle class suburbs; from completely disintegrated families and from effective loving families."[12] Males in the prostitution business have been found to enjoy the profession, merely tolerate it, or abhor selling their bodies.[13] While most male prostitutes wind up homeless, drug addicted, and/or in trouble with the law, some will thrive in the world of sexual exploration and exploitation.[14]

The majority of male prostitutes began street life as runaways and have been physically and sexually abused. In a study of adolescent prostitutes and child sexual abuse, Magnus Seng found that 77 percent of the prostitutes ran away from home on at least one occasion.[15] According to the National Center for Missing and Exploited Children, one in three runaway and homeless youth report prostituting themselves in the streets to acquire basic needs.[16] One study found that two-thirds of full-time male prostitutes were runaways.[17] Of those whose first sexual experience was with a male, over half reported being seduced, and two-thirds were paid for sexual relations. In another study of male prostitution, the average age for a male prostitute's first homosexual experience was 9.6 years.[18] Three-fifths of the males reported receiving payment of some type for their participation. On average, most male prostitutes' first sexual experience was with a male at least five years their senior.[19]

Male prostitution does not appear to be as related to coming from broken homes as female prostitution. A study examining age and socioeconomic status of male prostitutes found little evidence that these factors or broken homes were significantly associated with male entry into prostitution.[20] However, the families of male prostitutes were found to be larger than those of nonprostitutes, as well as more dysfunctional, such as incestuous and with substance abuse.

Most male prostitutes do not consider themselves to be homosexual but rather view their sexual behavior as something done solely for the money or other payment, such as drugs.[21] In one study where nearly 75 percent of the male prostitutes were identified as homosexual, only 6 percent defined themselves as gay.[22] However, this was contradicted by another study that found that two-thirds of the male prostitutes characterized themselves as homosexual or bisexual.[23]

Males who are involved in the sex trade industry as prostitutes tend to be self-destructive. Studies show that such males have high levels of psychopathology and are often immature, irresponsible, and unstable.[24] Male prostitutes have also been found to have a high rate of sexually transmitted diseases, HIV infection, drug addiction, and alcohol abuse.[25]

Male prostitutes and their johns have a "deep hatred" towards one another, according to experts on the male prostitution subculture.[26] "Both have to wrestle with conflicting emotions during their time together, often creating fantasies that are acted out in the course of the sexual encounter."[27]

Homosexual johns are often middle-aged and physically unappealing. Most tend to seek "bizarre and unusual sex acts which would not meet with acceptance in conventional gay society."[28]

Motivations For Entry Into Male Prostitution

Males typically enter and remain in prostitution for reasons that parallel female entry into the sex trade industry, including:

* Immediate need for food, clothing, and shelter.
* A means to make quick money.
* Drug or alcohol addiction.
* Dysfunctional family background.
* Sexual identity issues.
* Need for acceptance.
* Rejection by parents or guardians.
* Sexual experimentation.
* Adventure and thrills.
* Unemployment.
* Money for college tuition.
* Mental illness.
* Peer pressures.

Virtually all male prostitutes operate independent of pimps, in contrast to female prostitutes (particularly girl prostitutes).[29] As a result, males are responsible for their own earnings, shelter, scheduling of prostitution activities, and most aspects of their time in the business. This independence is lessened by the pressures of competition, stresses of substance abuse and money troubles, and the dangers that come with the territory of prostitution and street life.

MALE PROSTITUTION AND AIDS

Both male and female prostitutes are at risk for contracting AIDS just by the nature of their activities: frequent sexual contact, IV drug use, and disinhibitions that increase the risk of exposure to sexually transmitted diseases. Though much of the data on the relationship between AIDS/HIV and prostitution has focused on female prostitutes, male prostitutes have also been shown to have a high incidence of HIV infection.[30] This is based primarily on the sharing of dirty needles and tainted blood among IV drug-using male prostitutes and the transmission of bodily fluids infected with the AIDS virus, usually through anal intercourse. Some studies suggest that given their high rate of IV drug addiction, homosexual relations, and multiple homosexual and bisexual partners–male prostitutes may, in fact, have a greater risk of HIV infection than their female counterparts.[31] One study found that more than eight in ten homeless youth are involved in at least one high-risk behavior for contracting AIDS;[32] while another study concluded that youth engaging in homosexual relations with multiple and often anonymous partners are "in a high-risk subgroup among high-risk groups."[33]

Two recent studies illustrate the seriousness of the problem of AIDS among male prostitutes. In a study at a venereal disease clinic in New York City, 53 percent of the male prostitute sample tested HIV-seropositive.[34] A second study of male prostitutes, homosexual men, and male IV drug users in Italy found that 11 percent of the prostitutes tested positive for the HIV virus, compared to 17 percent of the homosexuals, and 49 percent of the IV drug users.[35] In both studies, the researchers found that male prostitutes represented a high-risk population for exposure to the AIDS virus.

Many experts believe that male prostitutes and their male clients, with their high-risk activities of prostitution, IV drug use, and frequent paid sex "may be or could become the major means through which HIV infection is passed into the general population."[36]

BOY PROSTITUTION

Boy prostitution is a subcategory of male prostitution. Most male prostitutes are over eighteen, but the number under eighteen is believed by some to be underrepresented in the literature and arrest statistics. Official data indicates that males under eighteen are far less likely to be arrested for prostitution and commercialized vice than males over eighteen.[37] However, since many boy prostitutes are arrested as runaways for curfew and loitering law violations and other charges, the actual number facing arrest may be greater.[38] Most male juveniles arrested for prostitution-related offenses are older teens. Three in four males under eighteen arrested for prostitution and commercialized vice in the United States in 2004 were sixteen and seventeen years of age.[39]

While many experts believe that girls are much more likely to be involved in prostitution than boys, some researchers have seen an increase in the incidence of boy prostitution.[40] Others suggest that this may actually be due to more boys being willing to disclose their involvement in prostitution.[41] Larger cities tend to have a higher proportion of juvenile male prostitution; however service providers in smaller cities have also reported an increase in boy prostitution. This may reflect a "migration to smaller urban areas, an increase in visibility due to heightened awareness, or the greater willingness of boys to use services."[42]

"Chickens" and "Chicken Hawks"

Boy prostitutes are typically identified on the street as *chickens,* while the homosexual men that solicit them are referred to as *chicken hawks* or *chicken queens.* These men are also known to law enforcement and child sexual abuse experts as child molesters and pedophiles (see Chapter 9). Much of the male juvenile prostitution takes place in big cities with a large gay population. Young boy prostitutes can also be found in the suburbs and rural areas or wherever opportunity presents itself. A typical example of a chicken-chicken hawk encounter can be seen in the following depiction by a police detective working in the sex offenses unit:

> The boy will usually find a set of marble steps, sit, and observe passing cars. Eye contact is the key. The "chicken hawk" will stare at the boy he feels could be a "hustler." If a period of eye contact is made between both, the "chicken hawk" will still circle the block several times, making eye contact at each passing. Finally the "chicken hawk" will nod and, if the boy returns the nod, a deal is in the making. At times, the "chickens" would work as teams, usually two together. If the customer wanted two boys he would use hand signals, indicating how many boys he wanted and how much he was paying.[43]

While most pedophiles prefer boy hustlers, many chicken hawks also solicit adult male prostitutes. Some desire chickens of a specific age or age group and "will not pick up any other boys who might be older or younger than he desires."[44] The typical chicken hawk is described as:

- Often middle aged.
- Gets along well with children, usually better than with adults.
- Sees the chicken as the sexual aggressor.
- Trends to be nonviolent.
- Often single, but sometimes married.
- Associated with other child molesters and chicken hawks.
- Is usually a white-collar worker or professional.
- Often pretends to be the boy prostitute's friend.[45]

Characterizing the Boy Prostitute

The first national study of male juvenile prostitution was undertaken by the Urban and Rural Systems Association of San Francisco.[46] It identified the following characteristics of boy prostitution and prostitutes:

- Boy prostitutes sell sexual favors primarily to pay for basic necessities, explore their sexuality, and to make contact with homosexual men.
- Money is the most important motivational factor for entering and remaining in prostitution.
- The average age of the male juvenile prostitute is sixteen.
- Most boy prostitutes are runaways or throwaways.
- Most boys involved in prostitution have been victims of sexual, physical, or mental abuse.
- Many male prostitutes come from dysfunctional or broken homes.
- A high percentage of teen prostitutes are high school dropouts or performed poorly in school.
- Pimps are almost nonexistent in the adolescent male prostitute subculture.
- Gay-identified boy prostitutes initially find the lifestyle exciting.
- Boy prostitutes often engage in other delinquent or criminal activities.

As many as half of all boy prostitutes are estimated to have been thrown out of the house due to sexual identity related problems.[47] The vast majority of adolescent male prostitutes are streetwalkers. According to D. Kelly Weisberg in her book, *Children of the Night,* 94 percent of boy prostitutes sold sex on the streets.[48] That notwithstanding, there are known boy brothels where young male prostitutes live and work. These are usually owned and operated by pimps. Joan Johnson refers to boys working in these brothels as occupying the lowest level of the juvenile male prostitution hierarchy.[49]

Categories of Boy Prostitutes

Researchers have divided boy prostitutes into categories and subcategories of prostitution. Weisberg identifies two distinct adolescent male prostitution subcultures: (1) the peer-delinquent subculture and (2) the gay subculture. For prostitutes in the

first subculture, prostitution is an integral aspect of delinquent street life. These adolescents engage indiscriminately in prostitution, drug dealing, panhandling, and petty criminal activity. They sell their sexual favors habitually as a way of making money, viewing prostitution as just one aspect of "hustling"–as the term is used to mean procuring more than one gives.

Youth in the gay subculture engage in prostitution for different reasons. Prostitution is one outlet for their sexuality. They find in the gay male subculture a means of identification, and prostitution satisfies their needs for social interaction with gay persons and for sexual partners. Simultaneously, it provides a way of making money, since the purchase and sale of sexual activity is a product of the sexual mores of that community.[50]

Within these subcultures exists a number of interchangeable subcategories as follows:

- **Situational prostitutes**–adolescent males who participate in prostitution activities only in certain situations and who tend to see prostitution as an occasional pastime.
- **Habitual prostitutes**–male juveniles involved in inner city street life in which prostitution is an integral part, along with such criminal activity as drug dealing, robbery and petty theft.
- **Vocational prostitutes**–boys who view teenage prostitution as a career or stepping stone or see themselves as professionals.
- **Avocational prostitutes**–vocational male juvenile prostitutes who regard their prostitution as part-time employment.[51]

In her study of teen prostitution, Johnson identified most adolescent male prostitutes as *street hustlers,* including homosexual, heterosexual, and bisexual prostitutes.[52] She described many as aggressive, drug addicts, and physically unappealing. Other types established were the *transvestite boy prostitute* and the *upper class adolescent male prostitute.* Upper class prostitutes tend to be better looking, better dressed, older, and more self-confident than lower class prostitutes.[53] Like upper class female prostitutes, these men typically ply their trade for escort services or have their own call boy service. Few upper class male prostitutes work as street hustlers.

Boy Prostitutes, Drugs, and Alcohol

Most boy prostitutes use and abuse alcohol, drugs, or both.[54] In a Huckleberry House Project study of male and female adolescent prostitution, 83 percent of the boy prostitutes had tried marijuana, while 77 percent had continued using it.[55] Another study reported that 29 percent of teenage boy prostitutes used hard drugs on a regular basis and 42 percent were heavy drinkers or alcoholics.[56] In Weisberg's study, the reason most prostitutes gave for using drugs was the pleasure received from "being high."[57] In a study by the California legislature of substance abuse and homeless youth, 63 percent of the teenage prostitutes with substance abuse problems did not believe they had a problem.[58] The study also found that 75 percent of the youth involved in prostitution had problems with substance abuse, compared to 36 percent of those not involved in prostitution activities.

Criminal Justice System Contact with Adolescent Male Prostitutes

Studies indicate that although boy prostitutes are more likely to engage in other offenses than girl prostitutes, they are less likely to come into contact with the criminal justice system. D. Sweeney estimated that 70 percent of male juvenile prostitutes never come into contact with the police;[59] while studies show that 75 percent of female juvenile prostitutes have had some contact with the criminal justice system.[60] When young male prostitutes are arrested, rarely is it for prostitution offenses. They are most likely to be arrested as runaways, for petty offenses, alcohol- and drug-related crimes, and violent offenses.[61]

Experts attribute the low rate of adolescent male prostitute contact with law enforcement to greater difficulty in identifying them compared to adolescent female streetwalkers.[62] Laws are also nonuniform from state to state with respect to what undercover officers are permitted to do in staking out and arresting young prostitutes. Male prostitutes tend to generally be more successful in avoiding police stings and entrapment than female prostitutes.

There are studies that contradict the view that boy prostitutes have little contact with law enforcement. For example, Weisberg reported a high rate of adolescent male prostitute involvement with the criminal justice system.[63] An estimated two-thirds of the prostitutes sampled had been arrested at least once, with prostitution-related crimes constituting 33 percent of the arrests.

NOTES

1. R. Barri Flowers, *Runaway Kids and Teenage Prostitution: America's Lost, Abandoned, and Sexually Exploited Children* (Westport: Greenwood Press, 2001), pp. 129–30; R. Barri Flowers, *Children and Criminality: The Child as Victim and Perpetrator* (Westport: Greenwood Press, 1986), p. 81.
2. R. Barri Flowers, *The Victimization and Exploitation of Women and Children: A Study of the Physical, Mental and Sexual Maltreatment in the United States* (Jefferson: McFarland, 1994), pp. 82, 172.
3. R. Barri Flowers, *Female Crime, Criminals and Cellmates: An Exploration of Female Criminality and Delinquency* (Jefferson: McFarland, 1995), pp. 103, 149.
4. Robin Lloyd, *For Money or Love: Boy Prostitution in America* (New York: Ballantine, 1976), p. 211.
5. R. Barri Flowers, *The Prostitution of Women and Girls* (Jefferson: McFarland, 2005), p. 134.
6. S. Caukins and N. Coombs, "The Psychodynamics of Male Prostitution," *American Journal of Psychotherapy 30* (1976): 441–51.
7. *Ibid.*, p. 441.
8. Donald M. Allen, "Young Male Prostitutes: A Psychosocial Study," *Archives of Sexual Behavior 9* (1980): 399–426.
9. Dan Waldorf and Sheigla Murphy, "Intravenous Drug Use and Syringe-Sharing Practices of Call Men and Hustlers," in Martin A. Plant, ed., *AIDS, Drugs, and Prostitution* (London: Routledge, 1990), pp. 109–31.
10. *Ibid.*
11. *Ibid.*
12. Allen, "Young Male Prostitutes," p. 418.
13. *Ibid.*, pp. 419–20; R. Barri Flowers, *Runaway Kids and Teenage Prostitution,* pp. 131–35.
14. Flowers, *The Prostitution of Women and Girls,* p. 137.
15. Magnus J. Seng, "Child Sexual Abuse and Adolescent Prostitution: A Comparative Analysis," *Adolescence 24* (1989): 671.
16. U.S. Department of Justice, Office of Juvenile Justice and Delinquency Prevention, *Prostitution of Children and Child-Sex Tourism: An Analysis of Domestic and International Responses* (Arlington: National Center for Missing & Exploited Children, 1999), p. 3.
17. Allen, "Young Male Prostitutes," pp. 409–18.
18. N. Coombs, "Male Prostitution: A Psychosocial View of Behavior," *American Journal of Orthopsychiatry 44* (1974): 782–98.
19. C. Earls and H. David, "A Psychosocial Study of Male Prostitution," *Archives of Sexual Behavior 18* (1989): 401–19.
20. Richard Green, *Sexual Science and the Law* (Cambridge: Harvard University Press, 1992), p. 194.
21. *Ibid.*; Caukins and Coombs, "The Psychodynamics of Male Prostitution," p. 446.
22. Coombs, "Male Prostitution," pp. 782–89.
23. Earls and David, "A Psychosocial Study of Male Prostitution," pp. 401–19.
24. Caukins and Coombs, "The Psychodynamics of Male Prostitution," p. 450; D. McNamara, "Male Prostitution in American Cities: A Socioeconomic or Pathological Phenomenon?" *American Journal of Orthopsychiatry 35* (1965): 204.
25. Flowers, *The Prostitution of Women and Girls,* p. 138; R. Barri Flowers, *Runaway Kids and Teenage Prostitution,* p. 135.
26. Caukins and Coombs, "The Psychodynamics of Male Prostitution," p. 446.
27. Flowers, *The Prostitution of Women and Girls,* p. 138; Joan J. Johnson, *Teen Prostitution*

(Danbury: Franklin Watts, 1992), p. 118.

28. Caukins and Coombs, "The Psychodynamics of Male Prostitution," pp. 446, 450; Green, *Sexual Science and the Law,* p. 194.

29. Flowers, *The Prostitution of Women and Girls,* pp. 138–39.

30. *Ibid.,* pp. 143–44; R. Barri Flowers, *Runaway Kids and Teenage Prostitution,* pp. 135–36.

31. Flowers, *The Prostitution of Women and Girls,* p. 143; Flowers, *The Victimization and Exploitation of Women and Children,* pp. 88–89; Waldorf and Murphy, "Intravenous Drug Use and Syringe-Sharing Practices of Call Men and Hustlers," pp. 109–27.

32. Cited in *Prostitution of Children and Child-Sex Tourism,* pp. 8, 86.

33. Jim A. Cates, "Adolescent Male Prostitution by Choice," *Child & Adolescent Social Work 6* (1989): 155–56.

34. M. A. Chiasson, A. R. Lifson, R. L. Stoneburner, W. Ewing, D. Hilderbrandt, and H. W. Jaffe, "HIV-1 Seroprevalence in Male and Female Prostitutes in New York City," Abstracts from the Sixth International Conference on AIDS (Stockholm, June, 1988).

35. U. Tirelli, D. Erranto, and D. Serraint, "HIV-1 Seroprevalence in Male Prostitutes in Northeastern Italy," *Journal of Acquired Immune Deficiency Syndromes 1* (1988): 414–15.

36. Martin A. Plant, "Sex Work, Alcohol, Drugs, and AIDS," in Martin A. Plant, ed., *AIDS, Drugs, and Prostitution* (London: Routledge, 1990), pp. 7–8.

37. U.S. Department of Justice, Federal Bureau of Investigation, *Crime in the United States: Uniform Crime Reports 2004* (Washington: Government Printing Office, 2005), pp. 287, 289.

38. *Ibid.,* p. 292; Flowers, *The Prostitution of Women and Girls,* p. 139.

39. *Uniform Crime Reports 2004,* p. 292.

40. *Prostitution of Children and Child-Sex Tourism,* p. 2.

41. *Ibid.*

42. *Ibid.*

43. Quoted in Alfred Danna, "Juvenile Male Prostitution: How Can We Reduce the Problem?" *USA Today 113* (May, 1988): 87.

44. *Ibid.,* p. 88.

45. R. Barri Flowers, *Runaway Kids and Teenage Prostitution,* p. 131; Flowers, *The Victimization and Exploitation of Women and Children,* p. 87.

46. Cited in Hilary Abramson, "Sociologists Try to Reach Young Hustlers," *Sacramento Bee* (September 3, 1984), p. A8.

47. Tamar Steiber, "The Boys Who Sell Sex to Men in San Francisco," *Sacramento Bee* (March 4, 1984), p. A22.

48. D. Kelly Weisberg, *Children of the Night; A Study of Adolescent Prostitution* (Lexington: Lexington Books, 1985), p. 61.

49. Johnson, *Teen Prostitution,* p. 110.

50. Weisberg, *Children of the Night,* p. 19.

51. *Ibid.,* p. 40.

52. Johnson, *Teen Prostitution,* p. 110.

53. *Ibid.,* pp. 111–12.

54. R. Barri Flowers, *Kids Who Commit Adult Crimes: Serious Criminality by Juvenile Offenders* (Binghamton: Haworth Press, 2002), p. 50.

55. Sparky Harlan, Luanne L. Rodgers, and Brian Flattary, *Male and Female Adolescent Prostitution: Huckleberry House Sexual Minority Youth Services Project* (Washington: U.S. Department of Health and Human Services, 1981), p. 22.

56. Allen, "Young Male Prostitutes," pp. 399–426.

57. Weisberg, *Children of the Night,* p. 58.

58. Cited in *Prostitution of Children and Child-Sex Tourism,* p. 9.
59. Cited in Stieber, "The Boys Who Sell Sex to Men in San Francisco," p. A22.
60. Weisberg, *Children of the Night,* pp. 124–28.
61. Flowers, *The Prostitution of Women and Girls,* p. 143; R. Barri Flowers, *Runaway Kids and Teenage Prostitution,* pp. 27–43.
62. R. Barri Flowers, *The Adolescent Criminal: An Examination of Today's Juvenile Offender* (Jefferson: McFarland, 1990), pp. 62–63.
63. Weisberg, *Children of the Night,* p. 75.

Part VI

EXPLAINING SEX CRIMINALITY

Chapter 16

THEORIES ON SEX CRIMES
AND CRIMINALS

The literature is replete with theories on the causes and factors of sexual offending and sex criminality. Many of these have been dismissed as empirically weak, biased, or otherwise seriously flawed. However, a number of longstanding theoretical perspectives on sex crimes and criminals continue to be widely supported by criminologists, social scientists, and other experts on sexual abuse and crimes. These include biological, psychological, social-based, childhood sexual victimization, cycle of abuse, sexual aggression, sexual addiction, and multiple-factor theories. This notwithstanding, no single hypothesis can account for the heterogeneous nature, characteristics, and motivations of the sex offender. Current theoretical approaches to sex crime causation will be explored in this chapter.

BIOLOGICAL THEORIES

Biological theories on sex offending contend that some persons are predisposed to or inherit tendencies to commit sexual crimes, or are otherwise biologically influenced in their sexual deviance. The origin of biological determinism is credited to Italian criminologist Cesare Lombroso.[1] Highly influenced by Charles Darwin's theory of evolution, Lombroso posited during the late nineteenth century that criminals are a product of atavism or throwbacks to primitive genetic forms. In his "born criminal" hypothesis, Lombroso found prostitutes in particular to possess certain primitive hereditary characteristics not present in normal women.[2] A number of early biological theorists contributed to this school of thought in explaining criminal behavior to one degree or another.[3] Most such propositions have been soundly rejected over the course of time as being unscientific, too simplistic, and irrational in explaining criminal behavior.

Modern biological research into genetic transmission of deviant behavior-including sexual offending, delinquency, and alcoholism–have examined criminality in terms of genetics, biochemistry, neuroscience, psychophysiology, endocrinology, and other behavioral sciences.[4] Some researchers have found a greater occurrence of certain biological conditions among sex offenders. The risk factors include "chromosomal abnormalities, congenital disturbances, hormonal abnormalities, and neuropsychological deficits."[5] The psychiatric term *pedophilia* implies that some individuals may have a predisposition to a sexual preference for children over adults.[6] Most biological theorists today also recognize the important influence of environmental variables in sex and violent criminality.

SOCIAL LEARNING THEORY

Social learning theory is believed by many to be the most significant theoretical perspective among professionals and researchers in the treatment of sexual offenders. First developed by Robert Burgess and Ronald Akers as differential association-reinforcement theory, the social learning theory proposes that sexual abuse and sexual violence are learned behaviors over the course of one's development.[7] This sexual deviancy is learned a number of ways. One is early exposure to sexual abuse as a witness or victim, which may result in the development of similar sexually abusive or aggressive tendencies. Learned sexual aggression can also occur through social interaction with other sexually aggressive or abusive individuals, who may represent their primary source of reinforcement. Exposure to pornographic or sexually explicit materials is also associated with normalizing such behavior in both child and adult sex offenders.[8]

Though social learning theory's general principles have been empirically supported, critics have posited that nonsocial reinforcement is more influential than social reinforcement in the causation of sexual aggression and other deviant behavior.[9] There are also questions about the ability of social learning theory to be adequately tested for its propositions.

STRESS THEORY

Stress theorists postulate that violent sexual behavior may result as a means to cope with severe stresses in a violent individual's life, either from a single trauma or the gradual accumulation of various sources of trauma. Robert Mawson held that such violent behavior may be directed towards a family member or a peer when the person experiencing stress wishes to continue the intense emotional physical contact with the victim, even if such person is the source of the stress.[10] Donna Hamparian's study further supports the stress theory of violence, finding that sexually violent delinquents are typically characterized by feelings of low self-esteem, weak impulse control, rage, lack of empathy towards others, and frustration.[11]

PERSONALITY-DISORDER THEORIES

Personality-disorder theories of sexual offending tend to focus on personality flaws and emotional disorders in explaining sexual abuse and sexually aggressive individuals. One influential personality-disorder theory is the psychopathic personality theory.[12] In modern psychiatry, the psychopath is generally defined as an individual who is antisocial, amoral, mentally unstable, hostile, egocentric, callous, and fearless while having limited social ties. According to William McCord and Joan McCord, who have done extensive research in psychopathology, the psychopath is characterized by guiltlessness and lovelessness, in particular.[13] The researchers found that the psychopathic personality originates in brain damage, physical trauma, and extreme childhood deprivation.

Psychologists have found that some psychopathic or sociopathic sex offenders suffer from attachment disorders. These occur when the normal physical and emotional attachment and bonding between a parent and child is absent.[14] The absence of such an attachment can cause such abused, neglected, or isolated children as adults to become antisocial, chronic career criminals, including sex offenders, with little regard for others, telling the truth, or experiencing guilt.

Another notable personality-disorder theory in explaining sexually violent behavior is the criminal personality theory. Established by Samuel Yochelson and Stanton Samenow after years of working with violent criminal patients, the theory proposes that violent offenders found normal family interaction to be dull and sought excitement.[15] Violent crime such as rape was found to be the ultimate form of excitement.

Personality theories have been criticized as empirically weak and, in effect, reject the body of evidence that supports social and environmental causes of sex criminality.

BRAIN DISORDER THEORIES

Some clinicians and researchers have studied the relationship between brain disorders and violent sex offenders. Some research has shown abnormal electroencephalogram (EEG) recordings of the brain activity in criminals, relating this to violent and aggressive behavior, limited impulse control, destructive tendencies, and weak social adaptation.[16] Studies have further linked brain dysfunction to such learning disabilities as dyslexia, aphasia, and hyperactivity which, according to some researchers, predisposes these individuals to violence and other antisocial behavior.[17]

Brain damage in violent sex offenders has been associated with a history of child abuse. One Canadian study reported that brain damage to the temporal lobes may be related to deviant sexual behavior.[18] Other findings have linked violent criminality to brain damage.[19] The significance of head trauma in the development of sexually abusive conduct can be seen in studies in which serious neuropsychological abnormalities were found in up to 96 percent of the sexual abusers sampled.[20]

SEXUAL ADDICTION THEORIES

Sexual addiction, defined as a "mood altering" dependence on sex, is seen by some experts as a prominent factor in explaining sexually violent behavior. Some sex addicts resort to sexual abuse and sexual violence to satisfy their cravings when normal sexual relations are insufficient or are adversely affected by guilt, shame, or emotional pain.[21] Other persons suffering from narcissistic wounds—any type of childhood trauma leaving the child unprepared for adult independence—may become sex addicts as a reflection of insecurities, fragility, selfishness, and psychological stresses.[22] These individuals often regard forbidden, secretive sex as a powerful and addictive drug.

Studies have found that a high percentage of sex abusers are, in fact, sex addicts. More than half the imprisoned sex offenders in a Wyoming survey were diagnosed as having a sexual addiction.[23] Another study found that nearly 40 percent of the rapists were considered sex addicts.[24] Around three out of every four child molesters are believed to be sex addicts.[25] Some prostitutes enter and remain in business due to sexual addiction and the addictiveness of the sex trade industry itself.[26]

The relationship between sexual addiction and childhood sexual abuse has been shown to be significant. According to the Institute for Behavioral Medicine, 81 percent of sex addicts studied reported being victims of child sexual abuse.[27] Seventy-two percent disclosed being physically abused, while 97 percent felt they were victimized by emotional abuse. For these individuals, sex is seen as a "pacifier and best friend," or medicine to cope with their emotional pain.[28]

Sexual addiction is often a progressive disorder, whereby the sexually traumatized child may ultimately become a sexually abusive child or adult.[29]

Though sex addicts represent only a minority of sex abusers, surveys show that sexually compulsive sex offenders can commit hundreds of sex crimes before being caught.[30]

THE CYCLE OF SEXUAL ABUSE AND SEXUAL OFFENDING THEORIES

Some theorists explain sexual abuse and violence as resulting from a pattern of intergenerational sexual offending. A cycle of sexual abuse and aberrant sexual behavior has been examined in both a biological and sociological context. Early researchers, such as Richard Dugdale[31] and Henry Goddard[32] documented the generations of prostitution, fornication, and delinquency within certain families. More recently some remote populations in the United States and Canada, where families have lived for generations, have been studied. The rate of sexual abuse victimization among these populations is believed to be quite high.[33]

The strong correlation between intrafamilial and intergenerational sexual or physical abuse and sex offenses or violent crimes has been supported in a number of other studies. Christopher Ounsted and colleagues postulated that violent parents often come from families where violence has passed from one generation to the next.[34] H. E. Simmons posited that "a brutal parent tends to produce a brutal child."[35] In a study of chronically violent juvenile offenders, Jeanne Cyriaque concluded that "violence-dominated lifestyles [of] . . . sexually and physically abusing families, particularly characterize juvenile murderers and sex offenders."[36]

While there is still much debate about the validity of intergenerational propositions on sexual offending and violent behavior, most sexual abuse experts give greater credence to the environmental and learned behavior cycle of sex offending than the biological determinants.

MULTIPLE-FACTOR THEORIES OF SEXUAL CRIMINALITY

In response to some of the weaknesses inherent in single-factor theories on sexual criminality, a number of multiple-factor theories have been forwarded in recent years. These theories address sexual offending in terms of multiple causes that separately and in combination create conditions that may result in sexual deviance. Though multiple approaches to explaining why sex crimes are committed are not without their own shortcomings, most criminologists and other experts in antisocial sexual behavior find such theories to be more substantive in understanding the processes through which sex offenders develop their patterns of behavior. Two of the more notable multiple-factor theories of sexual offending were proposed by David Finkelhor and S. E. Wolf.

Four-Factor Framework Theory

The four-factor framework theory of sexual abuse was put forth by Finkelhor in an attempt to explain why adults sexually abuse children.[37] Factor One involves the emotional congruence child abusers seem to have with children. Evidence indicates that child molesters regard children with special meaning, who they see as weak and nonthreatening.[38] Other factors contributing to emotional congruence with children include the child molester's own history of child abuse and identifying with their abuser.

Factor Two identifies the processes in which an adult becomes sexually aroused by a child. Studies show that when compared with nonchild abusers, many extra-familial child abusers find themselves more aroused by children than adults.[39] Given that a high percentage of child sex offenders were themselves victims of child sexual abuse, is to many evidence that "attraction to deviant stimuli has been conditioned or modeled through such early childhood sexual experiences."[40]

Factor Three explores why certain sex offenders are blocked from being able to satisfy their sexual and emotional needs through normal adult relationships. Finkelhor breaks this down into two types of blockage. The first, *developmental blockage,* takes place where the sex offender is unable to relate normally to peers. Research has shown that male child abusers often have trouble relating to women and have weak social skills and sexual anxieties.[41] The second, *situational blockage,* occurs when there is a normal adult relationship, per se, but an absence of a sexual relationship with a consenting adult.

Factor Four endeavors to understand why normal inhibitions against child sexual offending are either absent or overcome in the sex offender. Explanations include lack of impulse control, senility, learning difficulties, and substance abuse. An "incest avoidance mechanism" has also been considered empirically. This hypothesis proposes that stepfathers have less inhibitions in being sexually attracted to a child than biological fathers. This is supported by the much greater incidence of stepfather-stepdaughter incest than biological father-biological daughter incest as reported in the literature.[42]

Finkelhor also established four preconditions for sexual abuse to occur as follows:

- **Motivation to sexually abuse**–varies depending upon the abuser's background and circumstances.

- **Overcoming internal inhibitors**–by developing cognitive distortions in justifying behavior or using drugs or alcohol as disinhibitors.
- **Overcoming external inhibitors**–by creating situations in which the sexual abuse can occur and overcoming any external obstacles that may arise.
- **Overcoming the child victim's resistance**–through coaxing, coercion, intimidation, violence, or targeting children viewed as vulnerable or easy to molest.

The primary limitation of Finkelhor's four-factor theory of sexual offending is that it does not account for female sex abusers. This model further fails to explain in Factor Two why some people who have not been victims of child sexual abuse still become sex offenders. However, it does succeed as a theoretical framework in addressing the causes of child sexual abuse.

Sexual Assault Cycle Theory

A multifactor approach to explaining sexual offending was also formulated by Wolf. In incorporating developmental, social, cultural, and situational factors, his major premise is that early life results in the development of a certain type of personality and a predisposition to developing a deviant sexuality.[43] According to Wolf, sexual offenders' early experiences typically include sexual, physical, and emotional abuse, neglect, and growing up in a dysfunctional family. He postulates that this early history of abuse acts as "potentiators" in the development of sexual deviance. These potentiators cause the child to learn inappropriate behavioral patterns and, as an adult, to develop a self-image and feelings that promote being powerful and able to do as they please. Further, the potentiators weaken inhibitions against sexual offending so that the more potentiators in the individual's life, the greater the risk of becoming an adult sexual offender. Other disinhibitors in perpetrating sexual offenses include alcohol and drug use and pornography, which may increase arousal and/or the probability of acting out sexual fantasies.[44]

Wolf's cycle of offending was developed as a result of his work with adult sexual offenders in explaining the correlation between factors leading to sexual deviancy. The cycle typically starts with the sex offender possessing a poor self-image in which he expects failure or rejection. In defending against this, he becomes isolated, during which he copes through compensatory fantasies and sexual escapism.

The sex criminal then proceeds to plan the sexual offense, when and where, and grooms a potential victim. The offense tends to reflect the sex offender's own needs and desires, possibly increasing in severity over the course of time. Following the offense, the sex offender typically experiences a time of transitory guilt, alleviating this through distorted thinking and promises of not to repeat the offense. However, awareness that he has committed a sex crime results in a further blow to his self-image, taking him back to the beginning of the cycle of sexual offending.

According to Wolf, understanding a sex offender's cycle is critical in his assessment and treatment. Though many professionals support this model, it does have some drawbacks. For example, some sex offenders' developmental history and patterns of sexual offending fall outside the premise set forth in this model. The sexual assault cycle also fails to explain why many men with a history of victimization do not become sex offenders. Furthermore, though the theory can be said to account for most sex offenders, it is not applicable to all criminally sexual deviants. Nevertheless, Wolfe's multifactor approach to sexual offending is well regarded by those treating sex offenders in establishing a framework for understanding the development and dynamics of aberrant sexual behavior.

NOTES

1. Cesare Lombroso, *Crime, Its Causes and Remedies* (Boston: Little, Brown, 1918); Cesare Lombroso and William Ferrero, *The Female Offender* (New York; Appleton, 1900); Cesare Lombroso, *The Criminal Man* (Milan: Hoepli, 1876).

2. Lombroso and Ferrero, *The Female Offender;* R. Barri Flowers, *The Prostitution of Women and Girls* (Jefferson: McFarland, 2005), pp. 23–24.

3. *See, for example,* E. A. Hooten, *The American Criminal: An Anthropological Study* (Cambridge: Harvard University Press, 1939); S. Glueck and E. T. Glueck, *Physique and Delinquency* (New York: Harper & Row, 1956); Diana H. Fishbein, "Biological Perspectives in Criminology," in Dean G. Rojek and Gary F. Jensen, eds., *Exploring Delinquency: Causes and Control* (Los Angeles: Roxbury, 1996), pp. 102–8.

4. Fishbein, "Biological Perspectives in Criminology," p. 102; R. Barri Flowers, *The Adolescent Criminal: An Examination of Today's Juvenile Offender* (Jefferson: McFarland, 1990), pp. 111–17.

5. Robert E. Freeman-Longo and Geral T. Blanchard, *Sexual Abuse in America: Epidemic of the 21st Century* (Brandon: Safer Society Press, 1998), p. 57; F. Valcour, "The Treatment of Child Sex Abusers in the Church," in S. Rossetti, ed., *Slayer of the Soul* (Mystic: Twenty-Third Publications, 1990), pp. 44–66.

6. Freeman-Longo and Blanchard, *Sexual Abuse in America,* p. 57.

7. Robert L. Burgess and Ronald L. Akers, "A Differential Association-Reinforcement Theory of Criminal Behavior," *Social Problems 14* (1966): 128–47; Ronald L. Akers, *Deviant Behavior: A Social Learning Approach,* 3rd Ed. (Belmont: Wadsworth, 1985). *See also* A. Bandura, *Social Learning Theory* (Englewood Cliffs: Prentice Hall, 1977).

8. Freeman-Longo and Blanchard, *Sexual Abuse in America,* pp. 56–57.

9. Flowers, *The Adolescent Criminal,* pp. 130–31.

10. Robert Mawson, "Aggression, Attachment, Behavior, and Crimes of Violence," in Travis Hirshi and Michael Gottfredson, eds., *Understanding Crime* (Beverly Hills: Sage, 1981), p. 12.

11. Donna Hamparian et al., *The Violent Few* (Lexington: Lexington Books, 1978), p. 210.

12. Flowers, *The Adolescent Criminal,* pp. 120–21.

13. William McCord and Joan McCord, *The Psychopath* (Princeton: Van Nostrand, 1964).

14. Freeman-Longo and Blanchard, *Sexual Abuse in America,* p. 60; K. Magid and C. McKelvey, *High Risk Children Without a Conscience* (New York: Bantam, 1989); R. Hare, *Without Conscience: The Disturbing World of Psychopaths Among Us* (New York: Pocket, 1995).

15. Samuel Yochelson and Stanton E. Samenow, *The Criminal Personality,* Vol. 1 (New York: Jason Arsonson, 1976); Stanton E. Samenow, *Inside the Criminal Mind* (New York: Time Books, 1984).

16. Vicki Pollock, Sarnoff A. Mednick, and William F. Gabrielli, "Crime Causation: Biological Theories," in Sanford H. Kadish, ed., *Encyclopedia of Crime and Justice,* Vol. 1 (New York: Free Press, 1983).

17. Harold R. Holzman, "Learning Disabilities and Juvenile Delinquency: Biological and Sociological Theories," in C. R. Jeffrey, ed., *Biology and Crime* (Beverly Hills: Sage, 1979), pp. 77–86.

18. J. Pukins and R. Langevin, "Brain Correlates of Penile Erection," in R. Langevin, ed., *Erotic Preference: Gender Identity and Aggression in Men* (Hillsdale: Lawrence Erlbaum, 1985).

19. N. Pallone, *Rehabilitating Criminal Sexual Psychopaths* (New Brunswick: Transaction Publishers, 1990).

20. *See, for example,* A. Corley, D. Corley, J. Walker, and S. Walker, "The Possibility of Organic Left Posterior Hemisphere Dysfunction as a Contributing Factor in Sex-Offending Behavior," *Sexual Addiction & Compulsivity 1,* 4 (1994): 337–46.

21. Freeman-Longo and Blanchard, *Sexual Abuse in America,* pp. 63–64.

22. *Ibid.,* pp. 61–62.

23. G. Blanchard, "Differential Diagnosis of Sex Offenders: Distinguishing Characteristics of the Sex Addict," *American Journal of Preventive Psychiatry and Neurology 2,* 3 (1990): 45–47.

24. *Ibid.*

25. Freeman-Longo and Blanchard, *Sexual Abuse in America,* p. 63.

26. Flowers, *The Prostitution of Women and Girls,* p. 28.

27. P. Carnes, *Don't Call It Love* (New York: Bantam Books, 1991).

28. Freeman-Longo and Blanchard, *Sexual Abuse in America,* p. 64.

29. P. Carnes, *Out of the Shadows* (Minneapolis: CompCare, 1983).

30. R. Freeman-Longo and R. Wall, "Changing a Lifetime of Sexual Crime," *Psychology Today 20,* 3 (March, 1986), pp. 58–64.

31. Richard L. Dugdale, *The Jukes: A Study in Crime, Pauperism, and Heredity* (New York: Putnam, 1877).

32. Henry H. Goddard, *Feeblemindedness, Its Causes and Consequences* (New York: Macmillan, 1914).

33. Freeman-Longo and Blanchard, *Sexual Abuse in America,* p. 58.

34. Christopher Ounsted, Rhoda Oppenheimer, and Janet Lindsay, "The Psychopathology and Psychotherapy of the Families, Aspects Bonding Failure," in A. Frankin, ed., *Concerning Child Abuse* (London: Churchill Livingston, 1975).

35. H. E. Simmons, *Protective Services for Children,* 2nd Ed. (Sacramento, Citadel Press, 1970).

36. Jeanne Cyriaque, "The Chronic Serious Offender: How Illinois Juveniles 'Match Up'," *Illinois* (February, 1982), p. 4–5.

37. David Finkelhor, *Child Sexual Abuse: New Theory and Research* (New York: Free Press, 1984).

38. K. Howells, "Some Meanings of Children for Paedophiles," in M. Cook and F. Wilson, eds., *Love and Attraction* (Oxford: Pergamon, 1979).

39. Dawn Fisher, "Adult Sex Offenders: Who Are They? Why And How Do They Do It?"

in Tony Morrison, Marcus Erooga, and Richard C. Beckett, eds., *Sexual Offending Against Children: Assessment and Treatment of Male Abusers* (London: Routledge, 1994), p. 21.

40. Ibid.

41. J. H. Panton, "Personality Differences Appearing Between Rapists of Adults, Rapists of Children and Non-Violent Sexual Molesters of Children," *Research Communications in Psychology, Psychiatry and Behaviors 3,* 4 (1978): 385–93.

42. Fisher, "Adult Sex Offenders," p. 22; R. Barri Flowers, *The Victimization and Exploitation of Women and Children: A Study of Physical, Mental and Sexual Maltreatment in the United States* (Jefferson: McFarland, 1994), p. 64.

43. S. C. Wolf, "A Multifactor Model of Deviant Sexuality," paper presented at the Third International Conference on Victimology, Lisbon, 1984.

44. Fisher, "Adult Sex Offenders," p. 18.

Part VII

CRIMINAL JUSTICE SYSTEM AND SEX OFFENDERS

Chapter 17

SEX CRIME LAWS

S ex crime statutes have long since been in force in the United States, out-
lawing most types of sexual offenses including sexual homicide, rape,
incest, child molestation and sexual exploitation, prostitution, and other
criminal sexual paraphilias and perversions. However, before the late 1970s
some loopholes existed in the law. These made it difficult, if not impossible,
to prosecute certain types of sex offenders such as marital rapists and child
sexual exploiters, and to keep track of repeat or dangerous sex criminals in
the community. Furthermore, legislation was lacking to protect sex crime victims from character assassination and other attacks to their credibility in
favor of sex offender rights.

Public outcry about these injustices along with increased awareness about
child sexual abuse and other sexual offenses and offenders have since resulted in a number of reforms of sex crime laws. The feminist movement has
been influential in these reforms, particularly relating to criminalizing rape
in marriage and decriminalizing women's prostitution. In spite of the impact
of more sex crime laws in society, there is often nonuniformity between federal and state laws or from state to state. There is also much debate among
criminologists, social scientists and other sex crime experts on the effectiveness of sex crime statutes in reducing sex criminality and protecting citizens
from sex offenders.[1]

This chapter will examine sex crimes, sexual offenders, and the law.

RAPE CRIME LAWS

Forcible rape is considered a crime in every state. Legally defined as intercourse or sexual penetration of a woman by a man other than her husband,
by force and against her will, rape is a reflection of traditional common law
and statute law.[2] Rape laws have historically been meant to include all types

of rape. However, they excluded rapes in marriage, rapes where consensual issues conflicted with traditional law, rapes that could not be corroborated by physical evidence or a third party, and other types of forced sexual assaults that did not include unwanted intercourse of vaginal penetration.

Rape law reforms in recent years have addressed these discrepancies and issues, abolishing "several evidentiary rules that previously singled out rape as a crime to be tried differently from other crimes."[3] These included "the requirement that there be special corroboration in rape cases, proof of resistance, and special instructions to the jury about the need for caution in assessing the testimony of the victim."[4]

Rape has also been redefined in many rape statutes, making it a gender-neutral crime and broadening the acts that can be considered rape such as oral and anal forced sexual relations, sexual penetration with an object, and even inappropriate touching of private body parts.[5] In some instances, the term *rape* has been replaced with "criminal sexual assault," "sexual assault," or "sexual battery" in recognizing rape as a crime of violence as opposed to a sexual crime, per se.

Expanding the parameters of rape was seen by reformers as a means to increase the rate of conviction, assuming that "juries might convict more defendants on a wider range of offenses if the definitions and penalties were more closely tailored to fit the circumstances."[6] Violent criminal sexual assaults, such as sexually based murders, are a reflection of rape law reforms and homicide statutes in convicting and treating sexual offenders.

According to Richard Posner and Katharine Silbaugh in their book, *A Guide to America's Sex Laws,* rape reform laws in most states are based on the reforms seen in the Michigan statute,[7] the New York statute,[8] and the Model Penal Code.[9] The researchers wrote:

> The Model Penal Code emphasizes consent but avoids questions of the victim's subjective nonconsent as much as possible, focusing on outward manifestations of nonconsent such as physical resistance, corroborating testimony, or fresh complaint.
>
> . . . The Michigan statute removes the language of rape entirely from its code, relying instead on degrees of sexual assault. [It] was also the first to use gender-neutral language and to grade offenses equally regardless of the sexes of the parties, a practice that is now very common in sexual assault statutes.
>
> . . . The New York statute . . . is closer to the Model Penal Code. . . . [It] does not focus on the resistance of the victim to the extent that the Model Penal Code does, and it is possible to be guilty of the highest level of offense without severe physical injury to the victim or where the victim and the defendant are social companions.[10]

Rape Shield Laws

Rape shield laws further reflect efforts to reform rape laws and built-in biases. These statutes limit the admissibility of testimony with respect to a rape victim's prior sexual behavior. According to the federal rape shield statute in Federal Rule of Evidence 412, "evidence offered to prove a victim engaged in 'other sexual behavior' or to prove an alleged victim's sexual predisposition is generally inadmissible except under certain circumstances."[11] Additionally, testimony by a character witness regarding the reputation or beliefs about the sexual history of a rape victim is excluded.[12]

Many state rape shield statutes fall into line with the federal statute.[13] One study found that more than forty states had passed legislation placing limits on the ability of the defense to present evidence regarding the victim's sexual past.[14] However, some have argued that such laws violate the Sixth Amendment rights of the defendant to confront his accuser, resulting in the repeal of some states' rape shield laws.[15] Furthermore, even where rape shield statutes are in effect, judges still have the discretion in many instances to admit evidence about a victim's sexual history that they deem to be relevant to the defense's case.

Marital Rape Laws

A marital rape exemption prevented states from applying rape laws to husband rapists in this country until the mid 1970s. Fueled by the women's movement, in 1976 Nebraska became the first state to remove the marital rape exemption from the law. Two years later, Oregon became the first state to prosecute a spouse rapist who was still living with his wife victim at the time of the rape.[16] Today, marital rape is a crime in every state under at least one section of a state's sexual offense codes.[17] However, in thirty-three states, exemptions to prosecuting husbands and cohabitating mates who rape still exist under certain conditions.[18]

CHILD SEXUAL ABUSE LAWS

Since the mid 1970s, a number of important federal and state laws have been enacted to protect children from child sexual abuse and child sexual exploiters. These include laws against child abuse, incest, child molestation, child pornography, reporting laws, and a number of statutes aimed at helping to track down or keep track of child sex offenders.

Child Abuse Prevention and Treatment Act

The Child Abuse and Prevention and Treatment Act[19] became federal law in 1974 and was amended in 1978 under the Child Abuse Prevention and Treatment and Adoption Reform Act.[20] The act defined child abuse and neglect, while providing for

> (1) the establishment of a National Center on Child Abuse and Neglect, (2) increasing public awareness on child maltreatment, detection and reporting, (3) assisting states and local communities in developing more effective mechanisms for delivery of services to families, (4) providing training and technical assistance to state and local communities in dealing with the problem of child abuse and neglect, and (5) supporting research into causal and preventative measures in child victimizations.[21]

In order to qualify for federal funds, states are required to meet several criteria. These include a comprehensive definition of child abuse and neglect, specific reporting procedures for child abuse, and the investigation of reports of child abuse and neglect.

Incest and Child Molestation Laws

Incest is considered a felony in most states and a crime in every state, though definitions of what constitutes incest are not uniform.[22] According to the Model Penal Code, criminal incest is limited to sexual relations with "biological parents or other ancestors, descendants, and siblings of the whole or half blood, with relations between nonblood relatives only being incestuous as between a parent and child."[23] Most incest statutes are intended to prevent "sexual imposition by people in a position of familial power over others."[24] The majority of prosecutions for incest tend to involve incestuous fathers or stepfathers having sexual relations with daughters or stepdaughters, usually under or just over the legal age of consent.[25]

Other types of intrafamilial incest or intergenerational sexual abuse may fall under various sex crime laws including those pertaining to criminal sexual assault, statutory rape, age of consent, abuse of position of authority or trust, and other laws addressing criminal sexual paraphilias.[26]

Delayed discovery civil laws also exist in some states, allowing for the suspension of the statute of limitations in certain sexual abuse cases in which victims may have repressed memories or otherwise been unaware of the sexual abuse, preventing redress.[27] Court decisions involving delayed discovery have worked for and against child sexual abuse victims.[28]

Reporting Laws

Reporting of suspected child sexual abuse is mandated by law in all fifty states. All health care workers, including dentists and optometrists, are required to report possible child abuse. Penalties for failure to do so vary from state to state. In California, for example, failing to make a child abuse report is considered a misdemeanor and is punishable by a jail term of up to six months.[29] Studies have shown that there is often noncompliance in reporting the sexual abuse of children. A survey of physicians in Washington found that nearly six in ten did not report child sexual abuse, and two-thirds of the respondents believed it to be a private matter.[30] In a national survey of psychologists, one in four had never reported cases of suspected child abuse, while one in three had only reported it on some occasions.[31]

Background Screening Laws

In response to concerns about the sexual abuse and exploitation of children by child care personnel, federal and state legislation has been enacted in recent years to combat the problem. In 1993, the National Child Protection Act was passed by Congress, leading to changes and improvements in the national background check system and state statutes in complying with the act.[32] Today, there are comprehensive background screening laws for day care in forty-eight states.[33]

PORNOGRAPHY LAWS

A number of federal and state pornography statutes address the issues of use of, production, and transporting of pornography. The primary focus of pornography laws is on child pornography and pornographers and the sexual exploitation of children, including on the Internet.

Protection of Children Against Sexual Exploitation Act

The Sexual Exploitation Act of 1978 was designed to bridge the gap existing in federal laws against the sexual exploitation of children. The law sought to halt the production and dissemination of child pornography by prohibiting the transportation of children across state lines for purposes of sexual exploitation. Further, the legislation expanded the federal government's authority in prosecuting producers and distributors of child pornography. In specific, the law provides punishment for persons who use, employ, or persuade minors (defined as any persons under sixteen) to become involved in the production of visual or print materials that depict sexually explicit conduct if the producers know or have reason to know that the materials will be transported in interstate or foreign commerce or mailed. Punishment is also specifically provided for parents, legal guardians, or other persons having custody or control of minors and who knowingly permit a minor to participate in the production of such material.[34]

Stiff monetary penalties against child exploiters were also provided for in the act.

Other Federal Pornography Laws

Prohibitions against child pornography exist in other federal statutes as well. The Child Protection, Restoration and Penalties Enhancement Act of 1990 increased the prohibitions of Title 18 of the United States Code against pornographers and pimps concerning actions related to pornographic material that involves the sexual exploitation of children.[35] The Child Protection and Obscenity Enforcement Act required pornography producers to have proof of a subject's age and maintain a record of it.[36]

In 1995, President Clinton signed into law the child sex crime bill, increasing penalties for child pornographers and pimps, and those transporting minors for the purpose of prostitution and sexual exploitation.[37]

Federal Laws and Child Pornography on the Internet

The Internet has brought about a new means for child pornographers and molesters to sexually abuse and exploit children. Federal legislation has been enacted with mixed results in an attempt to protect children from Internet smut and other sexual exploitation. The Child Pornography Prevention Act of 1996 defines child pornography to include a visual depiction that appears to be of a minor engaged in sexually explicit acts.[38] The constitutionality of the act has been upheld in *United States v. Hilton*[39] and *The Free Speech Coalition v. Reno.*[40]

The Communications Decency Act of 1996 prohibited the online display of sexually explicit materials accessible to minors, with penalties of up to two years in prison and a $250,000 fine.[41] In 1997, the Supreme Court ruled the law unconstitutional in restricting the rights of free speech for adults,[42] upholding earlier federal court rulings.[43]

The Protection of Children from Sexual Predators Act of 1998 also targeted child pornography in cyberspace, including a "jurisdictional basis for prosecution if the visual depiction [of a minor] was produced using materials that were mailed, shipped, or transported in interstate or foreign commerce including by computer."[44]

The Child Online Protection Act was signed into law in 2000, with an aim of protecting minors from sexual material on the Internet seen as harmful.[45] The law was blocked from enforcement by several courts as unconstitutional, including the Supreme Court in 2004 in *Ashcroft v. American Civil Liberties Union.*[46]

State Pornography Laws

Since 1978, forty-eight states have drafted or improved upon legislation to combat child pornography and sexploitation of children.[47] One such example is a 1983 New York law, upheld by the Supreme Court, that prohibits the dissemination of child pornography irrespective of whether or not the material is judged to be legally obscene.[48] The ruling, in effect, upheld similar laws in twenty other states.[49]

PROSTITUTION LAWS

Prostitution is illegal in forty-nine states. Only in Nevada does legal prostitution exist in some rural counties, where brothel prostitutes are strictly regulated.[50] Anti-prostitution statutes vary from state to state. Payment for sexual acts is prohibited in thirty-eight states,[51] while solicitation laws are enforced in forty-four states and the District of Columbia.[52] Prostitution in other states is banned through curfew, loitering, and vagrancy statutes. Recently more efforts have been made to go after clients of prostitutes such as car seizure laws, which allows police to confiscate the vehicle of a person caught soliciting or procuring a prostitute.[53]

The legality of prostitution laws has been challenged by prostitute organizations such as COYOTE (Call Off Your Old Tired Ethics). For example, in *Coyote v. Roberts,* it was argued that Rhode Island's prostitution statutes prohibited consensual sexual acts without pay, in addition to paid sex.[54] Such challenges have mostly been unsuccessful in relation to overturning prostitution laws.

Child Prostitution Laws

Child prostitution is banned in all fifty states. Additionally, most states have prostitution statutes that directly target the patrons, pimps, and pornographers of child prostitutes. These include laws against pimping, pandering, procuring, and promoting prostitutes.[55] Other laws pertain to solicitation of a child for purposes of prostitution.[56]

Some states have passed legislation that makes parents criminally liable for allowing their children to participate in prostitution or for the failure to prevent such participation.[57] Other states have aiding, abetting, or accomplice statutes with respect to the solicitation or procurement of a juvenile into prostitution.[58]

On the federal level, child sexual exploitation is addressed through a number of statutes. The Mann Act, enacted in 1910, prohibits the transportation of a woman or girl in interstate or foreign commerce for purposes of prostitution or "any immoral practice."[59] The Mann Act went through some major revisions by Congress in 1986, including making it gender-neutral, changing "immoral practice" to any illegal sexual activity, and removing the "commercial" purposes requirement in transporting a minor across state lines.[60] The latter allows for criminal prosecution of a person in the transportation of a child for even noncommercial illegal sexual exploitation.

The Protection of Children from Sexual Predators Act of 1998 further clarified the statutes' parameters and definitions, adding attempt provisions while increasing penalties for child sexual predators under the Mann Act.[61] Other federal laws can be used in prosecuting child sexual exploiters, including the Racketeer Influenced and Corrupt Organizations Act (RICO).[62]

Americans who sexually exploit children in foreign countries can now also be prosecuted in the United States through the Prosecutorial Remedies and Other Tools to end the Exploitation of Children Today Act of 2003 (PROTECT Act), which became law in 2004.[63] It criminalized child sex tourism by U.S. citizens abroad, increasing penalties for persons who engaged in commercial sex acts with minors, and lessening the burden of proof in prosecuting them. A federal appeals court upheld the law in 2006.[64]

Sex Trafficking Laws

As part of the effort to combat human trafficking in the United States for purposes of forced labor and sexual exploitation, the Trafficking Victims Protection Reauthorization Act of 2005 (TVPRA) was enacted in 2006.[65] It renewed the Trafficking Victims Protection Act of 2000, the first major anti-trafficking law in this country.[66]

The TVPRA authorized new funds to investigate and prosecute domestic traffickers, strengthened penalties against traffickers, provided more services to protect, counsel and rehabilitate victims of sex trafficking; and monitor and battle human trafficking globally. The Act also allows for greater efforts in going after the people who pay to sexually abuse and exploit victims of sex trafficking.

SEXUAL PERVERSION LAWS

Many states have laws that prohibit sexual perversion or paraphilic acts, particularly those involving children and animals. These include bestiality, sodomy, necrophilia, voyeurism, exhibitionism, and obscenity-related offenses.[67] The crimes vary from misdemeanors to felonies, depending on the offense, victim, and state in which it occurs. In states where no applicable laws exist, offenders may be charged under more general child sexual abuse or sexual assault offenses. Indeed, studies show that most criminal paraphiliacs commit multiple paraphilias against multiple offenders including sex offenses such as pedophilia, rape, sadism, and homosexual acts.[68]

SEX OFFENDER REGISTRATION LAWS

Sex offender registration laws came about in recent years as a response to the increased public concern over the growing number of sex offenders in prison and, more importantly, those released into the community. Many were repeat offenders, sexually victimizing unsuspecting children or women. Today, all fifty states have passed legislation requiring sex offenders to register with a sex offender registry agency or local law enforcement agency.

In 2000, the federal Campus Sex Crimes Prevention Act was enacted to keep track of convicted, registered sex offenders enrolled in colleges and universities and/or who are employed or doing volunteer work on campus.[69] The law required that institutions of higher learning notify the campus population as to where information could be gathered on registered sex offenders.

The act amends the Jacob Wetterling Crimes Against Children and Sexually Violent Offender Registration Act as part of the Violent Crime Control and Law Enforcement Act of 1994.[70] The act mandated that all states create sex offender registry or lose federal funding. The statute further includes Megan's Law Amendments and requires the registration of juvenile sex offenders convicted as adults for certain kinds of sex crimes.

Critics argue that sex offender registration laws are ineffective, pointing out the percentage of noncompliance by convicted sex offenders, as well as problems in applying the law to children and teenage sex abusers.[71] However, in a fifteen-year study of California's sex offender registration statute, it was found to be effective in aiding law enforcement personnel to track down suspected sex offenders.[72]

COMMUNITY NOTIFICATION LAWS

Many states have taken further steps in trying to keep track of released violent sex offenders and keep the local citizens informed about their presence in the community. More than thirty states have enacted community notification statutes "that either make information about sex offenders available on request to individuals and organizations or that authorize or require probation and parole departments, law enforcement agencies, or prosecutor offices to disseminate information about released offenders to the community at large."[73]

Perhaps the most well-known community notification law is New Jersey's Megan's Law that was enacted in 1994.[74] It came as the result of the rape and murder of a seven-year-old girl, Megan Kanka, and her parents' efforts to make parents and other citizens aware of known sex offenders living in the community. The publicity associated with the law and its national support led to the passage of the federal Megan's Law in 1996.[75] It provided "a funding incentive for states to enact laws mandating the release of relevant registration information when necessary to protect the public."[76]

Community notification statutes can vary dramatically from state to state or even community to community. Little research has been done on the effectiveness of notification laws. An empirical study on the impact of such laws found no indication that recidivism of sex offenders was reduced by community notification laws.[77] However, the majority of law enforcement agencies believe that the laws are effective in helping them to protect the public and possibly preventing sex crimes in the future.[78]

DNA DATABASE LAWS

The importance of DNA in investigating sex crimes and other violent offenses has led to most states enacting DNA statutes. Legislation authorizing the creation of DNA databases has been passed by forty-two states and Congress.[79] According to the Justice Department: "The goal of such legislation is for investigators to be able to match the DNA profiles obtained from blood, semen, or saliva taken from crime scenes with the DNA profiles of convicted criminals who have been released from prison."[80]

Crimes falling under such state statutes include sex offenses, which commonly have a high rate of recidivism and biological evidence through which DNA can be obtained. Using DNA for trace evidence and other criminal investigation is considered crucial in identifying, apprehending, and exonerating persons suspected of sex crimes or other crimes of violence.

Enacting DNA legislation allows states to participate in the FBI's Combined DNA Index System (CODIS), enabling law enforcement agencies investigating sex crimes and violent offenses to share DNA information.[81] The North Carolina DNA Database Act of 1993 is seen as a model state DNA database statute. As the first state to draft legislation consistent with the FBI guidelines, North Carolina's database statute authorizes states to extract blood samples from inmates convicted of crimes of violence.[82]

SEXUAL PREDATOR LAWS

Sexual predator laws are another means by which states hope to protect the public from dangerous sex offenders. A number of states have enacted or are creating statutes that prevent convicted sexual predators confined to mental institutions and prisons who are deemed as too dangerous from being released, in spite of having served their complete criminal sentence.[83] The legislation allows for sex offenders to be held until it is determined that they no longer pose a threat to society.

Civil libertarians have challenged the constitutionality of sexual predator laws. However, in 1997 the Supreme Court upheld a Kansas law ruling that states can confine violent sexual predators beyond the term of their sentence if a judge or jury determines them to be mentally abnormal and/or a serious threat to commit new sex offenses if released.[84]

This has spawned new federal and state sexual predatory statutes.[85] Though well meaning, some see the laws as potentially abusive and costly while doing little to deter unknown dangerous sexual predators who are institutionalized or on the streets. Less than one percent of the sexual abusers in the United States are affected by sexual predatory laws.[86]

CHEMICAL CASTRATION LAWS

A few states have passed or are developing chemical castration sex offender laws in an effort to reduce the chances of reoffending by child molesters and other sexual abusers.[87] These laws require convicted sex offenders to take anti-androgen hormone treatment as a means to lower their sexual drive. The most commonly used anti-androgen drugs in the United States are Depo-Provera and Depo-Lupron. These medications lower blood serum testosterone levels in males. Testosterone is the hormone influencing the male sex drive and aggression.

Studies on the effectiveness of these drugs by sex offenders have generally indicated a reduced sexual drive and lower testosterone levels but are not seen as an adequate solution in and of themselves to prevent recurrence of sexual offending.[88] Anti-androgen drugs can also pose significant health risks to the sexual offender, and present ethical problems for physicians.[89] Furthermore, most repeat sex offenders are never caught, much less convicted and incarcerated. Therefore such an approach would only be applicable to a small percentage of sex abusers.

NOTES

1. U.S. Department of Justice, National Institute of Justice, *Sex Offender Community Notification* (Washington: Office of Justice Programs, 1997), p. 2; Robert E. Freeman-Longo and Geral T. Blanchard, *Sexual Abuse in America: Epidemic of the 21st Century* (Brandon: Safer Society Press, 1998), pp. 106–14.
2. R. Barri Flowers, *Women and Criminality: The Woman as Victim, Offender, and Practitioner* (Westport: Greenwood Press, 1987), pp. 28–29; Battelle Law and Justice Study Center Report, *Forcible Rape: An Analysis of Legal Issues* (Washington: Government Printing Office, 1977).
3. Carol Bohmer, "Rape and The Law," in Mary E. Odem and Jody Clay-Warner, eds., *Confronting Rape and Sexual Assault* (Washington: Scholarly Resources, Inc., 1998), p. 256.
4. *Ibid.*; Ronald J. Berger, Patricia Searles, and W. Lawrence Newman, "The Dimensions of Rape Reform Legislation," *Law and Society Review 22* (1988): 329–57.
5. Flowers, *Women and Criminality,* p. 29; Bohmer, "Rape and the Law," p. 257.
6. Bohmer, "Rape and the Law," p. 256. *See also* Hubert S. Feild and Leigh B. Bienen, *Jurors and Rape: A Study in Psychology and Law* (Lexington: Lexington Books, 1980).
7. Mich. Comp. Laws Ann. §§750.520a (1974), 750.5206b (1974), 750.520c (1974), 750.520d (1974), 750.520e (1974).
8. *See, for example,* N.Y. Penal Law §§130.35 (1965), 130.05 (1965), 130.40 (1965), 130.70 (1978).
9. The Model Penal Code refers to an American Law Institute drafted model or ideal criminal code. A number of state statutes include provisions of the Code.
10. Richard A. Posner and Katharine B. Silbaugh, *A Guide to America's Sex Laws* (Chicago: University of Chicago Press, 1996), pp. 6–7.
11. U.S. Department of Justice, Office of Juvenile Justice and Delinquency Prevention, *Prostitution of Children and Child-Sex Tourism: An Analysis of Domestic and International Responses* (Arlington: National Center for Missing & Exploited Children, 1999), p. 18; Fed. R. Evid. 412.
12. *Prostitution of Children and Child-Sex Tourism,* p. 18. *See also* John E. Myers, *Evidence in Child Abuse and Neglect Cases,* 3rd Ed. (New York: John Wiley & Sons, 1997).
13. *See, for example,* Ill. Ann. Stat. ch. 725, para. 5/115-7; R.I. Gen. Laws §11-37-13; Ala. Code §12-21-203.
14. Feild and Bienen, *Jurors and Rape.*
15. Bohmer, "Rape and the Law," p. 256; Lorraine Dusky, *Still Unequal: The Shameful Truth About Women and Justice in America* (New York: Crown, 1996), pp. 388–92.
16. Diana E. Russell, "Wife Rape and the Law," in Mary E. Odem and Jody Clay-Warner, eds., *Confronting Rape and Sexual Assault* (Wilmington: Scholarly Resources, Inc., 1998), pp. 73–75.
17. Patricia Mahoney and Linda M. Williams, "Sexual Assault in Marriage: Prevalence, Consequences, and Treatment of Wife Rape," in Jana L. Jasinski and Linda M. Williams,

eds., *Partner Violence: A Comprehensive Review of 20 Years of Research* (Thousand Oaks: Sage, 1998), p. 119.

18. *Ibid.*
19. P.L. 100–294 (1974).
20. P.L. No. 95–266, 92 Stat. 205 (1978).
21. 42 U.S.C. §5101–5106 (1974).
22. R. Barri Flowers, *The Victimization and Exploitation of Women and Children: A Study of Physical, Mental and Sexual Maltreatment in the United States* (Jefferson: McFarland, 1994), p. 61.
23. Posner and Silbaugh, *A Guide to America's Sex Laws,* p. 129.
24. *Ibid.,* p. 130.
25. *Ibid.*; Flowers, *The Victimization and Exploitation of Women and Children,* pp. 62–63.
26. Flowers, *The Victimization and Exploitation of Women and Children,* pp. 70–73; Posner and Silbaugh, *A Guide to America's Sex Laws,* pp. 5–7, 44–45, 111.
27. Richard Green, *Sexual Science and the Law* (Cambridge: Harvard University Press, 1992), pp. 168–71.
28. *See, for example, Tyson v. Tyson,* 727 P. 2d 226 (Wash. 1986); *DeRose v. Carswell,* 196 Cal. App. 3d 285 (1989).
29. Annotated California Codes, Penal Code Sections 11165 et. seq., 11172(e) West (1991).
30. J. James, W. Womack, and F. Strauss, "Physician Reporting of Sexual Abuse of Children," *Journal of the American Medical Association 240* (1978): 1145–46.
31. K. Pope, B. Tabachmick, and P. Keith-Spiegel, "Ethics of Practice: The Beliefs and Behaviors of Psychologists as Therapists," *American Psychologist 42* (1987): 993–1006.
32. U.S. Department of Justice, Office of Juvenile Justice and Delinquency Prevention, *A Report to the Nation: Missing and Exploited Children* (Arlington: National Center for Missing & Exploited Children, 1997), pp. 14–15.
33. *Ibid.*
34. 18 U.S.C. §2251, 2253–2254 (1978).
35. P.L. No. 101–647, §323, 104 Stat. 4789, 4818 (1990); *Prostitution of Children and Child-Sex Tourism,* p. 22.
36. 33 F. 3d 78 (D.C.C. 1994), *rehearing denied,* 47 F. 3d 1215 (1995), *cert denied,* 515 U.S. 1158 (1995).
37. Cited in R. Barri Flowers, *The Prostitution of Women and Girls* (Jefferson: McFarland, 2005), p. 151.
38. P.L. No. 104–208, §121, 110 Stat. 3009–26 (1996).
39. *United States v. Hilton,* No. 98–513, slip op. at 3 (1999), *rev'g* 999 F. Supp. 131 (D. Maine 1998).
40. N.D. Cal. WL 487758 (1997).
41. Cited in Flowers, *The Prostitution of Women and Girls,* p. 151.
42. *Ibid.*; Supreme Court ruling, Associated Press, June 26, 1997.
43. Flowers, *The Prostitution of Women and Girls,* p. 151.
44. *Prostitution of Children and Child-Sex Tourism,* p. 22; 18 U.S.C. §2251(a), as amended by Protection of Children from Sexual Predators Act, §201.
45. P.L. No. 106–554 (2000).
46. *Ashcroft v. American Civil Liberties Union* (2004).
47. Flowers, *The Victimization and Exploitation of Women and Children,* pp. 92–93.
48. Cited in Flowers, *The Prostitution of Women and Girls,* p. 152.
49. *Ibid.*
50. *Ibid.,* pp. 145–47, 154–61.

51. R. Barri Flowers, *Female Crime, Criminals and Cellmates: An Exploration of Female Criminality and Delinquency* (Jefferson: McFarland, 1995), p. 103.
52. *Ibid.*
53. Flowers, *The Prostitution of Women and Girls*, pp. 131–32.
54. *Coyote v. Roberts*, 502 F. Supp. 1342 (R.I. 1980).
55. *See, for example, Prostitution of Children and Child-Sex Tourism*, pp. 11–22.
56. *Ibid.*, pp. 14–15. *See also, for example*, Neb. Rev. Stat. §28–805; Kan. Stat. Ann. §21–3513; Cal. Penal Code §266h.
57. *See, for example*, Or. Rev. Stat. §167.017; Ariz. Rev. Stat. Ann. §13–3212; Nev. Rev. Stat. §201.360; S.D. Codified Laws Ann. §22–23–2; La. Rev. Stat. Ann. §14:82.1.
58. *See, for example*, Okla. Stat. Ann. tit. 21, §1029; Md. Ann. Code art. 27, §1; Mass. Gen. Laws Ann. ch. 272, §4A.
59. White Slave Traffic Act (Mann Act) of 1910, ch. 395, 36 Stat. 825, codified as amended at 18 U.S.C. §§2421–2424 (1998).
60. P.L. No. 99–628, §5 (1986), repealing and recodifying 18 U.S.C. §§2421–2423.
61. Protection of Children from Sexual Predators Act of 1998, P.L. No. 105–314, 112 Stat. 2974 (1998).
62. 18 U.S.C. §1962 (1982); *Prostitution of Children and Child-Sex Tourism*, p. 23.
63. "Americans Who Sexually Abuse Children Abroad Face Criminal Prosecution," (January 13, 2006), http://www.usembassy.at/en/policy/human_traff.htm.
64. Paul Elias, "Americans Can Be Prosecuted For Child-Sex Tours Overseas," (January 26, 2006), http://seattlepi.com.
65. Trafficking Victims Protection Reauthorization Act of 2005 (H.R. 972) (2005).
66. Trafficking Victims Protection Act of 2000; "President Signs H.R. 972, Trafficking Victims Protection Reauthorization Act," (January 10, 2006); http://www.whitehouse.gov/new/releases/2006/01/20060110-3.html; "New Law Strengthens Current Anti-Trafficking Effort, Attacks Domestic Demand," http://usinfo.state.gov/gi/Archive/2006/Jan/11-191763.html.
67. Posner and Silbaugh, *A Guide to America's Sex Laws*. *See also, for example, People v. Carrier*, 254 N.W. 2d 35 (Mich. App. 1977); Or. Rev. Stat. §166.087 (1993); *Chance v. State*, 268 S.E. 2d 737 (Ga. App. 1980).
68. G. Abel, M. Mittleman, J. Becker, J. Rathner, and J. Rouleau, "Predicting Child Molesters' Response to Treatment," *Annals of the New York Academy of Sciences 528* (1988): 223–34.
69. P.L. 106–386; Sec. 1601 (2000).
70. *A Report to the Nation*, p. 12; *Sex Offender Community Notification*, p. 1; A. K. Bedarf, "Examining Sex Offender Community Notification Laws," *California Law Review 83*, 3 (1995): 885–939.
71. Freeman-Longo and Blanchard, *Sexual Abuse in America*, pp. 107–8.
72. *Sex Offender Community Notification*, p. 1; 42 U.S.C. §14071 (1994).
73. *Sex Offender Community Notification*, p. 1.
74. *Ibid.*, p. 3; *A Report to the Nation*, p. 13; Freeman-Longo and Blanchard, *Sexual Abuse in America*, pp. 108–9.
75. *A Report to the Nation*, p. 13.
76. *Ibid.*
77. *Sexual Offender Community Notification*, p. 2.
78. *A Report to the Nation*, p. 13.
79. *Ibid.*, pp. 16–17.
80. *Ibid.*, p. 16.

81. *Ibid.*

82. *Ibid.*, p. 17.

83. Freeman-Longo and Blanchard, *Sexual Abuse in America,* pp. 112–14; Michelle Boorstein, Associated Press news report, June 26, 1997.

84. Michelle Boorstein, Associated Press news report, June 26, 1997; L. Greenhouse, "Sexual Predators Can Be Confined After Jail Term," *Rutland Herald* (June 24, 1997), p. 1.

85. Freeman-Longo and Blanchard, *Sexual Abuse in America,* p. 113.

86. *Ibid.*, p. 112.

87. *Ibid.*, pp. 110–11; Green, *Sexual Science and the Law,* pp. 222–27.

88. J. Bremer, *Asexualization* (New York: Macmillan, 1959); F. Berlin and C. Meinecke, "Treatment of Sex Offenders with Anti-androgenic Medication," *American Journal of Psychiatry 138* (1981): 601–7; N. Heim, "Sexual Behavior of Castrated Sex Offenders," *Archives of Sexual Behavior 10* (1981): 11–19.

89. Freeman-Longo and Blanchard, *Sexual Abuse in America,* pp. 110–12.

Chapter 18

ARRESTS AND SEX OFFENSES

Each year tens of thousands of people are arrested for sex-related offenses in the United States. Many of these individuals are ultimately convicted and sentenced to prison or juvenile facilities. However, most experts agree that the majority of sex offenders are not arrested–many of whom are repeat offenders–including rapists, incestuous sex offenders, child molesters, sex traffickers, and prostitutes.[1] For example, there was only a 41.8 percent clearance rate by law enforcement authorities for reported forcible rape in 2004, according to official statistics.[2] Clearance rate refers to solving a crime by the arrest of at least one person, charging them with a crime, and prosecution. In spite of the limitations in arrests of sex offenders as a crime measurement, it remains our most important means of identifying sex-related criminals, characterizing their patterns of behavior, and getting them off the streets. This chapter will examine arrest data on sex offenders and supplementary crime and victimization data on sex-related offenses.

UNIFORM CRIME REPORTS AND SEX CRIMES

Since 1929, the Federal Bureau of Investigation's Uniform Crime Reporting Program has been the preeminent means for collecting crime and arrest information in the United States, as reported from law enforcement agencies. In its annual report, *Crime in the United States: Uniform Crime Reports (UCR)*, the FBI provides details on arrests of individuals, including offender characteristics, arrest clearances, and arrest trends.[3] According to the *UCR*, in 2004 there were an estimated 148,790 arrests for sex crimes, as shown in Table 18.1. Arrest data was recorded for forcible rape, prostitution or commercialized vice, and sex offenses (except for forcible rape and prostitution). Arrests for prostitution and sex offenses were highest and nearly equal in number. Both were more than three times as likely to occur as forcible rape arrests.

Table 18.1
ESTIMATED SEX-RELATED ARRESTS, 2004[a]

Offense	Arrests
Forcible rape	18,693
Prostitution or commercialized vice	64,786
Sex offenses (except forcible rape and prostitution)	65,311
Total Sex Crime Arrests	148,790
Murder and nonnegligent manslaughter	9,998
Runaways	86,097
Total Other Arrests	96,095

a. Arrest figures are based on all reporting agencies and estimates from areas that did not report.

Source: Adapted from U.S. Department of Justice, Federal Bureau of Investigation, *Crime in the United States: Uniform Crime Reports 2004* (Washington: Government Printing Office, 2005), p. 297.

Additionally, there were 96,095 arrests for running away and murder and nonnegligent manslaughter. These offenses, in particular, are often sex-related before or after the fact and more of a direct reflection of sexual criminality in arrest figures than some other common factors of sex offenses such as drug or alcohol violations. The vast majority of these arrests were of persons charged with running away. Studies show that runaways are connected to sex crimes in several important ways. One is that most runaways have been victims of sexual abuse. Researchers have found that anywhere from two-thirds up to 90 percent of runaways have been sexually molested.[4] Second, a high percentage of runaways become victims of rape, child pornography, or other sexual offenses.[5] Third, the strong relationship between runaways and prostitution has been well documented (see Chapter 14).

Although only a relatively small percentage of total murders recorded in the United States are sexually motivated, the correlation between sex and homicide has been shown to be significant.[6] Most serial murders are sexually motivated,[7] along with most intimate murders.[8] In 2004, there were 156 sex-related known murders in this country, such as involving rape, prostitution, other sex offenses, and/or a romantic triangle; and likely many other sexual homicides that were attributed to other reasons or unknown to authorities.[9] (See also Chapter 1.)

The rate of sex-related arrests per 100,000 inhabitants in 2004 can be seen in Figure 18.1. Sex offenses and prostitution and commercialized vice had the

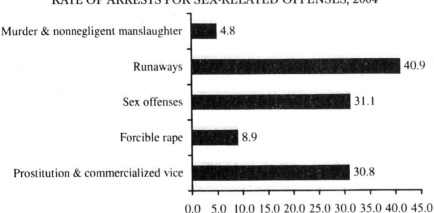

Figure 18.1
RATE OF ARRESTS FOR SEX-RELATED OFFENSES, 2004[a]

a. Number of arrests per 100,000 inhabitants.

Source: Derived from U.S. Department of Justice, Federal Bureau of Investigation, *Crime in the United States: Uniform Crime Reports 2004* (Washington: Government Printing Office, 2005), p. 281.

highest rates of arrest for actual sex offenses at 31.1 and 30.8, respectively. Each was more than three times the rate for forcible rape arrests. Overall, runaway arrests had the highest rate for sex-related offenses at 40.9. This was nearly nine times the rate for murder and nonnegligent manslaughter.

Table 18.2 compares the rate of arrests for sex-related offenses per 100,000 persons in different population groups in 2004. Sex offenders had the highest rates of arrests for all sex crimes in cities. Generally, the larger the city population, the higher the sex offense arrest rate is.[10] Among sex offenses, prostitution and commercialized vice had the highest arrest rate in cities, followed by sex offenses. Although the rate of arrests for forcible rape was higher in cities than metropolitan counties or suburban areas, it was well below that for other sex offenses in cities in 2004. Runaway arrest rates were highest for all sex-related offenses while murder and nonnegligent manslaughter arrest rates were the lowest.

Overall, metropolitan county arrest rates for sex-related offenses were slightly higher than suburban area arrest rates. Unlike city arrest rates, rates for sex-related offenses in metropolitan counties were highest for sex offenses, followed by forcible rape, and prostitution-related offenses. Runaway arrest rates were highest among all sex-related offenses, with homicide rates the lowest.

Arrest rates for forcible rape were higher in nonmetropolitan counties than metropolitan counties and suburban areas. The technical differences

Table 18.2
RATE OF ARRESTS FOR SEX-RELATED CRIMES,
BY POPULATION GROUP, 2004[a]

Offense charged	Cities	Metropolitan counties[b]	Non-metropolitan counties	Suburban areas[c]
Forcible rape	9.2	7.7	9.5	7.4
Prostitution and commercialized vice	42.7	7.0	0.8	7.0
Sex offenses (except forcible rape and prostitution)	33.2	26.3	26.7	25.1
Murder and nonnegligent manslaughter	5.2	3.9	3.5	3.0
Runaways	44.7	37.1	23.0	34.2

a. Number of arrests per 100,000 inhabitants.
b. Consists of metropolitan county law enforcement agencies.
c. Includes law enforcement agencies in cities with under 50,000 inhabitants and county law enforcement agencies within metropolitan areas, excluding agencies related to a central city.

Source: Adapted from U.S. Department of Justice, Federal Bureau of Investigation, *Crime in the United States: Uniform Crime Reports 2004* (Washington: Government Printing Office, 2005), pp. 282–83.

Table 18.3
ARRESTS FOR FORCIBLE RAPE, BY SEX AND AGE, 2004

Percent Distribution							
SEX		AGE					
Male	Female	Total all Ages	Under 18	18 and over	Under 15	Under 21	Under 25
98.5	1.5	100.0	16.3	83.7	6.2	30.6	45.7

Source: Derived from U.S. Department of Justice, Federal Bureau of Investigation, *Crime in the United States: Uniform Crime Reports 2004* (Washington: Government Printing Office, 2005), pp. 296–97.

between these suburban population groups can be found in the notes of Table 18.2. Nonmetropolitan county arrest rates were highest for sex offenses and runaways, and lowest for prostitution and commercialized vice and murder and nonnegligent manslaughter.

Forcible Rape Arrests

There were a total of 26,173 arrests for forcible rape reported by law

Figure 18.2
ARRESTS FOR FORCIBLE RAPE, BY RACE, 2004

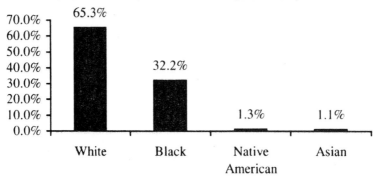

Note: Native American includes American Indian and Alaskan Natives. Asian includes Asians or Pacific Islanders.

Source: Derived from U.S. Department of Justice, Federal Bureau of Investigation, *Crime in the United States: Uniform Crime Reports 2004* (Washington: Government Printing Office, 2005), p. 298.

enforcement agencies in 2004.[11] The percent distribution for these arrests by sex and age of offender can be seen in Table 18.3. Forcible rape is predominantly an adult male sex offense. Nearly 99 percent of those arrested were male, while almost 84 percent were age eighteen and over. Although only 16.3 percent of the forcible rape arrestees were under the age of eighteen, a high percentage of persons charged with rape are young adults. More than three in ten individuals arrested for forcible rape in 2004 were under age twenty-one, while nearly half were younger than twenty-five.

Most persons arrested for forcible rape are white or black (see Figure 18.2). More than 65 percent of the arrestees in 2004 were white, while just over 32 percent were black. Blacks are over represented in rape arrests relative to their population figures. Slightly more than 1 percent of those arrested for forcible rape were of Native American or Asian descent, respectively.

Prostitution and Commercialized Vice Arrests

There were 64,786 arrests for prostitution and commercialized vice in 2004.[12] Table 18-4 shows sex and age comparisons of arrestees by percent distribution. This is the only sex offense in which females are arrested more often than males. Females accounted for 69.2 percent of prostitution-related arrests compared to 30.8 percent male arrests. The vast majority of persons arrested for prostitution activities are adults. Ninety-eight percent of those

Table 18.4
ARRESTS FOR PROSTITUTION AND COMMERCIALIZED VICE,
BY SEX AND AGE, 2004

Percent Distribution							
SEX		AGE					
Male	Female	Total all Ages	Under 18	18 and over	Under 15	Under 21	Under 25
69.2	30.8	100.0	2.0	98.0	0.2	12.2	25.4

Source: Derived from U.S. Department of Justice, Federal Bureau of Investigation, *Crime in the United States: Uniform Crime Reports 2004* (Washington: Government Printing Office, 2005), pp. 296–97.

Figure 18.3
ARRESTS FOR PROSTITUTION AND
COMMERCIALIZED VICE, BY RACE, 2004

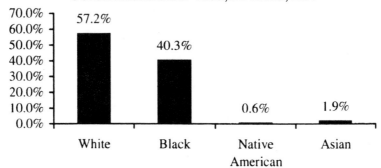

Note: Native American includes American Indian and Alaskan Natives. Asian includes Asians or Pacific Islanders.

Source: Derived from U.S. Department of Justice, Federal Bureau of Investigation, *Crime in the United States: Uniform Crime Reports 2004* (Washington: Government Printing Office, 2005), p. 298.

arrested in 2004 were age eighteen and over, while only 2 percent were under the age of eighteen and less than 1 percent under fifteen. More than 12 percent of arrestees were under twenty-one and over 25 percent younger than twenty-five.

Whites make up the majority of those arrested for prostitution, followed by blacks. As shown in Figure 18.3, 57.2 percent of the persons arrested for prostitution and commercialized vice in 2004 were white and, disproportionately, more than 40 percent were black. Asians were more than three times as likely to be arrested for prostitution as Native Americans. However,

Table 18.5
ARRESTS FOR SEX OFFENSES[a], BY SEX AND AGE, 2004

Percent Distribution							
SEX		AGE					
Male	Female	Total all Ages	Under 18	18 and over	Under 15	Under 21	Under 25
91.6	8.4	100.0	20.0	80.0	10.3	31.0	42.5

Source: Derived from U.S. Department of Justice, Federal Bureau of Investigation, *Crime in the United States: Uniform Crime Reports 2004* (Washington: Government Printing Office, 2005), pp. 296–97.

Figure 18.4
ARRESTS FOR SEX OFFENSES,[a] BY RACE, 2004

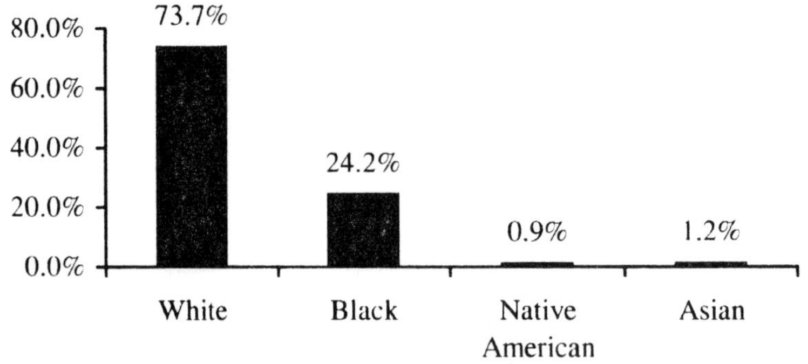

a. Excluding forcible rape and prostitution.

Note: Native American includes American Indian and Alaskan Natives. Asian includes Asians or Pacific Islanders.

Source: Derived from U.S. Department of Justice, Federal Bureau of Investigation, *Crime in the United States: Uniform Crime Reports 2004* (Washington: Government Printing Office, 2005), p. 298.

these groups represented only 1.9 and 0.6 percent of arrests for prostitution and commercialized vice, respectively.

Sex Offenses Arrests

FBI figures indicate that there were 65,311 reported arrests for sex offenses other than forcible rape and prostitution in 2004.[13] Table 18.5 reflects the percentages of arrestees by sex and age. Males and adults were much more likely to face arrests for sex offenses than females and juveniles. Nearly 92 percent of the arrestees for sex offenses were male, while just over 8 percent were

Figure 18.5
ARRESTS OF RUNAWAYS, BY AGE, RACE, AND SEX, 2004

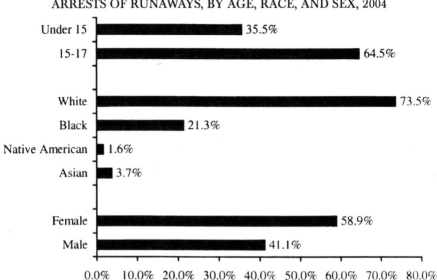

Note: Native American includes American Indian and Alaskan Natives. Asian includes Asians or Pacific Islanders.

Source: Derived from U.S. Department of Justice, Federal Bureau of Investigation, *Crime in the United States: Uniform Crime Reports 2004* (Washington: Government Printing Office, 2005), pp. 296–298.

female. Eighty percent of those arrested were age eighteen and over and 20 percent were under eighteen. More than 42 percent of the persons arrested for sex offenses were under twenty-five and 31 percent were under twenty-one. Juveniles were more likely to be arrested for sex offenses than other types of sex crimes. More than one in ten of the arrestees for sex offenses other than forcible rape and prostitution in 2004 were under the age of fifteen.

Whites accounted for nearly three in four persons arrested for sex offenses in 2004, as shown in Figure 18.4. Blacks made up almost one-fourth of the arrestees, while Asians and Native Americans constituted around 1 percent each of persons arrested for sex offenses.

UCR data does not record ethnic arrests such as Hispanics. However, studies show that Hispanics tend to be over represented in arrests for sex offenses and other crimes.[14]

Runaway Arrests

Law enforcement agencies reported 86,097 arrests of runaways in 2004.[15] Unlike other sex-related offenses, only juveniles can be arrested as runaways

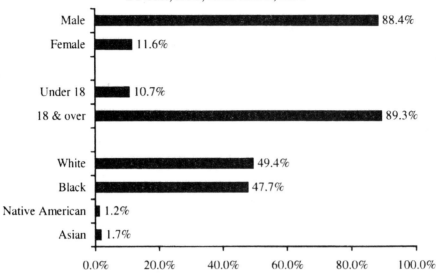

Figure 18.6
MURDER AND NONNEGLIGENT MANSLAUGHTER ARRESTS,
BY SEX, AGE, AND RACE, 2004

Note: Native American includes American Indian and Alaskan Natives. Asian includes Asians or Pacific Islanders.

Source: Derived from U.S. Department of Justice, Federal Bureau of Investigation, *Crime in the United States: Uniform Crime Reports 2004* (Washington: Government Printing Office, 2005), pp. 296–298.

(though many runaways may have engaged in prostitution activities upon their arrest, they are charged as runaways unless they are caught soliciting or performing sexual acts). Most individuals arrested for running away are female, white, and older teenagers, as shown in Figure 18.5. Females made up more than 58 percent of the runaway arrestees, while males accounted for just over 41 percent. More than 73 percent of those arrested for running away were white. Over 21 percent of the arrestees were black, 3.7 percent Asian, and 1.6 percent Native American. In more than six out of every ten arrests, the runaway was between the age of fifteen and seventeen, while nearly four in ten were under fifteen.

Murder and Nonnegligent Manslaughter Arrests

There were 9,998 persons arrested for murder and nonnegligent manslaughter in 2004.[16] A percent distribution of arrests by sex, age, and race can be seen in Figure 18.6. Nearly nine in ten persons arrested for murder and nonnegligent manslaughter were males, and age eighteen and over, with

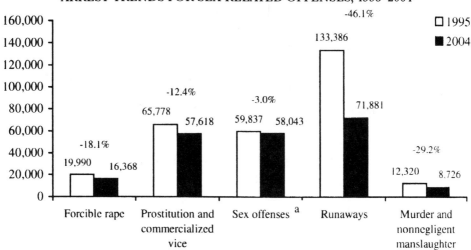

Figure 18.7
ARREST TRENDS FOR SEX-RELATED OFFENSES, 1995–2004

a. Excluding forcible rape and prostitution.

Source: Derived from U.S. Department of Justice, Federal Bureau of Investigation, *Crime in the United States: Uniform Crime Reports 2004* (Washington: Government Printing Office, 2005), pp. 284.

females and persons under eighteen constituting around 11 percent of the arrestees, respectively. Almost 48 percent of those arrested were black, well above their population figures, while more than 49 percent were white. Other races accounted for just under 3 percent of the arrests for murder and nonnegligent manslaughter.

Though males make up the majority of offenders and murder victims, females are much more likely to be the victims of sexually motivated murders such as rape murders, intimate murders, prostitute murders, child sexual abuse murders, and serial murders.[17] Moreover, some studies indicate that many more murders may be sex-related than the current data suggests.[18] (See also Chapter 1.)

Arrest Trends For Sex-Related Offenses

Arrests for sex-related crimes are on the decline, according to official indicators. As seen in Figure 18.7, between 1995 and 2004 arrests declined for every sex-related offense. Among sex crimes, arrests for forcible rape dropped the most at over 18 percent, while arrests for prostitution and commercialized vice fell by more than 12 percent and sex offense arrests declined 3 percent. For sex-related offenses, runaway arrests decreased by over 46 percent, while arrests for murder and nonnegligent manslaughter dropped by more than 29 percent.

Five-year arrest trends from 2000 to 2004 reveal similar overall declines in arrests for sex-related offenses.[19] Over the two-year span from 2003 to 2004, overall and female arrests for prostitution and commercialized vice rose slightly, while other figures for sex crime offense arrestees remained steady.[20]

Shortcomings of Uniform Crime Reports

In spite of the importance of the Uniform Crime Reporting Program in collecting crime and arrest data, its effectiveness in assessing the nature of sex offenses and offenders is limited. A number of prominent criminologists such as Marvin Wolfgang,[21] Donald Cressey,[22] and T. Sellin[23] have criticized official statistics for its shortcomings. Common criticisms include:

- Official statistics reflect only crimes known to law enforcement agencies.
- A reliance on percent changes in the total volume of serious offenses.
- The problem of what constitutes a crime (i.e., arrest, charge, conviction).
- The variance of *UCR* crime statistics.
- The differential enforcement of criminal arrests (such as for prostitution).
- Accommodating elements of the criminal justice system.
- The voluntary method of gathering arrest statistics.

There is also some evidence of manipulation of crime data by law enforcement agencies as a means of influencing public opinion or internal policies.[24] Current *UCR* data is inadequate as a true measure of sexual criminality because of the above and antiquated methodology.

NATIONAL INCIDENT-BASED REPORTING SYSTEM

The Uniform Crime Reporting Program has recently begun implementing a new system for collecting crime information from law enforcement agencies. The National Incident-Based Reporting System (NIBRS) is designed to eventually replace the *UCR* in presenting a more comprehensive picture of crime, criminal, and victim characteristics and dynamics. The NIBRS data collection includes information on "each incident and arrests with 22 crime categories. For each offense known to the police within these categories, agencies report information on incident, victim, property, offender, and arrestee."[25] Though not yet nationally representative, the NIBRS data on sex offenses promises to provide more detailed information on sex criminals and their victims for the next generation.

During 1998 there were 3,461 incidents of forcible rape reported to the NIBRS, representing almost 1 percent of all violent offenses.[26] Forcible rape as part of family violence constituted slightly more than 1 percent of the violence, or 1,380 incidents.[27] The NIBRS revealed that young child offenders tend to rape young child victims in total and family rape cases; whereas teenage offenders have teenage victims, and for family forcible rape the victims tend to be younger. Adult rapists are most likely to rape adults but for family rape, the victims tend to be under eighteen in two out of three cases.[28]

Shortcomings of the National Incident-Based Reporting System

The primary weakness of National Incident-Based Reporting System data on sex offenses and sex criminality is that the system has not yet been fully implemented; it is only used in less than a quarter of the states. Hence, NIBRS findings are not nationally representative. According to the *UCR*, one must "be mindful of several limitations particular to the study of the NIBRS data in general. . . . For instance, the NIBRS data collection cannot capture repeat calls to a given location. Additionally, no geographic identifiers are specific enough to support geographic mapping of the data."[29] Further, data quality "issues with the NIBRS are still evolving and statistical compatibility with other crime information systems remains to be studied."[30] It is still too soon to tell how effective the NIBRS will be in measuring some sexual offenses such as prostitution and child pornography; or offenses in which victims are not forthcoming, unable to talk about the victimization, or both victim and offender (such as a sexually assaulted prostitute).

NATIONAL CRIME VICTIMIZATION SURVEY

Supplementing the Uniform Crime Reporting Program in measuring crime in the United States is the Bureau of Justice Statistics' annual victimization report, *Criminal Victimization in the United States: A National Crime Victimization Survey (NCVS)*.[31] Begun in 1973, the *NCVS* provides details on victims of crime, crime in households, and trends using a representative sample of around 101,000 respondents age twelve or over who "not only are willing to report the crime but also understand what happened and how it happened."[32]

In the area of sexual crime and victimization, the *NCVS* measures the crimes of rape and sexual assault. According to the most recently available complete survey, there were an estimated 247,730 total rape or sexual assaults in the United States in 2002. Table 18.6 breaks these down by rape,

Table 18.6
ESTIMATED NUMBER AND RATE OF RAPE AND
SEXUAL ASSAULT VICTIMIZATION, BY SEX, 2002[a]

	Both sexes		Male		Female	
Type of crime	Number	Rate	Number	Rate	Number	Rate
All personal crimes	5,496,810	23.7	2,927,520	26.1	2,569,300	21.5
Crimes of violence	5,341,410	23.1	2,857,930	25.5	2,483,480	20.8
Completed violence	1,753,090	7.6	816,240	7.3	936,850	7.8
Attempted/threatened violence	3,588,320	15.5	2,041,690	18.2	1,546,630	13.0
Rape/sexual assault	247,730	1.1	31,640	0.3	216,090	1.8
Rape/attempted rape	167,860	0.7	22,610[b]	0.2[b]	145,240	1.2
Rape	90,390	0.4	4,100[b]	0.0[b]	86,290	0.7
Attempted rape[c]	77,470	0.3	18,520[b]	0.2[b]	68,950	0.5
Sexual assault[d]	79,870	0.3	9,030[b]	0.1[b]	70,840	0.6

a. Based on per 1,000 persons age 12 and over.

b. Estimate is based on about 10 or fewer sample cases.

c. Includes verbal threats of rape.

d. Includes threats.

Source: Adpted from U.S. Department of Justice, Bureau of Justice Statistics, *Sourcebook of Criminal Justice Statistics 2003* (Washington: Government Printing Office, 2005), p. 192.

attempted rape, and sexual assault, by sex, and the rate of victimization.

There were more rapes than sexual assaults, but more sexual assaults that included threats than attempted rapes. Females were much more likely to be victims of rape, attempted rape, and sexual assaults than males. There were 216,090 rape or sexual assault victimizations of females reported compared to only 31,640 of males. The rate of female sex crime victimization was nearly seven times greater than the male sex crime victimization rate.

The rate of rape and sexual assault victimization in 2003 was highest among persons age sixteen to thirty-four, whites, blacks, and non-Hispanics; and those with household incomes under $15,000.[33] Sex crime victims in 2002 were nearly twice as likely to be victimized by nonstrangers than strangers.[34] The *NCVS* reported that in 2002 victims of rape and sexual assault were more than five times as likely to perceive the crime as a single-offender victimization than multiple-offender victimization.[35]

Shortcomings of the National Crime Victimization Survey

The most glaring shortcoming of the *NCVS* with respect to sex crimes is its neglect of victims younger than twelve. Studies show that a high percentage of certain types of sexual crimes such as incest, pedophilia, and molestation involve child victims under the age of twelve.[36] Also, the failure of the *NCVS* to include such "victimless" crimes as prostitution limits its effectiveness as a measure of crime and victimization. Experts have found a strong correlation between prostitution and a number of sexual and nonsexual victimizations including rape, child molestation, intimidation, and physical assaults.[37] Other drawbacks of victimization surveys include excluding the following types of crimes:

- Crimes that the victim may not be aware of.
- Crimes in which the victim may have something to hide, possibly incriminating themselves (such as victims of child molestation who may also be sex offenders).
- Juvenile status offenders (many of whom may have run away from an abusive home).

Further criticism has been aimed at the *NCVS* for the underreporting of victimization through its program, lack of compatibility with other crime data, and the process of problems with its interviewing of crime victims.

NOTES

1. R. Barri Flowers, *Male Crime and Deviance: Exploring Its Cause, Dynamics, and Nature* (Springfield: Charles C Thomas, 2003), pp. 121–22, 221–24; R. Barri Flowers, *The Victimization and Exploitation of Women and Children: A Study of Physical, Mental and Sexual Maltreatment in the United States* (Jefferson: McFarland, 1994), pp. 98–110; U.S. Department of Justice, Federal Bureau of Investigation, *Crime in the United States: Uniform Crime Reports 2004* (Washington: Government Printing Office, 2005), pp. 28–29.
2. *Uniform Crime Reports 2004*, p. 29.
3. *Ibid.*, pp. 3–6.
4. R. Barri Flowers, *Runaway Kids and Teenage Prostitution: America's Lost, Abandoned, and Sexually Exploited Children* (Westport: Greenwood Press, 2001), pp. 41–43; R. Barri Flowers, *The Prostitution of Women and Girls* (Jefferson: McFarland, 2005), p. 96.
5. Flowers, *Runaway Kids and Teenage Prostitution*, pp. 46–47, 51–56; Flowers, *The Prostitution of Women and Girls*, pp. 93–98.
6. Flowers, *The Victimization and Exploitation of Women and Children*, pp. 156–67; *Uniform Crime Reports 2004*, pp. 20, 277; U.S. Department of Justice, Bureau of Justice Statistics, *Violence by Intimates: Analysis of Data on Crimes by Current or Former Spouses, Boyfriends, and Girlfriends* (Washington: Government Printing Office, 1998); R. Barri Flowers, *Murder, At The End of The Day and Night: A Study of Criminal Homicide Offenders, Victims, and Circumstances* (Springfield: Charles C Thomas, 2002), pp. 51–60; 159–77.
7. Flowers, *Murder, At The End of The Day and Night*, pp. 170–78; Robert K. Ressler, Ann W. Burgess, and John E. Douglas, *Sexual Homicide: Patterns and Motives* (New York: Lexington Books, 1988); Joel Norris, *Serial Killers* (New York: Anchor Books, 1988).
8. *Violence by Intimates;* Flowers, *Murder, At The End of The Day and Night*, pp. 51–61.

9. *Uniform Crime Reports 2004,* pp. 20–21, 24, 284–85.

10. *Ibid.,* pp. 281–82.

11. *Ibid.,* p. 29.

12. *Ibid.,* p. 290.

13. *Ibid.*

14. R. Barri Flowers, *Minorities and Criminality* (Westport: Greenwood Press, 1990), pp. 41–49.

15. *Uniform Crime Reports 2004,* p. 296.

16. *Ibid.,* p. 297.

17. *See, for example,* Flowers, *Murder, At The End of The Day and Night,* pp. 52, 160; *Violence by Intimates,* pp. 5–10; Flowers, *The Victimization and Exploitation of Women and Children,* p. 131; U.S. Department of Justice, Office of Juvenile Justice and Delinquency Prevention, *Prostitution of Children and Child-Sex Tourism: An Analysis of Domestic and International Responses* (Arlington: National Center for Missing & Exploited Children, 1999), pp. 6–7.

18. *Uniform Crime Reports 2004,* pp. 20–24; Flowers, *Male Crime and Deviance,* pp. 101–44.

19. *Uniform Crime Reports 2004,* p. 286.

20. *Ibid.,* pp. 288–89.

21. Marvin E. Wolfgang, "Uniform Crime Reports: A Critical Appraisal," *University of Pennsylvania Law Review 3* (1963): 408–38.

22. Donald R. Cressey, "The State of Criminal Statistics," *National Probation and Parole Association Journal 3* (1957): 230–41.

23. T. Sellin, "The Significance of Records of Crime," *The Law Quarterly Review 67* (1961): 489–504.

24. R. Barri Flowers, *Children and Criminality: The Child as Victim and Perpetrator* (Westport: Greenwood Press, 1986), p. 23.

25. *Uniform Crime Reports 2004,* p. 5.

26. U.S. Department of Justice, Federal Bureau of Investigation, *Crime in the United States: Uniform Crime Reports 1998* (Washington: Government Printing Office, 1999), p. 279.

27. *Ibid.,* p. 280.

28. *Ibid.,* pp. 277–83.

29. *Ibid.,* p. 289.

30. *Ibid.*

31. *Ibid.,* p. 407; U.S. Department of Justice, Bureau of Justice Statistics, *Criminal Victimization in the United States, 1994: A National Crime Victimization Survey Report* (Washington: Government Printing Office, 1997).

32. *National Crime Victimization Survey Report.*

33. U.S. Department of Justice, Bureau of Justice Statistics, *Sourcebook of Criminal Justice Statistics 2003* (Washington: Government Printing Office, 2005), p. 191.

34. *Ibid.*

35. *Ibid.,* pp. 204–5.

36. Flowers, *The Victimization and Exploitation of Women and Children,* pp. 56, 73; *Sexual Abuse of Children: Implications for Casework* (Denver: American Humane Association, 1967), p. 10; E. P. Sarafinio, "An Estimate of the Nationwide Incidence of Sexual Offenses Against Children," *Child Welfare 58,* 2 (1979): 127–34.

37. Flowers, *The Prostitution of Women and Girls,* pp. 49, 63–65, 84, 103; Anastasia Volkonsky, "Legalizing the 'Profession' Would Sanction the Abuse," *Insight on the News 11* (1995): 20; Mimi H. Silbert, "Delancey Street Study: Prostitution and Sexual Assault," summary of results, Delancey Street Foundation, San Francisco, 1982, p. 3.

Chapter 19

INCARCERATED SEX OFFENDERS

In spite of the fact that most persons who commit sex crimes manage to evade the law and justice, there are hundreds of thousands of sex offenders in jails, prisons, and juvenile custody facilities throughout the United States. Each year, many sex offenders are convicted and placed under correctional authority. There is considerable debate and controversy over what should be the proper treatment for convicted sex offenders, the level of effectiveness, and whether or not they can ever truly be rehabilitated.[1] Most sex offenders are recidivists, whether rapists, child molesters, prostitutes, or sexual murderers.[2] The majority of these offenders will be released back into the community at some point and will likely reoffend. This chapter will explore the extent and characteristics of incarcerated sex offenders in this country using the most current data available.

CONVICTED SEX OFFENDERS

Much of the data available on convicted and sentenced sex offenders comes from a number of Bureau of Justice Statistics (BJS) studies, surveys, censuses, and other statistical programs. This information covers institutional and community-based corrections. According to the BJS, on any given day there are an estimated 233,636 convicted sex offenders in the care, custody, or control of correctional institutions in the United States. The BJS defines sex offenders as offenders convicted of rape or sexual assault (including statutory rape, forcible sodomy, lewd acts with children, molestations, fondling, and other indecent practices). In Table 19.1, these offenders are broken down in relation to the total prison population and type of correctional sanction. Sex offenders constitute nearly 10 percent of offenders in State prisons and around 1 percent of Federal prison inmates; jailed sex offenders represent approximately 3.4 percent of the jail population; and sex

Table 19.1
CONVICTED SEX OFFENDERS, BY STATUS, 1994

	Total population	Sex offenders	
		Number	Percent
Probation	2,964,171	106,710	3.6
Jail 304,274	10,345	3.4	
State prisons	906,112	88,100	9.7
Federal prisons	87,515	875	1.0
Parole	690,159	27,606	4.0
Total	4,952,231	233,636	4.7

Source: U.S. Department of Justice, Bureau of Justice Statistics, *Sex Offenses and Offenders: An Analysis of Data on Rape and Sexual Assault* (Washington: Office of Justice Programs, 1997), p. 17.

offenders on probation and parole account for about 3.6 percent and 4 percent, respectively. In all, sex offenders make up nearly 5 percent of convicted offenders under correctional authority.

Persons convicted of rape and sexual assault represent an estimated 6 percent of offenders entering State prisons, and under 5 percent of inmates discharged from State prisons.[3] Sex offenders account for just over 4 percent of admissions to parole supervision, while constituting less than 4 percent of inmates discharged from parole supervision.[4] The ratio of sex offenders on conditional release to those incarcerated is 1.4 to 1, compared to the nearly 3 to 1 ratio for all convicted offenders.

JAIL INMATE SEX OFFENDERS

According to the BJS Special Report, *Profile of Jail Inmates, 2002,* there were 655,475 jail inmates in the United States at midyear in 2002.[5] Of these, 342,372 were convicted inmates and 178,035 were not convicted. Table 19.2 shows jail inmate sex offenders by detention status. More than one in four of all jail inmates' most serious offense was a crime of violence. Nearly 22 percent of convicted jail inmates' most serious offense was a violent offense, whereas almost 35 percent of unconvicted jail inmates were being held for a violent offense. Nearly four times as many unconvicted jail inmates as convicted ones' most serious offense was murder or nonnegligent manslaughter. Rape constituted less than 1 percent of the most serious offense for all jail inmates. Unconvicted jail inmates were more likely than convicted jail

Table 19.2
JAIL INMATE SEX OFFENDERS, BY DETENTION STATUS, 2002

| Most serious offense | Total | *Percent of jail inmates* | |
		Convicted	Unconvicted
Number of jail inmates	665,475ᵃ	342,372	178,035
Violent offenses	24.4%	21.6%	34.4%
Murderᵇ	2.5	1.6	5.7
Kidnapping	0.7	0.4	1.4
Rape	0.6	0.6	0.8
Other sexual assault	2.8	2.7	3.6
Public order offenses	24.9	29.1	20.2
Morals/drunkennessᶜ	1.7	1.8	1.5

a. Does not include inmates with unknown status for detention.

b. Includes nonnegligent manslaughter.

c. Includes commercialized vice, morals, unlawful assembly, drunkenness, vagrancy, and disorderly conduct.

Source: U.S. Department of Justice, Bureau of Justice Statistics, *Profile of Jail Inmates, 2002* (Washington: Office of Justice Programs, 2004), p. 3.

inmates to be in jail for rape. Nearly 3 percent of jail inmates' most serious offense committed was a sexual assault other than rape. Unconvicted inmates were slightly more likely than convicted inmates to be jailed for sexual assault. While less than 1 percent of jail inmates were detained for kidnapping, more than three times as many unconvicted as convicted inmates were in jail for kidnapping.

Almost one in four jail inmates' most serious offense was a public order offense. More than 29 percent of the convicted jail inmates had committed a public order offense compared to just over 17 percent of the unconvicted jail inmates. Almost 2 percent of these offenses involved morals and drunkenness offenses, including commercialized vice, unlawful assembly, and disorderly conduct. Convicted jail inmates were more likely to be in jail for morals and drunkenness charges than unconvicted inmates.

Characteristics of jail inmate sex offenders can be seen in Table 19.3. Overall most jail inmates were male, black, and non-Hispanic. There were nearly eight times as many males in jail as females in 2002, while around two times as many jail inmates were black or white as Hispanic. The most serious offense was a violent offense for more than one-quarter of jail inmates who were male, black, and Hispanic, with over one in five white inmates in jail for violent offenses.

Inmates in jail for murder and nonnegligent manslaughter tended to be

Table 19.3
CHARACTERISTICS OF JAIL INMATE SEX OFFENDERS, 2002

| | *Percent of jail inmates* | | | | |
| | *Sex* | | *Race/Ethnicity* | | |
Most serious offense	Male	Female	White[a]	Black[a]	Hispanic
Number of jail inmates	551,186	72,306	223,292	249,304	114,562
Violent offenses	26.5%	17.1%	21.8%	26.9%	27.1%
Murder[b]	2.7	1.8	1.6	3.0	3.1
Sexual offenses[c]	3.8	0.9	4.6	2.2	3.1
Public order offenses	25.5	20.8	31.0	18.0	27.5
Moral/drunkenness[d]	1.5	3.3	1.9	1.5	1.8

a. Includes only non-Hispanic jail inmates.
b. Includes nonnegligent manslaughter.
c. Includes rape or other sexual assault.
d. Includes commercialized vice, morals, unlawful assembly, vagrancy, disorderly conduct, and drunkenness.

Source: U.S. Department of Justice, Bureau of Justice Statistics, *Profile of Jail Inmates, 2002* (Washington: Office of Justice Programs, 2004), p. 4.

mostly Hispanic, black, and male. Males outnumbered females whose most serious offense was murder at 2.7 percent to 1.8 percent; while Hispanic and black jail inmates were nearly twice as likely as whites to be in jail for murder.

For sexual offenses such as rape and sexual assault, the jail inmate characteristics were somewhat different than those noted. The exception was by gender, where males were predominantly more likely to be in jail for sex offenses than females. White inmates (4.6 percent) were more than twice as likely as black inmates to have committed a most serious sexual offense; with 1.4 whites in jail as sex offenders for every Hispanic inmate detained for a sex offense.

Male jail inmates were more likely than female jail inmates to have a public order offense as the most serious offense, representing more than one in four males in jail, compared to around one in five females. Whites and Hispanics were more likely than blacks to be jail inmates for public-order offenses. For morals and drunkenness offenses, including commercialized vice and unlawful assembly, more than twice as many females were in jail as males, while whites and Hispanics were more likely than blacks to be jailed for morals and drunkenness charges.

Substance abuse is a significant factor in sex offenses perpetrated by jail inmates. The BJS reported in 2002 that around one-third of convicted jail inmates whose most serious offense was a sexual offense were under the influence of alcohol at the time of the crime, with more than one in five on drugs and almost half using both alcohol and drugs when committing the offense.[6]

STATE PRISON INMATE SEX OFFENDERS

State prisons in the United States held an estimated 88,100 sex offenders in 1994, according to the BJS analysis of data, *Sex Offenses and Offenders*.[7] Sex offenders accounted for nearly 10 percent of the prison population's 906,112 inmates (see Table 19.4). Almost half had been convicted of a violent offense. Nearly 4 percent of inmates convicted of a sexual offense were serving time for forcible rape, while 6 percent were in prison for other sexual assaults. Most of these involved fondling, molestation, lewd acts with children, and other sexual assaults.

Sex offenders are much more likely than other violent offenders incarcerated to have a history of convictions for violent sex crimes. Though inmate sex offenders account for about 20 percent of all violent offenders, they rep-

Table 19.4
SEX OFFENDERS IN STATE PRISON, BY TYPE OF SEX OFFENSE, 1994

Total State prison population
906,112

Convicted of a violent offense
47.4%

Convicted of rape or sexual assault
9.7%

Forcible rape	3.7%	Other sexual assault	6.0%
		Lewd acts with children	1.5%
		Statutory rape	0.2%
		Forcible sodomy	0.3%
		Fondling, molestation, and other sexual assaults	4.1%

Source: U.S. Department of Justice, Bureau of Justice Statistics, *Sex Offenses and Offenders: An Analysis of Data on Rape and Sexual Assault* (Washington: Office of Justice Programs, 1997), p. 18.

resent about two-thirds of all violent offenders who have a previous history of sex crimes.[8]

Characteristics of Inmate Sex Offenders

Table 19.5 shows characteristics of State prison inmates convicted of rape and sexual assault. Of an estimated 429,400 violent offenders in prison in 1994, 54,300 were convicted of sexual assault and 33,800 rape. Imprisoned violent sex offenders are predominantly male, white, eighteen to twenty-nine years of age, and divorced or never married. Males made up approximately 90 percent of inmates in State prison for rape or sexual assault. Over 52 percent of imprisoned rapists were white, nearly 44 percent black, and just over 4 percent other races. For sexual assault convictions, nearly three in four inmates were white. More than 20 percent of inmates incarcerated for sexual assault were black, and other races accounted for just over 3 percent of the total. Overall, black inmate sex offenders are over represented relative to their population figures.

One-third of convicted rapists were between the ages of eighteen and twenty-four and more than two in ten were twenty-five to twenty-nine years of age. More than 83 percent of inmates serving time for rape were between eighteen and thirty-nine. Around one-fourth of inmates convicted of sexual assault were eighteen to twenty-four years of age, while 17 percent were age twenty-five to twenty-nine. More than eight in ten prisoners serving time for sexual assault were eighteen to forty-four. Though most sexual offenders imprisoned are young, 7.4 percent of convicted rapists and 11.8 percent of imprisoned sexual assaulters in 1994 were age fifty or over.[9] The average age at the time of arrest of inmates serving time for rape and sexual assault was thirty-one and thirty-four, respectively.[10]

More than 40 percent of rape offenders and nearly 40 percent of sex assaulters in State prisons had never been married. Nearly 29 percent of incarcerated rapists and 35 percent of inmates in for sexual assault were divorced, while more than 20 percent of imprisoned sex offenders were married. Under 8 percent of rapists or sexual assaulters in prison were widowers or separated at the time of incarceration.

Around one-third of imprisoned sex offenders were using alcohol at the time the offense was committed. According to the BJS report, *Alcohol and Crime,* nearly 36 percent of offenders serving time for rape or sexual assault were drinking at the time of the offense.[11] This compares to around 32 percent of sex offenders on probation or in local jails, and nearly 27 percent of those in Federal prisons.[12]

Sex offenders in prison are much more likely to report having been victims of childhood physical or sexual abuse than other inmates. In a 1991 sur-

Table 19.5

CHARACTERISTICS OF IMPRISONED SEX OFFENDERS, 1994

	Offenders in State prison		
Characteristic	All violent	Rape	Sexual assault
Estimated number of offenders	429,400	33,800	54,300
Sex			
Male	96.2%	99.6%	98.8%
Female	3.8	0.4	0.2
Race			
White	48.1%	52.2%	73.9%
Black	48.2	43.7	22.8
Other	3.7	4.1	3.3
Age at arrest for current offense			
Less than 18	3.1%	0.6%	1.1%
18–24	38.1	33.7	23.6
25–29	22.1	20.9	17.0
30–34	15.0	17.7	16.3
35–39	8.8	10.9	13.4
40–44	5.0	4.1	10.2
45–49	3.4	4.8	6.6
50–54	1.7	2.9	4.4
55–59	1.5	3.2	4.2
60 or older			
Average age at arrest	29 yrs	31 yrs	34 yrs
Marital status			
Married	17.1%	22.1%	21.8%
Widowed	2.6	1.2	1.7
Divorced	21.4	28.5	35.0
Separated	5.6	6.2	4.9
Never married	53.3	42.0	36.6

Source: U.S. Department of Justice, Bureau of Justice Statistics, *Sex Offenses and Offenders: An Analysis of Data on Rape and Sexual Assault* (Washington: Office of Justice Programs, 1997), p. 21.

vey, nearly 40 percent of State prison inmates serving time for other sexual assault said they had been physically or sexually abused as children, while around 20 percent of convicted rapists reported being victims of child physical or sexual abuse.[13] This notwithstanding, about two-thirds of imprisoned sexual assaulters reported never having been abused sexually or physically during childhood.

Only a small percentage of imprisoned sex offenders used a firearm during the commission of the rape or other sexual assault in which they were convicted. The Justice Department reported in *Firearm Use by Offenders* that in 1997, of the 87,687 inmates in State prison for sexual assaults, an estimated 3 percent possessed a handgun or other firearm at the time of the crime.[14]

Trends in Imprisonment of Sex Offenders

Prisoner data indicates that more sex offenders are being convicted and more convicted sex offenders are being sent to prison. As shown in Figure 19.1, from 1980 to 1994 State prisoners convicted of rape or sexual assault went from an estimated 20,500 prisoners, or 6.9 percent of total prisoners, to 88,100 inmates, or 9.7 percent of all inmates. This represented an increase of 330 percent in imprisoned sex offenders compared to a 206 percent increase in the general prison population. Between 1980 and 1994, prisoners serving time for sex crimes other than rape had the second highest growth rate among violent offenders, increasing on average by more than 15 percent annually; while the number of convicted rapists in prison grew by an average of about 7 percent over the span.[15]

From 1985 to 1993, national data indicates that there has been little variation in the average sentence received for persons entering State prisons for

Figure 19.1
ESTIMATED NUMBERS OF SEX OFFENDERS[a] IN STATE PRISONS, 1980–1994

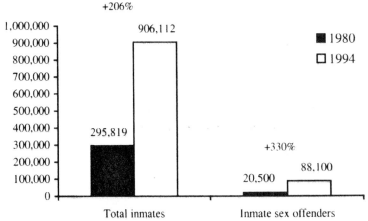

a. Includes prisoners convicted of rape or sexual assault.

Source: Adapted from U.S. Department of Justice, Bureau of Justice Statistics, *Sex Offenses and Offenders: An Analysis of Data on Rape and Sexual Assault* (Washington: Government Printing Office, 1997), p. 17.

the sex offenses of rape and sexual assault. Sentencing for rapists has been between twelve and thirteen years on average, while sexual assaulters admitted to prison have received an average sentence of between eight and nine years.[16] However, national figures have revealed that for sex offenders released from State prisons between 1985 and 1993, there was an increase in the average length of confinement and an increase in the percentage of the time served prior to being released. The average time served by discharged convicted rapists during the period increased from about 3.5 to 5 years, increasing the percentage of time served from around 38 percent to 50 percent. For sexual assaulters released from prison, the time served behind bars rose by around six months, from just over two years in prison to just under three years. The percentage of time served for inmates convicted of sexual assault rose from around 34 percent to 41 percent of the sentence over the span.[17]

Victims of Inmate Sex Offenders

The vast majority of imprisoned sex offenders had a single victim for which they were incarcerated. Nearly 86 percent of surveyed inmate rapists and almost 79 percent of inmate sexual assaulters reported victimizing one person in accounting for their incarceration.[18] Table 19.6 presents the characteristics of victims of sex offenders imprisoned for rape and sexual assault. Sex crime victims are far more likely to be female than male. More than 94 percentof rape victims and nearly 85 percent of sexual assault victims of imprisoned sex offenders were female. However, there were more than three times as many inmates serving time for sexual assaults as rapes in which the victim was a male.

Overall, sex crime victims of prisoners tend to be white but the percentage of white victims of sexual assault is higher than that of white rape victims. While nearly 68 percent of imprisoned rapists' victims were white, more than 76 percent of the inmate sexual assaulters' victims were white. More than one in four rape victims and about two in ten sexual assault victims of imprisoned sex offenders were black, with victims of other races for all sex crimes under 5 percent.

Most violent sex offenders in prison victimized persons under the age of eighteen. More than three-quarters of sexual assaulters serving time reported having victims age seventeen and under. Nearly 45 percent of the victims were age twelve or younger. Thirty-seven percent of rape victims of prisoners were under the age of eighteen. However, more than half of inmate rapists' victims were between the ages of eighteen and thirty-four. The median age of rape victims of inmates was twenty-two years old, compared to a median age of sexual assault victims of thirteen years old.

Table 19.6
VICTIMS OF INMATE SEX OFFENDERS[a]

| Characteristic | Violent offenders in State prison reporting single victis | | |
	All	Rape	Sexual assault
Sex of victim			
Male	55.8%	5.5%	15.2%
Female	44.2	94.5	84.8
Race			
White	64.5%	67.8%	76.4%
Black	29.8	27.6	20.1
Other	5.7	4.6	3.5
Age of victi			
12 or younger	9.9%	15.2%	44.7%
13 to 17	8.8	21.8	33.0
18 to 24	17.5	25.1	9.4
25 to 34	31.1	25.4	7.7
35 to 54	26.5	10.2	4.3
55 or older	6.3	2.3	0.9
Median age	29 yrs	22 yrs	13 yrs
Relationship to offender			
Family	12.9%	20.3%	37.7%
Spouse	2.5	1.2	0.6
Child/stepchild	6.1	14.0	25.9
Other relative	4.3	5.1	11.2
Intimate	5.5	9.1	6.2
Boyfriend/girlfriend	5.0	8.8	5.4
Ex-spouse	0.5	0.3	0.8
Acquaintance	34.7	40.8	41.2
Stranger	46.9	29.8	14.9

a. Includes person imprisoned for rape and sexual assault.

Source: U.S. Department of Justice, Bureau of Justice Statistics, *Sex Offenses and Offenders: An Analysis of Data on Rape and Sexual Assault* (Washington: Office of Justice Programs, 1997), p. 24.

While nearly half of all violent offenders in prison committed crimes against strangers, inmate sex offenders tended to victimize people they knew more often. Under 30 percent of incarcerated rapists and less than 15 percent of incarcerated sexual assaulters' victims were strangers. About 40 percent of inmates convicted of sexual assault and more than 20 percent of inmate rapists reported victimizing a family member. More than 9 percent of convicted rapists and over 6 percent of convicted sexual assaulters were in intimate relationships with their victims. However, more nonstranger victims of sex offender inmates were acquaintances. About 40 percent rape and sexual assault victims of inmates were reported to fall into this category.

INMATE INTIMATE SEX OFFENDERS

Most jail inmates convicted of a violent crime knew their victim. In about 60 percent of crimes of violence committed by jail inmates, the victim was an intimate, relative, friend or acquaintance.[19] About one in four inmates' crimes were against an intimate—a spouse or former spouse, boyfriend, girlfriend, or a significant other. Figure 19.2 identifies convicted sex offenders in jail by the relationship to the victim. More than 12 percent of intimate violence by a jail inmate involved rape or sexual assault. Over half the violence against other relatives and nearly one-fourth against friends or acquaintances of jail sex offenders was a sexual assault or rape. Other relevant findings on convicted intimate violent offenders in jail include:

- More than half had a history of having a restraining or protection order against them.
- Nearly four in ten had a criminal justice status, such as parole or probation, or a restraining order against them.
- More than half the jail inmates were drinking or using drugs at the time of

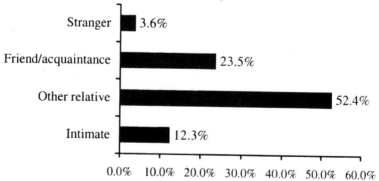

Figure 19.2
CONVICTED SEX OFFENDERS[a] IN LOCAL JAILS, BY RELATION TO VICTIM

a. Includes jail inmates convicted of rape and sexual assault.

Source: Adapted from U.S. Department of Justice, Bureau of Justice Statistics, *Violence by Intimates: Analysis of Data on Crime by Crrent or Former Spouses, Boyfriends, and Girlfriends* (Washington: Office of Justice Programs, 1998), p. 25.

the intimate offense.
• Around three in four jail inmates convicted of an intimate offense were recidivists, with more than half having previously committed violent offenses.[20]

Intimate violence represents a smaller part of overall violence perpetrated
by State prisoners than jail inmates. However, a greater proportion of intimate violence committed by prison inmates tends to involve sex offenses.
Just over 7 percent of violent offenders in State prisons were serving time for
violence against an intimate, compared to 9.8 percent against another relative, and 26.9 percent who victimized a friend or acquaintance. Fifty-six percent of violent offenders in prison committed crimes against strangers.
    Figure 19.3 breaks down sex offenders in State prisons by relationship to
their victims.
    More than 20 percent of intimate crimes of violence by inmates was a rape
or sexual assault, more than 60 percent of violent acts by prisoners was
against other relatives, and 30 percent against friends or acquaintances
involved a rape or sexual assault.
    Violent offenders in prison convicted of intimate violence were more like-
ly than other violent offenders to be serving time for homicide.[21] Conversely,
the rate of death or injury by victims of inmate intimate violence was higher
than that of victims of any other type of violent offender incarcerated.[22]
Nearly half the inmates in State prison for intimate violence killed the intimate, while almost 13 percent of the victims of intimate violence had been
raped or sexually assaulted.[23]

Figure 19.3
SEX OFFENDERS[a] IN STATE PRISONS, BY RELATIONSHIP TO VICTIM

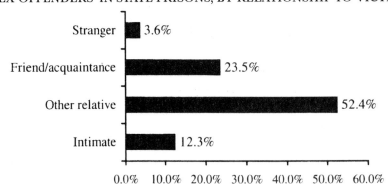

a. Includes prisoners convicted of rape or sexual assault.

Source: Adapted from U.S. Department of Justice, Bureau of Justice Statistics, *Violence by
Intimates: Analysis of Data on Crime by Crrent or Former Spouses, Boyfriends, and Girlfriends*
(Washington: Office of Justice Programs, 1998), p. 28.

Similar to intimate violence jail inmates, most prison inmates convicted of violence against an intimate used drugs or alcohol prior to committing the offense.[24]

CHILD SEXUAL VICTIMIZER INMATES

Around one-fifth of the inmates serving time in State prisons for violent crimes committed crimes against victims under the age of eighteen.[25] In more than half the crimes involving children, the child victim was younger than thirteen. Nearly 70 percent of inmates with child victims were incarcerated for child rape or a sexual assault, while two-thirds of all prisoners convicted of a sex offense had victimized a child.[26]

Table 19.7
OFFENSE DISTRIBUTION OF STATE PRISONERS
AND CHILD VICTIIZER INMATES, 1991

| | State prison inmates, by offense | | | |
| | All prisoners | | Child victiizers | |
Offense	*Number*	*Percent*	*Number*	*Percent*
All offenses	711,643	100.0%[a]	65,163	100.0%[a]
Violent offenses	327,958	46.1	61,037	93.7
Homicide	87,479	12.3	5,792	8.9
Murder	74,693	10.5	4,677	7.2
Negligent manslaughter	12,786	1.8	1,115	1.7
Kidnapping	8,369	1.2	1,508	2.3
Rape and sexual assault	66,482	9.3	43,552	66.8
Forcible rape	22,797	3.2	8,908	13.7
Forcible sodomy	2,036	0.3	1.741	2.7
Statutory rape	1,162	0.2	1,102	1.7
Lewd acts with children	10,799	1.5	10,799	16.6
Other sexual assault	29,688	4.2	21,002	32.2
Robbery	104,136	14.6	3,772	5.8
Assault	59,275	7.8	3,933	6.0
Aggravated assault	55,549	7.8	3,933	6.0
Child abuse	1,717	0.2	1,717	2.6
Simple assault	2,009	0.3	408	0.6
Other violent	2,217	0.3	355	0.5
Nonviolent offenses	383,685	53.9	4,126	6.3

a. Detail may not add to totals due to rounding.

Source: U.S. Department of Justice, Bureau of Justice Statistics, *Child Victimizers: Violent Offenders and Their Victims* (Washington: Office of Justice Programs, 1996). p. 1.

Table 19.7 reflects the offense distribution of State prisoners and the percentage with victims under eighteen in 1991. Overall, more than 9 percent of prisoners had committed crimes against children. This percentage more than doubled for violent offenses. There were 43,552 inmates serving time as child sexual victimizers. Around one-third of these were convicted of other sexual assaults, while nearly 17 percent committed lewd acts with children. Child rapists constituted almost 14 percent of inmates' sex offenses against children, with forcible sodomy and statutory rape representing under 5 percent of the offenses. Nearly 40 percent of all imprisoned sex offenders were convicted of forcible rape against a child; while more than 70 percent of prisoners serving time for other sexual assaults and more than 80 percent incarcerated for forcible sodomy had victims under eighteen years of age.

Table 19.8
VIOLENT CHILD VICTIMIZERS IN STATE PRISONS,
BY AGE OF VICTIM, 1991[a]

Violent offense		Prisoners serving time for crimes against children[b]		
	All	Victims age 12 or younger	Victims age 13 to 17	Percent with victims age 12 or younger
Total	60,285	33,287	26,998	55.2%
Homicide	87,479	12.3	5,792	8.9
Murder	74,693	10.5	4,677	7.2
Negligent manslaughter	12,786	1.8	1,115	1.7
Kidnapping	8,369	1.2	1,508	2.3
Rape and sexual assault	66,482	9.3	43,552	66.8
Forcible rape	22,797	3.2	8,908	13.7
Forcible sodomy	2,036	0.3	1.741	2.7
Statutory rape	1,162	0.2	1,102	1.7
Lewd acts with children	10,799	1.5	10,799	16.6
Other sexual assault	29,688	4.2	21,002	32.2
Robbery	104,136	14.6	3,772	5.8
Assault	59,275	7.8	3,933	6.0
Aggravated assault	55,549	7.8	3,933	6.0
Child abuse	1,717	0.2	1,717	2.6
Simple assault	2,009	0.3	408	0.6
Other violent	2,217	0.3	355	0.5

a. Excludes 752 cases for which the specific age of the victim was not reported.
b. Detail may not add to total due to rounding.

Source: U.S. Department of Justice, Bureau of Justice Statistics, *Child Victimizers: Violent Offenders and Their Victims* (Washington: Office of Justice Programs, 1996). p. 2.

Inmate child sexual victimizers in State prisons in 1991, by age of their victims, can be seen in Table 19.8. In all, there were 60,285 prisoners convicted of crimes against children.

More than 55 percent of the victims of child victimizers were age twelve or younger, while around 10 percent of all violent offenders reported victimizing children under the age of thirteen.[27] Older children were more likely to be targeted by inmate child sex offenders for forcible rape. However, in every other category of child sexual crime, child victimizers sexually assaulted or abused younger children. Sexual offenses typically described by imprisoned child victimizers with victims age twelve and under include fondling, child molestation, and indecent or lewd acts.

Figure 19.4 illustrates the high percentage of inmate child offenders' crimes against victims under the age of twelve. Nearly 90 percent of inmates serving time for child abuse victimized children age twelve and younger. Almost 70 percent of inmate sex offenders' lewd acts with children and

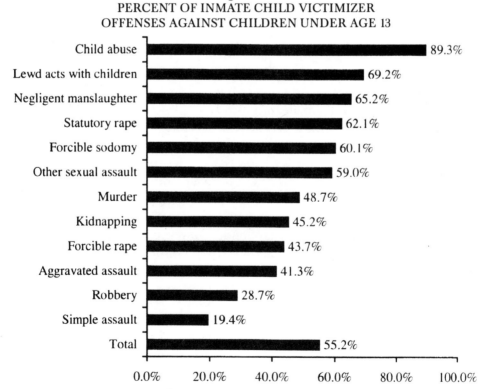

Figure 19.4
PERCENT OF INMATE CHILD VICTIMIZER
OFFENSES AGAINST CHILDREN UNDER AGE 13

Offense	Percent
Child abuse	89.3%
Lewd acts with children	69.2%
Negligent manslaughter	65.2%
Statutory rape	62.1%
Forcible sodomy	60.1%
Other sexual assault	59.0%
Murder	48.7%
Kidnapping	45.2%
Forcible rape	43.7%
Aggravated assault	41.3%
Robbery	28.7%
Simple assault	19.4%
Total	55.2%

Source: Adapted from U.S. Department of Justice, Bureau of Justice Statistics, *Child Victimizers: Violent Offenders and Their Victims* (Washington: Office of Justice Programs, 1996), p. 2.

around 60 percent who committed statutory rape, forcible sodomy, or other sexual assaults involved victims under thirteen years of age. More than 40 percent of forcible rape victims of child victimizers were younger children.

According to the BJS, most child sexual victimizers serving time are male, white, non-Hispanic, under thirty, high school graduates, and never married or divorced.[28] Around one-third of child victimizers in prison report coming from broken homes and being physically or sexually abused during childhood. Nearly 25 percent used alcohol at the time of the offense, while almost 14 percent of sexual offenders of children serving time used both alcohol and drugs while committing the offense.[29]

WOMEN INMATE SEX OFFENDERS

Women constitute only a small percentage of incarcerated sex offenders overall, but tend to have a higher rate of incarceration for sex offenses against children than total victims. They are also more likely than men to be serving time for prostitution-related charges. In 1994, women made up less than 2 percent of offenders in State prison for rape or sexual assault.[30] However, as child victimizers, females account for more than 3 percent of the prison population.[31] Under 1 percent of jail inmates whose most serious offense was a violent sex crime were female, according to a profile of jail inmates for 1996.[32]

However, 5.4 percent of jail inmates being held for morals charges—such as commercial vice—were female, or more than three times the percentage of males. Research on the most serious offense for women serving time in prison found a similar percent incarcerated for public order offenses such as prostitution and offenses against morals and decency.[33] The disparity in females-males serving time for prostitution-related offenses is reflected in the statistics.[34] Black women are more likely than women of other races to be arrested and incarcerated for prostitution or commercialized vice.[35]

Most incarcerated women sex offenders have been victims of sexual assaults and child sexual abuse,[36] and abused alcohol or drugs prior to conviction.[37]

JUVENILE INMATE SEX OFFENDERS

Sex offenders institutionalized under the age of eighteen are relatively rare. Just over 2 percent of jail inmates are age seventeen and under.[38] Only 1 percent of new court commitments to State prison for rape and sexual assault in 1996 were under eighteen, according to the Justice Department's study, *Juvenile Offenders and Victims: A 1999 Report.*[39] Sex offenses by juvenile new court commitments to State prison comprised a lower proportion of their overall offenses than sex offenses by adult new court commitments.

Most juvenile sex offenders are held in juvenile correctional facilities. In 1997, there were 105,790 delinquents and status offenders being held in public and private juvenile facilities in the United States.[40] Of these, 6 percent being held as delinquents were in residential placement for sexual assault offenses (see Table 19.9). Most of these were held in public facilities. Twice as many juvenile sexual assaulters were committed to rather than detained in public facilities. However, a slightly higher percentage (7 percent) of juvenile sex offenders were placed in private facilities rather than public facilities. Juvenile sexual assaulters in private facilities were more likely to be committed than detained.

More than one in five juvenile status offenders confined to juvenile facilities were held as runaways, often a precursor to juvenile prostitution.[41] Forty percent of runaways in public facilities were detained, while nearly 30 percent of runaways in private facilities were being detained. Five percent of juveniles in public facilities and 7 percent in private facilities were in residential placement for public order offenses, such as commercialized vice.

The vast majority of institutionalized juvenile sex offenders are male. According to the Office of Juvenile Justice and Delinquency Prevention's *Census of Juveniles in Residential Placement 1997,* 89 percent of juveniles in residential placement as delinquents were male.[42] There were more than thirteen times as many male juveniles being held for violent offenses as female

Figure 19.5
JUVENILE SEX ASSAULTERS IN RESIDENTIAL PLACEMENT,
BY RACE AND HISPANIC ORIGIN, 1997

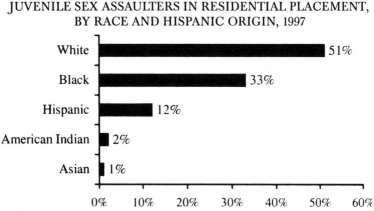

Source: Derived from U.S. Department of Justice, Office of Justice Programs, *Juvenile Offenders and Victims: 1999 National Report* (Washington: Office of Juvenile Justice and Delinquency Prevention, 1999), p. 195.

Table 19.9
JUVENILE DELINGQUENTS AND STATUS OFFENDERS
IN RESIDENTIAL PLACEMENT FACILITIES, 1997

Percent of juvenile offenders in residential placement

Most serious offense	All facilities	Public facilities			Private facilities		
		Total	Committed	Detained	Total	Committed	Detained
Delinquency	99,913	74,552	50,163	23,819	24,361	21,515	2,450
	100%	100%	100%	100%	100%	100%	100%
Person	36	37	39	31	33	33	31
Sexual assault	6	5	6	3	7	7	5
Property	32	31	33	26	37	37	36
Drug	9	9	9	9	11	11	9
Public order	10	10	10	10	11	10	12
Other public order	5	5	5	5	7	6	7
Technical violation[a]	13	14	9	24	9	8	13
Status offense	6,877	1,783	973	695	5,094	3,852	716
	100%	100%	100%	100%	100%	100%	100%
Running away	22	27	15	40	20	18	29

a. Includes violations of probation, parole, and valid court order.

Source: U.S. Department of Justice, Bureau of Justice Statistics, *Juvenile Offenders and Victis: 1999 National Report* (Washington: Office of Juvenile Justice and Delinquency Prevention, 1999), p. 188.

juveniles in 1997. However, there were nearly four times as many females as males in residential placement as status offenders. Females accounted for 63 percent of the juveniles held in public and private facilities as runaways.

White youths constituted more than half the juvenile sexual assaulters being held in residential facilities in 1997, as shown in Figure 19.5. One-third of juveniles in residential placement for sexual assaults were black, while Hispanic youths made up 12 percent of the juvenile sexual assaulters. Only 3 percent of the juveniles in residential facilities for sexual assault were American Indian or Asian. Around half of all juveniles held for public order offenses such as prostitution-related, are white with about one-third black, 15 percent Hispanic, and 4 percent other racial minorities.[43]

According to experts in child abuse, the majority of juvenile sex offenders have been sexually or physically abused or victimized through emotional abuse, neglect, or abandonment.[44]

NOTES

1. *See, for example,* W. L. Marshall, T. Ward, R. Jones, P. Johnston, and H. E. Barbaree, "An Optimistic Evaluation of Treatment Outcome with Sex Offenders," *Violence Update 1,* 7 (1991): 1, 8, 10–11; David Briggs, "The Management of Sex Offenders in Institutions," in Tony Morrison, Marcus Erooga, and Richard C. Beckett, eds., *Sexual Offending Against Children: Assessment and Treatment of Male Abusers* (London: Routledge, 1994), pp. 129–45.

2. U.S. Department of Justice, Bureau of Justice Statistics, *Sex Offenses and Offenders: An Analysis of Data on Rape and Sexual Assault* (Washington: Office of Justice Programs, 1997), pp. 25–27; R. Barri Flowers, *The Prostitution of Women and Girls* (Jefferson: McFarland, 2005); R. Barri Flowers, *Murder, At The End of The Day and Night: A Study of Criminal Homicide Offenders, Victims, and Circumstances* (Springfield: Charles C Thomas, 2002), pp. 159–78; Brian Lane and Wilfred Gregg, *The Encyclopedia of Serial Killers* (New York: Berkley, 1995).

3. *Sex Offenses and Offenders,* p. 17.

4. *Ibid.*

5. U.S. Department of Justice, Bureau of Justice Statistics Special Report, *Profile of Jail Inmates, 2002* (Washington: Office of Justice Programs, 2004), p. 1.

6. *Ibid.,* p. 8.

7. *Sex Offenses and Offenders,* p. 17.

8. *Ibid.,* p. 23.

9. *Ibid.,* p. 21.

10 *Ibid.*

11. U.S. Department of Justice, Bureau of Justice Statistics, *Alcohol and Crime* (Washington: Government Printing Office, 1998), p. 21.

12. *Ibid.*

13. *Sex Offenses and Offenders,* p. 23.

14. U.S. Department of Justice, Bureau of Justice Statistics Special Report, *Firearm Use by Offenders* (Washington: Office of Justice Programs, 2001), p. 4.

15. *Sex Offenses and Offenders,* p. 18.

16. *Ibid.*, p. 19.
17. *Ibid.*, p. 20.
18. *Ibid.*, p. 23.
19. U.S. Department of Justice, Bureau of Justice Statistics, *Violence by Intimates: Analysis of Data on Crimes by Current or Former Spouses, Boyfriends, and Girlfriends* (Washington: Office of Justice Programs, 1998), p. 25.
20. *Ibid.*, pp. 25–27.
21. *Ibid.*, p. 28.
22. *Ibid.*, p. 29.
23. *Ibid.*
24. *Ibid.*, pp. 26–27; R. Barri Flowers, *Drugs, Alcohol and Criminality in American Society* (Jefferson: McFarland, 1999), pp. 157–79.
25. U.S. Department of Justice, Bureau of Justice Statistics, *Child Victimizers: Violent Offenders and Their Victims* (Washington: Office of Justice Programs, 1996), p. 3.
26. *Ibid.*
27. *Ibid.*, p. 2.
28. *Ibid.*, p. 5.
29. *Ibid.*, p. 7.
30. *Sex Offenses and Offenders*, p. 21.
31. *Child Victimizers*, p. 5.
32. *Profile of Jail Inmates, 2002*, p. 4.
33. R. Barri Flowers, *Female Crime, Criminals and Cellmates: An Exploration of Female Criminality and Delinquency* (Jefferson: McFarland, 1995), pp. 228–29.
34. *Ibid.*, p. 105; Flowers, *The Prostitution of Women and Girls,* pp. 145–48; D. Kelly Weisberg, *Children of the Night: A Study of Adolescent Prostitution* (Lexington: Lexington Books, 1985), pp. 124–28.
35. Flowers, *Female Crime, Criminals and Cellmates*, p. 105; Marilyn G. Haft, "Hustling for Rights," in Laura Crites, ed., *The Female Offender* (Lexington: Lexington Books, 1976), p. 212.
36. Flowers, *The Prostitution of Women and Girls,* pp. 106–12; Flowers, *Female Crime, Criminals and Cellmates,* pp. 233–34; U.S. Department of Justice, Bureau of Justice Statistics Special Report, *Survey of State Prison Inmates, 1991: Women in Prison* (Washington: Government Printing Office, 1994), pp. 3–6.
37. Flowers, *Female Crime, Criminals and Cellmates*, pp. 227–29; Survey of State Prison Inmates, 1991, p. 9.
38. *Profile of Jail Inmates, 2002*, p. 2.
39. U.S. Department of Justice, Office of Justice Programs, *Juvenile Offenders and Victims: 1999 National Report* (Washington: Office of Juvenile Justice and Delinquency Prevention, 1999), p. 209.
40. *Ibid.*, p. 188.
41. *Ibid.*; Flowers, *The Prostitution of Women and Girls,* pp. 89, 97–98.
42. *Juvenile Offenders and Victims*, p. 199.
43. *Ibid.*, p. 195.
44. Flowers, *The Prostitution of Women and Girls,* pp. 83–84, 105–12; R. Barri Flowers, *The Victimization and Exploitation of Women and Children: A Study of Physical, Mental and Sexual Maltreatment in the United States* (Jefferson: McFarland, 1994), p. 66, 84–86.

REFERENCES

Abel, G., J. Becker, J. Cunningham-Rathner, and J. Rouleau. (1987). "Self-Reported Sex Crimes of 561 Nonincarcerated Paraphiliacs." *Journal of Interpersonal Violence 2,* 6: 3–25.

___, M. Mittleman, J. Becker, J. Rathner, and J. Rouleau. (1988). "Predicting Child Molesters' Response to Treatment." *Annals of the New York Academy of Sciences: 528:* 223–34.

Abramson, Hilary. "Sociologists Try to Reach Young Hustlers." *Sacramento Bee* (September 3, 1984), p. 48.

Adams, C. (1993). "I Just Raped My Wife! What Are You Going to Do About It, Pastor?" In E. Buchwald, P. Fletcher, and M. Roth, eds. *Transforming a Rape Culture.* Minneapolis: Milkweed Editions.

Adler, Freda. (1975). *Sisters in Crime: The Rise of the New Female Criminal.* New York: McGraw-Hill.

Akers, Ronald. (1985). *Deviant Behavior: A Social Learning Approach.* 3rd Ed. Belmont: Wadsworth.

Allen, Clifford. (1949). *The Sexual Perversions and Abnormalities.* London: Oxford University Press.

Allen, Donald M. (1980). "Young Male Prostitutes: A Psychosocial Study." *Archives of Sexual Behavior 9:* 399–406.

American Humane Association. (1966). *Protecting the Child Victim of Sex Crimes.* Denver: American Humane Association.

___. (1967). *Sexual Abuse of Children: Implications for Casework.* Denver: American Humane Association.

___. (1968). *Child Victims of Incest.* Denver: American Humane Association.

___. (1978). *National Reporting Study of Child Abuse and Neglect.* Denver; American Humane Association.

American Psychiatric Association. (1987). *Diagnostic and Statistical Manual of Mental Disorders.* 3rd Ed. Washington: American Psychiatric Association.

Amir, Menachem. (1971). *Patterns in Forcible Rape.* Chicago: University of Chicago Press.

Arbetter, Sandra. (1995). "Family Violence: When We Hurt the Ones We Love." *Current Health 22,* 3: 6.

Arias, I., M. Samios, and K. D. Leary. (1987). "Prevalence and Correlates of Physical Aggression During Courtship." *Journal of Interpersonal Violence 2,* 1: 82–90.

Bachman, R., and L. E. Saltzman. (1994). *Violence Against Women: A National Crime Victimization Survey Report.* Washington: Bureau of Justice Statistics.

Bagley, C. (1992). "Characteristics of 60 Children and Adolescents with a History of Sexual Assault Against Others: Evidence from a Comparative Study." *Journal of Forensic Psychiatry 3,* 2.

Bales, Kevin, and Steven Lize. (2005). *Trafficking in Persons in the United States.* Unpublished

Report to the National Institute of Justice. Washington: U.S. Department of Justice.

Bandura, A. (1977). *Social Learning Theory.* Englewood Cliffs: Prentice Hall.

Barchis, V. (1983). "The Question of Marital Rape." *Women's Studies International Forum 6:* 383.

Barnard, C. P. (1989). "Alcoholism and Sex Abuse in the Family: Incest and Marital Rape." *Journal of Chemical Dependency Treatment 3:* 131–44.

Barnett, S., F. Corder, and D. Jehu. (1989). "Group Treatment for Women Sex Offenders." *Practice 3:* 148–59.

Baron, Larry, and Murray A. Straus. (1984). "Sexual Stratification, Pornography, and Rape in the United States." In Neil M. Malamuth and Edward Donnerstein, eds. *Pornography and Sexual Aggression.* Orlando: Academic Press.

Barry, Kathleen. (1979). *Female Sexual Slavery.* Englewood Cliffs: Prentice-Hall.

Bateman, Py. (1998). "The Context of Date Rape." In Barrie Levy, ed. *Dating Violence: Young Women in Danger.* Seattle: Seal Press.

Battelle Law and Justice Study Center Report. (1977). *Forcible Rape: An Analysis of Legal Issues.* Washington: Government Printing Office.

Bedarf, A. R. (1995). "Examining Sex Offender Community Notification Laws." *California Law Review 83,* 3: 885–939.

Bender, L., and A. Blau. (1937). "The Reactions of Children to Sexual Problems with Adults." *American Journal of Orthopsychiatry 8,* 4: 500–18.

Benjamin, Henry, and R. E. L. Masters. (1964). *Prostitution and Morality.* New York: Julian Press.

Bensinger, Gad J. (2001). "Trafficking of Women and Girls." *Crime & Justice International 17,* 56: 11–13.

Bergen, R. K. (1996). *Wife Rape: Understanding the Response of Survivors and Service Providers.* Thousand Oaks: Sage.

Berger, Ronald J., Patricia Searles, and W. Lawrence Newman. (1988). "The Dimensions of Rape Reform Legislation." *Law and Society Review 22:* 329–57.

Berlin, F., and C. Meinecke. (1981). "Treatment of Sex Offenders with Anti-androgenic Medication." *American Journal of Psychiatry 138:* 601–7.

Berliner, L., and J. R. Wheeler. (1987). "Treating the Effects of Sexual Abuse on Children." *Journal of Interpersonal Violence 2:* 415–24.

Bernard, M. L., and J. L. Bernard. (1983). "Violent Intimacy: The Family as a Model For Love Relationships." *Family Relations 32:* 283–86.

Bidwell, L., and P. White. (1986). "The Family Context of Marital Rape." *Journal of Family Violence 1:* 277–87.

Billingham, R. E., and A. R. Sack. (1987). "Conflict Resolution Tactics and the Level of Emotional Commitment Among Unmarrieds." *Human Relations 40:* 59–74.

Blanchard, G. (1990). "Differential Diagnosis of Sex Offenders: Distinguishing Characteristics of the Sex Addict." *American Journal of Preventive Psychiatry and Neurology 2,* 3: 45–47.

Block, Carolyn R., and Antigone Christakos. (1995). "Chicago Homicide From the Sixties to the Nineties: Major Trends in Lethal Violence." In U.S. Department of Justice. Office of Juvenile Programs. *Trends, Risks, and Interventions in Lethal Violence: Proceedings of the Third Annual Spring Symposium of the Homicide Research Working Group.* Washington: National Institute of Justice.

Blume, E. Sue. (1998). *Secret Survivors: Uncovering Incest and Its Aftereffects in Women.* New York: Random House.

Bohmer, Carol. (1998). "Rape and the Law." In Mary E. Odem and Jody Clay-Warner, eds. *Confronting Rape and Sexual Assault.* Wilmington: Scholarly Resources, Inc.

Bovard, James. (1995). "Safeguard Public Health: Legalize Contractual Sex." *Insight on the*

News 11: 20.

Bowker, Lee H. (1978). *Women, Crime, and the Criminal Justice System.* Lexington: Lexington Books.

Bracey, Dorothy H. (1979). *"Baby-Pros": Preliminary Profiles of Juvenile Prostitution.* New York: John Jay Press.

Bremer, J. (1959). *Asexualization.* New York: Macmillan.

Briere, J., and N. A. Malamuth. (1983). "Predicting Self-Reported Likelihood of Sexually Abusive Behavior: Attitudinal Versus Sexual Explanations." *Journal of Research in Personality* 17: 315–23.

Briggs, David. (1994). "The Management of Sex Offenders in Institutions." In Tony Morrison, Marcus Erooga, and Richard C. Beckett, eds. *Sexual Offending Against Children: Assessment and Treatment of Male Abusers.* London: Routledge.

Brodsky, Stanley L., and Susan C. Hobart. (1978). "Blame Models and Assailant Research." *Criminal Justice and Behavior 5:* 379–88.

Browne, A. (1987). *When Battered Women Kill.* New York: Macmillan.

___. (1993). "Violence Against Women by Male Partners: Prevalence, Outcomes, and Policy Implications." *American Psychologist 48,* 10: 1077–87.

Brownmiller, Susan. (1975). *Against Our Will: Men, Women and Rape.* New York: Simon & Schuster.

Burgess, Ann W. (1984). *Child Pornography and Sex Rings.* Lexington: Lexington Books.

___, A. N. Groth, L. L. Holmstrom, and S. M. Sgroi. (1978) *Sexual Assault of Children and Adolescents.* Lexington: Lexington Books.

Burgess, Robert L., and Ronald L. Akers. (1966). "A Differential Association-Reinforcement Theory of Criminal Behavior." *Social Problems 14:* 128–47.

Burt, Martha R. (1980). "Cultural Myths and Support for Rape." *Journal of Personality and Social Psychology 38:* 217–30.

Burton, L. (1968). *Vulnerable Children.* New York: Schocken Books.

Buss, D. M. (1994). *The Evolution of Desire.* New York: Basic Books.

Campbell, J. C (1989). "Women's Response to Sexual Abuse in Intimate Relationships." *Health Care for Women International 10:* 335–46.

___. (1992). "If I Can't Have You, No One Can: Issues of Power and Control in Homicide of Female Partners." In J. Radford and D. E. Russell, eds. *Femicide: The Politics of Woman Killing.* Boston: Twayne.

___, and P. Alford. (1989). "The Dark Consequences of Marital Rape." *American Journal of Nursing:* 946–49.

Carnes, P. (1983). *Out of the Shadows.* Minneapolis: CompCare.

___. (1991). *Don't Call It Love.* New York: Bantam Books.

Cates, Jim A. (1989). "Adolescent Male Prostitution by Choice." *Child & Adolescent Social Work 6:* 155–56.

Caukins, S., and N. Coombs. (1976). "The Psychodynamics of Male Prostitution." *American Journal of Psychotherapy 30:* 441–51.

Center for Policy Research. *Stalking in America.* July, 1997.

Chiasson, M. A., A. R. Lifson, R. L. Stoneburner, W. Ewing, D. Hilderbrandt, and H. W. Jaffe. "HIV-1 Seroprevalence in Male and Female Prostitutes in New York City." *Abstracts from the Sixth International Conference on AIDS.* Stockholm, June, 1988.

Clark, Lorenne M., and Debra J. Lewis. (1977). *Rape: The Price of Coercive Sexuality.* Toronto: Canadian Women's Educational Press.

Clinard, Marshall B. (1957). *Sociology of Deviant Behavior.* New York: Holt, Rinehart & Winston.

Cohen, Albert K. (1965). "The Sociology of the Deviant Act; Anomie Theory and Beyond."

Sociological Review 2: 5–14.

Cohen, M. L., R. F. Garofalo, R. Boucher, and T. Seghorn. (1971). "The Psychology of Rapists." *Seminars in Psychiatry 3:* 302–27.

Coleman, J. C. (1972). *Abnormal Psychology and Modern Life.* Glenview: Scott, Foresman and Co.

Commission on Obscenity and Pornography. (1971). *Technical Report of the Commission on Obscenity and Pornography: Legal Analysis.* Vol. 2, Washington: Government Printing Office.

The Commonwealth Fund. *First Comprehensive National Survey of American Women.* July, 1993.

Coombs, N. (1974). "Male Prostitution: A Psychosocial View of Behavior." *American Journal of Orthopsychiatry 44:* 782–89.

Corley, A., D. Corley, J. Walker, and S. Walker. (1994). "The Possibility of Organic Left Posterior Hemisphere Dysfunction as a Contributing Factor in Sex-Offending Behavior." *Sexual Addiction & Compulsivity 1,* 4: 337–46.

Cormier, B. S., and S. P. Simons (1969). "The Problem of the Dangerous Sexual Offender." *Canadian Psychiatric Association 14:* 329–34.

Courtois, Christine. (1988). *Healing the Incest Wound.* New York: W. W. Norton.

Cressey, Donald R. (1957). "The State of Criminal Statistics." *National Probation and Parole Association Journal 3:* 230–41.

Crowley, Maura G. (1977). "Female Runaway Behavior and Its Relationship to Prostitution." Master's thesis, Sam Houston State University. Institute of Contemporary Corrections and Behavioral Sciences.

Curtis, L. A. (1976). "Present and Future Measures of Victimization in Forcible Rape." In M. J. Walker and S. L. Brodsky, eds. *Sexual Assault.* Lexington: D.C. Heath.

Cyriaque, Jeanne. "The Chronic Serious Offenders: How Illinois Juveniles 'Match Up'." *Illinois* (February 1982), pp. 4–5.

Daly, Martin, and Margo Wilson. (1982). "Homicide and Kinship." *American Anthropologist 84:* 372–78.

Danna, Alfred. "Juvenile Male Prostitution: How Can We Reduce the Problem?" *USA Today 113* (May 1988): 87.

Davis, Kingsley. (1937). "The Sociology of Prostitution." *American Sociological Review 2:* 744–55.

Dietz, P. E. (1986). "Mass, Serial and Sensational Homicides." *Bulletin of the New York Academy of Medicine 62:* 477–91.

Dobash, R. E., and R. P. Dobash. (1979). *Violence Against Wives.* New York: Free Press.

Donat, Patricia L., and John D'Emilio. (1988). "A Feminist Redefinition of Rape and Sexual Assault: Historical Foundations and Change." In Mary E. Odem and Jody Clay-Warner, eds. *Confronting Rape and Sexual Assault.* Wilmington: Scholarly Resources, Inc.

Drucker, D. (1979). "The Common Law Does Not Support a Marital Exemption for Forcible Rape." *Women's Rights Law Reporter 5:* 2–3.

Drummond, Isabel. (1953). *The Sex Paradox.* New York: Putnam.

Dube, R., and M. Herbert. (1988). "Sexual Abuse of Children Under 12 Years of Age: A Review of 511 Cases." *Child Abuse and Neglect 12:* 321–30.

Dugdale, Richard L. (1877). *The Jukes: A Study in Crime, Pauperism, and Heredity.* New York: Putnam.

Dusky, Lorraine. (1996). *Still Unequal: The Shameful Truth About Women and Justice in America.* New York: Crown.

Dyer, M. (1988). "Exhibitionism/Voyeurism." In D. M. Dailey, ed. *The Sexual Unusual.* New York: Harrington Press.

Earls, C., and H. David. (1989). "A Psychosocial Study of Male Prostitution." *Archives of Sexual Behavior:* 401–19.

Eby, K. K., J. C. Campbell, C. M. Sullivan, and W. S. Davidson. (1995). "Health Effects of

Experiences of Sexual Violence for Women with Abusive Partners." *Health Care for Women International 16:* 563–76.

The Enablers. (1978). *Juvenile Prostitution in Minnesota: The Report of a Research Project.* St. Paul: The Enablers.

Estes, Richard J., and Neil A. Weiner. (February 7, 2006). "The Commercial Sexual Exploitation of Children in the U.S., Canada and Mexico; Executive Summary." Philadelphia: Center for the Study of Youth Policy.

Eve, R. A. (1985). "Empirical and Theoretical Findings Concerning Child and Adolescent Sexual Abuse: Implications for the Next Generation of Studies." *Victimology: An International Journal 10:* 97–109.

Ewing, Charles P. (1997). *Fatal Families: The Dynamics of Intrafamilial Homicide.* Thousand Oaks: Sage.

Faris, Robert E. (1955). *Social Disorganization.* New York: Ronald Press.

Farrior, Stephanie. (1997). "The International Law on Trafficking in Women and Children for Prostitution: Making it Live Up to its Potential." *Harvard Human Rights Journal 10:* 10–12.

Fasset, Byron, and Bill Walsh. (1994). "Juvenile Prostitution: An Overlooked Form of Child Sexual Abuse." *The APSAC Advisor 7,* 1: 30.

Faugier, Jean, and Mary Sargeant. (1997). "'Boyfriends,' 'Pimps' and 'Clients'." In Graham Scambler and Annette Scambler, eds. *Rethinking Prostitution: Purchasing Sex in the 1990s.* London: Routledge.

Feild, Hubert S., and Leigh B. Bienen. (1980). *Jurors and Rape: A Study in Psychology and Law.* Lexington: D.C. Heath.

"Female Victims: The Crime Goes On." (1984). *Science News 126:* 153.

"Final Report of the Supreme Court Task Force on Courts' and Communities' Response to Domestic Abuse." Submitted to the Supreme Court of Iowa, August, 1994.

Finkelor, David. (1979). *Sexually Victimized Children.* New York: Free Press.

___. (1984). *Child Sexual Abuse: New Theory and Research.* New York: Free Press.

___, and Diana Russell. (1984). "Women as Perpetrators." In David Finkelhor, ed. *Child Sexual Abuse: New Theory and Research.* New York: Free Press.

___, Gerald Hotaling, I. A. Lewis, and Christine Smith. (1990). "Sexual Abuse in a National Survey of Adult Men and Women: Prevalence, Characteristics, and Risk Factors." *Child Abuse and Neglect 14:* 19–28.

___, and Kersti Yllo. (1985). *License to Rape: Sexual Abuse of Wives.* New York: Holt, Rinehart & Winston.

___, and Richard Ormrod. (2004). *Child Pornography: Patterns From NIBRS.* Washington: Office of Juvenile Justice and Delinquency Prevention.

___, and Richard Ormrod. (2004). *Prostitution of Juveniles: Patterns From NIBRS.* Washington: Office of Juvenile Justice and Delinquency Prevention.

___, Sharon Araji, Larry Baron, Angela Browne, Stephanie Peters, and Gail Wyatt. (1986). *A Sourcebook on Child Sexual Abuse.* Beverly Hills: Sage.

Fishbein, Diana H. (1996). "Biological Perspectives in Criminology." In Dean G. Rojeck and Gary F. Jensen, eds. *Exploring Delinquency: Causes and Control.* Los Angeles: Roxbury.

Fisher, B. S., F. T. Cullen, and M. G. Turner. (2000). *The Sexual Victimization of College Women.* Washington: National Institute of Justice.

Fisher, Dawn. (1994). "Adult Sex Offenders: Who Are They? Why and How Do They Do It?" In Tony Morrison, Marcus Erooga, and Richard C. Beckett, eds. *Sexual Offending Against Children: Assessment and Treatment of Male Abusers.* London: Routledge.

Fitzpatrick, Joan. (2003). "Trafficking as a Human Rights Violation: The Complex Intersection of Legal Frameworks for Conceptualizing and Combating Trafficking." *Michigan Journal of*

International Law 24: 1143.

Flexner, Abraham. (1914). *Prostitution in Europe.* New York: Century.

Flinn, M. V. (1988). "Mate Guarding in a Caribbean Village." *Ethnology and Sociobiology 9:* 1–28.

Flowers, R. Barri. (1986). *Children and Criminality: The Child as Victim and Perpetrator.* Westport: Greenwood Press.

___. (1987). *Women and Criminality: The Woman as Victim, Offender, and Practitioner.* Westport: Greenwood Press.

___. (1989). *Demographics and Criminality: The Characteristics of Crime in America.* Westport: Greenwood Press.

___. (1990). *The Adolescent Criminal: An Examination of Today's Juvenile Offender.* Jefferson: McFarland.

___. (1990). *Minorities and Criminality.* Westport: Greenwood Press.

___. (1994). *The Victimization and Exploitation of Women and Children: A Study of Physical, Mental and Sexual Maltreatment in the United States.* Jefferson: McFarland.

___. (1995). *Female Crime, Criminals and Cellmates: An Exploration of Female Criminality and Delinquency.* Jefferson: McFarland.

___. (1996). *The Sex Slave Murders.* New York: St. Martin's Press.

___. (1999). *Drugs, Alcohol and Criminality in American Society.* Jefferson: McFarland.

___. (2000). *Domestic Crimes, Family Violence and Child Abuse: A Study of Contemporary American Society.* Jefferson: McFarland.

___. (2001). *Runaway Kids and Teenage Prostitution: America's Lost, Abandoned, and Sexually Exploited Children.* Westport: Greenwood Press.

___. (2002). *Kids Who Commit Adult Crimes: A Study of Serious Juvenile Criminality and Delinquency.* Binghamton: Haworth Press.

___. (2002). *Murder, At The End of the Day and Night: A Study of Criminal Homicide Offenders, Victims, and Circumstances.* Springfield: Charles C Thomas.

___. (2003). *Male Crime and Deviance: Exploring Its Causes, Dynamics, and Nature.* Springfield: Charles C Thomas.

___. (2004). *Persuasive Evidence.* New York: Dorchester.

___. (2005). *Justice Served.* New York: Dorchester.

___. (2005). *The Prostitution of Women and Girls.* Jefferson: McFarland.

___. (2006). *State's Evidence.* New York: Dorchester.

___, and H. Loraine Flowers. (2001). *Murders in the United States: Crimes, Killers and Victims of the Twentieth Century.* Jefferson: McFarland.

Forward, Susan, and C. Buck. (1978). *Betrayal of Innocence: Incest and Its Devastation.* Los Angeles: J. P. Tarcher.

Freeman-Longo, Robert E., and Geral T. Blanchard. (1998). *Sexual Abuse in America: Epidemic of the 21st Century.* Brandon: Safer Society Press.

___, and R. Wall. "Changing a Lifetime of Sexual Crime." *Psychology Today 20,* 3 (March, 1986), pp. 58–64.

Freud, Sigmund. (1933). *New Introductory Lectures in Psychoanalysis.* New York: W. W. Norton.

Frieze, I. H. (1983). "Investigating the Causes and Consequences of Marital Rape." *Signs 8,* 3: 532–53.

Fromuth, M., and B. Burkhart. (1980). "Childhood Sexual Victimization Among College Men: Definitional and Methodological Issues." *Violence and Victims 2,* 4: 241–53.

Frontline. (February 7, 2006). "Sex Slaves." http://www.pbs.org/wgbh/pages/frontline/slaves/etc/stats.html.

Gager, Nancy, and Cathleen Schurr. (1976). *Sexual Assault: Confronting Rape in America.* New

York: Grosset and Dunlap.

Gebhard, Paul H., John H. Gagnon, Wardell B. Pomeroy, and Cornelia V. Christenson. (1965). *Sex Offenders: An Analysis of Types*. New York: Harper & Row.

Geis, Gilbert. (1978). "Rape-in-Marriage: Law and Law Reform in England, the United States, and Sweden." *Adelaide Law Review 6,* 2: 285.

Gelles, Richard J. (1987). *The Violent Home*. Beverly Hills: Sage.

George, L. K., I. Winfield, and D. G. Blazer. (1992). "Sociocultural Factors in Sexual Assault: Comparison of Two Representative Samples of Women." *Journal of Social Issues 48,* 1: 105–25.

Giobbe, Evelina. (1992). "Juvenile Prostitution: Profile of Recruitment." In Ann W. Burgess, ed. *Child Trauma I: Issues and Research*. New York: Garland Publishing.

Glueck, S., and E. T. Glueck. (1956). *Physique and Delinquency*. New York: Harper & Row.

Goddard, Henry H. (1914). *Feeblemindedness, Its Causes and Consequences*. New York: Macmillan.

Goldsmith, Barbara. "Women on the Edge: A Reporter at Large." *New Yorker 69* (April 26, 1993), pp. 64–67, 74–78.

Goldstein, Paul J. (1979). *Prostitution and Drugs*. Lexington: Lexington Books.

Gomes-Schwartz, B., J. M. Horowitz, and A. P. Caldarelli. (1990). *Child Sexual Abuse: The Initial Effects*. Beverly Hills: Sage.

Goodall, Richard. (1995). *The Comfort of Sin: Prostitutes and Prostitution in the 1990s*. Kent: Renaissance Books, 1995.

Goodwin, Jean. (1981). "Suicide Attempts in Sexual Abuse Victims and Their Mothers." *Child Abuse and Neglect 5:* 217–21.

___, Lawrence Cormier, and John Owen. (1983). "Grandfather-Granddaughter Incest: A Trigenerational View." *Child Abuse and Neglect 7:* 163–70.

Gorman, Christine. "Liquid X." *Time 148* (September 30, 1996), p. 64.

Gray, Diana. (1971). "Turning Out: A Study of Teenage Prostitution." Master's thesis, University of Washington.

Green, Richard. (1992). *Sexual Science and the Law*. Cambridge: Harvard University Press.

Greenberg, Joel. (1980). "Incest Out of Hiding." *Science News 117,* 4: 218–20.

Greenwald, Harold. (1970). *The Elegant Prostitute: A Social and Psychoanalytic Study*. New York: Walker and Co.

Griffin, S. (1971). "Rape: The All-American Crime." *Ramparts 10:* 26–35.

Gross, Andrea. "A Question of Rape." *Ladies Home Journal 110,* 11 (November 1993), p. 170.

Groth, A. Nicholas, and J. Birnbaum. (1979). *Men Who Rape: The Psychology of the Offender*. New York: Plenum.

___, Ann W. Burgess, and Lynda L. Holmstrom. (1977). "Rape: Power, Anger, and Sexuality." *American Journal of Psychiatry 34:* 1239–43.

Guio, M., A. Burgess, and R. Kelly. (1980). "Child Victimization: Pornography and Prostitution." *Journal of Crime and Justice 3:* 65–81.

Haberman, Paul W., and Michael M. Baden. (1978). *Alcohol, Other Drugs, and Violent Death*. New York: Oxford University Press.

Haft, Marilyn G. (1976). "Hustling for Rights." In Laura Crites, ed. *The Female Offender*. Lexington: Lexington Books.

Hale, Ellen. "Center Studies Causes of Juvenile Prostitution." *Gannet News Service* (May 21, 1981).

Hammer, Emanuel, and Bernard Glueck. (1957). "Psychodynamic Patterns in Sex Offenders: A Four Factor Theory." *Psychiatric Quarterly 31:* 167–73.

Hamparian, Donna, et al. (1978). *The Violent Few*. Lexington: Lexington Books.

Hare, R. (1995). *Without Conscience: The Disturbing World of Psychopaths Among Us*. New York:

Pocket.

Harlan, Sparky, Luanne L. Rodgers, and Brian Flattery. (1981). *Male and Female Adolescent Prostitution: Huckleberry House Sexual Minority Youth Services Project.* Washington: U.S. Department of Health and Human Services.

Hazelwood, R. R., P. E. Dietz, and J. Warren. (1992). "The Criminal Sexual Sadist." *FBI Law Enforcement Bulletin 61:* 12–20.

Heim, N. (1981). "Sexual Behavior of Castrated Sex Offenders." *Archives of Sexual Behavior 10:* 11–19.

Heller, M. A., S. M. Ehrlich, and D. Lester. (1984). "Childhood Cruelty to Animals, Firesetting and Enuresis as Correlates of Competence to Stand Trial." *Journal of General Psychology 110:* 151–53.

Hersch, Pamela. "Coming of Age on City Streets." *Psychology Today* (January, 1988), pp. 28–37.

Hickey, E. W. (1991). Sexual Murderers and Their Victims. Pacific Grove: Brooks/Cole.

Hirschfield, Magnus. (1956). *Sexual Abnormalities: The Origins, Nature and Treatment of Sexual Disorders.* New York: Emerson.

Holzman, Harold R. (1979). "Learning Disabilities and Juvenile Delinquency: Biological and Sociological Theories." In C. R. Jeffrey, ed. *Biology and Crime.* Beverly Hills: Sage.

Hooten, E. A. (1939). *The American Criminal: An Anthropological Study.* Cambridge: Harvard University Press.

Hornblower, Margot. "The Skin Trade." *Time 141* (June 21, 1993), p. 44.

Horos, Carol. (1974). *Rape.* New Canaan: Toby Publishing.

Howard, Julie. "Incest: Victims Speak Out." *Teen* (July 1985), p. 31.

Howells, K. (1979). "Some Meanings of Children for Paedophiles." In M. Cook and F. Wilson, eds. *Love and Attraction.* Oxford: Pergamon.

Hughes, Donna M., Janice G. Raymond, and Carol J. Gomez. (2001). *Sex Trafficking of Women in the United States: International and Domestic Trends.* North Amherst: Coalition Against Trafficking in Women.

Hyde, Margaret O., and Elizabeth H. Forsyth. (1997). *The Sexual Abuse of Children and Adolescents.* Brookfield: Millbrook Press.

Ivey, G. (1993). "Psychodynamic Aspects of Demonic Possession and Satanic Worship." *South African Journal of Psychology 23:* 186–94.

Jabainville, H. D. (1905). *La Familie Celtique: Et de Droit Compare.* Paris: Librarie Emile Boullon.

James, J., W. Womack, and F. Strauss. (1978). "Physician Reporting of Sexual Abuse of Children." *Journal of the American Medical Association 240:* 1145–46.

James, Jennifer. (1972). "Two Domains of Streetwalker Argot." *Anthropological Linguistics 14:* 174–75.

___. (1973). "Prostitutes-Pimp Relationships." *Medical Aspects of Human Sexuality 7:* 147–63.

___. (1976). "Motivations for Entrance into Prostitution." In Laura Crites, ed. *The Female Offender.* Lexington: Lexington Books.

___. (1977). "Prostitutes and Prostitution." In Edward Sagarin and Fred Montanino, eds. *Deviants: Voluntary Actors in a Hostile World.* Morrison: General Learning Press.

___. (1980). *Entrance into Juvenile Prostitution.* Washington: National Institute of Mental Health.

Janus, M. D., A. McCormack, A. W. Burgess, and C. R. Hartman. (1987). *Adolescent Runaways.* Lexington: Lexington Books.

Johnson, A. G. (1980). "On The Prevalence of Rape in the United States." *Signs: Journal of Women in Culture and Society 6:* 136–46.

Johnson, Hilary. "Violence Against Women: Is Porn to Blame?" *Vogue 175* (September 1985), p. 678.

Johnson, Joan J. (1992). *Teen Prostitution.* Danbury: Franklin Watts.

Kahn, T. J., and M. A. Lafond. (1988) "Treatment of the Adolescent Sex Offender." *Child and Adolescent Social Work Journal 5.*

Kandel, Minouche. (1992). "Whores in Court: Judicial Processing of Prostitutes in the Boston Municipal Court in 1990." *Yale Journal of Law and Feminism 4:* 346.

Kanin, E. J. (1957). "Male Aggression in Dating-Courtship Relations." *American Journal of Sociology 63:* 197–204.

___, and S. R. Parcell. (1977). "Sexual Aggression: A Second Look at the Offended Female." *Archives of Sexual Behavior 6:* 67–76.

Kaplan, M., J. Becker, and J. Cunningham-Rathner. (1988). "Characteristics of Parents of Adolescent Incest Perpetrators: Preliminary Findings." *Journal of Family Violence 3,* 3: 183–91.

Karen, Robert. "The World of the Middle Class Prostitute." *Cosmopolitan 217* (March 1987), pp. 202–7.

Katz, Sedelle, and Mary A. Mazur. (1979). *Understanding the Rape Victim: A Synthesis of Research Findings.* New York: John Wiley & Sons.

Kelleher, Michael D., and C. L. Kelleher. (1998). *Murder Most Rare: The Female Serial Killer.* New York: Dell.

Kelly, L., L. Regan, and S. Burton. (1991). *An Exploratory Study of the Prevalence of Sexual Abuse in a Sample of 16–21 Year Olds.* London: CSAU, North London Polytechnic.

Keppel, Robert D., and William J. Birnes. (1997). *Signature Killers: Interpreting the Calling Cards of the Serial Murderer.* New York: Pocket Books.

Kilpatrick, D. G., C. C. Best, B. E. Saunders, and L. J. Vernon. (1988). "Rape in Marriage and in Dating Relationships: How Bad is it For Mental Health?" *Annals of the New York Academy of Sciences 528:* 335–44.

___, C. L. Best, L. J. Veronen, A. E. Amick, L. A. Villeponteaux, and G. A. Ruff. (1985). "Mental Health Correlates of Criminal Victimization: A Random Community Survey." *Journal of Consulting and Clinical Psychology 53,* 4: 866–73.

___, C. N. Edmunds, and A. K. Seymour. (1992). *Rape in America: A Report to the Nation.* Charleston: Medical University of South Carolina, Crime Victims Research and Treatment Center.

Kinsey, A. C., W. B. Pomeroy, and C. E. Martin. (1948). *Sexual Behavior in the Human Male.* Philadelphia: W. B. Saunders.

Klemmack, Susan H., and David L. Klemmack. (1976). "The Social Definition of Rape." In Mary J. Walker and Stanley L. Brodsky, eds. *Sexual Assault.* Lexington: Lexington Books.

Koss, Mary P. (1987). "Outrageous Acts and Everyday Seductions: Sexual Aggression and Victimization Among College Students." Paper presented at Romance, Rape and Relationships: A Conference on Teen Sexual Exploitation. Seattle.

___. (1988). "Hidden Rape: Sexual Aggression and Victimization in a National Sample of Students in Higher Education." In Ann W. Burgess, ed. *Rape and Sexual Assault II.* New York: Garland Publishing.

___, and C. A. Gidyez. (1985). "Sexual Experiences Survey: Reliability and Validity." *Journal of Consulting and Clinical Psychology 53:* 422–23.

___, C. A. Gidyez, and N. Wisniewski. (1987). "The Scope of Rape: Incidence and Prevalence of Sexual Aggression and Victimization in a National Sample of Higher Education Students." *Journal of Consulting and Clinical Psychology 55,* 2: 167–70.

___, K. E. Leonard, D. A. Beezley, and C. J. Oros. (1985). "Non-stranger Sexual Aggression: A Discriminant Analysis of the Psychological Characteristics of Undetected Offenders." *Sex Roles 12:* 981–92.

___, T. E. Dinero, C. A. Siebel, and S. L. Cox. (1988). "Stranger and Acquaintance Rape: Are There Differences in the Victim's Experience." *Psychology of Women Quarterly 12:* 1–24.

Krafft-Ebing, Richard von. (1965). *Psychopathic Sexualis.* New York: Stein and Day.

Kuehl, Sheila. (1998). "Legal Remedies for Teen Dating Violence." In Barrie Levy, ed. *Dating Violence: Young Women in Danger.* Seattle: Seal Press.

Lane, Brian, and Wilfred Gregg. (1995). *The Encyclopedia of Serial Killers.* New York: Berkley.

Lane, K. E., and P. A. Gwartney-Gibbs. (1985). "Violence in the Context of Dating and Sex." *Journal of Family Issues 6,* 1: 45–59.

Lange, W. R., et al. (1987). "HIV Infection in Baltimore: Antibody Seroprevalence Rates Amongst Parenteral Drug Abusers and Prostitutes." *Maryland Medical Journal 36:* 757–61.

Lankester, D., and B. Meyer. (1986). "Relationship of Family Structure to Sex Offense Behavior." Paper presented at First National Conference on Juvenile Sexual Offending. Minneapolis.

LeBlanc, Adrian N. "I'm a Shadow." *Seventeen 52* (March 1993), pp. 214–16.

Lederer, Laura, ed. (1980). *Take Back The Night: Women on Pornography.* New York: William Morrow.

Lee, Linda. "The World (and Underworld) of the Professional Call Girl." *New Woman* (January 1988), pp. 60–63.

Leidholdt, Dorchen A. (2003). "Prostitution and Trafficking in Women: An Intimate Relationship." *Journal of Trauma Practice 2,* 3/4: 167–83.

Lester, David. (1995). *Serial Killers: The Insatiable Passion.* Philadelphia: The Charles Press.

Leuchtag, Alice. (1995). "The Culture of Pornography." *The Humanist 55:* 4–6.

Levin, J., and J. A. Fox. (1985). *Mass Murder.* New York: Plenum.

Lidz, R., and T. Lidz. (1969). "Homosexual Tendencies in Mothers of Schizophrenic Women." *Journal of Nervous Mental Disorders 149:* 229.

Lieberman Research Inc. *Domestic Violence Campaign Tracking Survey.* Conducted for The Advertising Council and the Family Violence Prevention Fund. July-October, 1996.

Lloyd, Robin. (1976). *For Money or Love: Boy Prostitution in America.* New York: Ballantine.

Lombroso, Cesare. (1876). *The Criminal Man.* Milan: Hoepli.

___. (1918). *Crime, Its Causes and Remedies.* Boston: Little, Brown.

___, and William Ferrero. (1900). *The Female Offender.* New York: Appleton.

Longino, Helen E. (1980). "Pornography, Oppression, and Freedom: A Closer Look." In Laura Lederer, ed. *Take Back the Night: Women on Pornography.* New York: William Morrow.

Lonsway, Kimberly A., and Louise F. Fitzgerald. (1994). "Rape Myths: In Review." *Psychology of Women Quarterly 18:* 133–64.

Lundberg-Love, Paula, and Robert Geffner. (1989). "Date Rape: Prevalence, Risk Factors, and a Proposed Model." In Maureen Piroz-Good and Jan Stets, eds. *Violence in Dating Relationships.* New York: Praeger.

Lunde, D. T. (1979). *Murder and Madness.* New York: W. W. Norton.

MacDonald, J. M. (1971). *Rape Offenders and Their Victims.* Springfield: Charles C Thomas.

Machotka, P., F. S. Pittman, and K. Flomenhaft. (1967). "Incest as a Family Affair." *Family Process 6:* 98.

MacNamara, D. (1965). "Male Prostitution in American Cities: A Socioeconomic or Pathological Phenomenon?" *American Journal of Orthopsychiatry 35:* 204.

Magid, K., and C. McKelvey. (1989). *High Risk Children Without a Conscience.* New York: Bantam.

Mahoney, Patricia, and Linda M. Williams. (1998). "Sexual Assault in Marriage: Prevalence, Consequences, and Treatment of Wife Rape." In Jana L. Jasinski and Linda M. Williams, eds. *Partner Violence: A Comprehensive Review of 20 Years of Research.* Thousand Oaks: Sage.

Makepeace, J. M. (1981). "Courtship Violence Among College Students." *Family Relations 30:* 97–102.

___. (1988). "The Severity of Courtship Violence Injuries and Individual Precautionary Measures." In G. T. Totaling, D. Finkelhor, J. T. Kilpatrick, and M. A. Straus, eds. *Family Abuse and Its Consequences: New Directions in Research.* Newbury Park: Sage.

"Marital Rape: Drive for Tougher Laws is Passed." *New York Times* (May 15, 1987), p. A16.

Marshall, L. L., and P. Rose. (1987). "Gender, Stress and Violence in Adult Relationships of a Sample of College Students." *Journal of Social and Personal Relationships 4:* 219–316.

Marshall, W. L., and A. Eccles. (1991). "Issues in Clinical Practice with Sex Offenders." *Journal of Interpersonal Violence 6:* 68–93.

___, and H. E. Barbaree. (1990). "Outcome of Cognitive-Behavioral Treatment." In W. L. Marshall, D. R. Laws, and H. E. Barbaree, eds. *Handbook of Sexual Assault.* New York: Plenum.

___, T. Ward, R. Jones, P. Johnston, and H. E. Barbaree. (1991). "An Optimistic Evaluation of Treatment Outcome with Sex Offenders." *Violence Update 1,* 7: 1, 8, 10–11.

Mathis, J. L. (1972). *Clear Thinking About Sexual Deviations.* Chicago: Nelson-Hall.

Matthews, R., J. K. Matthews, and K. Speltz. (1989). *Female Sexual Offenders: An Exploratory Study.* Orwell: Safer Society Press.

Mawson, Robert. (1981). "Aggression, Attachment, Behavior, and Crimes of Violence." In Travis Hirshi and Michael Gottfredson, eds. *Understanding Crime.* Beverly Hills: Sage.

Mayer, Adele. (1983). *Incest: A Treatment Manual for Therapy with Victims, Spouse, and Offenders.* Holmes Beach: Learning Publications.

McCarthy, L. (1981). "Investigation of Incest: Opportunity to Motivate Families to Seek Help." *Child Welfare 60:* 679–89.

McCord, William, and Joan McCord. (1964). *The Psychopath.* Princeton: Van Nostrand.

McCormack, Arlene, et al. (1986). "Runaway Youths and Sexual Victimization: Gender Differences in an Adolescent Runaway Population." *Child Abuse and Neglect 10:* 392–93.

McCoy, Kathy. "Incest: The Most Painful Family Problem." *Seventeen 43* (June, 1984), p. 18.

McFarlane, J., B. Parker, K. Soeken, and L. Bullock. (1992). "Assessing for Abuse During Pregnancy." *Journal of American Medical Association 267,* 23: 3176–78.

McKeganey, Neil, and Mariana Barnard. (1996). *Sex Work on the Streets: Prostitutes and Their Clients.* Bristol: Taylor and Francis.

McKinney, K. (1986). "Measures of Verbal, Physical, and Sexual Dating Violence." *Free Inquiry into Creative Sociology 14,* 1: 55–60.

Meddis, Sam. "Teen Prostitution Rising, Study Says." *USA Today* (April 23, 1984), p. 3A.

Medlicott, R. (1967). "Parent-Child Incest." *Australian Journal of Psychiatry 1:* 180.

Meiselman, K. C. (1978). *Incest: A Psychological Study of Causes and Effects with Treatment Recommendations.* San Francisco: Jossey-Bass.

Mercy, J. A., and L. E. Saltzman. (1989). "Fatal Violence Among Spouses in the United States, 1976–85." *American Journal of Public Health 79:* 595–99.

Mezey, Gillian, and Michael King. (1998). "The Effects of Sexual Assault on Men: A Survey of Twenty-two Victims." In Mary E. Odem and Jody Clay-Warner, eds. *Confronting Rape and Sexual Assault.* Wilmington: Scholarly Resources, Inc.

Miller, B. (1988). "Date Rape: Time For a New Look at Prevention." *Journal of College Student Development 29:* 553–55.

___, and J. Marshall. (1987). "Coercive Sex on the University Campus." *Journal of College Student Personnel 28,* 1: 38–47.

Miller, Stuart J. (1982). "Foreword." In Anthony M. Scacco, Jr., ed. *Male Rape: A Casebook of Sexual Aggression.* New York: AMS Press.

Millet, Kate. (1971). "Prostitution: A Quartet for Female Voices." In Vivian Gornick and Barbara K. Moran, eds. *Women in a Sexist Society*. New York: New American Library.

Mithers, Carol L. "Incest: The Crime That's All in the Family." *Mademoiselle 96* (June, 1984), p. 127.

Mohr, Johan W., R. Edward Turner, and M. B. Jerry. (1964). *Pedophilia and Exhibitionism*. Toronto: University of Toronto Press.

Molnar, Beth E., et al. (1998). "Suicidal Behavior and Sexual/Physical Abuse Among Street Youth." *Child Abuse and Neglect 22:* 213–14.

Money, J. (1990). "Forensic Sexology." American Journal of Psychotherapy 44: 26–36.

Moran, Susan. (1993). "New World Havens of Oldest Profession." *Insight on the News 9:* 12–16.

Morneau, Robert H., and Robert R. Rockwell. (1980). *Sex, Motivation and the Criminal Offender*. Charles C Thomas.

Mrazek, Patricia B. (1981). "Definition and Recognition of Child Sexual Abuse: Historical and Cultural Perspectives." In Patricia Mrazek and C. Henry Kempe, eds. *Sexually Abused Children and Their Families*. New York: Pergamon Press.

Myers, John E. (1997). *Evidence in Child Abuse and Neglect Cases*. 3rd Ed. New York: John Wiley & Sons.

Nadelson, Carol G., and Malkah T. Notman. (1977). "Emotional Repercussions of Rape." *Medical Aspects of Human Sexuality 11:* 16–31.

National Institute of Justice and Centers for Disease Control and Prevention. *Prevalence, Incidence, and Consequences of Violence Against Women: Findings from the National Violence Against Women Survey*. November, 1988.

National Resource Center on Domestic Violence. (1999). *Domestic Violence*. Harrisburg: Pennsylvania Coalition Against Domestic Violence.

Newton, M. (1993). *Raising Hell*. New York: Avon Books.

Norris, Joel. (1988). *Serial Killers*. New York: Anchor Books.

Northern Ireland Research Team. (1991). *Child Sexual Abuse in Northern Ireland*. Belfast: Greystone.

O'Brien, Michael. (1991). "Taking Sibling Incest Seriously." In M. Quinn-Patton, ed. *Family Sexual Abuse: Frontline Research and Evaluation*. Beverly Hills: Sage.

O'Brien, Shirley. (1983). *Child Pornography*. Dubuque: Kendall/Hunt.

O'Callaghan, Dave, and Bobbie Print. (1994). "Adolescent Sexual Abusers: Research, Assessment and Treatment." In Tony Morrison, Marcus Erooga, and Richard C. Beckett, eds. *Sexual Offending Against Children: Assessment and Treatment of Male Abusers*. London: Routledge.

O'Carroll, Tom. (1980). *Pedophilia: The Radical Case*. Boston: Alyson Publications.

O'Keefe, N., K. Brockopp, and E. Chew. (1986). "Teen Dating Violence." *Social Work 31:* 465–68.

O'Neill-Richard, Amy. (1999). *International Trafficking in Women in the United States: A Contemporary Manifestation of Slavery and Organized Crime*. Washington: Center for the Study of Intelligence.

Odem, Mary E., and Jody Clay-Warner, eds. (1998). *Confronting Sexual Assault and Rape*. Wilmington: Scholarly Resources, Inc..

Office of the Press Secretary. (July 16, 2004). "Fact Sheet: Human Trafficking: A Modern Form of Slavery." http://www.whitehouse.gov/news/releases/2004/07/20040716-3.html.

Ogilvie, Beverly A. (2004). *Mother-Daughter Incest: A Guide for Helping Professionals*. Binghamton: Haworth Press.

Ounsted, Christopher, Rhoda Oppenheimer, and Janet Lindsay. (1975). "The Psychopathology and Psychotherapy of the Families, Aspects Bounding Failure." In A.

Frankin, ed. *Concerning Child Abuse.* London: Churchill Livingston.

Packer, Herbert L. (1968). *The Limits of the Criminal Sanction.* Stanford: Stanford University Press.

Pagelow, M. D. (1981). "Factors Affecting Women's Decision to Leave Violent Relationships." *Journal of Family Issues 2,* 4: 391–414.

___. (1984). *Family Violence.* New York: Praeger.

Pallone, N. (1990). *Rehabilitating Criminal Sexual Psychopaths.* New Brunswick: Transaction Publishers.

Panton, J. H. (1978). "Personality Differences Appearing Between Rapists of Adults, Rapists of Children and Non-Violent Sexual Molesters of Children." *Research Communications in Psychology, Psychiatry and Behaviors 3,* 4: 385–93.

Parrot, Andrea, and Laurie Bechhofer, eds. (1991). *Acquaintance Rape: The Hidden Crime.* New York: John Wiley & Sons.

Patai, Frances. (1982). "Pornography and Woman Batering: Dynamic Similarities." In Maria Roy, ed. *The Abusive Partner: An Analysis of Domestic Battering.* New York: Van Nostrand Reinhold.

Peacock, P. L. (1995). "Marital Rape." In V. R. Wiehe and A. L. Richards, eds. *Intimate Betrayal: Understanding and Responding to the Trauma of Acquaintance Rape.* Thousand Oaks: Sage.

Pence, E., and M. Paymar. (1993). *Education Groups for Men Who Batter: The Duluth Model.* New York: Springer.

Pierce, L. H., and R. L. Pierce. (1990). "Adolescent/Sibling Incest Perpetrators." In L. Horton, B. Johnson, L. Roundy, and D. Williams, eds. *The Incest Perpetrator: A Family Member No One Wants to Treat.* Beverly Hills: Sage.

Plant, Martin A. (1990). "Sex Work, Alcohol, Drugs, and AIDS." In Martin A. Plant, ed. *AIDS, Drugs, and Prostitution.* London: Routledge.

___, ed. (1990). *AIDS, Drugs, and Prostitution.* London: Routledge.

Podolsky, E. (1966). "Sexual Violence." *Medical Digest 34:* 60–63.

Pollack, Otto. (1950). *The Criminality of Women.* Philadelphia: University of Philadelphia Press.

Pollock, Vicki, Sarnoff A. Mednick, and William F. Gabrielli. (1983). "Crime Causation: Biological Theories." In Sanford H. Kadish, ed. *Encyclopedia of Crime and Justice.* Vol. 1. New York: Free Press.

Pope, K., B. Tabachmick, and P. Keith-Spiegel. (1987). "Ethics of Practice: The Beliefs and Behaviors of Psychologists as Therapists." *American Psychologist 42:* 993–1006.

Porterfield, Kay M. "Are Women as Violent as Men?" *Cosmopolitan 197* (September, 1984), p. 276.

Posner, Richard A., and Katharine B. Silbaugh. (1996). *A Guide to America's Sex Laws.* Chicago: University of Chicago Press.

"President Signs H.R. 972, Trafficking Victims Protection Reauthorization Act." (January 10, 2006) http://www.whitehouse.gov/news/releases/2006/01/20060110-3.html.

Pryor, Douglas W. (1996). *Unspeakable Acts: Why Men Sexually Abuse Children.* New York: New York University Press.

Puig, A. (1984). "Predomestic Strife: A Growing College Counseling Concern." *Journal of College Student Personnel 25:* 268–69.

Pukins, J., and R. Langevin. (1985). "Brain Correlates of Penile Erection." In R. Langevin, ed. *Erotic Preference: Gender Identity and Aggression in Men.* Hillsdale: Lawrence Erlbaum.

Rada, Richard T. (1978). *Clinical Aspects of the Rapist.* New York: Grune and Stratton.

Rader, Dotson. "I Want to Die So I Won't Hurt No More." *Parade Magazine* (August 18, 1985), pp. 4–6.

Randall, M., and L. Haskell. (1995). "Sexual Violence in Women's Lives." *Women 1,* 1: 6–31.

Rappaport, R. G. (1988). "The Serial and Mass Murderer." *American Journal of Forensic Psychiatry 9,* 1: 39–48.

Reinhardt, J. M. (1957). *Sex Perversions and Sex Crimes.* Springfield: Charles C Thomas.

Renvoize, Jean. (1982). *Incest: A Family Pattern.* London: Routledge & Kegan Paul.

Report of the Special Rapporteur on the Sale of Children, Child Prostitution and Child Pornography. (1996). United Nations Economic and Social Council. Commission on Human Rights, 52nd Sess.

Ressler, Robert K., Ann W. Burgess, and John E. Douglas. (1988). *Sexual Homicide: Patterns and Motives.* New York: Lexington Books.

Riggs, D. S., D. G. Kilpatrick, and H. S. Resnick. (1992). "Long-Term Psychological Distress Associated with Marital Rape and Aggravated Assault: A Comparison to Other Crime Victims." *Journal of Family Violence 7,* 4: 283–96.

Riskin, L. I., and M. P. Koss. (1987). "Sexual Abuse of Boys: Prevalence and Descriptive Characteristics of the Childhood Victimizations." *Journal of Interpersonal Violence 2:* 309–19.

Rooney, Rita. "Children For Sale: Pornography's Dark New World." *Reader's Digest* (July, 1983), pp. 52–56.

Roscoe, B., and J. E. Callahan. (1985). "Adolescents' Self-Report of Violence in Families and Dating Situations." *Adolescence 20:* 545–53.

Rosenberg, J. (1989). *Fuel on the Fire: An Inquiry into "Pornography" and Sexual Aggression.* Orwell: Safer Society Press.

Rosenberg, M. J. and J. M. Weiner. (1988). "Prostitution and AIDS: A Health Department Priority." *American Journal of Public Health 78:* 418.

Rosenbleet, Charles, and Barbara J. Pariente. (1973). "The Prostitution of the Criminal Law." *American Criminal Law Review 11:* 373.

Rotheram-Borus, Jane, et al. (1966). "Sexual Abuse History and Associated Multiple Risk Behavior in Adolescent Runaways." *American Journal of Orthopsychiatry 66:* 390–91.

Rovner, Sandy. "Healthtalk: Facing the Aftermath of Incest." *Washington Post* (January 6, 1984), p. D5.

Rumbelow, Donald. (1988). *Jack the Ripper: The Complete Casebook.* Chicago: Contemporary Books.

Russell, Diana E. (1983). *Intra-Family Child Sexual Abuse: Final Report to the National Center on Child Abuse and Neglect.* Washington: U.S. Department of Health and Human Services.

___. (1984). *Sexual Exploitation: Rape, Child Abuse, and Workplace Harassment.* Beverly Hills: Sage.

___. (1986). *The Secret Trauma: Incest in the Lives of Girls and Women.* New York: Basic Books.

___. (1990). *Rape in Marriage.* New York: Macmillan.

___. (1998). "Wife Rape and the Law." In Mary E. Odem and Jody Clay-Warner, eds. *Confronting Rape and Sexual Assault.* Wilmington: Scholarly Resources, Inc.

Sagarin, E. (1976). "Prison Homosexuality and Its Effect on Post-Prison Sexual Behavior." *Psychiatry 39:* 245–57.

Samenow, Stanton E. (1984). *Inside the Criminal Mind.* New York: Time Books.

Sarafino, E. P. (1979). "An Estimate of the Nationwide Incidence of Sexual Offenses Against Children." *Child Welfare 58,* 2: 127–34.

Satchel, Michael. "Kids for Sale: A Shocking Report on Child Prostitution Across America." *Parade Magazine* (July 20, 1986), pp. 4–6.

Schecter, Marshall D., and Leon Roberge. (1976). "Sexual Exploitation." In Ray E. Helfer and C. Henry Kempe, eds. *Child Abuse and Neglect: The Family and The Community.* Cambridge: Ballinger.

Schroder, Theodore. (1915). "Incest in Mormanism." *American Journal of Urology and Sexology 11:* 409–16.

Schultz, Leroy C. (1975). "The Child as a Sex Victim: Socio-Legal Perspectives." In Israel Drapkin and Emilo Viano, eds. *Victimology: A New Focus.* Vol. 5. Toronto: D.C. Heath.

Schwendinger, Julia R., and Herman Schwendinger. (1983). *Rape and Inequality.* Beverly Hills: Sage.

Scully, Diana, and Joseph Marolla. (1983). "Incarcerated Rapists: Exploring a Sociological Mode." *Final Report for Department of Health and Human Services.* Washington: Government Printing Office.

Sears, D. (1991). *To Kill Again.* Wilmington: Scholarly Resources.

Seghorn, T. K., R. A. Prentky, and R. J. Baucher. (1987). "Childhood Sexual Abuse in the Lives of Sexually Aggressive Offenders." *Journal of the American Academy of Child and Adolescent Psychiatry 26:* 262–67.

Sellin, T. (1961). "The Significance of Records of Crime." *The Law Quarterly Review 67:* 489–504.

Seng, Magnus. (1989). "Child Sexual Abuse and Adolescent Prostitution: A Comparative Analysis. *Adolescence 24:* 671.

Serrill, Michael S. "Defiling the Children." *Time 141* (June 21, 1993), pp. 52–56.

"Sex Researcher's Report: The Men Raped by Women." *San Francisco Chronicle* (March 15, 1982), p. 5.

Sheffield, Carole J. (1984). "Sexual Terrorism." In Jo Freerman, ed. *Women: A Feminist Perspective.* 4th Ed. Mountain View; Mayfield.

Sidler, M. (1971). *On the Universality of the Incest Taboo.* Stuttgart: Enke.

Sigelman, C. K., C. J. Berry, and K. A. Wiles. (1984). "Violence in College Students' Dating Relationships." *Journal of Applied Social Psychology 14,* 6: 530–48.

Silbert, Mimi H. (1980). *Sexual Assault of Prostitutes: Phase One.* Washington: National Institute of Mental Health.

___. (1982). "Delancey Street Study: Prostitution and Sexual Assault." Summary of results. Delancey Street Foundation. San Francisco.

___, and Ayala M. Pines. (1982). "Entrance into Prostitution." *Youth & Society 13:* 471–73.

___, and Ayala M. Pines. (1981). "Occupational Hazards of Street Prostitutes." *Criminal Justice and Behavior 8:* 397.

Simari, C. Georgia, and David Baskin. (1982). "Incestuous Experiences Within Homosexual Populations: A Preliminary Study." *Archives of Sexual Behavior 11:* 329–44.

Simmons, H. E. (1970). *Protective Services for Children.* 2nd Ed. Sacramento: Citadel Press.

Simons, Ronald, and Les B. Whitbeck. (1991). "Sexual Abuse as a Precursor to Prostitution and Victimization Among Adolescents and Homeless Women." *Journal of Family Issues 12:* 375.

Sitton, J. (1993). "Old Wine in New Bottles: The Marital Rape Allowance." *North Carolina Law Review 72:* 261–89.

Skrobanek, Siripon, S. Boonpakdee, and C. Jantateroo. (1997). *The Traffic in Women: Human Realities of the International Sex Trade.* New York: Zed Books Ltd.

Stanmeyer, William A. (1984). *The Seduction of Society.* Ann Arbor: Servant Books.

Stark, Evan, and Anne Flitcraft. *Surgeon General's Workshop on Violence and Public Health Source Book.* Presented at the Surgeon General's Workshop on Violence and Public Health. Leesburg: October 1985.

Stets, J. E., and M. A. Piroz-Good. (1989). "Patterns of Physical and Sexual Abuse for Men and Women in Dating Relationships: A Descriptive Analysis." *Journal of Family Violence 4,* 1: 63–76.

Stiebler, Tamer. "The Boys Who Sell Sex to Men in San Francisco." *Sacramento Bee* (March 4, 1984), p. A 22.

Stoenner, H. (1972). *Child Sexual Abuse Seen Growing in the United States.* Denver: American Humane Association.

Sugarman, David B., and Gerald T. Hotaling. (1998). "Dating Violence: A Review of Contextual and Risk Factors." In Barrie Levy, ed. *Dating Violence: Young Women in Danger.* Seattle: Seal Press.

Svalastoga, K. (1962). "Rape and Social Structure." *Pacific Sociological Review 5:* 48–53.

Sweet, Ellen. "Date Rape." *Ms./Campus Times* (October 1985), p. 58.

Tannahill, Reay. (1980). *Sex in History.* New York: Stein and Day, 1980.

Thomas, William I. (1907). *Sex and Society: Studies in the Sexual Psychology of Sex.* Boston: Little, Brown.

Thompson, W. E. (1986). "Courtship Violence: Toward a Conceptual Understanding." *Youth and Society 18,* 2: 162–76.

Tirelli, U., D. Erranto, and D. Serraino. (1988). "HIV-1 Seroprevalence in Male Prostitutes in Northeast Italy." *Journal of Acquired Immune Deficiency Syndrome 1:* 414–15.

Troup-Leasure, Karyl, and Howard N. Snyder. (2005). *Statutory Rape Known to Law Enforcement.* Washington: Office of Juvenile Justice and Delinquency Prevention.

Ugarte, Marisa B., Laura Zarate, and Melissa Farley. (2003). "Prostitution and Trafficking of Women and Children From Mexico to the United States." *Journal of Trauma Practice 2,* 3/4: 145–65.

UN Protocol to Prevent, Suppress and Punish Trafficking in Persons. (February 14, 2006) http://www.unodc.org/unodc/en/trafficking_protocol.html.

U.S. Department of Health and Human Services. *Research Symposium on Child Sexual Abuse: May 17–19, 1988.* Washington: National Center on Child Abuse and Neglect, 1988.

U.S. Department of Justice. (1986). *Attorney General's Commission on Pornography: Final Report.* Vol. 1. Washington: Government Printing Office.

___. Bureau of Justice Statistics. (1994). *Survey of State Prison Inmates, 1991: Women in Prison.* Washington: Government Printing Office.

___. Bureau of Justice Statistics. (1996). *Child Victimizers: Violent Offenders and Their Victims.* Washington: Government Printing Office.

___. Bureau of Justice Statistics. (1997). *Criminal Victimization in the United States, 1994: A National Crime Victimization Survey Report.* Washington: Government Printing Office.

___. Bureau of Justice Statistics. (1997). *Sex Offenses and Offenders: An Analysis of Data on Rape and Sexual Assault.* Washington: Office of Justice Programs.

___. Bureau of Justice Statistics. (1998). *Alcohol and Crime.* Washington: Government Printing Office.

___. Bureau of Justice Statistics. (2005). *Family Violence Statistics: Including Statistics on Strangers and Acquaintances.* Washington: Office of Justice Programs.

___. Bureau of Justice Statistics. (2005). *Sourcebook of Criminal Justice Statistics 2003.* Washington: Government Printing Office.

___. Bureau of Justice Statistics Factbook. (1998). *Violence by Intimates: Analysis of Data on Crimes by Current or Former Spouses, Boyfriends and Girlfriends.* Washington: Government Printing Office.

___. Bureau of Justice Statistics Special Report. (1988). *Children Traumatized in Sex Rings.* Arlington: National Center for Missing & Exploited Children.

___. Bureau of Justice Statistics Special Report. (1992). *Child Sex Rings: A Behavioral Analysis, For Criminal Justice Professionals Handling Cases of Child Sexual Exploitation.* Arlington: National Center for Missing & Exploited Children.

___. Bureau of Justice Statistics Special Report. (2001). *Firearm Use by Offenders.* Washington: Office of Justice Programs.

___. Bureau of Justice Statistics Special Report. (2004). *Profile of Jail Inmates, 2002.* Washington: Office of Justice Programs.

___. Bureau of Justice Statistics Special Report. (2005). *Sexual Violence Reported by Correctional Authorities, 2004.* Washington: Office of Justice Programs.

___. Federal Bureau of Investigation. (1985). "The Men Who Murdered." *FBI Law Enforcement Bulletin 62:* 2–6.

___. Federal Bureau of Investigation. (1998). *Crime in the United States: Uniform Crime Reports 1999.* Washington: Government Printing Office.

___. Federal Bureau of Investigation. (2004). *Crime in the United States: Uniform Crime Reports 2005.* Washington: Government Printing Office.

___. National Institute of Justice. (1997). *Sex Offender Community Notification.* Washington: Office of Justice Programs.

___. National Institute of Justice. (2005). *Sexual Assault on Campus: What Colleges and Universities Are Doing About It.* Washington: Office of Justice Programs.

___. Office of Justice Programs. (1999). *Juvenile Offenders and Victims: 1999 National Report.* Washington: Office of Juvenile Justice and Delinquency Prevention.

___. Office of Juvenile Justice and Delinquency Prevention. (1992). *Child Molesters: A Behavioral Analysis, For Law Enforcement Officers Investigating Cases of Child Sexual Exploitation.* Arlington: National Center for Missing & Exploited Children.

___. Office of Juvenile Justice and Delinquency Prevention. (1997). *A Report to the Nation: Missing and Exploited Children.* Arlington: National Center for Missing & Exploited Children.

___. Office of Juvenile Justice and Delinquency Prevention. (1999). *Prostitution of Children and Child-Sex Tourism: An Analysis of Domestic and International Responses.* Arlington: National Center for Missing & Exploited Children.

U.S. Department of State. (2005). *Trafficking in Persons Report.* Washington: Office to Monitor and Combat Trafficking in Persons. http://www.state.gov/g/tip/ris/tiprpt/2005/46606.htm.

U.S. Immigration and Customs Enforcement. (January 11, 2006) "2,300 Smuggling, Trafficking Convictions Since 2003." http://www.usembassy.at/en/policy/human_traff.htm.

"U.S., Moldovan, Romanian Cooperation Leads to Sex Tourist Arrests." (January 13, 2006) http://www.USInfo.state.gov.

"U.S. Report on Rape Cases Cites Victims' Frustrations with Law." *New York Times* (March 25, 1985), p. A 17.

Ullman, S. E., and J. M. Siegel. (1993). "Victim-Offender Relationship and Sexual Assault." *Violence and Victims 8,* 2: 121–34.

Urquiza, Anthony J., and Maria Capra. (1990). "The Impact of Sexual Abuse: Initial and Long-Term Effects." In Mic Hunter, ed. *The Sexually Abused Male.* New York: Lexington Books.

Valcour, F. (1990). "The Treatment of Child Sex Abusers in the Church." In S. Rossetti, ed. *Slayer of the Soul.* Mystic: Twenty-Third Publications.

van Dam, Carla. (2001). *Identifying Child Molesters: Preventing Child Sexual Abuse by Recognizing the Patterns of the Offenders.* Binghamton: Haworth Press.

Vander Mey, Brenda J., and Ronald L. Neff. (1986). *Incest as Child Abuse: Research and Applications.* New York: Praeger.

Vanderbilt, Heidi. "Incest-A Chilling Report." *Lear's* (February 1992): 52–62.

VAWnet Applied Research Forum. National Electronic Network on Violence Against

Women. (1999). "Marital Rape." National Resource Center on Domestic Violence. San Francisco.

Vetter, Harold J., and Ira J. Silverman. (1978). *The Nature of Crime.* Philadelphia: W. B. Saunders.

Volkonsky, Anastasia. (1995). "Legalizing the 'Profession' Would Sanction the Abuse." *Insight on the News 11:* 20–22.

Waldorf, Dan, and Sheigla Murphy. (1990). "Intravenous Drug Use and Syringe-Sharing Practices of Call Men and Hustlers." In Martin A. Plant, ed. *AIDS, Drugs, and Prostitution.* London: Routledge.

Walker, Lenore E. (1984). *The Battered Woman Syndrome.* New York: Springer.

Weinberg, S. Kirson. (1966). *Incest Behavior.* New York: Citadel Press.

Weinrott, M. R. and M. Saylor. (1991). "Self-Report of Crimes Committed by Sex Offenders." *Journal of Interpersonal Violence 6,* 3: 286–300.

Weisberg, D. Kelly. (1985). *Children of the Night: A Study of Adolescent Prostitution.* Lexington: Lexington Books.

Wellman, Mary. (1993). "Child Sexual Abuse and Gender Differences: Attitudes and Prevalence." *Child Abuse and Neglect 17:* 539–47.

West, Dorothy. (1982). "I Was Afraid to Shut My Eyes." In Anthony M. Scacco, Jr., ed. *Male Rape: A Casebook of Sexual Aggression.* New York: AMS Press.

Westermarch, Edward. (1921). *The History of Human Marriage.* 5th Ed. New York: Macmillan.

Whatley, M. (1993). "For Better or Worse: The Case of Marital Rape." *Violence and Victims 8:* 29–39.

Whitcomb, Debra, Edward DeVos, and Barbara E. Smith. (1998). *Program to Increase Understanding of Child Sexual Exploitation, Final Report.* Education Development Center, Inc. and ABA Center on Children and the Law.

Widom, Cathy S., and Joseph B. Kuhns. (1996). "Childhood Victimization and Subsequent Risk for Promiscuity, Prostitution and Teenage Pregnancy: A Prospective Study." *American Journal of Public Health 86:* 1611.

___, and M. Ashley Ames. (1994). "Criminal Consequences of Childhood Sexual Victimization." *Child Abuse and Neglect 18:* 303, 310, 312.

Wiehe, Vernon R. (1990). *Sibling Abuse: Hidden Physical, Emotional and Sexual Trauma.* Lexington: Lexington Books.

Wijers, Marjan, and Lin Lap-Chew. (1997). *Trafficking in Women: Forced Labor and Slavery-like Practices in Marriage, Domestic Labor, and Prostitution.* Utrecht: STV.

Williams, L. S. (1984). "The Classic Rape: When Do Victims Report?" *Social Problems 31,* 4: 459–67.

Wilson, Colin. (1998). *The Mammoth Book of True Crime.* New York: Carroll & Graf.

Wilson, Margo I., and Martin Daly. (1993). "Spousal Homicide Risk and Estrangement." *Violence and Victims 8:* 3–15.

___. (1995). "Uxoricide." In U.S. Department of Justice. Office of Justice Programs. *Trends, Risks, and Interventions in Lethal Violence: Proceedings of the Third Annual Spring Symposium of the Homicide Research Working Group.* Washington: National Institute of Justice.

Winick, Charles, and Paul M. Kinsie. (1971). *The Lively Commerce: Prostitution in the United States.* Chicago: Quadrangle Books.

Wolf, S. C. (1984). "A Multifactor Model of Deviant Sexuality." Paper presented at the Third International Conference on Victimology. Lisbon.

Wolfgang, Marvin E. (1963). "Uniform Crime Reports: A Critical Appraisal." *University of Pennsylvania Law Review 3:* 408–38.

Woolston, Howard B (1921). *Prostitution in the United States.* New York: Century.

Yates, Gary L., et al. (1991). "A Risk Profile Comparison of Homeless Youth Involved in Prostitution and Homeless Youth Not Involved." *Journal of Adolescent Health 12:* 547.

Yochelson, Samuel, and Stanton E. Samenow. (1976). *The Criminal Personality.* Vol. 1. New York: Jason Arsonson.

Zaccaro, John Jr. "Children of the Night." *Women's Day* (March 29, 1988), p. 137.

INDEX

defined as, 111
historical, 126
multidimensional, 126
solo, 112, 125
syndicated, 112, 125–126
transition, 112, 125
See also Child molestation; Child pornography; Pornography; Sex trafficking
Child sex tourism (CST), 133, 135, 137
defined, 137
See also Child sexual abuse; Sex trafficking; Sexual abuse
Child sex tourists, 137
prosecution of, 137
See also Child sexual abuse; Prostitution;
Sex trafficking
Child sexual abuse, 6, 67, 76–77, 94–95,
103–105, 112–113, 121, 174, 187, 200,
211–213, 254
advocating, 112–113
child molestation, v, 5, 65, 75, 103–113,
141, 144, 149, 211, 237, 253
and child sex rings, 125–126
defined as, 76
estimates of, 104
hidden form of, 94
incidence of, 103–105
intrafamilial, 76, 103
laws, 211–213
pedophilia, 109–111
and running away, 174
types of female child sexual abusers,
87–88
See also Child molestation; Incest; Sexual
abuse
Child sexual abuse laws, 211–213
Child sexual exploiters, 125
characterizing, 125
See also Child molesters; Child pornographers; Child sexual abuse
Childhood Sensuality Circle, 112
Children and Criminality (Flowers), 78
Children of the Night (Weisberg), 188
Children's Internet Protection Act (CIPA),
127
Christakos, Antigone, 9
Christian Coalition, 127

Clark, Lorenne M., 32
Clinton, President, 214
Cohen, Albert K., 110
Coleman, J. C., 143
Combined DNA Index System (CODIS),
219
Commercialized vice, 6, 172, 181, 187,
224–230, 233–234, 254–255
arrests for, 224–230, 233–234
See also Prostitutes; Prostitution; Sex traf-
ficking; Substance abuse
Communications Decency Act of 1996, 127,
214
Conjugal rape, 38, 45
See also Date rape; Marital rape; Rapist(s)
Community notification laws, 218
Coombs, N., 183
Coprolagnia, viii, 144–145
See also Child molester(s); Child molesta-
tion; Child sexual abuse
Coprophilia, 109
See also Coprolagnia
Corder, F., 89
Cormier, B. S., 7
Courtois, Christine, 52
Covenant House, 175
COYOTE (Call Off Your Old Tired Ethics),
215
Coyote v. Roberts, 215
Cressey, Donald R., 234
*Crime in the United States: Uniform Crime
Reports* (UCR), 224
Crime Victims Research and Treatment
Center (CVC), 41
Criminal personality theory, 199
Criminal Victimization in the United States:
A National Crime Victimization Survey
(NCVS), 235
The Criminality of Women (Pollak), 163
Crowley, Maura G., 174
Cultural transmission theory, 163
Cunningham-Rathner, J., 96
"Cyber sex," 127
See also Child molestation; Child sexual
abuse
Cycle of sexual abuse and sexual offending
theories, 201
Cyriaque, Jeanne, 201

arrest rates, 225–226
arrested as, 171–172, 190, 225, 231–232
arrests of, 228–232
and boy prostitution, 187–188, 190
and child sexual abuse, 104, 174, 225
girl, 171–172
and girl prostitution, 171–174
and male prostitutes, 181, 184
and physical abuse, 174
and pimps, 173
and prostitution, 224–225
See also Boy prostitutes; Child abuse;
    Child pornography; Child sexual
    abuse; Girl prostitutes; Incest;
    Prostitution
Russell, Diana E., 25, 27, 41–44, 53, 57, 67,
    88
Russell, George, 146

S

Sadism, v, 12–13, 66, 106, 109, 123, 142,
    145, 217
Sadistic/obsessive rapists, 46
    See also Forcible rape; Rapist(s)
Sadistic rapists, 29
Sadomasochism, 168
Sagawa, Josei, 147
Same sex rape, 24, 61–68
    institutional, 67
    See also Forcible rape; Incarcerated sex
        offenders; Rape; Rapist(s)
Samenow, Stanton E., 199
Sarrel, Philip, 64
Satanism, 141, 147–149
    See also Ritualistic sex abuse
Saylor, M., 81
Schechter, Marshall D., 81
Schizophrenia, 144, 176
Schurr, Cathleen, 25
Schwendinger, Herman, 31
Schwendinger, Julia R., 31
Scully, Diana, 31
Sears, D., 146
Sellin, T., 234
Seng, Magnus J., 184
Serial killers, 6, 13–14, 145–149, 162, 176
    and bestiality, 145
    female sexual, 14

of prostitutes, 13–14, 162, 176
sexual, 145–146, 155
See also Homicide(s); Murder(s); Serial
    murder(s)
Serial murder(s), 12–15, 167
    See also Homicide(s); Murder(s); Serial
        killers
Sex addicts, 200
    See also Prostitution; Sexual addiction
        theories
Sex crime laws, 209–220
    background screening laws, 213
    chemical castration laws, 219–220
    child pornography on the Internet,
        214–215
    child prostitution laws, 215–216
    child sexual abuse laws, 211–213
    community notification laws, 218
    DNA database laws, 218–219
    federal laws, 214–215
    incest and child molestation laws, 212
    marital rape laws, 211
    pornography laws, 213–215
    prostitution laws, 215–216
    rape crime laws, 209–211
    rape shield laws, 211
    reporting laws, 213
    sex offender registration laws, 217
    sex trafficking laws, 216–217
    sexual perversion laws, 217
    sexual predator laws, 219
    state pornography laws, 215
    See also Uniform Crime Reports (UCR)
Sex criminality, v, 62, 199
    See also Sexual abuse; Sexual criminality
Sex criminals, v, 197–204
    theories on, 197–204
    See also Human traffickers, Incarcerated
        sex offenders; Laws; Sex traffickers
Sex-for-sale industry, 132
Sex offender(s), v, 13, 79, 81, 110, 121, 141,
    145, 198, 203, 217, 224–237
    adolescent, 96–97
    adult, 198, 202
    characteristics of inmate, 244–246
    and chemical castration laws, 219
    child sexual victimizer inmates, 251–254
    compulsive, 201
    convicted, 217, 239–240